Movements in Or_
Communication Research

Movements in Organizational Communication Research is an essential resource for anyone wishing to become familiar with the current state of organizational communication research and key trends in the field. Seasoned organizational communication scholars will find that the book provides unique insights by way of the intergenerational dialogue that is found in the book, as well as the contributors' stories about their scholarly trajectories. Those who are new to the field will find that the book enables them to familiarize themselves with the field and become a part of the organizational communication scholarly community in an inviting and accessible way.

Key features of the book include:

- A review of current issues and future directions in 13 topical areas of organizational communication research
- Intergenerational dialogue and collaboration between both established and emerging scholars in their specialty areas
- Reflections by the authors on their scholarly trajectories and how they became a part of the field
- Discussion questions at the end of each chapter that prompt reflections and debate

The book also features online resources for instructors:

- Sample course syllabus
- Suggested case studies from the book *Cases in Organization and Managerial Communication* to align with this book's chapters

The book is recommended as the anchor text for introductory graduate-level courses and upper-level undergraduate courses in organizational communication. It is also an excellent supplementary text for advanced doctoral-level courses in organizational communication, and courses in related fields such as organization studies, organizational behavior, and management.

Jamie McDonald (Ph.D., University of Colorado Boulder) is an Assistant Professor in the Department of Communication at the University of Texas at San Antonio, USA. His research interests include identity and difference at work, occupational segregation, and feminist and queer approaches to organizing. His work has appeared in peer-reviewed journals such as *Communication Theory*, *Management Communication Quarterly*, *Management Learning*, the *Journal of Applied Communication Research*, and *Gender, Work, and Organization*.

Rahul Mitra (Ph.D., Purdue University) is an Assistant Professor in the Department of Communication at Wayne State University, USA. His research focuses on sustainable organizing, corporate responsibility, and careers/work discourses. His work has appeared in peer-reviewed journals such as *Management Communication Quarterly*, the *Journal of Applied Communication Research*, *Human Relations*, *Environmental Communication*, and *Journal of Business Ethics*.

Movements in Organizational Communication Research

Current Issues and Future Directions

Edited by
Jamie McDonald and Rahul Mitra

Routledge
Taylor & Francis Group

NEW YORK AND LONDON

First edition published 2019
by Routledge
52 Vanderbilt Avenue, New York, NY 10017

and by Routledge
2 Park Square, Milton Park, Abingdon, Oxon, OX14 4RN

Routledge is an imprint of the Taylor & Francis Group, an informa business

British Library Cataloguing-in-Publication Data
A catalogue record for this book is available from the British Library

Library of Congress Cataloging-in-Publication Data
A catalog record for this book has been requested

ISBN: 978-1-138-30444-4 (hbk)
ISBN: 978-1-138-30446-8 (pbk)
ISBN: 978-0-203-73008-9 (ebk)

Typeset in Sabon
by Apex CoVantage, LLC

Visit the eResources: www.routledge.com/9781138304468

Contents

Contributors

William C. Barley (Ph.D., Northwestern University) is an Assistant Professor of Communication at the University of Illinois at Urbana-Champaign. His research explores how individuals use technology to overcome the challenges of diverse teams in the modern workplace.

Patrice M. Buzzanell (Ph.D., Purdue University) is Chair and Professor of the Department of Communication at the University of South Florida and Endowed Visiting Professor for the School of Media and Design at Shanghai Jiaotong University. In addition to being a Fellow and serving as Past President of the International Communication Association, she also has served as President of the Council of Communication Associations and the Organization for the Study of Communication, Language and Gender. She became a Distinguished Scholar of the National Communication Association (NCA) in 2017. Her research focuses on career, work–life policy, resilience, gender, and engineering design in micro–macro contexts.

George Cheney (Ph.D., Purdue University) is Professor of Communication at the University of Colorado-Colorado Springs. He is also affiliated with the University of Utah, the University of Waikato, NZ, and Mondragon University, Basque Country, Spain. He is the author or co-author of ten books and over 100 articles and chapters. He is writing and speaking on a range of topics for community and popular venues.

Stephanie L. Dailey (Ph.D., University of Texas at Austin) is an Assistant Professor in the Department of Communication Studies at Texas State University. Her research seeks to understand how people learn about and feel part of organizations. Specifically, she is interested in issues of membership and identity across three contexts: health, social media, and training.

Jennifer Ervin (Ph.D., University of Arizona) is a post-doctoral associate studying medical decision-making teams in the University of Pittsburgh's Department of Critical Care Medicine. She also teaches organizational behavior in the Tepper School of Business at Carnegie Mellon.

Gail T. Fairhurst (Ph.D., University of Oregon) is a Distinguished University Research Professor of Organizational Communication at the University of Cincinnati. She specializes in organizational and leadership communication processes, including those involving paradox, problem-centered leadership, and framing. She is a Fellow of the International Communication Association, Distinguished Scholar of the National Communication Association, and Fulbright Scholar.

Jeremy Fyke (Ph.D., Purdue University) is an Assistant Professor in Communication Studies and Corporate Communication at Belmont University. His research includes corporate social responsibility, consulting, leadership development, crisis communication, and ethics. He is lead editor of *Cases in Organizational and Managerial Communication: Stretching Boundaries* (Routledge, 2017).

Guowei Jian (Ph.D., University of Colorado Boulder) is Professor of Communication at Cleveland State University. He studies and teaches organizational communication, leadership, and intercultural communication. He is especially interested in the process of communication and culture in constructing leadership and identity and managing organizational change.

Joann Keyton (Ph.D., The Ohio State University) is Professor of Communication at North Carolina State University. She is the editor of *Small Group Research*, a founder of the Interdisciplinary Network for Group Research, and was honored with the 2011 Gerald Phillips Award for Distinguished Applied Communication Scholarship by the National Communication Association.

Jared Kopczynski is a Ph.D. candidate in the Department of Communication at the University of Colorado Boulder. His research aims to understand how organizations might better serve society, which includes focusing on critical approaches to valuation and issues of corporate social responsibility.

Michael W. Kramer (Ph.D., University of Texas at Austin) is Professor and Chair in the Department of Communication at the University of Oklahoma. His research examines the assimilation/socialization process for employees or volunteers. In addition, he studies group processes, including leadership and decision-making. He explores these issues in a variety of profit and nonprofit organizations.

Timothy R. Kuhn (Ph.D., Arizona State University) is a Professor in the Department of Communication at the University of Colorado Boulder. His research addresses the constitution of authority and agency in organizational action, with particular attention to how knowledge, identities, and conceptions of value emerge in sociomaterial and power-laden communication practices.

Laurie Lewis (Ph.D., University of California at Santa Barbara) is a Professor of Communication at Rutgers University. She is author of *Organizational Change: Creating Change Through Strategic Communication*, and co-editor of the *International Encyclopedia of Organizational Communication*, as well as numerous academic publications on topics related to organizational change and stakeholder communication. Her research investigates how organizations work most effectively through collaboration, stakeholder engagement, input solicitation, and high-quality participative processes. She is a Fellow at the Rutgers Center for Organizational Leadership.

Shawna Malvini Redden (Ph.D., Arizona State University-Tempe) is an assistant professor in the Communication Studies Department at California State University, Sacramento. She studies and teaches organizational communication and qualitative methods, centering on issues of identity, emotion, change, and workplace relationships.

Steven K. May (Ph.D., University of Utah) is an Associate Professor in the Department of Communication at the University of North Carolina at Chapel Hill. His research interests include organizational ethics and corporate social responsibility, with a particular focus on ethical dilemmas, as well as ethical practices of dialogue, transparency, participation, courage, and accountability. His books include *The Handbook of Communication Ethics*, *The Handbook of Communication and Corporate Social Responsibility*, *The Debate Over Corporate Social Responsibility*, *Case Studies in Organizational Communication: Ethical Perspectives and Practices* and *Engaging Organizational Communication Theory and Research: Multiple Perspectives*, each of which has won a top book award from national and international associations.

Katharine E. Miller is a doctoral candidate in the Lamb School of Communication at Purdue University. She studies organizational communication with emphasis in corporate social responsibility (CSR) and research methods. Her work includes qualitative and interdisciplinary approaches to CSR, as well as broader issues surrounding organizational identity, rhetoric, and engagement.

Dennis K. Mumby (Ph.D., Southern Illinois University, Carbondale) is the Cary C. Boshamer Distinguished Professor of Communication at the University of North Carolina at Chapel Hill. He has published numerous books and articles exploring the relationships among discourse, power, gender, and organizing. He is a Fellow of the International Communication Association and a National Communication Association Distinguished Scholar.

Patricia S. Parker (Ph.D., University of Texas at Austin) is Chair of the Department of Communication at the University of North Carolina at Chapel Hill, where she is also an Associate Professor of Organizational Communication. Her current research and teaching are focused on decolonizing approaches to social justice leadership and community-based organizing.

Jessica A. Pauly (Ph.D., Purdue University) is an Assistant Professor for the Department of Communication at Utah Valley University. She is an organizational communication scholar with particular interest in identity, social change, religion, and gender. Jessica has published articles on how women who identify as Catholic and feminist negotiate these two seemingly conflicting identities, as well as faculty perspectives of the service-learning pedagogy.

Mie Plotnikof (Ph.D., Copenhagen Business School) is Associate Professor at the Danish School of Education, Aarhus University, Denmark. She studies the role of communication and discourse in the public governance of various policy areas, focusing on power, resistance, organizing and identity. Her work is published in such journals as *International Journal of Public Sector Management*, *The Innovation Journal*, and *Nordic Journal of Working Life Studies*, plus in several edited volumes.

Marshall Scott Poole (Ph.D., University of Wisconsin) is the David L. Swanson Professor of Communication at the University of Illinois at Urbana-Champaign. His research interests include group and organizational communication, communication technology, organizational innovation, and interorganizational collaboration.

Surabhi Sahay (Ph.D., Rutgers University) is Assistant Professor of Corporate Communication at Pennsylvania State University at Abington. Her research is primarily focused on understanding the implications of participatory designs offered to stakeholders during organizational change. Surabhi's research spans various contexts where she has used a range of methodologies to collect data. She has also co-authored various articles and book chapters.

Matthew W. Seeger (Ph.D., Indiana University) is Dean of the College of Fine, Performing and Communication Arts and Professor in the Department of Communication at Wayne State University. His research concerns crisis and risk communication, health promotion and communication, crisis response and agency coordination, the role of media, including new media, crisis and communication ethics, failure of complex systems, and post-crisis renewal.

Katie Sullivan (Ph.D., University of Utah) is an Assistant Professor of Communication at the University of Colorado-Colorado Springs, and a visiting scholar in the Department of Business Administration at Lund University, Sweden. Katie's research explores issues such as the intersections between professionalization and embodiment, diversity in organizations and occupations, and the role of branding in public life.

Sarah J. Tracy (Ph.D., University of Colorado Boulder) is Professor and Co-Director of The Transformation Project in the Hugh Downs School of Human Communication at Arizona State University Tempe. Her research and teaching focus on qualitative research methods and organizational communication, with specific emphases in compassion, well-being, workplace bullying, emotional labor, and burnout.

Acknowledgments

We would have never have been able to produce this book without the guidance, support, and encouragement of all the extraordinary mentors who have shaped our scholarly careers and trajectories over the years. Though not an exhaustive list, we would particularly like to acknowledge Karen Lee Ashcraft, Chantal Benoit-Barné, Boris Brummans, Patrice Buzzanell, Stacey Connaughton, François Cooren, Ann Cunliffe, Debbie Dougherty, Gail Fairhurst, Radhika Gajjala, Tim Kuhn, and Sarah Tracy for their tremendous mentorship that has made this book possible.

This book would also have never been possible without the outstanding contributions provided by the authors whose work is included in this volume. We are deeply grateful for your contributions and for your support of the project.

We are also greatly indebted to our graduate student assistants, Quentin Hemphill and Brittany Potter. Quentin helped with the preparation of the manuscript for submission and Brittany provided tremendous assistance in the production stage by compiling the book's index.

Lastly, we acknowledge the support that we received from our respective institutions—the University of Texas at San Antonio and Wayne State University—which provided each of us with a generous course release that helped make the book possible.

1 Introduction to the Field and to the Volume

Jamie McDonald and Rahul Mitra

Organizational communication is a flourishing field of inquiry and a vibrant scholarly community. Although a relatively young subfield of communication with its origins dating back to the 1960s and 1970s (Conrad and Sollitto 2017), the Organizational Communication Division is now among the largest divisions of both the United States–based National Communication Association and the International Communication Association. The field is in constant movement and has a tremendous theoretical, methodological, and topical scope, which is clearly documented in the three handbooks of organizational communication that have been published to date (Jablin and Putnam 2001, Jablin et al. 1987, Putnam and Mumby 2014).

"Organizational communication" refers to much more than the study of communication *within* organizations; that is, understanding organizations as already-formed entities within which we study communication processes. Such a view of organizations represents what is commonly referred to as the "container metaphor," which has been extensively problematized (Putnam and Nicotera 2009, Putnam et al. 1996, Smith 1993, Taylor and Van Every 2000). Rather than take organizations as taken-for-granted and already-formed entities, much organizational communication scholarship is concerned with the ways in which organizing and organizations are accomplished through communication. This research thus underscores how organizations are dynamic entities that are constantly (re)produced through organizing processes, which are fundamentally communicative (Brummans et al. 2014, Weick 1979). In this sense, organizations can be conceptualized as discursive constructions that cannot exist without communication (Fairhurst and Putnam 2004). Researching organizational communication through this lens implies that communication is not what needs to be explained—rather, communication is what explains organizational phenomena (Ashcraft et al. 2009).

Although the field of organizational communication is now well established, discerning the uniqueness of organizational communication scholarship and the identity of the field has been and continues to be heavily debated (e.g., Ashcraft et al. 2009, Broadfoot and Munshi 2007,

Mumby and Ashcraft 2006, Mumby and Stohl 1996, 2007). In one influential piece that sought to establish organizational communication as a unique field of inquiry, Mumby and Stohl (1996) suggested that the field is defined by four problematics that all organizational communication scholars address in some way in their scholarship: the problematics of voice, rationality, organization, and the organization–society relationship. These problematics include whose voices are heard; what counts as knowledge; what is and what counts as an organization; and how society, culture, organizations, and communication are interdependent and shape each other. More recently, Ashcraft, Kuhn, and Cooren (2009) put forth that organizational communication research is differentiated from research in other similar fields (e.g., management and organizational behavior) by a constitutive view of communication; that is, viewing communication as not merely expressing but also generating and constituting social and organizational realities for both internal and external stakeholders, even as these internal-versus-external boundaries are increasingly tenuous.

As Mumby and Stohl (2007: 269) have stated, "any effort to 'discipline' a field of study will, by definition, engage in acts of inclusion and exclusion." As such, disciplining the field of organizational communication is ultimately a political endeavor. Because of the political nature of setting boundaries around what organizational communication scholarship is and is not, Broadfoot and Munshi (2007: 253) have questioned the relevance of discerning disciplinary boundaries altogether and suggested that we instead break "down boundaries of discipline, space, language, and worldviews." They noted that this is particularly important considering that the scope of organizational communication scholarship is often problematically assumed to be limited to the boundaries of the U.S. and to Euro-American intellectual traditions (Broadfoot and Munshi 2007).

In this volume, we adopt a broad view of organizational communication and do not attempt to establish clear boundaries that distinguish the field from allied disciplines. Rather, we contend that all scholarship that examines the relationship between *communication* and *organizing/organization* falls within the purview of the field of organizational communication—regardless of the institutional affiliation and location of the authors, the language of this scholarship, and what intellectual traditions the scholarship draws from. Importantly, we do not claim that only those who identify as organizational communication scholars produce this scholarship, as a great deal of research in fields such as management, organization studies, and sociology also examines the relationship between communication and organizing/organization in some way. Rather than attempting to establish boundaries that separate organizational communication from these allied fields, we prefer to build connections among and with them by emphasizing how they overlap and, together, enhance our understanding of organizational communication processes.

Because of the enormous body of scholarship that examines the relationship between communication, organizing processes, and organization, those who are new to the study of organizational communication may find it overwhelming. As we discuss in the following section, the principal aim of this book is to make familiarizing oneself with the field, finding one's niche within the field, and becoming a part of the organizational communication scholarly community much less daunting, and more inviting and accessible.

Why This Book?

The starting point for this volume was a Facebook post in which Rahul was crowdsourcing for books that are ideally situated for advanced undergraduate and graduate students who are being introduced to organizational communication for the first time. When we took such a course as graduate students in the late 2000s, we had both been assigned an edited book published by Steve May and Dennis Mumby (2005), which served this purpose perfectly with its engaging tone and robust overview of key approaches to organizational communication. Over the course of a conversation that ensued from Rahul's post, we realized that there was a need for a similar book with the same inviting tone as May and Mumby's, but with an updated overview of the field that accounts for developments in organizational communication research and practice— "movements" in the field—over the past 15 years. After reaching out to key figures in the organizational communication community, we found a great level of enthusiasm for such a book and decided to pursue this project.

We understand "movements" in the field to mean not just shifts in specific paradigms or approaches to a topic (or the world in general), but ongoing contestations of what these topics really mean to different actors, who gets to speak and/or set the terns of these conversations, shifting values and norms over time and space. Early in our planning, we sought to ensure that this book would be distinct not only in its tone but also in its approach to reviewing key trends in the field. Thus, a distinguishing feature of the book is that each chapter is coauthored by a senior scholar, who is recognized as an established expert on the chapter's topic, and at least at least one "junior" scholar whom that senior scholar has mentored in some way and who is conducting cutting-edge research in his or her own right. The moniker "junior" might well be misleading, since the reader will find that these authors range widely from current graduate students to well-established researchers collaborating with their former advisors and mentors. On the one hand, then, this coauthorship is meant to remind us that we are all, at different stages of our careers, moving across and perennially learning new dimensions, theories, methods, and perspectives—and thus, both "junior" and "senior." On the other hand, this coauthorship highlights how such perspectives, theories, and methods have shifted and evolved over the years for scholars working perchance on similar theories and concepts, so that a central feature of this book is prompting intergenerational dialogue and collaboration among scholars in their speciality areas.

Another key feature of this book is that, in addition to providing a review of scholarship in their areas of specialty, the authors discuss their scholarly trajectories and how they became a part of the field. The reflections and stories about authors' scholarly careers enable readers to not just become acquainted with organizational communication research, but also with the scholars themselves. As such, the book accounts for the human and practical component of doing research, thereby showing the myriad connections between scholars and their scholarship. The stories shared by our contributing authors may be particularly enlightening to those who are new to the field, and/or who are in the process of finding their own scholarly interests, as they provide insight into how both personal and professional experiences come together to shape scholarly trajectories in particular ways. Thus, in yet another iteration of the "movements" theme, readers will learn not only how key topics and themes have shifted (and continue to shift and be contested) but also how and why leading figures in the field have themselves been "moved" to study what they do—the underlying stories, experiences, and values that continue to shape their scholarship and the broader field.

In line with the goals of the book stated previously, each contributed chapter includes the following elements: (1) a discussion of how the authors found their way into studying the topic at hand, (2) a review of current issues and future directions in this area, (3) a discussion of the practical applications of the research that is reviewed, and (4) reflections on future directions for organizational communication scholars to explore. Together then, the chapters enable readers to become familiar with key themes addressed by organizational communication scholars, current issues in the field, as well as the organizational communication scholarly community.

Organization of the Book

The book is divided into 15 chapters, with Chapters 2–14 written by experts in topical areas of inquiry within the field of organizational communication. The first topical chapter, Chapter 2, is written by Tim Kuhn and Jared Kopczynski and is devoted to explicating the relationship among three foundational concepts in organizational communication studies: structure, process, and agency. In particular, the authors explore how these concepts and the relationship between them are viewed through the lens of two different and contrasting perspectives: systems theory and process philosophy.

In addition to structure, process, and agency, power and resistance are also fundamental concepts to understanding organizational communication processes. In Chapter 3, Dennis Mumby and Mie Plotnikof examine the relationship between power and resistance in organizational settings, which organizational communication scholars have been exploring over the past three decades. The authors note that the dominant forms of power and resistance that we see in organizational settings have evolved significantly over time, from coercive, to consensual, to governmental forms of power.

In Chapter 4, Steve May, Jeremy Fyke, and Katharine Miller build upon Chapter 3's discussion of power and resistance by exploring organizational ethics, corporate social responsibility, and sustainability. Although each of these topics has its own literature, the authors show how the literatures are intertwined and how research in these areas enables us to understand the constantly evolving and contested relationship between organizations and society.

Identity, identification, and branding are fundamental concepts to understanding organizational communication processes. In Chapter 5, George Cheney and Katie Sullivan discuss how these concepts and the relationship between them have evolved over the course of the more than three decades that they have been explored in organizational communication scholarship. To explain these complex and shifting concepts, the authors offer references to personal experiences, work trends, popular culture, and contemporary social issues.

In Chapter 6, Michael Kramer and Stephanie Dailey explore the relationship between organizational socialization and organizational culture. Although these areas of study are most often treated separately, their discussion shows how they inform each other. In particular, the authors explore the socialization processes through which individuals join, participate in, and leave organizations, as well as how one's understanding of organizational culture shifts through these socialization processes.

Chapters 7 and 8 are each devoted to exploring the ways in which various forms of difference matter in organizations and shape organizational experiences. In this regard, Chapter 7, cowritten by Jessica Pauly and Patrice Buzzanell, specifically focuses on gender and sexuality, whereas Chapter 8, cowritten by Patricia Parker and Jamie McDonald, addresses difference, diversity, and inclusion more broadly. In this volume, we decided to have separate chapters for gender and difference because of their distinct origins and historical trajectories in organizational communication scholarship, which has resulted in there being much more scholarship about gender than about other forms of difference such as race, class, and disability. However, we recognize that separating scholarship on gender and difference is problematic because it foregrounds gender as a special form of difference that deserves special attention, while grouping all other forms of difference under a generic umbrella term (Ashcraft 2009). As such, although we felt that it was important to have two separate chapters for gender and difference in this book, we hope that this will be less necessary in the future as scholars increasingly examine the ways in which multiple forms of difference are intersectional, intertwined, and inseparable.

In Chapter 9, Sarah Tracy and Shawna Malvini Redden review scholarship on emotions and relationships in organizational settings. As such, they address topics such as the commodification and control of emotion at work, stress, burnout, and bullying. They also discuss research on prosocial emotions at work, which include humor, compassion, resilience, emotional intelligence, and mindfulness.

Chapter 10, cowritten by Jennifer Ervin and Joann Keyton, focuses on group decision-making and collaboration—crucial processes in all organizational settings. In this chapter, the authors discuss five key areas of group communication research: information and influence, group polarization, the hidden profile, groupthink, and the functional theory of group decision-making. The authors also address more recent areas of concern for group communication scholars, such as research on diversity among group members and the use of technology in group communication processes.

In Chapter 11, Guowei Jian and Gail Fairhurst review organizational communication research on leadership, perhaps one of the most widely studied organizational phenomena. The authors draw on four discursive lenses to organize the tremendous amount of research on this topic: (1) leadership as an objective phenomenon, (2) leadership as an interpretive accomplishment, (3) leadership as a form of power and control, and (4) leadership as dialogue and practice.

Change is constant in organizational life, and Chapter 12 is devoted to reviewing research that explores the complex dynamics of organizational change. In this regard, coauthors Laurie Lewis and Surabhi Sahay discuss how both implementers of change and stakeholders communicate during change, as well as current trends in research regarding change management.

Chapter 13 reviews research on networks and technology, two ubiquitous features of organizational life. In this chapter, William Barley and Marshall Scott Poole introduce key concepts in these lines of research and subsequently discuss the complex and dynamic relationship between networks and technology. In particular, they explore how the shifting nature of technology has impacted the nature of social networks, how advances in technology influence how we think about and study social networks, and how our understandings of social networks impact both technology and how we study it.

Chapter 14, written by Matthew Seeger and Rahul Mitra, is the final topical chapter and explores research on crisis and resilience in organizational settings. The authors conceptualize crises as communicative phenomenons and discuss how organizations, agencies, and communities can learn from crisis events to develop and strengthen their underlying resilience and incorporate discourses of long-term renewal.

The book concludes with Chapter 15, in which we bring together the different concepts, ideas, and frameworks discussed by contributing authors and advance a movement-inspired lens for organizational communication. We also outline how key clusters of technological, social-ecological, and cultural-generational changes might shape future directions for the field.

Editor Positionalities

Partially because of the stories and reflections offered by the authors in each of their chapters, reflexivity is a key theme that cuts across the book. By reflexivity, we refer to the processes through which we critically reflect on our positionalities and how our positionalities shape the ways in which we view and act in the world (Cunliffe 2003). These positionalities are shaped by many elements, including personal identities and experiences, philosophical assumptions about research, and our particular interests, values, and ideologies. When conducting research, engaging in reflexivity is crucial to account for the ways in which our positionalities shape aspects of the research process such as *what* we research, *why* we research it, and *how* we conduct and present research (Cunliffe 2002, Hibbert et al. 2014, Tomkins and Eatough 2010). Or, as the old adage goes, you can't really know where you are going until you know where you have been. As editors, we thus provide reflexive accounts in the following sections that discuss our positionalities in the field, which have ultimately shaped how we have organized the book and how we understand these ongoing movements in organizational communication research.

Jamie's Positionality in the Field

I first encountered the field of organizational communication while pursuing my bachelor's and master's degrees in the Department of Communication at the Université de Montréal, Canada. Although I didn't know it when I first entered that department, it is commonly referred to as the home of the "Montréal School" of organizational communication. As Tim Kuhn and Jared Kopczynski discuss in Chapter 2 of this volume, one of the defining characteristics of the Montréal School is a constitutive approach to both communication and organizing. As such, my early training in the field was very much grounded in the idea that communication constitutes organization and organizing, as well as in qualitative, discursive approaches to research.

During my time as a master's student, I became increasingly intrigued by critical and feminist approaches to organizational communication—an interest that was without a doubt sparked by presenting on this topic in a course taught by Consuelo Vásquez. As a doctoral student at the University of Utah and the University of Colorado Boulder, I pursued this interest by specializing in organizational communication research on identity and difference. For my dissertation, I conducted 2 years of ethnographic fieldwork at an organization seeking to increase the representation of women in the male-dominated field of computing and information technology and explored the tensions and contradictions that emerged during this process.

The ultimate goals of my research are to highlight how multiple facets of difference shape organizational experiences in ways that are both embedded within and reinforce power relations, as well as to explore ways of creating more just and inclusive organizing practices. To achieve these goals, I adopt multiple (meta)theoretical lenses, including interpretive, critical, feminist, and queer approaches to communication inquiry. For instance, interpretivism leads me to view communication as a constitutive process through which meaning is co-created among various actors, rather than simply transmitted. In line with critical approaches, my research is also premised on the assumption that communication is a value-laden, political process through which social actors strive to shape reality in ways that serve particular interests. Relatedly, my feminist commitments lead me to examine how meanings of difference are embedded into the social construction of reality in ways that constrain agency and reinforce extant relations of power. Moreover, queer theory leads me to view identity categories as both fluid and normalizing constructs, as well as to critique the dominant discourses that construct certain forms of difference as taken-for-granted and others as less valued. All of these (meta) theoretical lenses are explored in greater detail throughout the book, particularly in Chapter 8.

As an early career scholar, I have been enthralled by how many new developments in the field since I first began my doctoral studies, 10 years ago at the time of writing. New frameworks have emerged, new theories have been developed, and our understanding of organizational life has expanded significantly as a result. Looking forward, I'm excited to see how the field continues to develop over the next ten years and how these developments contribute to our knowledge of organizational communication processes.

Rahul's Positionality in the Field

I always wanted to get a master's degree, but I was never sure when, where, or in what. After majoring in Economics during my undergraduate years, and then obtaining a certification in Print Journalism,

I embarked on a career in business journalism in my native India, and was content—for a while, at least—to be done with school. Gradually, however, I began to realize that the life of a journalist wasn't meant for me, although I loved learning about and reporting the strategic decisions that companies undertook and tracing their social impacts on the ground. I decided to switch careers and worked for a large public relations firm, as a Senior Executive in Investor Relations, trying to see if I liked it better. Working as an Investor Relations practitioner was fascinating, because it allowed me access to deeper fundamentals and leadership processes within companies, which journalism only afforded me now and then. I was working with top leadership of these companies to devise strategies and practices that would fundamentally transform their organizations— or strengthen existing cores—to attract investors and funders. That got me thinking—as much as I love my work, are there specific reasons and drivers that make these "best practices" *best*, after all? And, can I be a part of uncovering those practices on the ground?

Enter graduate school.

To be honest, I had little idea what organizational communication was when I applied for a master's program in "Public Relations/ Organizational Communication" at Bowling Green State University in early 2007. The public relations part I knew—or thought I knew— based on my work as a journalist and investor relations specialist, and I assumed that "organizational communication" was merely an American spin on corporate communications work—where the organization messaged investors, media, customers, and other external stakeholders to further its strategic goals. Nor was I particularly interested in research or theory-building for the sake of theory-building; from the start, I was interested in using theoretical knowledge to apply to real-life situations, like the latest launch of a new product or crisis control, as I had dealt with during my professional career. "Theory" itself was an alien word.

In hindsight, much has changed, and I am incredibly grateful for it. My initial plans to complete a 1-year master's degree and return to working in industry were entirely disrupted by the joy I found in doing research, and upon my realization of the many topics, themes, methods, and impacts organizational communication involves. At the same time, my scholarly career has indubitably been shaped by my professional history and practical leanings, as my approach toward organizational communication research—and this book—has always been in terms of the applied lessons and social impacts of such research. The specific topics I have studied have shifted over the years—from corporate social responsibility to sustainable organizing to building resilient institutions and back again—and, while I have been satisfied at the fluidity of my research program, what has remained steadfast is my commitment to the "so what?" question. That is, before undertaking a new study or project, I have always sought to answer—for myself as the researcher, for participants in my research projects, and for broader communities and institutions—what practical and applied use it might have. In doing so, I have not only sought to ground the generation of organizational communication theory in everyday use and relevance, but also to make it more . . . human.

Try that, as you read the chapters in this book. After reading about the wonderful new developments in theory, method, and scope of organizational communication research, ask yourself how they have potentially shaped your understanding and experience of the world and organizations around you. Challenge yourself—and both contemporary organizations and this body of research—so *what?*

Moving Forward with the Book

In this brief introduction, we have introduced the field of organizational communication as an interdisciplinary area of inquiry that examines the relationship between communication and organizing/organization. The subsequent chapters build upon this introduction and, together, demonstrate the broad array of topics and perspectives with which organizational communication scholars engage. The chapters will, without a doubt, enhance your understanding of organizational communication processes, but it is important to remember that this understanding will never be complete. Indeed, all bodies of knowledge are always in movement as new research is published and new ideas are explored, and the field of organizational communication is no different (see Chapter 15 of this volume). As you familiarize yourself with organizational communication research, we thus encourage you to continue to ask questions about what remains to be explored—as these questions contribute to spurring future developments in the field, charting new directions for scholars to explore, and enriching the always evolving body of knowledge about the relationship between communication and organizing/organization.

Discussion Questions

1. What do you think of when you hear the words "organizational communication"? What do you expect to learn from this book?
2. Why do you think that debates continue as to what distinguishes organizational communication from allied fields? Do you think that establishing disciplinary boundaries is necessary? Why or why not?
3. What does it mean to engage in reflexivity? Why is reflexivity such an important part of the scholarly process?
4. What topical areas are you the most excited to read about? Why?

References

Ashcraft, K. L. 2009. "Gender and Diversity: Other Ways to "Make a Difference," in Alvesson, M., Bridgman, T. and Willmott, H. (eds.), *The Oxford Handbook of Critical Management Studies*, Oxford, UK: Oxford University Press, pp. 304–327.

Ashcraft, K. L., Kuhn, T. and Cooren, F. 2009. "Constitutional Amendments: 'Materializing' Organizational Communication," in Brief, A. and Walsh, J. (eds.), *The Academy of Management Annals*, New York: Routledge, pp. 1–64.

Broadfoot, K. J. and Munshi, D. 2007. "Diverse Voices and Alternative Rationalities: Imagining Forms of Postcolonial Organizational Communication," *Management Communication Quarterly*, 21, 249–267.

Brummans, B. H. J. M., Cooren, F., Robichaud, D. and Taylor, J. R. 2014. "Approaches to the Communicative Constitution of Organizations," in Putnam, L. L. and Mumby, D. K. (eds.), *The SAGE Handbook of Organizational Communication: Advances in Theory, Research, and Methods*, Thousand Oaks, CA: SAGE, pp. 173–194.

Conrad, C. and Sollitto, M. 2017. History of Organizational Communication. In Scott, C. R. and Lewis, L. K. (eds.) *International Encyclopedia of Organizational Communication*. Malden, MA: Wiley.

Cunliffe, A. L. 2002. "Reflexive Dialogical Practice in Management Learning," *Management Learning*, 33, 35–61.

Cunliffe, A. L. 2003. "Reflexive Inquiry in Organizational Research: Questions and Possibilities," *Human Relations*, 56, 983–1003.

Fairhurst, G. T. and Putnam, L. L. 2004. "Organizations as Discursive Constructions," *Communication Theory*, 14, 5–26.

Hibbert, P., Sillince, J., Diefenbach, T. and Cunliffe, A. 2014. "Relationally Reflexive Practice: A Generative Approach to Theory Development in Qualitative Research," *Organizational Research Methods*, 17, 278–298.

Jablin, F. M. and Putnam, L. L. (eds.) 2001. *The New Handbook of Organizational Communication: Advances in Theory, Research, and Methods*, Thousand Oaks, CA: SAGE.

Jablin, F. M., Putnam, L. L., Roberts, K. and Porter, L. (eds.) 1987. *Handbook of Organizational Communication: An Interdisciplinary Perspective*, Newbury Park, CA: SAGE.

May, S. and Mumby, D. K. (eds.) 2005. *Engaging Organizational Communication Theory & Research: Multiple Perspectives*, Thousand Oaks, CA: SAGE.

Mumby, D. K. 2007. "(Re)Disciplining Organizational Communication Studies: A Response to Broadfoot and Munshi," *Management Communication Quarterly*, 21, 268–280.

Mumby, D. K. and Ashcraft, K. L. 2006. "Organizational Communication Studies and Gendered Organization: A Response to Martin and Collinson," *Gender, Work, and Organization*, 13, 68–90.

Mumby, D. K. and Stohl, C. 1996. "Disciplining Organizational Communication Studies," *Management Communication Quarterly*, 10, 50–72.

Putnam, L. L. and Mumby, D. K. (eds.) 2014. *The SAGE Handbook of Organizational Communication*, Thousand Oaks, CA: SAGE.

Putnam, L. L. and Nicotera, A. M. (eds.) 2009. *Building Theories of Organization: The Constitutive Role of Communication*, New York: Routledge.

Putnam, L. L., Phillips, N. and Chapman, P. 1996. "Metaphors of Communication and Organization," in Clegg, S., Hardy, C. and Nord, W. (eds.), *Handbook of Organization Studies*, Thousand Oaks, CA: SAGE, pp. 375–408.

Smith, R. C. 1993. Images of Organizational Communication: Root-Metaphors of the Organization-Communication Relation. *International Communication Association conference*. Washington, DC.

Taylor, J. R. and Van Every, E. J. 2000. *The Emergent Organization: Communication as Its Site and Surface*, Mahwah, NJ: Lawrence Erlbaum.

Tomkins, L. and Eatough, V. 2010. "Towards an Integrative Reflexivity in Organisational Research," *Qualitative Research in Organizations and Management*, 5, 162–181.

Weick, K. E. 1979. *The Social Psychology of Organizing*, Reading, MA: Addison-Wesley.

2 Organizational Structures, Processes, and Agency

Timothy R. Kuhn and Jared Kopczynski

In the popular consciousness, the relationship between structure, process, and agency tends to evoke the menace embodied in a particular organizational form: bureaucracy. Although bureaucracies can bring positive outcomes, like preventing abuses of power and safeguarding democracy, cautionary tales are far more common. From Ben Franklin's statement on how a salaried governmental administration caters to office holders' avarice and ambition (see Bryan 1906) to Kafka's nightmarish-yet-amorphous anxiety generated by a rigid and byzantine legal system to depictions of soul-crushing monotony seen in films such as *Office Space*, the bureaucratic form is an enduring frustration. Bureaucracies are designed to constrain agency, curb exploitation, and produce predictable processes, but they develop architectural rigidities and ideological prejudices that suggest that organizing processes may be more complex than pronouncements about bureaucratic malice can capture.

Beyond these social concerns about bureaucracy, our interests in structure, process, and agency are also personal. For Jared, the topic has represented a long-term struggle with competing ideas that resist integration. During happy hours and seminars in his MA program, a good friend consistently shouted, "It's the capitalist structure" in response to any contemporary problem. Often swayed by this line of thinking, but hesitant to commit, he would say, "But people can't be so easily controlled" only to be interrupted by a quick response about how agency is a myth. At this impasse, other colleagues would chime in with their refrain that it's best to understand problems by focusing on local communication processes. Oscillating between these poles, Jared has often wondered how to best approach organizational problems.

For Tim, the interest in structure came around the family dinner table when he was growing up. Throughout Tim's teenage years, his father was a line manager at a natural foods manufacturing plant. In response to perfunctory nightly questions about how his day had gone, Tim's father would recount disagreements occurring that day, typically involving superiors who were invariably short-sighted, ignorant, and spiteful. He was the protagonist in these tales: always correct about the issues at play, never harboring a hidden agenda, undeniably wronged by abuses of power. Those stories carried lessons about the arbitrariness of organizational authority, the capriciousness of decision-making, and the dangers of being subject to the whims of those structurally superordinate.

In this chapter, our aim is not to resolve the personal tensions that led us to these topics, but rather to review organizational communication thinking on structure, process, and agency. This is both an important and daunting task, since these concepts form the substrate upon which most of the field—as covered in the following chapters in this book—have been established (though, as is evident across those chapters, that substrate takes on diverse forms in different scholarly traditions). Although structure, process, and agency are frequently invoked in organizational communication scholarship, they are seldom defined. So, as a starting point, we define *structure* as simply an arrangement of elements and their connections (like rules, responsibilities, and communication patterns), which demonstrates organizational order. *Processes*, in contrast, are the activities or tasks that enact the organization and accomplish its varied aims (and not merely its formally sanctioned goals); they are the site of action. *Agency*, finally, is the ability of social actors—usually individual persons, but also including groups and organizations—to make independent choices and to engage in autonomous action. We shall return to these basic conceptions as we review organizational communication's engagement with these terms.

The Ascendancy of Systems Theorizing in Organizational Communication

From a contemporary vantage point, it may seem hard to think of organizations as anything other than *systems*, collections of elements in definite relationship to one another that form a whole, set off from the environment by a (permeable) boundary. For many decades, the term has shaped conceptions of what organizations are and how they (should) operate. But it was not always so: the language and logic of systems entered organization theory through the natural sciences, though the widespread influence of general systems theory only in the middle of the twentieth century (von Bertalanffy 1968). Leading social scientists like Parsons (1956) borrowed from natural science models to portray the entirety of society as a system.

Systems theory spread to organization studies and came to occupy a central place in our field because it arrived with other bodies of management and organization theory that presented systems as logical ways to frame organizations. This move was marked most prominently by Katz and Kahn's (1966) depiction of organizations as open systems, but systems-based conceptions of organizations can be found throughout much of the earliest theorizing about organizations (Pondy and Mitroff 1979). Systems models were also adopted in the communication field when scholars began to see the wholeness of systems as a communicative accomplishment: As Barnett (1997: 2) summarizes, "One emergent property of the components' interaction is the organization itself. It was through communication among the components that their behavior could be coordinated, making it possible for the organization to achieve its goals." Communication, in this view, is a process (one among many) occurring within systems; these processes are generally understood as coordinated sets of changes in structures unfolding over time, linked to one another either causally or functionally, and propelled by some generative mechanism (Poole 2013).

In much systems thinking, *structure* and *process* are posed as complementary: processes occur within structures, which are designed to guide and direct action. Structure is often positioned as stable and enduring; process is about movement and change in those same structures. For instance, in studies of leadership, structure is seen as constraining (and enabling) organizational processes; it can thus serve as a substitute for supervision in that it guides and directs actors (e.g. employees) in their carrying out of processes (Kerr and Jermier 1978). *Agency*, in systems theorizing, is associated with an actor's responsiveness to cues from inside and outside the system, an ability to monitor and plan its action, its awareness of other agents, and an ability to make actions meaningful in the stream of activity (Poole 2014). Agents and their agency are key to establishing goals that guide ongoing action, as well as to configuring and modifying structures and processes to meet those aims. In systems theorizing, therefore, structure, process, and agency are intimately intertwined in the ongoing production of the system and the performance of its functions.

In what follows, we shall not devote much space to recounting the tenets and assertions of systems theory (given its coverage in the sources mentioned previously), but shall instead focus on how a few lines of thought within systems theorizing advance particular models of structure, process, and agency (for a framework for categorizing systems models, see Poole 2014)—and then also consider how those influences carry on in contemporary organizational communication scholarship.

Structural-Functionalism and Configurational Approaches

In the communication field in the 1970s, a debate raged about the standards by which we should judge explanations of communicative phenomena (Farace et al. 1977). One stance suggested that a search for generally applicable *laws*, theoretical statements about relationships between two or more events or variables that hold irrespective of situation (or that are at least predictable given situational constraints), was what communication studies needed to pursue. A second held that the proper aim of communication scholarship is the understanding of the *rules* that human agents develop and enforce in shaping social action; the goal in this view is to understand the regulation of interaction within particular settings, relationships, and communities. And a third position built upon systems theorizing to suggest that communication inquiry should examine the logical relations between components of a given *system* (e.g. dyad, family, group, or organization) and strive to explain how communication makes the relationships between elements of that system obtain. One outgrowth of this third view—systems approaches to theorizing communication—became known as *structural-functionalism*.

Structural-functionalism examines how the actions that enable a system to adjust or adapt to its environment occur. It requires a specification of the components, boundaries, and environment of a system; some characteristic essential for the system's persistence; and an explanation for how the system's structural features keep that characteristic alive (Monge 1977, Pavitt 1994). Structure, here, is "the network of relationships and roles throughout the organization. Structure enables the organization to meet its objectives efficiently and in an orderly manner" (Goldhaber 1986: 42). Structures thus guide and channel processes and are preserved when they perform useful functions for the system, such as achieving goals, maintaining its features, and innovating to meet ongoing challenges (Farace et al. 1977).

Communication, in a structural-functional rendering, is a process occurring *within* the system that produces integration of components (e.g. agreements on values or a shared culture), defines members' role expectations, and coordinates disparate activities. There can, of course, be patterns of communication, networks of relationships and messages that qualify as "communication structure," but this factor is important only to the extent that it provides a mechanism that generates or reinforces the system's ability to carve out a niche within its environment (Johnson 1993, Monge and Contractor 2003). Structural-functional scholarship tends, therefore, to focus on the structures that bring about order and advantage with respect to the demands of a system's environment.

Structural-functional theorizing tends to see agency as an outcome of the system and its structures, and often portrays systems themselves as the sites of agency. Structural-functional analysts see systems as having or displaying agency in the extent to which they monitor the environment, establish goals, receive feedback, and solve problems in attaining those goals. By way of example, functional analyses of small-group interaction (Hirokawa et al. 1996, Hirokawa and Salazar 1999) argue that the quality of a group's decision is an outcome of its ability to perform critical decision functions. Here, persons are seen to be interacting, and the communication process is where decisions occur, but the unique capacities of persons, as well as the possibility that the process *creates* the group and its enactment of exigencies, is not an element of the theory. Agency, for Hirokawa and colleagues, is generally understood to be circumscribed by the system and its structural features, including the goals it establishes. Consequently, structural-functional analyses are limited in their ability to explain intentional and creative departures from system equilibria.

A second systems-based approach begins with a recognition of varied organizational types, seeing those types as particular combinations of structures and processes that satisfy different organizational aims and outcomes. These *configurational* models assert that organizational forms (and processes) can be adapted to the exigencies of the environment and the needs of the organization with respect to its position in that environment. Bureaucracies, as mentioned in the introduction, are configurations designed to meet particular aims, and labels such as *postbureaucratic, participative, high reliability, learning,* and *stakeholder* speak to differences in organizational designs, outcomes, and practices. The forms and processes pursued by these types of organizations are understood to be contingent on the environment in which the organization finds itself, as well as on the aims of strategic managers.

Perhaps the most well-known approach along these lines is Mintzberg's typology of structural forms in *The Structuring of Organizations*. There, he defines organizational structure as "the sum total of ways in which the organization divides its labor into distinct tasks and then achieves coordination among them" (1979: 2; emphasis removed). He presents five mechanisms for the coordination of work: mutual adjustment, direct supervision, the standardization of work processes, the standardization of outputs, and the standardization of skills. Varied organizational configurations employ these mechanisms differently, developing communication structures that suit varied organizational strategies (Lawrence and Lorsch 1967). Accordingly, communication processes are central elements of configurational theorizing, a welcome inclusion following the systems theories of earlier vintage. And though there is debate about the novelty and persistence of "new" organizational forms like those mentioned in the preceding paragraph (Lammers 1989, McPhee and Poole 2001), the desire to theorize how organizations respond to social, economic, and technological changes has made configurational approaches key components of systems theorizing.

Structuration Theory

In the 1970s and 1980s, sociologist Anthony Giddens (among other contributors) developed structuration theory, one of the most influential contemporary social theories. Positioned as a *meta*theory, structuration aims to guide theories of more situated phenomena by shaping their explanations of social relations unfolding across time and space. This theory has attracted considerable attention across the social sciences, and its uptake in communication has been strong for several decades (Banks and Riley 1993).

Structure and the Duality of Structure

In the structural-functional theorizing introduced previously, structure was portrayed as a force external to human action, one that serves as a constraint on activity. Structuration, in contrast, conceives of structure as simultaneously constraining *and* enabling action. Structure is not outside the practices it constitutes; it exists only as it is instantiated in the interaction of agents.

This is so because structures, here, are composed of rules and resources. For Giddens, *rules* are generalizable procedures, not always understood at a level at which agents can put them into words. Rules assist agents in assigning meaning to practices and outcomes; they also dictate the manner in which practices may be carried out. *Resources*, on the other hand, supply agents with control over the material features of their environment or other agents. But structures are not explanatory devices on their own: When agents follow the rules and employ the resources implicated in structures, their action is shaped and directed by those rules and resources. This is the notion of the *duality of structure*, where "the structural properties of social systems are both medium and outcome of the processes they recursively organize" (Giddens 1984: 25). One implication of the duality of structure is that communication is key, because structures "only exist through being applied and acknowledged in interaction—they have no reality independent of the social practices they constitute" (Poole et al. 1985: 76). All situated practices are *social* in nature, and the patterning of social practices implies the creation of meanings. Every practice draws on *numerous* rules and resources; systems, therefore, also always incorporate *multiple* structures. For these reasons, the *relationships between* structures, and how those relationships play out in communication practices, are vital to understanding structuration.

The Status of Agency

Agency, for Giddens, is the expression of the "knowledgeability" of agents in action. The patterned activities of agents compose social *systems*, the majority of which are constructed in those agents' routine activities. Agency, then, is impossible without knowledgeability, the degree to which the actor understands the reasons for his or her action. And, because agency revolves around knowledgeability for Giddens, it is a uniquely human characteristic; neither collectives (as in structural-functionalism, as previously discussed), nor human–nonhuman hybrids (as in the Montréal School, as discussed in the following pages) can be considered agents.

Also associated with the notion of knowledgeability is that agency involves the capacity to act, or to act otherwise (to choose a course of action other than that normatively prescribed). In other words, agency means that an actor has the ability to produce an effect: "agency concerns the events of which an individual is the perpetrator, in the sense that the individual could, at any phase in a given sequence of conduct, have acted differently. Whatever happened would not have happened if that individual had not intervened" (Giddens 1984: 9). An important concern, then, is not only agents' *intended* outcomes of their actions but also the *unintended consequences*. Giddens notes that unintended consequences are often closely connected to institutionalized practices (normal, everyday activities), and thus the production and reproduction of *systems*. Thus, what transpires in an earlier context influences the conditions of action later and, when the actions that produce the unintended consequences are routinized, the influences on the subsequent context can stabilize into recognizable social and organizational forms.

Contemporary Structurationist Research in Organizational Communication

Communication scholars who investigate structure tend to concentrate on either technology (especially in groups) or communication networks. Because these topics are covered in Chapters 9 and 12 of this volume, however, we illustrate structuration-inspired scholarship with two additional lines of research. First is McPhee and colleagues' "Four Flows" model of organizational constitution (McPhee and Zaug 2000, McPhee and Iverson 2009). One of the three "pillars" (Schoeneborn et al. 2014) of what has become known as *Communication as Constitutive of Organization*, or CCO, scholarship, the Four Flows model suggests that organizations comprise four analytically distinct types of communication: membership negotiation (recruitment, socialization, and identification), organizational self-structuring (defining the organization's aims and procedures), activity coordination (interdependently accomplishing organizational tasks), and institutional positioning (setting the organization in the larger environment, in relation to the other entities and stakeholders upon which its existence depends). Each type of communication, on its own, involves complex negotiations of meaning enacting the duality of structure, but when the Four Flows intersect, an organization—as distinct from other social collectives or groupings—can be said to exist (Iverson et al. 2018). The resulting system need not be understood as a seamlessly integrated whole simply because the flows overlap; indeed, some of the more interesting insights generated from the (relatively limited amount of) empirical research into the Four Flows model indicates that examining the unintended consequences emerging from tensions between the flows could be a fruitful line of inquiry (e.g. Browning et al. 2009, Lutgen-Sandvik and McDermott 2008, Shumate and O'Connor 2010).

A second illustration is *structurating activity theory*, a melding of structuration and cultural-historical activity theory (Engeström 1993).

Canary (2010; Canary and McPhee 2009) developed this perspective to address how knowledge—policy-oriented knowledge in particular—is a product of activity systems composed of interrelated people, communities, practices, artifacts, resources, a division of labor, and the objective(s) toward which the system(s) is/are oriented. Building on claims key to both its intellectual inspirations, structurating activity theory portrays contradictions between elements as normal operations of systems. These contradictions not only chart the system's trajectory but also can lead to important transformations in activity and, ultimately, alter agents' knowledgeability. Research employing structurating activity theory is still in its early stages, but scholars have used the theory to explore, among other things, a network of organizations seeking to reduce ethnic conflict in the former Soviet Union (Foot and Groleau 2011) and cancer screening conversations (Canary et al. 2015), demonstrating its broad utility and heuristic capacities.

Summary of Systems Theorizing

Research drawing inspiration from systems theories tends to position structure—rather than process or agency—as taking precedence in understandings of organizational communication. Structure, particularly in structural-functional and configurational renderings, is designed to fit organizational needs, and process and agency are understood to be dependent on structural choices. Structuration theory differs somewhat in its attention to the intricate interplay between agency and structure and, as seen in the examples presented previously, novel questions and approaches to understanding organizations can emerge from making communication process the point at which structure and agency—which, for Giddens at least, are only analytically separable—meet. Even in structurationist research, however, structure tends to maintain its conceptual grip, often being preferred over agency in explanations of social phenomena. Table 2.1 depicts these differences in systems approaches. In the next section (as well as in the far-right column of the table), we present a theoretical move that does not simply argue that this emphasis should be rectified (as if it were taking the "other side"), but one that seeks to eradicate the very separation guiding systems theorizing.

The Development of an Ontological Departure: Process Philosophy

An alternate starting point for examinations of organizing involves a radical re-conception of organizations and organizing practices. Based on a novel ontological stance, theory in this vein refuses to see processes (like communication) as simply a property of a system; in other words, *process* is not merely the action term that complements (and shapes)

Table 2.1 Differences in Systems Approaches

	Systems Approaches	Structuration Theory	Process Philosophy
	Structural Functionalism and Contingency Theorizing		
Guiding Question	How does a system adapt to its environment?	How are systems (re)constituted in communicative practice?	How do organizational phenomena (e.g., knowing and organizing) emerge, develop, and change across time and space? Structure is but a moment selected from an ongoing stream of processes.
Conception of Structure	Network of relationships and roles. Structures emerge to serve organizational needs with respect to environmental demands.	Composed of rules and resources and always already contingent upon processes. Structural contradictions normal in complex systems.	
Conception of Process	Guided and constrained by structure. Processes are activities within systems that allow for system cohesion and persistence.	Simultaneously mediated by and constitutive of structure.	Anti-substantialist: Social reality is continuous flow of interconnected and fluctuating activities.
Conception of Agency	Collectives display agency in monitoring the environment, establishing goals, interpret feedback, and solve problems.	Agency is the ability of knowledgeable human actors to deploy to produce an effect; patterning produces (un)intended consequences.	The accomplishment of action by multiple and hybrid actors—human and nonhuman together.
Conception of Communication	The process of information exchange, which produces internal integration for efficient operations. Includes forms of work coordination and sense-making with respect to environmental demands.	The site for the (re)production of the duality of structure—the interplay of structure and agency.	Site of struggles over meaning that constitute contingent and temporary social realities.

structure. Instead, process *is* social reality—it is in the conduct and flow of practice that what we conceive of as entities, knowledge, and phenomena exist. Drawing on a diverse set of theorists, including Alfred North Whitehead, Henri Bergson, Charles Sanders Peirce, John Dewey, and Ilya Prigogine, process philosophers depict the world as a continuous flow of interconnected and fluctuating activities, rather than as a set of determinate relationships between fixed entities.

Despite drawing on a long lineage of philosophical thought, process thinking in organization studies only gained significant traction in the 1990s. To establish a legitimate place on the academic stage, process philosophies leveled several critiques of conventional systems-based theorizing. They charge that systems views employ a mechanistic model of the world, where the objective existence of independent entities like persons, markets, environments, buildings, artifacts, languages, and organizations are taken for granted; they evince a *representationalist epistemology*, in which our depictions are taken to be more or less accurate renderings of the assumedly identifiable objects and generative mechanisms populating the external world (Chia 1999). In systems theorizing, processes are peripheral to the primary interest, structure: "All important processual phenomena are presumed to sediment into durable and measurable aspects of structure. Structures are then taken to be the relevant empirical data for the explanation of social order" (Boden 1994: 12). Systems models thus have a tendency to (a) treat settings and situations (including organizational environments) as deterministic—such that agency and novelty are rendered peripheral, which hampers explanations of change; (b) render organizations as containers within which communication occurs, portraying communication as derivative of the "real" mechanisms driving organizational action; and (c) simplify the messiness, contingency, and ambiguity of organizing.

In contrast, process-oriented perspectives urge scholars to examine how and why the emergence, development, and modification of organizational phenomena happen as they do. From a process ontology, there is a distinction to be made in conceptions of process. *Weak process views* describe a temporal evolution in entities (such as persons, groups, or organizations), but assume a continuity in the identities of those entities over time (Langley and Tsoukas 2016). Simply considering how an organizational unit changes its actions or structures from one point in time to another does not involve the sort of radical break away from a representationalist epistemology offered by process philosophy (Cummings et al. 2016). In other words, when processes are depicted as taking place within already-constituted structures, a weak process view is operating. A *strong process view*, in contrast, sees the world as a whole, including organizational phenomena, as always *becoming*. In a strong process view, the "entity" (such as persons, groups, or organizations) is not something to which events happen; instead, "it" is *constituted by* the events in which it both participates and is invoked. Constitutive conceptions of communication—where communication is seen as the force generating and sustaining social and organizational realities, as described in the following subsection—exemplify a stance that has taken a strong process stance to heart.

From a strong-process perspective, analysts' interests shift to the experiences that constitute and invoke the entity in question. As Langley and Tsoukas (2016: 5) explain, "To be sensitive to process means, among other things, to be alert to capture and understand others' and one's own evolving experience." Experience thus becomes a tool with which to understand the development and deployment of agency in the process of organizing. Experiences, moreover, are inherently *heterogeneous* in the sense that they occur anew each time and are embedded in a particular temporal flow, even if we linguistically categorize the experiences as fitting a particular type. Moreover, in expressing a preference for process, this approach does not deny the existence of objects, entities, or structures; instead, these are taken to be "transient appearances in the flow of time" (Hernes 2014: 41) that are captured by situated actors for particular purposes. Another way of saying this is that a process ontology hinges on a recognition of continual change, but "does not, though some fools project such a conclusion into it, postulate a world in which everything is always in radical flux" (Connolly 2013: 401). The aim is instead to analyze, in detail, the complex communicative activities that constitute, organize, maintain, and alter those objects, entities, and structures.

A key moment in the development of a process vision of organizing was the publication of Karl Weick's (1969, 1979) *The Social Psychology of Organizing*. Positioning his work in direct contrast to a book introduced in the preceding section, Katz and Kahn's (1966) *The Social Psychology of Organizations*, Weick's use of the gerund organiz*ing* signaled an important shift. He began by asking about how we organize and showed that what we take to be organizations are always accomplished and sustained in communication. For Weick, organizations have no inherent reality beyond the behavioral patterns and cognitive structures of those creating them; they are nothing more than interlocked behavioral patterns and structures of belief that are repeated and stabilized. This is reflected in his conception of organizing: "A consensually validated grammar for reducing equivocality by means of sensible interlocked behaviors. To organize is to assemble ongoing interdependent actions into sensible sequences that generate sensible outcomes" (Weick 1979: 3). Given this focus, Weick suggests that analysts need to examine enactment (the *creation* of inputs from environments to be processed by organizing), sensemaking, and interaction. Traditional systems models, as suggested previously, are inadequate for this task; what is required is a sensitivity to communication processes, co-evolution, and becoming (Weick 2010). Not only was his model of organizing attractive to organizational communication scholars (Bantz 1989, Bantz and Smith 1977, Weick and Browning 1986) but it also helped to establish the centering of language and communication in the larger organization studies field.

Process-Based Organizational Communication Research

Because a process ontology constitutes a radical break with conventional thinking, process-based conceptions of organization are rarely represented in textbooks the way systems theory is. Yet there are several lines of organizational communication scholarship that draw inspiration from process ontologies. Here we overview two: knowing and knowledge management, and the Montréal School's version of CCO.

Knowing as Organizational Processes

For several decades, analysts have heralded the development of an information economy, one in which organizational performance hinges on an ability to accumulate and capitalize on knowledge. Early scholarship thus sought to manage knowledge in the organizational interest by creating systems that would capture knowledge from individuals, protecting knowledge possessed by the organization, moving knowledge to where it was needed, and capitalizing on amassed stocks of knowledge (Barley et al. 2018). Such efforts at knowledge management (KM) depict knowledge as a commodity, an entity that can be possessed, stored, and transferred; they tend to see knowledge as a matter of cognition and organizations as systems.

More recently, however, scholars influenced by a process ontology have been developing an alternative stance on knowledge and KM. Starting by shifting, linguistically, to a verb—to the gerund *knowing* (and *learning*) rather than the noun *knowledge*—this view asserts that we know too little about how organizationally relevant activity is actually accomplished; *to know* implies involvement in a complex array of people, things, discourses, and practices spread across time and space (Brown and Duguid 2001, Gherardi 2000, Orlikowski 2002). This move is warranted because the process ontology outlined previously directs our attention to the "performative, provisional, dynamic, ongoing, often mundane production of a social practice . . . knowing is a practical accomplishment, and solutions to problematic situations encountered in organizing are always interactively realized" (Kuhn 2014: 483). Process-based theorists often advocate for studying neither the person (as knower) nor abstract knowledge (as object), but the *community of practice*: A "site" where belonging, identity, and collectivity are continually reconstructed through participation in a joint enterprise (Wenger 1998). KM thus shifts to shaping the community and its practices, not amassing knowledge.

In organizational communication, research stemming from this process-oriented vision is interested in how a diverse assortment of elements get configured to produce "knowledgeable" action. Scholars in this stream have, accordingly, examined how heterogeneity across a community requires *meta*communication (Kuhn and Porter 2011), how agency and structure are deployed in fashioning assessments of expertise (Yoon et al. 2016), and how the location of expertise and authority shift in response to organizational contingencies (Kuhn and Rennstam 2016, Rennstam 2012). A concern raised about work of this sort, however, is that in its attention to process and community, it runs the risk of ignoring or obscuring the power and domination that typically characterizes organizing (Contu and Willmott 2003, Kuhn and Jackson 2008). Framing communication as a process of *struggle over meaning* (Mumby 2005) can allow analysts to probe and dissect what "counts" as knowledge and expertise in a given context, and what consequences particular associations create. Research on the often-invisible work associated with process experts and unpaid (and frequently gendered) labor (Treem and Barley 2016), as well as on agents' resistance to forms of control in knowledge-intensive work (Kärreman and Rylander 2008, Lyon 2005), represents a line of process-oriented thinking that takes the struggle over meaning seriously.

Montréal School CCO

A second example of organizational communication scholarship inspired by the turn to a process ontology is Montréal School CCO theorizing. This body of work has, since the mid-1990s, risen in prominence in organizational communication scholarship as a novel approach to understanding organization and organizing. A complete summary of this theorizing is beyond the scope of this chapter (Ashcraft et al. 2009, Brummans et al. 2014, Schoeneborn et al. 2014) but, at a basic level, Montréal School scholars are concerned with understanding how communication practices construct and organize the practices we come to recognize as "organizational." This is accomplished through a complex set of concepts and theoretical commitments that configure structure, process, and agency in rather divergent ways from that traditionally seen in communication scholarship, which leads them to see organization not as a system of interdependent components, but as networks of practices and conversations, collective experiences, texts "authored" through communication, or "figures" deployed in conversation to shape action. These conceptions are, needless to say, a sharp break with systems models of formal organizations.

Two interrelated concepts provided the initial groundwork for Montréal School CCO: the text/conversation dialectic and distanciation. In the first major introduction to Montréal theorizing, Taylor et al. (1996)

examined the dialectical relationship between texts and conversations, which serves as both the basis of organizing and their model of communication. Put simply, *text* refers to the content of interaction, whereas *conversation* refers to the situated process of speaking and interpreting. The relationship between text and conversation is dialectical "because the activities of interpretation are themselves interpretable, the conversation is in turn the matter of text" (Taylor et al 1996: 4). Coordination and control (i.e., *organizing*) occurs as actors, both in local settings and those dispersed across space and time, draw on and interpret texts, engage in interaction, and reinterpret their conversations as texts.

Although the text/conversation dialectic describes how actors organize, the concept of distanciation explains how networks of conversations *scale up* to the "entities" we often think of as organizations. As Taylor et al. (1996: 7) explained, "What we are accustomed to calling *organization* is at once actual (a network of conversations) and symbolic (a perceived actor, embodying the community as a whole). The symbolic dimension is text mediated." As the textualized results of conversations escape the conditions of their originating conversations, they gain a facticity that can infuse many distributed conversations. And when that textualization is taken to be representative of the whole network of conversations, it can become taken as itself an actor (an entity) which can then guide and direct subsequent conversations (Kuhn 2008).

Although these concepts were central to the initial building blocks of Montréal School CCO, later writings have continued to press further into process thinking. A process ontology is more fully realized by some of the recent work from Cooren and colleagues, utilizing concepts such as *ventriloquism*. Although a number of other concepts could be discussed here—presentification (Benoit-Barne and Cooren 2009) or spacing (Vásquez 2013), to name two—ventriloquism helps demonstrate how Montréal School theorizing is dependent upon conceptualizing agency as distributed. In other words, agency is not possessed by a single agent (and is not limited to human actors and their knowledgeability, as in structuration theory), but because action always involves heterogeneous elements coming together—think persons enrolling other persons, using tools, occupying space, deploying artifacts, enlisting rules, crafting language, and the like—agency cannot be reduced to any particular element (Brummans 2006, Kuhn and Burk 2014). Agency, in other words, is always hybrid, a property of a multiplicity of entities acting conjointly. Cooren et al. (2013) draw on ventriloquism as a metaphor for understanding communication as a constitutive activity dependent on this form of distributed agency. As they explain, "A ventriloqual approach to communication presumes that 'things' besides human beings are continuously inviting and expressing themselves in human interactions, which gives us deeper insight into the things that contribute to the enactment of situations" Cooren et al. 2013: 262) A Montréal School approach to communication and organization thus directs attention to the immense complexity involved in an action as seemingly simple as an organizational member speaking *for* an organization. Put another way, instead of saying that the person spoke on behalf of the organization, we might focus on how the organization and the person were *both* ventriloquized through the act of speaking.

The theoretical framework developed by the Montréal School has been used to provide insights on a wide range of phenomena. A key empirical project on *Médecins sans Frontières* (Doctors without Borders) demonstrates the usefulness of this approach (Benoit-Barné and Cooren 2009, Cooren et al. 2008, Cooren et al. 2013). For the sake of brevity, we discuss Benoit-Barné and Cooren's (2009) study, which focused on the challenge of asserting authority as members spread across large and remote geographic regions. They demonstrate that authority is not *possessed* by individuals (or positions) within an organization but is instead *accomplished* as actors "make present" authority in interactions. For example, an organizational actor might direct attention toward a printed organizational policy and, in so doing, act in conjunction with the policy to shape decisions (i.e., accomplish authority). Benoit-Barné and Cooren (2009: 26) demonstrate how humans and "things" (material objects, policies, or organizations) *co*-produce authority, "which allows scholars to show how interactions are constantly dislocated through presentification by bringing to the floor sources of authority that might at first sight appear absent." This demonstrates how taken for granted concepts such as "authority" are reimagined through Montréal School thinking and process ontology.

Summary of Process-Based Theorizing

The two exemplars of organizational communication scholarship (knowing/KM and the CCO scholarship of the Montréal School) exhibit the novelty offered by a process ontology, but also display its conceptual challenges. As evident in the preceding subsections, these efforts to rework literature on knowledge and organizational existence require conceptual shifts, expansions of vocabularies, and alterations in our criteria to assess the quality of scholarship. Placing emphasis on process as the genesis of organizational existence and action positions structures as but moments in ongoing flows, shaped by the actions of a heterogeneous mix of human and nonhuman agents. In comparison to systems theory, a process ontology is in its infancy, yet it has attracted the interest of a host of communication scholars interested in pursuing its repercussions for research and practice.

Discussion

Previously, we explored the intersections between structure, process, and agency as they have played out in two of the dominant conceptual frames in the organizational communication field: systems theory and a process ontology. These issues are cornerstones of the field that have received a great deal of study, and our exposition showed a variety of ways of understanding their relationships. In traditional versions of systems theory (structural-functional and configurational approaches), structure is understood as driving process and agency, whereas structuration theory seeks a fundamental interdependence—a *duality*, rather than a dualism—between the concepts. A process ontology takes this further by foregrounding flux and transformation—not in the sense that apparent solidity is denied, but such that the constitution of entities of all sorts, including actors and organizations, must be explained through communicative practice.

How the field conceives of structure, process, and agency is important for at least three reasons. First, to reiterate a point made previously, these are fundaments of the organizational communication field. Not only do we talk colloquially about organizations as systems and communication as a process, but much of our theorizing draws (even if only implicitly) on these frames.

Second, these bodies of work bear implications for both pedagogy and organizational action. In both structuration theory and in process thinking, the presence of tensions, contradictions, and paradoxes is portrayed as a common, everyday fact of organizational life; exposing and practitioners to these literatures can help them see the ubiquity of these phenomena and to locate their source(s) in communicative practice (Trethewey and Ashcraft 2004). Moreover, exploring the connections between structure, process, and agency—and CCO thinking in particular—can overcome the tendency to take organizations for granted and, instead, to see them as the ongoing accomplishments continually (re) created in dispersed communicative practices (Kuhn and Schoeneborn 2015). Both moves position communication as key to explaining how organizations exist, persist, and transform.

A third implication is particularly aligned with a process ontology's stance on knowing. In a recent review, Barley et al. (2018) note that the lion's share of KM literature—produced primarily in the field of strategic management—insists upon the need for knowledge *integration*. This means that most KM programs seek to create similarity in the knowledge possessed by persons within a given organizational unit, or an organization as a whole, and do so by extracting knowledge from its locations and making it public, often through electronic repositories. Fostering knowledge sharing, and eliminating hoarding, is seen as a crucial KM task because strategic management's guiding desire favors organizational interests over those of individual employees. A process-based conception of KM, in contrast, argues against the need to integrate or assimilate the knowledge of actors across a unit and, instead, would direct attention to the mundane practices that stitch together heterogeneous forms of knowing. It also highlights the benefits of differentiation, even if contrasting practices generate conflict and uncertainty (Bruns 2013, Kuhn and Porter 2011). Not only is highlighting difference more aligned with most people's experiences of organizational life than is an integrationist frame, it also carries the potential to draw attention to divergent models of valuing knowledge in organizations, as well as to sources of ongoing change (and innovation) that might escape the gaze of those not attuned to complex dynamics of knowing (Gehman et al. 2013, Nicholls 2009).

In sum, the triumvirate of structure, process, and agency are core notions for theorizing and practicing organizational communication. What our review has laid bare is that these notions do not have a single and straightforward meaning; rather, the frame from which we understand the interplay of these terms shapes the theory, research, and practice generated. It is additionally clear, though, that these frames are in continual development—seen not merely in the growth of process ontologies, but the advent of new versions of systems theories associated with complexity and relationality (Kuhn et al. 2017). These complicate the division we have presented here, suggesting that the field's understandings of structure, process, and agency will continue to evolve and serve as ongoing sources of intellectual inspiration.

Discussion Questions

1. If you were studying the creation of a new student organization at your university, how might systems and process approaches complement one another in posing research questions and in determining what to analyze? How would they contrast?

2. In systems theorizing, decisions are often a key unit of analysis. What resources do the versions of systems theory discussed here provide for explaining the forces that shape decision-making in organizations? And to what would one look to explain how managers make poor decisions?

3. How might the organizational impacts of communication technologies be understood from a systems perspective? How would one's view of these technologies change if we saw them (as well as organizations) in process terms?

4. What does the attention to *knowing* in communities of practice highlight that would be missed in approaches that conceive of *knowledge* as an entity to be managed?

5. How do the different approaches discussed in this chapter allow us to think about what an organization is and does (i.e., the *constitution* of an organization)?

30 *Kuhn and Kopczynski*

References

Ashcraft, K. L., Kuhn, T. and Cooren, F. 2009. "Constitutional Amendments: 'Materializing' Organizational Communication," in Brief, A. and Walsh, J. (eds.), *The Academy of Management Annals*, New York: Routledge, pp. 1–64.

Banks, S. P. and Riley, P. 1993. "Structuration as an Ontology for Communication Research," in Deetz, S. A. (ed.), *Communication Yearbook 16*, Newbury Park, CA: SAGE, pp. 167–196.

Bantz, C. R. 1989. "Organizing and 'The Social Psychology of Organizing'," *Communication Studies*, 40, 231–240.

Bantz, C. R. and Smith, D. H. 1977. "A Critique and Experimental Test of Weick's Model of Organizing," *Communication Monographs*, 44, 171–184.

Barley, W. C., Treem, J. W. and Kuhn, T. 2018. "Valuing Multiple Trajectories of Knowledge: A Critical Review and Research Agenda for Knowledge Management Research," *Annals of the Academy of Management*, 12, 278–317.

Barnett, G. A. 1997. "Organizational Communication Systems: The Traditional Perspective," in Barnett, G. A. and Thayer, L. (eds.), *Organization—Communication Emerging Perspectives V: The Renaissance in Systems Thinking*, Greenwich, CT: Ablex, pp. 1–46.

Benoit-Barné, C. and Cooren, F. 2009. "The Accomplishment of Authority through Presentification: How Authority is Distributed Among and Negotiated by Organizational Members," *Management Communication Quarterly*, 23, 5–31.

Boden, D. 1994. *The Business of Talk: Organizations in Action*, Cambridge, UK: Polity Press.

Brown, J. S. and Duguid, P. 2001. "Knowledge and Organization: A Social-Practice Perspective," *Organization Science*, 12, 198–213.

Browning, L. D., Greene, R. W., Sitkin, S. B., Sutcliffe, K. M. and Obstfeld, D. 2009. "Constitutive Complexity: Military Entrepreneurs and the Synthetic Character of Communication Flows," in Putnam, L. L. and Nicotera, A. M. (eds.), *Building Theories of Organization: The Constitutive Role of Communication*, New York: Routledge, pp. 89–116.

Brummans, B. H. J. M. 2006. "The Montréal School and the Question of Agency," in Cooren, F., Taylor, J. R. and Van Every, E. (eds.), *Communication as Organizing: Empirical and Theoretical Explorations in the Dynamic of Text and Conversation*, Mahwah, NJ: Lawrence Erlbaum Associates, pp. 197–211.

Brummans, B. H. J. M., Cooren, F., Robichaud, D. and Taylor, J. R. 2014. "Approaches to the Communicative Constitution of Organizations," in Putnam, L. L. and Mumby, D. K. (eds.) *The SAGE Handbook of Organizational Communication*. 3rd ed., Thousand Oaks, CA: SAGE, pp. 173–194.

Bruns, H. C. 2013. "Working Alone Together: Coordination in Collaboration across Domains of Expertise," *Academy of Management Journal*, 56, 62–83.

Bryan, W. J. (ed.) 1906. *The World's Famous Orations*, New York: Funk and Wagnalls.

Canary, H. E. 2010. "Constructing Policy Knowledge: Contradictions, Communication, and Knowledge Frames," *Communication Monographs*, 77, 181–206.

Canary, H. E., Bullis, C., Cummings, J. and Kinney, A. Y. 2015. "Structuring Health in Colorectal Cancer Screening Conversations: An Analysis of Intersecting Activity Systems," *Southern Communication Journal*, 80, 416–432.

Canary, H. E. and McPhee, R. D. 2009. "The Mediation of Policy Knowledge: An Interpretive Analysis of Intersecting Activity Systems," *Management Communication Quarterly*, 23, 147–187.

Chia, R. 1999. "A 'Rhizomatic' Model of Organizational Change and Transformation: Perspectives from a Metaphysics of Change," *British Journal of Management*, 10, 209–227.

Connolly, W. E. 2013. "The 'New Materialism' and the Fragility of Things," *Millennium*, 41, 399–412.

Contu, A. and Willmott, H. 2003. "Re-Embedding Situatedness: The Importance of Power Relations in Learning Theory," *Organization Science*, 14, 283–296.

Cooren, F., Brummans, B. H. J. M. and Charrieras, D. 2008. "The Coproduction of Organizational Presence: A Study of Medicins Sans Frontiers in Action," *Human Relations*, 61, 1339–1370.

Cooren, F., Matte, F., Benoit-Barné, C. and Brummans, B. H. J. M. 2013. "Communication as Ventriloquism: A Grounded-in-Action Approach to the Study of Organizational Tensions," *Communication Monographs*, 80, 255–277.

Cummings, S., Bridgman, T. and Brown, K. G. 2016. "Unfreezing Change as Three Steps: Rethinking Kurt Lewin's Legacy for Change Management," *Human Relations* 69, 33–60.

Engeström, Y. 1993. "Developmental Studies of Work as a Testbench of Activity Theory: The Case of Primary Care Medical Practice," in Chaiklin, S. and Lave, J. (eds.), *Understanding Practice*, New York: Cambridge University Press, pp. 64–103.

Farace, R., Monge, P. and Russell, H. 1977. *Communicating and Organizing*, Reading, MA: Addison-Wesley.

Foot, K. and Groleau, C. 2011. "Contradictions, Transitions, and Materiality in Organizing Processes: An Activity Theory Perspective," *First Monday*, 16.

Gehman, J., Treviño, L. K. and Garud, R. 2013. "Values Work: A Process Study of the Emergence and Performance of Organizational Values Practices," *Academy of Management Journal*, 56, 84–112.

Gherardi, S. 2000. "Practice-Based Theorizing on Learning and Knowing in Organizations," *Organization*, 7, 211–223.

Giddens, A. 1984. *The Constitution of Society: Outline of the Theory of Structuration*, Berkeley, CA: University of California Press.

Goldhaber, G. M. 1986. *Organizational Communication*, Dubuque, IA, Wm. C. Brown.

Hernes, T. 2014. *A Process Theory of Organization*, New York: Oxford.

Hirokawa, R. Y., Erbert, L. and Hurst, A. 1996. "Communication and Group Decision-Making Effectiveness," in Hirokawa, R. Y. and Poole, M. S. (eds.), *Communication and Group Decision Making*. 2nd ed., Thousand Oaks, CA: SAGE, pp. 269–300.

Hirokawa, R. Y. and Salazar, A. 1999. "Task-Group Communication and Decision-Making Performance," in Frey, L. R., Gouran, D. S. and Poole, M. S. (eds.), *The Handbook of Group Communication Theory and Research*, Thousand Oaks, CA: SAGE, pp. 167–191.

Iverson, J. O., McPhee, R. D. and Spaulding, C. W. 2018. "Being Able to Act Otherwise: The Role of Agency in the Four Flows at 2-1-1 and Beyond," in Brummans, B. H. J. M. (ed.), *The Agency of Organizing: Perspectives and Case Studies*, New York: Routledge, pp. 59–81.

Johnson, J. D. 1993. *Organizational Communication Structure*, Norwood, NJ: Ablex.

Kärreman, D. and Rylander, A. 2008. "Managing Meaning through Branding: The Case of a Consulting Firm," *Organization Studies*, 29, 103–125.

Katz, D. and Kahn, R. L. 1966. *The Social Psychology of Organizations*. New York: Wiley.

Kerr, S. and Jermier, J. M. 1978. "Substitutes for Leadership: Their Meaning and Measurement," *Organizational Behavior and Human Performance*, 22, 375–403.

Kuhn, T. 2008. A Communicative Theory of the Firm: Developing an Alternative Perspective on Intra-Organizational Power and Stakeholder Relationships, *Organization Studies*, 29, 1227–1254.

Kuhn, T. 2014. "Knowledge and Knowing in Organizational Communication," in Putnam, L. L. and Mumby, D. K. (eds.), *Handbook of Organizational Communication*. 3rd ed., Thousand Oaks, CA: SAGE, pp. 481–502.

Kuhn, T. and Burk, N. 2014. "Spatial Design as Sociomaterial Practice: A (Dis)organizing Perspective on Communicative Constitution," in Cooren, F., Vaara, E., Langley, A. and Tsoukas, H. (eds.), *Language and Communication at Work: Discourse, Narrativity, and Organizing*, Oxford, UK: Oxford University Press, pp. 147–172.

Kuhn, T. and Jackson, M. 2008. "Accomplishing Knowledge: A Framework for Investigating Knowing in Organizations," *Management Communication Quarterly*, 21, 454–485.

Kuhn, T. and Porter, A. J. 2011. "Heterogeneity in Knowledge and Knowing: A Social Practice Perspective," in Canary, H. and McPhee, R. D. (eds.), *Communication and Organizational Knowledge: Contemporary Issues for Theory and Practice*, New York: Routledge, pp. 39–56.

Kuhn, T. and Rennstam, J. 2016. "Expertise as a Practical Accomplishment Among Objects and Values," in Treem, J. and Leonardi, P. (eds.), *Where Is Expertise? Communication and Organizing in the Information Age*, Oxford, UK: Oxford University Press, pp. 25–43.

Kuhn, T. and Schoeneborn, D. 2015. "The Pedagogy of CCO," *Management Communication Quarterly*, 29, 295–301.

Kuhn, T. R., Ashcraft, K. L. and Cooren, F. 2017. *The Work of Communication: Relational Perspectives on Working and Organizing in Contemporary Capitalism*, New York: Routledge.

Lammers, C. J. 1989. "Transcience and Persistence of Ideal Types in Organization Theory," *Research in the Sociology of Organizations* 6, 205–224.

Langley, A. and Tsoukas, H. 2016. "Introduction: Process Thinking, Process Theorizing and Process Researching," in Langley, A. and Tsoukas, H. (eds.) *The SAGE Handbook of Process Organization Studies*, Thousand Oaks, CA: SAGE, pp. 1–25.

Lawrence, P. R. and Lorsch, J. W. 1967. *Organization and Environment: Managing Differentiation and Integration*, Boston, MA: Graduate School of Business Administration, Harvard.

Lutgen-Sandvik, P. and McDermott, V. 2008. "The Constitution of Employee-Abusive Organizations: A Communication Flows Theory," *Communication Theory*, 18, 304–333.

Lyon, A. 2005. "'Intellectual Capital' and Struggles Over the Perceived Value of Members' Expert Knowledge in a Knowledge-Intensive Organization," *Western Journal of Communication*, 69, 251–271.

McPhee, R. D. and Iverson, J. O. 2009. "Agents of Constitution in Communidad: Constitutive Processes of Communication in Organizations," in Putnam, L. L. and Nicotera, A. M. (eds.), *Building Theories of Organization: The Constitutive Role of Communication*, New York: Routledge, pp. 49–87.

McPhee, R. D. and Poole, M. S. 2001. "Organizational Structures and Configurations," in Jablin, F. M. and Putnam, L. (eds.), *The New Handbook of Organizational Communication: Advances in Theory, Research, and Methods*, Thousand Oaks, CA: SAGE, pp. 503–543.

McPhee, R. D. and Zaug, P. 2000. "The Communicative Constitution of Organizations: A Framework for Explanation," *The Electronic Journal of Communication/La Revue Electronique de Communication*, 10.

Mintzberg, H. 1979. *The Structuring of Organizations*, Englewood Cliffs, NJ: Prentice-Hall.

Monge, P. 1977. "The Systems Perspective as a Basis for the Study of Human Communication," *Communication Quarterly*, 25, 19–29.

Monge, P. and Contractor, N. S. 2003. *Theories of Communication Networks*, New York: Oxford University Press.

Mumby, D. K. 2005. "Theorizing Resistance in Organization Studies: A Dialectical Approach," *Management Communication Quarterly*, 19, 19–44.

Nicholls, A. 2009. "'We Do Good Things, Don't We?': 'Blended Value Accounting' in Social Entrepreneurship," *Accounting, Organizations and Society*, 34, 755–769.

Orlikowski, W. J. 2002. "Knowing in Practice: Enacting a Collective Capability in Distributed Organizing," *Organization Science*, 13, 249–273.

Parsons, T. 1956. "Suggestions for a Sociological Approach to the Theory of Organizations—II," *Administration and Society*, 1, 225–239.

Pavitt, C. 1994. "Theoretical Commitments Presupposed by Functional Approaches to Group Discussion," *Small Group Research*, 25, 520–541.

Pondy, L. and Mitroff, I. 1979. "Beyond Open Systems Models of Organization," in Cummings, L. L. and Staw, B. M. (eds.), *Research in Organizational Behavior*, Greenwich, CT: JAI Press, pp. 3–39.

Poole, M. S. 2013. "On the Study of Process in Communication Research," *Annals of the International Communication Association*, 36, 371–409.

Poole, M. S. 2014. "Systems Theory," in Putnam, L. L. and Mumby, D. K. (eds.), *The SAGE Handbook of Organizational Communication: Advances in Theory, Research, and Methods*. 3rd ed., Thousand Oaks, CA: SAGE, pp. 49–74.

Poole, M. S., Seibold, D. R. and McPhee, R. D. 1985. "Group Decision-Making as a Structurational Process," *Quarterly Journal of Speech*, 71, 74–102.

Rennstam, J. 2012. "Object-Control: A Study of Technologically Dense Knowledge Work," *Organization Studies*, 33, 1071–1090.

Schoeneborn, D., Blaschke, S., Cooren, F., McPhee, R. D., Seidl, D. and Taylor, J. R. 2014. "The Three Schools of CCO Thinking: Interactive Dialogue and Systematic Comparison," *Management Communication Quarterly*, 28, 285–316.

Shumate, M. and O'Connor, A. 2010. "The Symbiotic Sustainability Model: Conceptualizing NGO–Corporate Alliance Communication," *Journal of Communication*, 60, 577–609.

Taylor, J. R., Cooren, F., Giroux, H. and Robichaud, D. 1996. "The Communicational Basis of Organization: Between the Conversation and the Text," *Communication Theory*, 6, 1–39.

Treem, J. W. and Barley, W. C. 2016. "Explaining the (De)valuaiton of Process Experts in Contemporary Organizations," in Treem, J. W. and Leonardi, P. M. (eds.), *Expertise, Communication, and Organization*, Oxford, UK: Oxford University Press, pp. 213–231.

Trethewey, A. and Ashcraft, K. L. 2004. "Practicing Disorganization: The Development of Applied Perspectives on Living with Tension," *Journal of Applied Communication Research*, 32, 81–88.

Vásquez, C. 2013. "Spacing Organization (or How to be Here and There at the Same Time)," in Robichaud, D. and Cooren, F. (eds.), *Organization and Organizing: Materiality, Agency, and Discourse*, New York: Routledge, pp. 127–149.

von Bertalanffy, L. 1968. *General System Theory: Foundations, Development, Applications*, New York: George Brazilier.

Weick, K. E. 1969. *The Social Psychology of Organizing*, Reading, MA: Addision-Wesley.

Weick, K. E. 1979. *The Social Psychology of Organizing*, New York: McGraw-Hill.

Weick, K. E. 2010. "The Poetics of Process: Theorizing the Ineffable in Organization Studies," in Hernes, T. and Maitlis, S. (eds.), *Process, Sensemaking, and Organizing*, Oxford, UK: Oxford University Press, pp. 102–111.

Weick, K. E. and Browning, L. D. 1986. "Argument and Narration in Organizational Communication," *Journal of Management*, 12, 243–259.

Wenger, E. 1998. *Communities of Practice: Learning, Meaning, and Identity*, Cambridge, UK: Cambridge University Press.

Yoon, K., Gupta, N. and Hollingshead, A. B. 2016. "Judging the Competence (and Incompetence) of Co-Workers," in Treem, J. W. and Leonardi, P. M. (eds.) *Expertise, Communication, and Organizing*, Oxford, UK: Oxford University Press, pp. 123–144.

3 Organizing Power and Resistance

Dennis K. Mumby and Mie Plotnikof

This chapter explores the relationship between power and resistance in the context of work and organizations, with a particular focus on the communicative, discursive processes of power and resistance. We do this by examining some key research traditions in this area—traditions that encompass both Fordist and post-Fordist work contexts. Historically speaking, the Fordist organizational form emerged in the early twentieth century and was dominant until the late 1970s, while post-Fordist work arrangements began to emerge in the wake of the crisis of capitalism in the 1970s. Our goal in the chapter is to explore how, in the course of the various transformations of work and organization during the twentieth and early twenty-first centuries, there have been concomitant shifts in the nature of workplace struggle; that is, in the relationships between power, resistance, and organizing. As a particular economic mode of production, capitalism is incentivized to transform the labor process because, as Marx observed, the rate of profit tends to fall as markets become more competitive and saturated. As such, conceiving of new ways to intensify the labor process is one of the only ways to regain a competitive edge. Such transformations, however, always occur in an economic and political context of struggle, as workers inevitably push back against efforts to extract more and more surplus value from their labor. Power and resistance, then, are defining, constitutive dynamics of the labor process that take on particular features under capitalism. Indeed, as Boltanski and Chiapello (2002: 2) state, "Capitalism needs it enemies" in order to retain its dynamism. In this chapter, we delve into the changing nature of these features.

In some respects, we view this chapter as a frame through which the other chapters in this book can be read. Processes of power and resistance underpin, define, and constitute organizational communication; they are the medium and outcome of everyday organizing. Thus, organizational communication phenomena such as organizational identity and identification, culture, gender, difference, decision-making, emotion and relationships, and so forth are all inflected by the power and politics of everyday organizational life. As you read this collection, we encourage you to think about how each of the topics covered might be read through the dialectical lens of power and resistance.

The chapter takes the following form. First, we provide brief narrative accounts of how we developed our particular research interests. Second, we explore research and new themes in the area of organizational power and resistance. Third, we develop a practical application of this research with data examples from a study of new public governance. Finally, we briefly discuss directions for future research.

Personal Reflections

Dennis' Narrative

I've been studying power and resistance for longer than I care to remember. My very first publication, coauthored with a fellow grad student, was written as a course paper for a philosophy seminar and, although it wasn't about organizational communication, it focused on the relationships between discourse, ideology, and power (Mumby and Spitzack 1983). The opening of that first publication (about the ideological effects of television news) stated: "Language plays a fundamental role in the structuring of experience. Social realities are constituted, sedimented, and reified for members of a community through discourse" (Mumby and Spitzack 1983: 162). More than 35(!) years later, I am still motivated by the relationship between discourse and human experience, although I'd like to think I've learned a few things in that time and am addressing it in more thoughtful ways.

The turn to studying organizations as a site of power and resistance came shortly after I wrote that first article. Work and organizations provided me with an interesting context in which to study the ways in which social actors collectively constructed social realities. At that time, the study of organizations as cultures was beginning to emerge, and I was frustrated that while this literature explored organizations as social constructions, there was little or no attention paid to the dynamics of political struggle in this social construction process. How people make sense of the world and create meanings is never politically innocent, but always emerges out of struggles between different stakeholder interests. My next few publications, then, both critiqued the political neutrality of the organizational culture movement, and built a case for taking more seriously the relationships among communication, power, and organization (Mumby 1988). For me, it was important to be part of the development of a critical tradition (drawing on neo-Marxist and post-structuralist theory) that developed the idea that not only were organizations constructed through communication processes, but that this construction process was both medium and outcome of power and politics.

Since those early days I've expanded my research agenda in order to (a) more fully comprehend the incredibly complex ways that communication, power, and organizing intersect; and (b) better account for the changing features of work and organization itself, exploring the shift from Fordism to post-Fordism with the emergence of neoliberal capitalism. I have written about: the intersection of gender, organizing, and power (Ashcraft and Mumby 2004); resistance practices and organizing (Mumby et al. 2017); humor, power, and organization (Mumby 2009); how we might better understand power as an endemic feature of everyday organization life (Mumby 2015); and, more recently, the role of branding in the emergence of new forms of "organizing beyond organization" (Mumby 2016). I've also published a textbook as a way of trying to bring all of these ideas to the classroom (Mumby 2013). In all of this research my goal has been to figure out how people go about individual and collective meaning-making in everyday organizing contexts that are not of their own making. How do people exercise agency in situations where their power is limited? What is the role of communication in mediating and constructing the struggle among different organizational stakeholders? How has communication played a pivotal role in the very shaping of capitalist relations of production?

Mie's Narrative

My very first exam at university was on Michel Foucault's (1979a) discussion of disciplinary power. As an undergraduate in educational psychology, this subject was overwhelming, and although I passed the examination I felt that my understanding was limited, which fueled further curiosity. As such, I struggled on with this in simultaneous confusion and comprehension, inspired by such quotations as the following:

> This form of power that applies itself to immediate everyday life categorizes the individual, marks him by his own individuality, attaches him to his own identity, imposes a law of truth on him that he must recognize and others have to recognize in him. It is a form of power that makes individuals subjects. There are two meanings of the word "subject": subject to someone else by control and dependence, and tied to his own identity by a conscience or self-knowledge. Both meanings suggest a form of power that subjugates and makes subject to.
>
> (Foucault 1994: 331)

Puzzled by the power relations of discourse, subjectivity, and agency, it seemed the more I thought I knew, the more I also knew that I did not know. This resulted in theoretical and empirical explorations of post-structuralist developments in educational psychology about various educational issues (Davies 2006).

My interest in the management and organization of education started during my Master's and was cemented during my doctoral study about challenges of contradicting public governance discourses and the struggles over meaning and matter (Barad 2003) among actors in the education sector (Plotnikof 2015a). As I entered the field of management and organization, I was searching for critical theorizing that could help me untangle and destabilize the complex discursive-material constructions I found in my empirical data (Plotnikof and Zandee 2016). Hence, discovering the fields of organizational communication (Putnam and Mumby 2014) and discourse (Phillips and Oswick 2012) was a great relief, and they became my new "home." Ever since, Foucault and these related critical scholars have delightedly haunted and challenged my work.

Inspired by such, my work questions relations of power, discourse, subjectification, and organization—with a specific focus on normative dimensions, and on how subjects, practices, policies, and technologies are communicatively entangled, thereby co-constituting possible ways of doing, managing, and organizing work-life. Inherent in this is a curiosity about how communicative struggles and practices take the form of selves, others, and social ordering—and especially how this demarcates and (re)produces normativity. For instance, I have explored the communicatively constituted organizing of collaborative educational policy-making, thereby conceptualizing tensional meaning negotiations and resistance (Plotnikof 2015b). Also, I have investigated identity struggles of managers influenced by competing public governance discourses through concepts of subjectification and positioning (Plotnikof 2016b). Furthermore, I have critically discussed contradictions of hierarchy, marketization, and collaboration within neoliberal governance forms in education by theorizing their value-laden discursive practices and tensions (Plotnikof 2016a). As such, my work aims at developing critical accounts and complex understandings of managing and organizing in a discursive nexus of hierarchy, market competition, and collaboration—often within the education area. I do this by exploring the constitutive dynamics and effects of such neoliberal tendencies through organizational communication approaches.

Communicative struggles are still an interest of mine—as is the field of education. However, these days I am investigating the tensional relations of power/resistance and dis/organizing between dominating and marginal discourses in education policy. Both Dennis and I see the co-constitutive dynamics of dis/organization to be a central research topic to which organizational communication approaches can contribute. In addition to challenging the often-taken-for-granted foregrounding of organizational order as the primary and most optimal state of affairs, they can also expand knowledge about the correlations of dis/order, mis/managing, and dis/organizing of everyday life under various neoliberal governance forms (Mumby 2016, Putnam et al. 2016). A related aspect, which we also explore in our work, is the norms of difference endemic in such dis/organizing processes and the gendering performativity and effects produced thereby (Ashcraft and Mumby 2004). To this end, we see organizational communication as a key field through which to enhance theorizing of the co-constitutive, re- or counterproductive, and politicizing effects of such norms of difference. This includes an interest in studying norm-critical practices of diversity management, and their construction of resistance to these norms, which relates to discussions of critical performativity across organizational communication and critical management studies (Parker 2001, 2016, Pullen et al. 2017). We view organizational communication studies as critical to further advancing these research areas.

Research Traditions in Studies of Power and Resistance

Research on organizational power and resistance is largely—though by no means exclusively—defined by the critical tradition in organizational communication and management studies, and it is that tradition that we focus on in this chapter. Historically, mainstream management and organization studies have eschewed the study of power and control because it flies in the face of long-held beliefs about organizations as rational sites of cooperation. As Burawoy (1979) has pointed out, however, mainstream management research is founded on the two rather paradoxical assumptions that organizations are (a) characterized by cooperative behavior oriented toward common goals, and (b) in need of mechanisms of control to maintain organizational goals. Where conflict is recognized (e.g. in the famous Hawthorne Studies of the 1920s–1930s) it is viewed as the result of idiosyncratic behaviors and psychological maladjustment of individual employees behaving emotionally rather than rationally. Multiple studies have shown, however, that the managerial view of "misbehavior" as aberrant overlooks the essential rationality of such "misbehavior" in contexts where following managerial and corporate goals is not in workers' best interests (e.g. working harder can result in pay cuts or layoffs due to overproduction). The critical tradition, then, sees worker responses to power and control as one half of a dialectic that has emerged from a system replete with asymmetries of power; where the power of capital far outweighs that of the average worker, and the interests behind those power asymmetries exist in contradiction.

The critical tradition takes its cue from Marx (1967), whose classic analysis of the capitalist mode of production exposed the material and structural contradictions at its heart. Marx's analysis of the capitalist labor process demystified how what appears as the "just equivalence" of exchange (workers freely selling their labor power to capitalists at the going market rate) obscures the exploitation of labor on which the sphere of circulation and capital accumulation depends. Marx showed how the distinctive character of capitalism is the subordination of the human capacity to produce use values to the exploitive demands of the capitalist, whose concern is to create commodities that realize exchange value greater than the cost of production. In capitalism, then, exchange value is more important than use value (capitalists don't care what their factories make, as long as they make a profit). However, profit depends on the appropriation of surplus value from labor by paying it less than the value it adds to the labor process. As a result, capitalism is in a constant state of flux, with continual revolutionizing of production and constant redesign of the labor process to secure the extraction of surplus value.

Marx argued that workers are key to the process of surplus value extraction precisely because capital purchases not a fixed amount of labor, but labor power (i.e., the *potential* to labor for a particular time). As such, labor power is always indeterminate because it has flexibility and plasticity, embodied as it is in the figure of a live human being. Thus, conflict is an inherent part of capitalism because the employer cannot access the commodity purchased (labor power) without going through the embodied person of the worker. Under these circumstances, the capitalist needs to convert labor power to actual labor in as efficient a manner as possible. From a capitalist perspective, the most efficient way to achieve this is through a control imperative that enables the legal purchase of labor power to be converted into actual labor and hence surplus value. As we will see, there are numerous forms of control that capitalism enacts in order to intensify the labor process and hence maximize the production of surplus value, but precisely because work is embodied, workers tend to resist these efforts at control. Indeed, it is this problem of resistance (and the concomitant indeterminacy of labor) that management has been trying to solve in increasingly complex ways since the emergence of industrial capitalism (while increasingly trying to make it seem like they are not trying to control workers).

In the rest of the chapter, we examine the dialectic of power and resistance in the context of evolving forms of work within capitalism. In this sense, we follow Foucault's (1980: 95) well-known dictum that "where there is power, there is resistance, and yet, or rather consequently, this resistance is never in a position of exteriority in relation to power." As capitalism has adapted to both economic and political challenges, the character of the power-resistance dialectic has also changed. As we hope to demonstrate, "struggle is not merely derivative but determinative of capitalism's development" (Burawoy 1985: 48).

Power as Coercion

One of the most direct and unvarnished ways in which the labor process is intensified is through forms of power that operate coercively. Much of early capitalism adopted direct forms of control aimed simply at keeping workers at their tasks. This included use of punch clocks to dictate the beginning and end of the working day (adopted as early as the 1700s in the UK), company spies to identify trouble makers and union sympathizers (Henry Ford employed his own security service to surveil and attack union organizers) and, of course, various forms of technology. Indeed, the early twentieth century witnessed the introduction of both Taylorist scientific management principles and moving assembly line technology to both simplify and deskill work and limit workers' autonomy and ability to control the speed of work (Taylor 1911/1934). As Braverman (1974) showed in his famous analysis, Taylorism intensified the labor process through the development of a managerial monopoly over knowledge about work (previously the possession of skilled workers), using this monopoly to separate the conception of work from its execution. Hence, brain (management) and hand (workers) became not only divided under monopoly capitalism but hostile, as workers were reduced to deskilled appendages to the labor process and denied any autonomy. Taylorism, then, was less about increasing technical efficiency and more about wresting control of the labor process from workers and giving it to management. Moreover, Braverman argues, subsequent theories of management (e.g. human relations, human resource management, etc.) do not replace scientific management, but rather function to psychologically adjust workers to the new reality of Taylorized labor processes.

The use of coercive control processes is both a medium and outcome of worker resistance to capitalist efforts to intensify the labor process. Taylor developed scientific management as a response to "systematic soldiering"—a deliberate and coordinated effort by workers to restrict output in the face of management efforts to speed up work (which often resulted in either reduction of workers' piece rates or laying off of workers). Moreover, despite these intensive control efforts (often aimed at the very body of the employee) workers continued to find ways to resist, for example, by sabotaging machines, "working to rule" (i.e. refusing to do overtime), and engaging in organized and "wildcat" strikes. Thus, Burawoy (1985: 41) suggests that,

> [r]ather than a separation of conception and execution, we find a separation of workers' conception and management's conception, of workers' knowledge and management's knowledge. The attempt to enforce Taylorism leads workers to recreate the unity of conception and execution, but in opposition to management rulings.

Of course, coercive forms of control have not disappeared in the 100 years or more since the introduction of Taylorism and the moving assembly line. Indeed, one might argue that today's workers are far more subject to surveillance than early or mid-twentieth-century workers, with the advent of sophisticated software that tracks employees' every move. For example, Levy (2015) shows how truck driving—a profession whose members are traditionally fiercely independent and espouse the rhetoric of the "open road"—has become tightly controlled through a software-based "fleet management system." Under the old system of paper log books, truckers were able to subvert control efforts by completing log books in a post hoc manner. Under the new system, however, an electronic on-board recorder (EOBR) constantly collects real-time data that tells a central control system precisely where each trucker is at all times. As such, employers can largely eliminate trucker autonomy and "local knowledge."

An even more extreme example of coercive workplace surveillance is Amazon's close tracking of the movements of warehouse employees as they rush to fill orders. Amazon recently patented technology for a wristband worn by all warehouse workers. The wristbands "use ultrasonic tracking to identify the precise location of a worker's hands as they retrieve items. One of the patents outlines a haptic feedback system that would vibrate against the wearer's skin to point their hand in the right direction" (Solon 2018). Here, workers' movements are not only monitored but also dictated, thus reducing the amount of time spent locating items. Frederick Taylor would have been proud! Increasingly, then, and particularly for low-paid and contingent workers, electronic surveillance is the norm rather than the exception as companies seek to gain advantage over their competitors in speed and quality of service.

Power as Consent

While coercive forms of power are effective under certain circumstances and, indeed, dominated organizational life in the early twentieth century, in the last few decades organizations have increasingly moved toward consensual models of powers. As Willmott (1993) has pointed out, the goal here is not to control employee behavior, but rather to manage how they think and feel. Burawoy (1979) described this shift as one from "despotic" to "hegemonic" regimes, capturing the evolving efforts of capitalism to secure the production of surplus value. Indeed, critical organization studies research over the past 30 years has been devoted to understanding how these "hegemonic" forms of power shape everyday organizational life. Much of this research is rooted in neo-Marxism and critical theory, drawing on the works of Gramsci (1971), Althusser (1971), and Habermas (1984, 1987), among others, to examine how communication, power, and ideology intersect to construct organizational realities.

A consistent theme in this work is the focus on organizations as political sites of sense-making and meaning formation in which struggles over stakeholder interests occur. In this context, power is exercised not by directly shaping organizational behavior, but by the ideological process of communicatively constructing systems of meaning that organization members internalize and enact "spontaneously." These ideological control systems have simultaneous "loose-tight" properties (Weick 1976); that is, employees are given the freedom to exercise considerable autonomy within an organizational value system that carefully circumscribes the range of options for such autonomy.

In many respects, the "corporate culture" movement of the 1980s (Peters and Waterman 1982) represented the apogee of efforts to ideologically construct the autonomous selves of employees in ways that served the corporate goals of productivity and profit. Thus, when corporations began speaking about the need for "strong cultures" in the early 1980s, they were really speaking about the need to capture workers "within a complex process of social engineering" (Willmott 1993: 522) such that every employee activity is consistent with and reproduces the carefully engineered value system of the corporation. Kunda, for example, explores how a high-tech company engages in "normative control" of employees by "controlling the underlying experiences, thoughts, and feelings that guide their actions" (Kunda 1992: 11). As such, workers are driven by internal commitment to corporate goals. Importantly, Kunda (1992) argues that the real object of control under the corporate culture movement is the employee's self; to be truly devoted to the corporation, the ideal employee sees little distinction between their own system of beliefs and values and those of the corporation.

In this sense, we might say that the exercising of power within the corporate culture management strategy is both top-down and bottom-up. That is, while corporations carefully and systematically indoctrinate employees with their corporate vision (e.g. through "culture boot camps"), employees also engage in forms of self-discipline whereby they might experience forms of anxiety, guilt, and shame if they view themselves as failing to live up to the standards of the corporate culture.

What are the possibilities for employee resistance within this apparently totalizing disciplinary process? While corporations envisioned a single, monolithic culture with which all employees identified, in practice such a vision often translated into multiple subcultures that adhered to greater or lesser degrees to the formal culture. As many studies have demonstrated, organizational employees have an almost infinite ability to appropriate hegemonic corporate meanings and rework them in oppositional ways. The corporate culture movement is rooted in managing meanings, and thus struggle and resistance also occur on the terrain of meaning; employees deploy irony, cynicism, joke-telling, and so forth as a way to undermine managerial efforts to shape a singular organizational reality (e.g. Collinson 1988, Fleming 2007, Fleming and Spicer 2002). For example, Collinson's (1988) well-known study of a shop-floor culture examines how blue-collar workers used humor as a form of resistance to management's top-down efforts to introduce a new, more "friendly" workplace culture. Workers perceived the new "corporate culture" as an attempt to co-opt them and undermine their bargaining position within the organization. Thus, while power as consent is largely managed through the discursive construction of particular organizational realities, resistance to such power is also rooted in discourse as employees push back against managerial efforts to shape such realities, often performing a kind of "semiotic jujitsu" (Klein 2001) in which the discourse of management is used against itself to construct alternative readings and realities.

While many organizations still talk about their "culture," in many respects the very notion of a strong corporate culture as a specific managerial strategy has been assigned to the trash heap of history. This occurred for a couple of reasons. First, there was a good deal of backlash—from both employees and social commentators—about the "cult-like" character of many strong cultures that created claustrophobic work environments that stifled creativity and innovation. Second, and more significantly, the shift in the 1980s to a neoliberal political and economic philosophy fundamentally changed the relationship between the individual and work, the employee and the organization. As Fleming (2014: 878) put it,

> management ideology suddenly encourages the 'whole person' in the workplace, with individual difference, diversity and 'life' more generally becoming key organizational motifs... . [M]anagers ought to tap the pre-existing and unique social capabilities of employees, rather than attempt to hammer them into an identikit image of the firm.

While such a shift might be seen as an effort to develop a more "humane" workplace (Ross 2003), it actually reflects a significant transformation in the ways that power is exercised in organizational life. In the next section we examine power as "governmentality."

Power as Governmentality

We have given the first two forms of power relatively short shrift because we want to focus more extensively on "governmental" forms of power (Foucault 1979b, 2008). Governmentality is, we argue, the form of power that most effectively characterizes how organizing operates in twenty-first century neoliberal capitalism. Indeed, it represents a significant shift from earlier forms of power, radically transforming the relationships among work, self, and organization. While power through consent operated via a homogenizing logic in which all employees were (at least ideally) ideologically interpellated into the same organizational reality, governmental power operates according to a logic of differentiation; that is, "through the organized proliferation of individual difference" (McNay 2009: 56). How does this make sense as an exercise of power? How does the proliferation of difference rather than sameness and conformity function as a form of power in contemporary organizing?

To understand this, we need to understand governmentality as the principal form of power within neoliberal capitalism. Neoliberalism as a political and economic philosophy has emerged in the last 30 years as a response to the classical liberalism exercised through Keynesian capitalism in the three decades following World War II. Rooted in a view of government as a mitigator of the worst excesses of capitalism, Keynesian capitalism sought to create a social democracy that provided security for its citizens through government programs such as social security, healthcare programs, stable, long-term employment (guaranteed through a social contract between workers and employers), and so forth. Neoliberalism, on the other hand, is driven by the fear of excessive state intervention, and thus is premised on minimizing the role of the state and allowing market principles to flourish across all spheres of life, including work, family, relationships, and education. At the center of this privileging of the market is the sovereign individual, defined as an entrepreneur of him- or herself. In this sense,

> [n]eoliberalism is . . . a theory of political economic practices that proposes that human wellbeing can be best advanced by liberating individual entrepreneurial freedoms and skills within an institutional framework characterized by strong private property rights, free markets, and free trade.
>
> (Harvey 2005: 2)

From a neoliberal perspective, society functions most effectively when individuals are free to engage in self-regulation and self-promotion, unencumbered by the state. In such a context, the only role of the state is to provide the conditions under which such a process of marketization can flourish. However, as a number of scholars have pointed out, these self-regulating abilities of individuals are carefully managed; they are "shaped and normalized in large part through the powers of expertise" (Miller and Rose 1990: 2). Thus, beginning in the 1980s, and consonant with the rise of neoliberal economic policies, a new political discourse developed in which employees were constructed as entrepreneurial individuals who sought to actualize themselves in all spheres of life, including work. Employees are increasingly viewed as in search of meaning, responsibility, and fulfillment in work itself, rather than as seeking emancipation from work viewed as simply a means to an end.

This new "problematization" of the self–work relationship (Miller and Rose 1990) is consistent with the neoliberal view of the market as providing the "grid of intelligibility" for all spheres of life. Under a system of governmentality, individuals are encouraged to view themselves as "human capital" engaged in a permanent process of enterprise as the means to increase the value of that capital. In this sense, the market is extended "to the entire social body and to generalize it inside the whole social system that, normally, does not pass through or is not authorized by the market" (Foucault 2008: 248).

Important within this system of governmentality is the normalization of risk and insecurity. While under the classic liberalism of Keynesian economics the goal was to mitigate risk and provide security for citizens, under neoliberalism risk and insecurity are normalized as a necessary and constitutive feature of control; an actual instrument of governance through insecurity (Lorey 2015). As Lorey (2015: 11) argues, "In neoliberalism precarization becomes 'democratized.'" If precarity is the norm, then there is no longer a separation between free subjects (in the classic liberal sense of social actors free to pursue their own economic self-interest) and the precarious; those who are free are also precarious. Thus, for Lorey, the function of what she terms "governmental precarization" is to create subjects who accept precarity as the norm, an inevitable and necessary feature of self-governance within neoliberalism. Under post-Fordism and neoliberalism, then, risk is spread increasingly downward, marking a shift from "venture capital" under Fordism to "venture labor" under post-Fordism (Neff 2012). In this sense, the implicit separation of labor and capital under Fordism is eliminated under neoliberalism. Everyone is a venture capitalist, but of their own human capital.

Organization studies research has increasingly focused on how the ubiquity of the market as the grid of intelligibility has led to the "corporate capture" of all spheres of life within capital. While under previous regimes of control the primary locus of struggle was between capital and labor "at the point of production" (Burawoy 1979), today the primary locus of struggle is between capital and "life itself" (Fleming 2014). In this sense, the capitalist mode of production has escaped the factory walls (what Marx called the "hidden abode of production") to encompass all of society, such that we now effectively live in a "social factory" (Gill and Pratt 2008, Lazzarato 2004) within which all aspects of life create the potential for capitalist valorization. As Böhm and Land (2012) argue, capitalism is now characterized by a "new hidden abode" in which the social becomes economic, and the central question for critical analysts of work and organization becomes: How does the production of meaning and subjectivity intersect with the capitalist valorization process?

From an organizational communication perspective, communication is constitutive of economic value within neoliberal capitalism. As Lazzarato (2004: 190) has argued, "Contemporary capitalism does not first arrive with factories; these follow, if they follow at all. It arrives with words, signs, and images." Thus, the production of value within an employment relationship is subordinated to the production and organization of subjects within social relations (Böhm and Land: 225).

The question of the communicative production of the (free) subject within neoliberalism is therefore increasingly central to understanding how organizing processes operate in twenty-first-century capitalism. A number of authors, including McRobbie (2016), Fleming (2014, 2017), Marwick (2013), Kuhn et al. (2017) and Mumby (2016, 2018), have explored this question, examining the communicative processes through which governmentality constructs social actors as human capital/enterprising subjects. In the following, we provide a brief empirical example of how such governmental processes can unfold. As indicated earlier, the "grid of intelligibility" of the market frames all domains, including the public sector. Thus, we examine one area of governmentality in the public governance of education.

New Public Governance as Neoliberal Capitalism: The Governmentality of Co-Creating Value

In this brief case study, we illustrate how the study of power and resistance has practical implications for understanding the unfolding of organizing at the level of everyday life, and how this shapes employee identity struggles. In particular, we focus on governmentality as an everyday, endemic form of power in contemporary organizing. We examine how employees must simultaneously negotiate discourses of empowerment and subjection as they operate as "free" subjects of neoliberal governmentality, even within the public sphere of education (a sphere traditionally seen as exempt from marketization discourses under classic liberalism).

New Public Governance (NPG) has emerged as a public management discourse highlighting the potential of networks, partnership, and collaborative governance arrangements to deal with so-called "wicked problems" and public innovation demands (Ansell and Torfing 2014, Osborne 2006). As such, it is often seen as a post–New Public Management (NPM) tendency; where NPM aims for competitive market incentives to improve public policy and services, NPG seeks to innovate and produce public value by means of stakeholder involvement and cross-sector collaboration. The expectations for such a collaborative form of governance to enable public innovation are great:

> As a means of 'doing more with less' . . . [it] brings together a range of stakeholders, variously from the public, for-profit and non-profit sectors as well as users and citizens themselves, in interactive arenas that facilitate the cross-fertilization of ideas, mutual and transformative learning and the development of joint ownership of new solutions.
>
> (Hartley et al. 2013: 828)

NPG thus relocates its economic locus for value production from market competition to cross-sector collaboration, relational contracts, and the co-creation of involved actors as human capital. In this way, NPG can be read as a neoliberal capitalist discourse and practice that produces power through a form of governmentality, which encourages stakeholders to realize the innovative potential of collaboration and co-create "more" value for fewer financial resources, such that 2 + 2 may become 5.

This form of governmentality works through motivating organizational members and stakeholders to offer themselves as collaborative resources—as human capital who participate in co-creating value, in the name of responding to "wicked problems," fiscal crises, and innovating public policy and services for the sake of our future society. Far from accomplishing a kind of win-win situation, however, critical organizational communication studies have shown how this form of governance is constituted in practice through discursive tensions between, for example, hierarchical, market, and collaborative power-resistance relations (Bergmann 2018, Hardy et al. 2005, Koschmann et al. 2012, Plotnikof 2015b, 2016a, 2016b). Moreover, critical scholars unpack how communicative processes of NPG organize work and structure collaborations in ways that create precarious subject effects on workers, insofar as they must always be available, knowledgeable, and recognizable as human capital for public value production.

To illustrate this point, we provide a data extract from a Danish case study of two local governments' education departments that initiated cross-sector collaborations to improve local education policy and services. In this case, the collaborations included public, private, and civil sectors (politicians, administrators, union representatives, education staff, children, and parents). Ethnographic methods included shadowing the public servants involved in facilitating these collaborative encounters. The public servants were key actors in the local production of NPG practices, particularly in the organization and motivation of selves and others as human capital to come together and co-create "more for less." Following, we see Stuart, Head of Department, and Marsha, a civil servant, both working in the education department, but from two different local governments:

Stuart: We, public managers and servants, used to translate between political and professional logics. Typically, education practice is quality managed in a written quality report presented to a political committee once a year. But now we hear the politicians requesting these collaborative encounters and their more authentic communication in meetings with educational stakeholders and citizens. And that means it removes me as a translating part in the chain of command. I rather become someone who is to assure that the collaboration occurs and creates public value . . . Collaborative facilitation is really about orchestrating different kinds of processes, right? And being empowered to do that. You know, how can we initiate and frame meaningful collaborative encounters as part of our new role? As part of the public governance of, in our situation, the education area.

Marsha: At the moment we are discussing another cross-sector initiative, and I've been asked for a plan, so I'm figuring it out. You know, I've told my boss that if we do it collaboratively then we shouldn't decide it all yet, then we need to find the answers with the stakeholders—they are the drivers. But it's not easy, because the stakeholders are also a struggle to deal with, you know, so I also have to think of how to motivate them, both before and during the process. It's really frustrating, really, because I'm not sure what they will do and say, so assuring that the collaboration creates value is central. But it's also what makes it all worth it, you know, this is the challenging part, because here our knowledge and development of education matters. This is not just about numbers, budgets, strategy, this is where we can make a real difference, this is where all this actually can be of value to the kids . . . I really think it's assuring the best knowledge sharing and decision-making about the value of education, but it's sometimes necessary to be strategic, too. So, I also work a lot with traditional control-data for bench-marking and budgets, but to create space and arguments for the necessity of collaborating as well. But it is frustrating and confusing often. I feel like its two different logics and languages—sometimes I'm going mental—because I never know which one is the right one. I just have to be ready to respond accordingly and take the opportunity to show the potential of collaboration when it is an advantage—politically, financially, or educationally. So I strategize a lot. I need to always be ready to see these opportunities, but it is not easy.

In the first extract, Stuart explains how the turn to NPG has changed the role of managers and other civil servants from translators between policy and frontline practice to facilitators of collaboration between stakeholders in order to assure public value co-creation. Although this change removes him from a certain position in the chain of command, he chooses to discursively enact his new role as "empowered" to orchestrate collaborative governance processes, which he constructs by means of positively charged words such as "authentic communication" and "meaningful encounters."

In the second extract, Marsha uses different discursive practices to construct cross-sector collaboration positively as a process of "finding answers together" with stakeholders, who are seen as "drivers." Like Stuart, she positions herself as a facilitator; however, in so doing, she not only constructs stakeholders as drivers but also as challenging to collaborate with, and thus she "struggles" and needs to "motivate" them. Even though she subjects herself to the ideal of NPG as collaborative innovation, her discursive self-positioning also includes frustrations regarding: (a) dealing with stakeholders, with making herself and others available as human capital and with assuring that this creates public value; and (b) the different operating logics, invoking tensions between NPM and NPG discourses. Marsha uses terms like "control," "budget," and "benchmarking" about the former, and "best knowledge sharing and decision-making" and "value of education" concerning the latter, thereby stressing this as the better of the two logics. Nevertheless, her positioning also emphasizes strategic use of the opposing discursive practices, depending on their legitimacy in different situations. Hence, as she subjects herself to collaborative governance forms as ideal, she also empowers herself to strategize between competing logics of NPG and NPM. In doing so, however, she struggles with constructing legitimacy—"responding accordingly"—and with constructing "opportunity" and "advantages" for enabling collaboration between different stakeholders as the human capital to co-create public value.

Key actors like Marsha are thus subjected to the performance of identity struggles invoked by discursive tensions between these competing logics. On the one hand, Marsha is constructing her professional identity through NPM discourse and related practices, for example, benchmarking; on the other hand, she is constantly stressing and pushing the NPG agenda to position herself and others as important human resources that co-create value. Two related issues can be emphasized here: First, such tensional struggle produces challenging subject positions for involved actors to perform identity work by negotiating opposing discursive logics. Second, the governmental power that is thereby produced seems to create "free" subjects, but they are only recognized as "free" by positioning themselves as human capital available for various forms of value production. This governmental power, then, may make subjects appear as "free," but affects them in problematic ways; that is, by producing "insecurity" that make them "go mental," hence making them and their work precarious accomplishments (which, of course, must be continually *re*accomplished on a daily basis).

In sum, NPG discourses and associated practices may express ideals of stakeholder-involvement in cross-sector collaboration as a "meaningful," "authentic," and "knowledge-sharing" way of appropriating local resources for innovating and co-creating value. Yet, the tension-filled governmental power relations of collaborative organizing, alongside other existing governance discourses (e.g. NPM), require key actors to position themselves and others as collaborative resources. As a result, people like Marsha experience ongoing identity struggles related to their subject positions as human capital who are enjoined to contribute to value production under the neoliberal model of new public governance.

Conclusion and Recommendations for Future Research

In this chapter, we have tried to provide a sense of the evolving relationships between communication, power, resistance, and organizing. The evolution from coercive, to consensual, to governmental forms of power reflects increasingly sophisticated understandings on the part of capital and its agents of how the indeterminacy of labor power can be made more determinate. Moreover, each evolution relies on an increasingly complex conception of the employee as subject; that is, as both subject *to* control processes and as an autonomous subject who exercises agency and struggles against these control processes.

From an organizational communication perspective, one of the biggest challenges for future research is to create more nuanced understandings and critiques of the processes through which the scope of capital accumulation has been expanded under neoliberal capitalism. While under Fordist capitalism the creation of surplus value took place largely "at the point of production" (Burawoy 1979) in the factory setting (where the principal point of antagonism was between capital and labor), under neoliberal capitalism the production of economic value has escaped the boundaries of the formal organization to encompass life itself. The market "grid of intelligibility" encompasses all aspects of life, including the public sphere. Hence, the principal point of antagonism is no longer between capital and labor, but between capital and everyday life. Moreover, while the production of value under Fordism pivoted around the indeterminacy of labor power (and the efforts of capital to make it determinate), under neoliberalism the production of value now pivots around the indeterminacy of meaning; that is, how is capital able to capture the sense-making practices and identity work of actors' everyday life in ways that can be turned into human capital and monetized? If "life itself" is the new terrain of capital, what are the possibilities for resisting this expanded form of corporate capture? Recent essays (e.g. Ashcraft 2017, Gagnon and Collinson 2017, Wilhoit and Kisselburgh 2017) all speak to important efforts to study "life itself" beyond traditional work and organizational spaces and explore how forms of resistance are flourishing.

As critical scholars, we thus need to think in terms of more expansive conceptions of what counts as "organizational communication." We can no longer afford to conceive of organizations as specific sites of communicative organizing; we must broaden the scope of the field to include not only the study of the (communicative) production of organization, but also the communicative organization of (capitalist) production. Communication not only constitutes organization; it also constitutes capital.

Discussion Questions

1. The three forms of power are presented as historically succeeding one another, but to what degree is there evidence of all three forms of power (and resistance to them) in contemporary organizations?
2. Using the chapter's discussion of governmentality as a framework, identify how power operates in the "gig" economy. How are workers for companies such as Fiverr, Uber, and Airbnb (or identify a company of your own) subject to governmental forms of power?
3. To what extent do you agree with Boltanski and Chiapello's claim that "capitalism needs its enemies?" What does this tell us about the nature of capitalism?
4. From a critical perspective, what does it mean to say that the principal struggle in contemporary capitalism is between capital and labor? Historically, how have capitalist organizations managed this struggle? In contemporary work under neoliberalism, what does it mean to say that the principle struggle is now between capital and life rather than between capital and labor? Provide some examples of this capital–life struggle.

References

Althusser, L. 1971. *Lenin and Philosophy*, New York: Monthly Review Press.
Ansell, C. and Torfing, J. 2014. *Public Innovation through Collaboration and Design*, New York: Routledge.
Ashcraft, K. L. 2017. " 'Submission' to the Rule of Excellence: Ordinary Affect and Precarious Resistance in the Labor of Organization and Management Studies," *Organization*, 24, 36–58.
Ashcraft, K. L. and Mumby, D. K. 2004. *Reworking Gender: A Feminist Communicology of Organization*, Thousand Oaks, CA: SAGE.
Barad, K. 2003. "Posthumanist Performativity: Toward an Understanding of How Matter Comes to Matter," *Signs: Journal of Women in Culture and Society*, 28, 801–831.
Bergmann, R. 2018. "Co-existing Logics of Change: The Case of the Danish Associational Development Championships," *Journal of Civil Society*, Advance online publication.
Böhm, S. and Land, C. 2012. "The New 'Hidden Abode': Reflections on Value and Labour in the New Economy," *The Sociological Review*, 60, 217–240.
Boltanski, L. and Chiapello, E. 2002. *The New Spirit of Capitalism*, Paper presented at the The Conference of Europeanists, Chicago, IL.
Braverman, H. 1974. *Labor and Monopoly Capital: The Degradation of Work in the Twentieth Century*, New York: Monthly Review Press.
Burawoy, M. 1979. *Manufacturing Consent: Changes in the Labor Process under Monopoly Capitalism*, Chicago: University of Chicago Press.
Burawoy, M. 1985. *The Politics of Production: Factory Regimes under Capitalism and Socialism*, London: Verso.

Collinson, D. 1988. "Engineering Humor": Masculinity, Joking and Conflict in Shop-Floor Relations," *Organization Studies*, 9, 181–199.

Davies, B. 2006. "Subjectification: The Relevance of Butler's Analysis for Education," *British Journal of Sociology of Education*, 27, 425–438.

Fleming, P. 2007. "Sexuality, Power and Resistance in the Workplace," *Organization Studies*, 28, 239–256.

Fleming, P. 2014. "When 'Life Itself' Goes to Work: Reviewing Shifts in Organizational Life through the Lens of Biopower," *Human Relations*, 67, 875–901.

Fleming, P. 2017. "The Human Capital Hoax: Work, Debt and Insecurity in the Era of Uberization," *Organization Studies*, 38, 691–705.

Fleming, P. and Spicer, A. 2002. "Workers' Playtime? Unravelling the Paradox of Covert Resistance in Organizations," in Clegg, S. (ed.), *Management and Organization Paradoxes*, Amsterdam: John Benjamins, pp. 65–85.

Foucault, M. 1979a. *Discipline and Punish: The Birth of the Prison* (Sheridan, A., Trans.), New York: Vintage.

Foucault, M. 1979b. Governmentality. *Ideology and Consciousness*, 6, 5–21.

Foucault, M. 1980. *The History of Sexuality: An Introduction* (Hurley, R., Trans., Vol. 1), New York: Vintage.

Foucault, M. 1994. *Power: Essential Works of Foucault 1954–1984, Vol. 3.*, Éditions Gallimard.

Foucault, M. 2008. *The Birth of Biopolitics: Lectures at the Collège de France, 1978–1979* (Burchell, G., Trans.), Basingstoke, UK: Palgrave MacMillan.

Gagnon, S. and Collinson, D. L. 2017. "Resistance through Difference: The Co-Constitution of Dissent and Inclusion," *Oranization Studies*, 38, 1253–1276.

Gill, R. and Pratt, A. 2008. "In the Social Factory? Immaterial Labour, Precariousness and Cultural Work," *Theory, Culture & Society*, 25, 1–30.

Gramsci, A. 1971. *Selections from the Prison Notebooks* (Hoare, Q. and Smith, G. N., Trans.), New York: International Publishers.

Habermas, J. 1984. *The Theory of Communicative Action: Reason and the Rationalization of Society* (McCarthy, T., Trans. Vol. 1), Boston: Beacon Press.

Habermas, J. 1987. *The Theory of Communicative Action: Lifeworld and System* (McCarthy, T., Trans. Vol. 2), Boston: Beacon Press.

Hardy, C., Lawrence, T. B. and Grant, D. 2005. "Discourse and Collaboration: The Role of Conversations and Collective Identity," *The Academy of Management Review*, 30, 58–77.

Hartley, J., Sørensen, E. and Torfing, J. 2013. "Collaborative Innovation: A Viable Alternative to Market-Competition and Organizational Entrepreneurship, *Public Administration Review*, 73, 821–830.

Harvey, D. 2005. *A Brief history of Neoliberalism*, New York: Oxford University Press.

Klein, N. 2001. *No Logo*, London: Flamingo Press.

Koschmann, M., Kuhn, T. and Pharrer, M. 2012. "A Communicative Framework of Value in Cross-Sector Partnerships," *Academy of Management Review*, 37, 332–354.

Kuhn, T., Ashcraft, K. and Cooren, F. 2017. *The Work of Communication: Relational Perspectives on Working and Organizing in Contemporary Capitalism*, New York: Routledge.

Kunda, G. 1992. *Engineering Culture: Control and Commitment in a High-Tech Corporation*, Philadelphia: Temple University Press.

Lazzarato, M. 2004. "From Capital-Labour to Capital-Life," *Ephemera*, 4, 187–208.

Levy, K. E. C. 2015. "The Contexts of Control: Information, Power, and Truck-Driving Work," *The Information Society*, 31, 160–174.

Lorey, I. 2015. *State of Insecurity: Government of the Precarious* (Derieg, A., Trans.), London: Verso.

Marwick, A. 2013. *Status Update: Celebrity, Publicity and Attention in the Social Media Age*, New Haven, CT: Yale University Press.

Marx, K. 1967. *Capital* (Moore, S. and Aveling, E., Trans.), New York: International Publishers.

McNay, L. 2009. "Self as Enterprise: Dilemmas of Control and Resistance in Foucault's *The Birth of Biopolitics*," *Theory, Culture & Society*, 26, 55–77.

McRobbie, A. 2016. *Be Creative: Making a Living in the New Culture Industries*, Cambridge, UK: Polity Press.

Miller, P. and Rose, N. 1990. "Governing Economic Life," *Economy and Society*, 19, 1–31.

Mumby, D. K. 1988. *Communication and Power in Organizations: Discourse, Ideology, and Domination*, Norwood, NJ: Ablex.

Mumby, D. K. 2009. "The Strange Case of the Farting Professor: Humor and the Deconstruction of Destructive Communication," in Lutgen-Sandvik, P. and Sypher, B. D. (eds.), *Destructive Organizational Communication: Processes, Consequences, and Constructive Ways of Organizing*, New York: Routledge, pp. 316–338.

Mumby, D. K. 2013. *Organizational Communication: A Critical Approach*, Thousand Oaks, CA: SAGE.

Mumby, D. K. 2015. "Organizing Power," *Review of Communication*, 15, 19–38.

Mumby, D. K. 2016. "Organizing Beyond Organization: Branding, Discourse, and Communicative Capitalism," *Organization*, 23, 884–907.

Mumby, D. K. 2018. "Targeting Alex: Brand as Agent in Communicative Capitalism," in Brummans, B. H. J. M. (ed.), *The Agency of Organizing: Perspectives and Case Studies*, New York: Routledge, pp. 98–122.

Mumby, D. K. and Spitzack, C. 1983. "Ideology and Television News: A Metaphoric Analysis of Political Stories," *Communication Studies*, 34, 162–171.

Mumby, D. K., Thomas, R., Martí, I. and Seidl, D. 2017. "Resistance Redux," *Organization Studies*, 38, 1157–1183.

Neff, G. 2012. *Venture Labor: Work and the Burden of Risk in Innovative Industries*, Cambridge, MA: MIT Press.

Osborne, S. P. 2006. "The New Public Governance?" *Public Management Review*, 8, 377–387.

Parker, M. 2001. "Fucking Management: Queer, Theory and Reflexivity," *Ephemera*, 1, 36–53.

Parker, M. 2016. "Queering Queer," *Gender, Work and Organization*, 23, 71–73.

Peters, T. and Waterman, R. M. 1982. "*In Search of Excellence*," New York: Harper and Row.

Phillips, N. and Oswick, C. 2012. "Organizational Discourse: Domains, Debates, and Directions," *Academy of Management Annals*, 6, 435–481.

Plotnikof, M. 2015a. *Challenges of Collaborative Governance*, Copenhagen Business School.

Plotnikof, M. 2015b. "Negotiating Collaborative Governance Designs: a Discursive Approach," *The Innovation Journal*, 20, 1–20.

Plotnikof, M. 2016a. "Changing Market Values? Tensions of Contradicting Public Management Discourses: A Case from the Danish Daycare Sector," *International Journal of Public Sector Management*, 29, 659–674.

Plotnikof, M. 2016b. "Letting Go of Managing? Struggles over Managerial Roles in Collaborative Governance," *Nordic Journal of Working Life Studies*, 6, 109–128.

Plotnikof, M. and Zandee, D. 2016. "Meaning Negotiations of Collaborative Governance: A Discourse-Based Ethnography," in Pedersen, A. R. and Humle, D. M. (eds.), *Doing Organizational Ethnography*, New York: Routledge, pp. 137–159.

Pullen, A., Harding, N. and Phillips, M. 2017. "Introduction: Feminist and Queer Politics in Critical Management Studies," in Pullen, A., Harding, N. and Phillips, M. (eds.), *Feminist and Queer Theorists Debate the Future of Critical Management Studies*, Bingley, UK: Emerald, pp. 1–11.

Putnam, L. L., Fairhurst, G. T. and Banghart, S. 2016. "Contradictions, Dialectics, and Paradoxes in Organizations: A Constitutive Approach," *The Academy of Management Annals*, 10(1), 65–171.

Putnam, L. L. and Mumby, D. K. (2014). *The SAGE Handbook of Organizational Communication: Advances in Theory, Research, and Methods*, Thousands Oaks, CA: SAGE.

Ross, A. 2003. *No-Collar: The Humane Workplace and its Hidden Costs*, New York: Basic Books.

Solon, O. 2018, January 31. "Amazon Patents Wristband that Tracks Warehouse Workers' Movements," *The Guardian*, Retrieved from www.theguardian.com/technology/2018/jan/31/amazon-warehouse-wristband-tracking

Taylor, F. W. 1911/1934. *The Principles of Scientific Management*, New York: Harper and Brothers [originally published 1911].

Weick, K. E. 1976. "Educational Organizations as Loosely-Coupled Systems," *Administrative Science Quarterly*, 21, 1–19.

Wilhoit, E. D. and Kisselburgh, L. G. 2017. "The Relational Ontology of Resistance: Hybridity, Ventriloquism, and Materiality in the Production of Bike Commuting as Resistance," *Organization*, Advance online publication.

Willmott, H. 1993. "Strength is Ignorance; Slavery is Freedom: Managing Culture in Modern Organizations," *Journal of Management Studies*, 30, 515–552.

4 Ethics, Corporate Social Responsibility, and Sustainability

Steven K. May, Jeremy P. Fyke, and Katharine E. Miller

This chapter explores the interrelated phenomena of organizational ethics, corporate social responsibility, and sustainability. Each, in its own right, has emerged as a key issue in the theory and practice of organizational communication. Taken together, they represent a substantive shift in the ways in which we engage, critique, and create new forms of organizing. As Stan Deetz (1992) noted some time ago, the business organization has become the central institution in modern society, often eclipsing the state, family, church, and community in power. Organizations pervade modern life by providing personal identity, structuring time and experience, influencing education and knowledge production, and directing news and entertainment. Increasingly, they also shape the discursive and material production of values that are embedded in ethics codes, values statements, professional training and development, volunteerism programs, community-based initiatives, climate-change efforts, supply-chain management, and even in organizational mission, strategy, and operations, in some cases. We see this transition through the blurring of boundaries between for-profit and not-for-profit organizations and the emergence of trends such as conscious capitalism and new hybrid forms that focus on the triple bottom line of economic, social, and environmental dimensions of organizations. We anticipate that such trends will become even more pronounced in the future and, as such, it is incumbent upon organizational communication scholars to consider the opportunities and challenges of such practices.

This chapter examines organizational ethics, corporate social responsibility, and sustainability, focusing on their history, current research, practical applications, and directions for future research. We begin by offering some initial insights regarding how and why we came to study these phenomena.

Our Stories

Steve's Story

My interest in organizational ethics and, by extension, corporate social responsibility and sustainability, developed via a long and indirect path.

In many respects, my research trajectory has been the convergence of lived experience and scholarly influence from mentors. As a youth, one of my earliest memories of the nature and impact of work was driving by striking Whirlpool factory workers, late at night, as my family returned from visits to my grandparents' house. I can vividly remember the image of union workers huddled around metal barrels, burning wood to stay warm in the cold of winter. Although I didn't realize it at the time, I was learning lessons about equity and fairness related to working conditions, wages, and, ultimately, power and resistance.

Once in college at Purdue University, I double-majored in Journalism and Public Relations. Again, unbeknownst to me, I was already beginning to navigate a kind of dialectical tension regarding the ethical responsibilities of company and career. On the one hand, I was motivated to critique powerful institutions, learning how to be an investigative journalist on the heels of Vietnam and the civil rights movement and in the midst of Watergate. On the other hand, I learned that a more lucrative career option was to help companies engage in rhetorical appeals to pursue their interests and engage in crisis management when misconduct was uncovered. It wasn't until my junior year, though, that I discovered organizational communication and one influential reading that gave voice to the key tensions in my life: Studs Terkel's *Working*. Never before had I been exposed to the raw, human emotions of work in the natural, accessible, and sometimes profound language of workers themselves. From that reading assignment, in a course taught by Cynthia Stohl, those workers' voices resonated and reverberated, articulating for me both the opportunities and challenges of work.

As an M.A. student at Purdue, I was fortunate to be a part of lively scholarly conversations that reflected, in many ways, the ferment in the field at the time. Linda Putnam, a mentor of mine, had recently edited a ground-breaking volume on interpretive approaches to organizational communication with Michael Pacanowsky. The field of organizational communication was opening up, both theoretically and methodologically. At Purdue, there was a strong ethical impetus in the work that was being conducted by others such as Charles Redding, Phil Tompkins, Nick Trujillo, and George Cheney. I, in turn, sought out Cynthia Stohl and Linda Putnam to help me imagine how to create social support at work in response to pervasive stress.

As a Ph.D. student at the University of Utah, with the guidance of Len Hawes, Mary Strine, and Buddy Goodall, I was introduced to a set of theoretical perspectives—critical theory, poststructuralism, and postmodernism—that enabled me to integrate the cultural and the organizational, always around key tensions of work such as how to create organizations that are simultaneously productive and humane, responsible and responsive. Binaries faded away and dialectics that blurred realms of life came to the fore—public and private, labor and leisure, work and family. As always, I remained intrigued by practices that both enabled and constrained ethical action in and around organizations.

That sense of dialectics remains at the heart of ethics, corporate social responsibility, and sustainability for me. What practices enable and/or constrain ethical behavior in organizations? How do CSR initiatives simultaneously contribute to the public good and also further corporate colonization of the lifeworld? In what ways are companies able to engage in constructive environmental change, yet remain viable, financially? These questions led me to organize a series of Forum essays in *Management Communication Quarterly* in 2003 that sought to introduce corporate social responsibility to organizational communication scholars and to critique the sometimes simplistic and overly optimistic research on the topic at the time. The quality of those essays and the ongoing dialogue that ensued at conferences and casual conversations was the impetus for *The Debate Over Corporate Social Responsibility*, with George Cheney and Juliet Roper, and *The Handbook of Communication and Corporate Social Responsibility*, with Oyvind Ihlen and Jennifer Bartlett. In recent years, I have continued to wrestle with tensions between ethics/performance, agency/structure, internal/external, and material/symbolic dimensions of work. I see this chapter with Jeremy and Katharine as an extension of that legacy, but with their own unique contributions and insights that are reformulating our understanding of ethics, CSR, and sustainability.

Jeremy's Story

My start to these topics began in 2008, on spring break in my first year of my Ph.D. at Purdue. On the patio of my parents' home in Wimberley, Texas, my father and I were discussing Rick Warren's best-selling book, *The Purpose-Driven Life*, which I had recently begun reading. At one point my father asked a question that stays with me even today—"What about a purpose-driven *company*?" At the time, not knowing anything about the place I now call my scholarly home, I thought it was such an original and fascinating concept to consider.

Along more scholarly lines, what I was really interested in—and fascinated by—were the very questions that drive my work now. Questions like "Why?," "What else is out there?," and "How?" In an organizational setting, these questions have translated into: "*Why* do organizations really exist, beyond making money, delivering goods and services, etc.?"; "*What else is out there* for organizations to strive for?"; and "*How* can organizations best function to make the most difference with their talent and resources?" In short, these are questions that have occupied individuals for millennia—fundamental questions of purpose and existence.

Fast-forward 2 years later, and I secured an internship at a "purpose-driven" (Mitra and Fyke 2017) consulting and leadership development firm as a 7-week field study for my dissertation. During that project, my eyes were opened and my mind blown, as I was introduced to all of the topics that now occupy nearly every keystroke when I write—chiefly, conscious capitalism and corporate social responsibility, ethics, consulting, and ethical leadership development. From that 7-week study emerged my dissertation, entitled "Doing 'The Work' of Conscious Capitalism: Leading Change and Changing Leaders," along with my first publication based on that data set (Fyke and Buzzanell 2013).

In all, I continue to ask fundamental questions about the existence of the institutions that have a loud voice in our society; questions about the "business-society relationship" (Fyke et al. 2016). In the end, for me, it all circles back to *purpose*.

Katharine's Story

As someone once professionally bound to work in the corporate world, I've always been interested in the idea or goal of doing "good" work— or finding meaning and purpose in my career, whether it be through my individual work or through that of my employer. Thus, I've had a passion for nonprofit organizations and those contexts in which this kind of work is possible and perhaps even encouraged. As a senior in Corporate Communication at Marquette University in the fall of 2013, I was required to take Corporate Social Responsibility (CSR) as my capstone class. As I was introduced to the concept, I became enamored with this idea that organizations as a whole are fulfilling needs or demands by both internal and external entities to move beyond the sole pursuit of profit maximization—or being able to succeed at both simultaneously. Thus began my academic passion and change in post-undergraduate path to pursue a graduate degree. My master's thesis focused on the internal perspectives of CSR held by employees under the directive and support of Jeremy as my advisor, as well as through the guidance and work of Steve. My journey academically has since progressed throughout the first 2 years of my Ph.D. program to various areas and dynamics of CSR—from considering this from a meaningful work perspective to implications for training and development—and, most recently, sustainability. Writing this chapter, I've been in the process of furthering my research program in these areas through a study abroad opportunity at the Copenhagen Business School and in narrowing a dissertation project.

We hope these personal reflections provide a sense of how and why we have chosen to pursue research in organizational ethics, corporate social responsibility, and sustainability. In some cases, our scholarly direction was purposeful and intentional, while in others it was unexpected and fortuitous. Regardless of the reasons for our research foci, however, it is also important to better understand how and why each of these realms of scholarship developed in the field of organizational communication and to articulate where we see them headed in the future.

Why Organizational Ethics, Corporate Social Responsibility, and Sustainability?

Nearly from the outset of the field, scholars of organizational communication have raised concerns about ethics in/through organizations (Cheney et al. 2011). Charles Redding, considered by many to be a central figure in modern organizational communication, crystallized the emphasis on ethics when he explained that organizations are, ultimately, ethical systems of practice. Back in 1982, he noted that "the preponderance of everyday problems that plague all organizations are either problems that are patently ethical or moral in nature, or they are problems in which deeply embedded ethical issues can be identified" (p. 2).

Despite the widely publicized scandals in both the for-profit and the not-for-profit sectors worldwide and the related rise of corporate social responsibility and sustainability (see, for example, May et al. 2007), the broader field of ethics has continued to hold a marginal status in the theory and practice of organizational communication

The stakes for ethics can be particularly high and raise a number of questions that foreground why ethics are so important: How do organizations impact our economic, political, social, and environmental systems? How safe is a particular product or service? How should employees be hired, trained, evaluated, and compensated? What role should our organizations have in our communities? Whose definition of "ethics" is dominant in an increasingly global economy? How should wealth be created and distributed? These questions are certainly not exhaustive and, ultimately, revolve around basic ethical expectations of organizations such as the following: (a) creating a decent product/service that provides a public good at a fair price; (b) fostering equitable treatment of employees that affords them safe working conditions, a living wage, and opportunities for growth and development; (c) establishing fair treatment of customers, suppliers, and competitors; (d) using accurate advertising and marketing strategies; (e) facilitating a sense of responsibility to the local communities in which they operate; (f) enhancing our democratic potential as a country; and (g) producing a reasonable return on investments, while minimizing the externalization of costs onto others (Gini 2005).

There are several reasons that ethics are critical, including risk management, organizational functioning, market positioning, and civic positioning, among others (Paine 2003). In recent years, many organizational leaders have concluded that ethics improves performance and, ultimately, the bottom line. We now understand, for example, that nearly a quarter of the workforce is likely to leave a company because of ethical concerns (May 2013). Similarly, prospective employees consider a company's values and integrity when making employment decisions. Consumers have increasingly begun to make buying decisions on the basis of company reputation. Although these performance-based rationales for organizational ethics have expanded in recent years, other leaders assert that it is the right thing to do. They have concluded that organizations should be fair, honest, respectful, responsive, trustworthy, accountable, and responsible, regardless of whether it serves the organization's self-interest (Fyke et al. 2016).

Communities also have a say in why organizational ethics are vital. They want employers to provide good, sustainable jobs that promote economic development. Communities also expect that for-profit organizations will pay their fair share of taxes in exchange for the public benefits provided to them. Not-for-profit organizations are expected to understand community challenges and to address them as effectively as possible. Communities also increasingly demand that organizations do no harm—that they don't unduly disrupt democratic political principles, negatively affect the environment, or damage the social fabric. In short, they call for ethical behaviors that enable economic, political, social, and environmental justice (Schaefer et al. 2011).

This broader perspective on ethics is central to a related realm of CSR research. While organizational ethics research often prioritizes the individual/employee, CSR scholars, by contrast, focus on the organization–society relationship. CSR enjoys a close relationship with sustainability and ethics, and specifically as an exemplar or subset of what Mitra and Buzzanell term "sustainable organizing," the commitment to "transforming extant social systems" (2015: 133). CSR work in organizational communication fits under a larger umbrella of work that centers the organization–society relationship as a key problematic (Fulk 2014), along with related topics such as cross-sector partnerships (Koschmann et al. 2012) and globalization (Stohl and Ganesh 2014).

One way of viewing the *why* of CSR is to see CSR as a way for businesses to *legitimize* their practices (Fyke et al. 2016) to a range of stakeholders with competing interests. In other words, businesses, in their efforts to pursue normative *corporate* aims (e.g. profit, providing goods and services), must also attend to the *social* (e.g. ethics, giving back, solving social problems). Furthermore, public perceptions of legitimacy include (a) whether an organization's product and/or service creates a public good, and (b) how an organization treats employees (e.g., regarding issues such as sexual harassment, discrimination, a living wage, etc.).

In the United States, CSR began as a form of philanthropy attributable to less government provision for social welfare—business "gave back," voluntarily, because they were getting much from society. Howard R. Bowen's classic 1953 book, *The Social Responsibilities of the Businessman*, highlights the important social call for businesses to promote public welfare (e.g. social justice, standards for living, economic security).

Recent work on CSR reporting shows how companies use reports to signal their legitimacy—their license to operate—either routinely or in response to public claims (see Bartlett 2014). Societal demands evolve over time, so CSR is a way for companies to align their practices with what society wants. For instance, companies operating in more responsible manners toward the environment (i.e. sustainability) is largely a response to increasing demands from society at all levels, notably global concerns about climate change. Corporate social responsibility is a way of responding to general demands, or specific issues, risks, or crises, for instance, workplace violence, accidents, or other misgivings (see Palenchar et al. 2014).

By contrast, if communication about CSR activities does not reflect reality, it damages an organization's legitimacy. Related here is work on greenwashing and pinkwashing. As often seen in sustainability research, greenwashing denotes a situation in which word and deed conflict, if not contradict—companies say they are doing one thing but the practices suggest otherwise. CSR, in this case, amounts to another form of corporate spin, window dressing, or storytelling (Becker-Olsen and Guzmán 2017). Similarly, with pinkwashing, companies claim to care about women's health issues such as breast cancer without having genuine CSR practices that affect said issues (Moscato 2018).

The third strand of research we address, "sustainability," is a broad term for specific efforts organizations execute otherwise known as social responsibility. But, *why* sustainability? From an organizational standpoint, corporate sustainability is most often linked to sustainable development—or, the idea that we must meet present needs without compromising those of future generations (Mitra 2016, Rasche et al. 2017). Thus, one view of sustainable development and broader sustainability efforts is one that posits CSR as a way for businesses to contribute to such development and, in turn, make change on a macro level to entire societies (Rasche et al. 2017). Traditionally, the argument for why organizations should adopt sustainable practices refers to a win-win solution for both the corporation and surrounding environment—otherwise known as the "business case" for social responsibility (Ihlen and Roper 2011) related to the triple bottom line of economic, social, and environmental concern. Additionally, from an ethical standpoint and related to the case for CSR, the "moral case" for sustainability encourages organizations to engage in such efforts because it is simply the right thing to do.

In organizational communication scholarship, research has been conducted on the reasons that companies engage in sustainability—either as a specific type of CSR or as a broader contribution to society through sustainable development. Often, sustainability-as-CSR is seen as a way for organizations to be legitimized. Most often, sustainability is connected to the environment. Corporations have increasingly taken stances toward environmental concerns in response to ecological or social pressures, among others. Thus, research has explored topics of corporate environmentalism (Bullis and Ie 2007), corporate "eco-talk" or the "greening of organizations," through the rise of crisis communication regarding environmental calamities (Livesey and Graham 2007), and green marketing and greenwashing (Becker-Olsen and Guzmán 2017).

As such, sustainability research has explored the driving forces behind the reasons that organizations seek to engage in sustainability in one way, shape, or form. Like CSR, there has been debate that these efforts are misleading or a form of "greenwashing" or "aspirational" in their communication that misaligns with current or future action (Christensen et al. 2013). However, more positive reviews include topics on purpose-driven organizations (Mitra and Fyke 2017) and the connection between successful corporate sustainability and organizational culture (Baumgartner 2009). Communicatively, organizations talk about sustainability issues for various reasons—marketing, business, or social (Signitzer and Prexl 2008). Considering the triple bottom line, therefore, has been an argument for adopting sustainable practices.

Where Are Organizational Ethics, CSR, and Sustainability Research Located and *Whom* Do They Address?

When scholars have studied organizational ethics, they have focused either exclusively on internal dynamics or external conditions, commonly on individuals *within* organizations. Internally, scholars have studied a range of organizational practices such as identity formation, leadership, decision-making, whistleblowing, and organizational culture, among others.

The existing research on organizational ethics, though, has focused primarily on individuals and extensively on leadership and decision-making, respectively. At the discrete, individual level, scholars have sought to understand the moral character of employees and how it affects ethical behavior. Conrad (1993), in one of the earliest volumes on ethics in organizational communication, refers to the "ethical nexus" of personal values, ethics, and decision-making. Scholars have shown particular interest in the morality of leaders, including their capacity for ethical reasoning (Collinson 2005) and their ability to translate communication into responsible leadership (Seeger and Ulmer 2003). Other researchers have explored how leaders manage ethical risk, in general, and via crisis management (Novak and Sellnow 2009). Finally, on the dark side of leadership, scholars have also acknowledged a range of unethical behaviors such as bullying among leaders (Lutgen-Sandvik 2008) and the ethical implications of downsizing on employees (Fairhurst et al. 2002).

Scholars such as Jeffrey Kassing (2011) have studied the role of ethics, dissent, and whistleblowing in organizations. As Gossett and Kilker (2006) have noted, employees who experience job dissatisfaction because of ethical concerns may often turn outside the organization to express voice and resistance, including whistleblowing. Whistleblower research, in particular, has sought to better understand the relationship between ethical perspectives of whistleblowers (Contu 2014) and their desire to correct imbalances of power and secrecy by circumventing institutional mechanisms to gain redress outside the organization.

Beyond the individual level of analysis, organizational ethics research has recently shifted its focus toward practices embedded within organizational culture. Such research explores how organizational structures can either enable or constrain ethical behavior. Historically, organizational ethics scholars have paid attention to the effect of organizational culture, and how ethics codes and other formal policies impact the willingness of employees to address ethical issues at work (Hoffman and Schwartz 2015). Further, scholars have argued that, in order to understand how seemingly good people make unethical decisions at work, we need to acknowledge the role of dialogic communication, transparency, participation, accountability, and ethical courage (Nadesan, 2011, Stohl and Cheney 2001). For instance, Fyke, Trisler, and Lucas (2018) recently demonstrated the illusiveness of courage in contexts in which leadership entwines with sexuality. Notably, in the Penn State sexual abuse scandal, top leaders demonstrated a stunning lack of courage when faced with a sexualized context. In all, researchers from this perspective assume that context matters—rather than just personal morality—in organizational ethics.

Finally, scholars who have studied ethics from an external vantage point tend to consider broader cultural conditions, such as neoliberalism, post-Fordism, and related theories of the firm. As Cheney and Cloud (2006: 503) explained, any ethics-based research about organizations needs to account for the "material, political, and social constraints of global consumer capitalism." Similarly, our culturally and legally derived "theories of the firm" (Kuhn and Ashcraft 2003) also significantly affect our ethical expectations of companies, as well as how the public responds to misconduct. Scholars who address the impact of cultural discourses on organizational ethics have also critiqued taken-for-granted assumptions about "the market" (Cheney et al. 2010), the relationship between labor and management (Cloud 2005), and our fundamental understanding of what constitutes work itself (Gini 2000). Such work encourages researchers interested in ethics to challenge naturalized conceptions of communication (Christensen et al. 2008) by taking into account broader notions of stewardship that consider production, consumption, and, ultimately, the cultural legitimacy of organizations (Melé 2009).

The *where* and *who* questions are important to CSR, as well, because CSR has audience considerations at its foundation. Placing "social" next to "corporate" suggests wider concerns beyond the firm's financial interests. In this vein, various iterations of CSR have emerged in recent years including corporate social performance, corporate citizenship, and stakeholder theory. As Garriga and Melé (2004) noted, these approaches are all part of the "complex and unclear" territory of the broader CSR field of study and practice. Each of these approaches broadens the frame of reference for CSR, and enlightens *whom* is impacted by corporate actions and activities, and which actors and audiences are recipients of CSR communications.

The great majority of CSR work concerns external audiences, such as by creating CSR reports that target shareholders, community groups, activists, and the like. There are, perhaps, good reasons for the relative lack of research on the internal context of CSR, most notably difficulties gaining access to employees and/or internal CSR documents (May and Roper 2014). Indeed, Katharine faced that situation in a study of employees. Specifically, not only was access difficult but, interestingly, it was difficult for the company—a prominent, large, and highly recognizable financial management firm—to even locate the appropriate employees "responsible" for, or with sufficient knowledge of, CSR. Such a dilemma is perhaps an interesting finding in its own right.

Arguably the most comprehensive study of employees from a CSR perspective is Dana Cloud's research on Boeing workers where she argues that perhaps a company's greatest responsibility is to its employees (Cloud 2007). She further noted that, to truly explore the interests of workers, one must critique the basics of capitalism, which often requires the exploitation of workers in the name of profit. Such a critical view of CSR is increasingly common, especially in organizational communication work (May and Roper 2014). Another recent study by Chen and Hung-Baesecke (2014) found that manager behaviors affected employee participation in CSR activities, specifically by leading by example, advocating CSR's importance, and facilitating involvement in CSR work. Likewise, Mory, Wirtz, and Göttel (2017) studied the impact that internal CSR has on affective and normative organizational commitment. Internally directed CSR efforts positively impact affective commitment—the extent to which you enjoy your job—and seem to have minimal impact on normative commitment—the extent to which you feel you should stay in your job. Finally, new research from Cone Communications (Cone 2017) demonstrated that citizens increasingly demand that companies stand *up* for social issues that matter to them—domestic job growth (the number one reported issue), racial equality, women's rights, cost of higher education, etc. For instance, citizens have recently called on corporations to cut ties with the National Rifle Association (NRA) in light of the February 2018 shooting in Parkland, Florida. Companies such as Hertz, Enterprise Rent-A-Car, MetLife, and Symantec have ended discount programs for NRA members and/or severed ties altogether, largely because of pressure generated online via #BoycottNRA.

Further, May and Roper (2014) provided a brief overview of internally directed CSR work under the umbrella of interpretive approaches to CSR. They noted that internal CSR work often concerns management and/or leadership viewpoints rather than employees. For example, Burchell and Cook (2006) took an insider's view to explore managerial attitudes toward stakeholder dialogue and its effect on corporate strategy. Although studies of the impact of dialogue are rare, such work would seem to exemplify one of Mitra and Buzzanell's (2015) agenda items for sustainability work, broadly speaking: the emphasis on understanding how organizational policies are subject to shift in light of sociohistorical influences. In other words, in Burchell and Cook's case, stakeholder dialogue/engagement is but one example of how a wide variety of actors (re)constitute organizational policy.

While sizable literature has explored the reasons that organizations may take on sustainable and socially responsible initiatives, much work from a communicative standpoint lies within the internal–external organizational dimensions. Exploring sustainability from an external standpoint presents an interdisciplinary convergence between organizational communication and public relations. Examples include work that has examined how organizations position themselves as sustainable leaders and is discursively constructed via policy (Roper 2011) and the role of stakeholder engagement in achieving sustainability (Collins et al. 2005). Additionally, much work has considered how corporations discuss sustainable development in their reporting efforts (Feller 2004). O'Connor and Gronewold (2013) examined environmental sustainability reports from international petroleum companies focusing on competitive advantage and institutional language use related to CSR. The article also addressed the increase in non-financial reporting around sustainable efforts in response to stakeholder pressure. Here, the terms "CSR" and "sustainability" were used simultaneously in referring to specific organizational efforts.

Furthermore, scholars have explored sustainability from an external perspective in considering how organizations engage with their surrounding environment. For example, Cooren's (2001) seminal piece on the Great Whale River case explored the nature of organizational coalitions with a controversial environmental issue at the center. Similarly, Norton (2007: 146) presented organizing environmental control through public participation processes—exploring the contribution of involving broader interest groups in "developing better environmental policy."

Perhaps the largest area of sustainability research, according to Mitra (2016), explores communication surrounding corporate-environmental impact. For example, Ihlen (2009) examined how global organizations rhetorically framed issues of climate change in their non-financial reporting. Likewise, Livesey (2002) took a Foucauldian approach to Shell's social report, revealing "links between discourse and changing social practices of sustainable development while simultaneously uncovering aspects of the power-knowledge dynamics at play" (Livesey 2002: 314) in what was, at the time, an entirely new form of corporate reporting—integrating economic, environmental, and social impacts.

The discussion of sustainability situated internally, much like CSR, is relatively limited in comparison to an external perspective. Much focus related to the internal dimension has been on the topics of sustainable supply chain management, sustainable business model, and organizational collaboration for environmental and sustainable causes—all more widely discussed in management and production disciplines. However, Mitra and Buzzanell (2018) took an insider's view; specifically, they analyzed the sensemaking of work by sustainability practitioners. Similarly, they situate sustainability in a meaningful work context, once again examining professionals and highlighting complexities and tensions in the discursive process of meaning-making within sustainable work. In short, both studies demonstrated the rather ineffective and vague nature of implementing sustainable practices, thus highlighting the traditional macro-level approach to understanding sustainability in and around organizations, and a need for more micro and individualistic examination.

How? Practical Implications of Ethics, CSR, and Sustainability Research

As we look back through our chapter thus far, it strikes us that one need only to look for times when these topics were absent—for example, ethical misgivings, failing to balance corporate and social aims, unsustainable actions—to see that they are inherently practical. For organizational ethics practice, the goal is to develop "ethical agility" that improves ethical awareness, strengthens ethical judgment, and, ultimately, produces ethical action (May 2013). To date, much of the applied research in organizational ethics has focused on the practical (and often, formalized) norms, policies, and procedures that enable ethical behavior (Seeger et al. 2009). For instance, organizations can consider the role of training and development in fostering ethical decision-making. At the organizational level, scholars have more commonly espoused the benefits of robust ethics codes (Schwartz 2001).

For their part, organizational leaders have launched ethics programs, mission-driven strategies, values initiatives, and cultural change efforts. In addition, companies have created ethics officers, high-level ethics committees, ethics ombudspersons, codes of ethics, grievance procedures, ethics hotlines, and ethics task forces. Finally, companies have attempted to strengthen their relationships with various stakeholders, developing programs on the environment, which aligns directly with sustainability practice, as well as human rights, work–family balance, corporate volunteerism, community assistance, product safety, customer service, and philanthropy, among others.

Meanwhile, CSR's practical promise offers a way to view the ways in which organizations can fulfill their ethical duties—perhaps ethics is the goal and CSR is the vehicle. Indeed, in 1979 Archie Carroll noted that

CSR encompasses the economic, legal, discretionary, and *ethical* expectations of society. The classic, practical view of CSR is philanthropy—essentially, giving back for getting much. Another view of CSR that is quite a departure from philanthropy is strategic CSR (Porter and Kramer 2006). CSR that is strategic is seen as core to the firm's operations: its decision making, execution, overall strategy, and day-to-day operations. From this standpoint, a company will and should only undertake a CSR initiative, program, or campaign if it is core to its business and thus helps it in the long run. It seeks mutual benefit rather than one-way payoffs.

Two examples help illustrate strategic CSR. First, consider IBM's "Smarter Planet." On one hand, Smarter Planet might appear to be CSR in a traditional sense—it connects business aims with societal needs—but it is much more business strategy than *just* CSR. It represents a sophisticated business strategy for IBM that has problem solving and helping society at its core. By contrast, consider Enterprise's partnership with the Arbor Day Foundation for its 50 Million Tree program, whereby it pledges to plant 1 million trees over the next 50 years to offset carbon emissions from its car rentals. Such a program arguably falls somewhere in the middle of philanthropy and strategic CSR. The trees are not really core to its operations; rather, they essentially help make up for potential damage caused by their core operations.

Another view of strategic CSR relevant for organizational communication scholars is that it resembles a discourse of hope, a less common angle on the topic that counterbalances inherent skepticism from critical scholars (May and Roper 2014). Specifically, nodding toward the sustainability of CSR, Zorn and Collins (2007) are optimistic about how complex problems—climate change, finite resources, income inequality—call for greater transparency and accountability. Additionally, these authors noted that communication practices are vital for moving CSR inward and operational to a firm's core operations. We argue that strategic CSR might represent a positive, more sustainable, shift in that direction.

Thus, by extension, activities often associated with "sustainability" include introducing or altering of certain organization policies, creating products or services to address largely environmental issues including pollution, water or other natural resource use, and on a broader scale, enhance stakeholder relations (Linnenluekcke and Griffiths 2010). In an age of increased concern for environmental conservation and climate change, the role of business in society, and sustainability have become top-of-mind for organizational leaders in the face of growing pressure to respond to societal and environmental issues (Valente 2017). Thus, organizational communication is a fitting space to further explore sustainability initiatives promised and enacted by organizations, both internally and externally.

From an external standpoint, sustainability is a natural application for CSR. In other words, organizations are taking on sustainable initiatives to undoubtedly fill some need often related to the environment or broader community outreach. On the broader sense, the debate of corporate sustainability calls for a need for organizations to go beyond talk and contribute to the larger environment and society (Rasche et al. 2017).

Indeed, the issue of sustainability talk versus action holds practical promise. Are organizations truly committed to sustainable development through the full integration of such principles into their very culture and operations? Or, are these efforts simply aspirational in the hope of responding to crucial societal concerns and are, in fact, just "window dressing." The practical promise of sustainability is that it can take the form of "systemic resilience" (Mitra 2016). Here, there is continuous interaction and mutually beneficial dialogue between an organization and its stakeholders within the larger, complex environment. For example, this line of research shows how organizations are transforming communities through the perspective of eco-localism (Ganesh and Zoller 2014).

Within the past decade, CSR and (corporate) sustainability have converged both conceptually and in practice (Valente 2017)—often analogous in their communication, reporting, and enactment in organizational contexts. In fact, perhaps the most popular conceptualization is sustainability *as* CSR. As Mitra (2016: 2) noted, "Organizational ethics and CSR have long been the cornerstone of organizational communication scholarship, examining the economic, environmental, social, and discretionary responsibilities of managers and firms to their various stakeholders." Here, sustainability is an avenue for CSR initiatives—focused primarily on environmental and social elements—and considering sustainable development from either a voluntary, altruistic standpoint, or contributing to profit maximization. Thus, related research has often presented CSR and sustainability as interrelated and integrated in practice (O'Connor and Gronewold 2013).

We see sustainability as part of the larger, overarching umbrella of CSR as a specific way for organizations to employ responsible initiatives and goals. Sustainability can be conceptualized as an ongoing process "across government, nonprofit, and for-profit entities to enable sustainable development" (Mitra 2016: 1). Common to its conceptualization is the idea of intergenerational and long-term sustainment—providing a similar or better world for future generations. Ranging from commitment to reducing effects of climate change to protection of natural resources to waste management and the like, sustainability most commonly refers to environmental impact and conservation. From this view, sustainability is not contained or constricted within the boundaries of organizations, but rather considers the wider contributions made by individual companies (Montiel 2008).

Conclusion and Future Directions

As can be seen from our discussion of research and practice in organizational ethics, corporate social responsibility, and sustainability, we believe that they are distinct, but related, realms of scholarship. Here, we offer suggestions for future research for each area.

Steve's Directions for Future Ethics Research

Nearly 40 years after Charles Redding compared organizational ethics research to "wandering in a lonely desert" (Redding 1982), we encourage organizational communication scholars to take up his admonition to seriously consider ethics, in all its facets. As the broadest of the three phenomena discussed in this chapter, as I have discovered throughout my career, the possible avenues for ethics-oriented organizational communication are nearly limitless; however, I encourage scholars to direct their efforts towards three levels of analysis—individual, organizational, and cultural. At the individual level, we certainly need to continue studies of ethical leadership, since executives set the ethical tone for behavior. Yet, we also need to understand the complex ethical tensions that mid- and lower-level employees face in their day-to-day work experiences. Thus, we should explore the ethical dilemmas, contradictions, and paradoxes that are common for today's workers in their regular workdays. Further, scholars should begin to study the unique complexities of different jobs, occupations, and industries. While ethical challenges are pervasive, they are not equally distributed in and across organizations.

At the organizational level, we need to understand the specific practices that enable and/or constrain ethical action in organizations. While organizations tend to focus on ethical compliance, organizational communication scholars can set their sights higher, on aspirational ethics. We can begin by exploring ethics through the life cycle of employment—recruitment, selection, socialization, assessment/evaluation, and exit. We need to account for the relationship between formal organizational prescriptions (e.g. mission, codes, values statements) and informal, mundane practices (e.g. language, storytelling, ritual) around ethics.

Finally, at the cultural level, we can study how our culture has valued—and is currently valuing—work and how our related assumptions frame what we see as acceptable and unacceptable behavior at work. We should explore how work produces particular identities for us and their ethical implications. Broader cultural analyses of ethics can also allow us to consider the blurring of boundaries such as private/public, labor/leisure, and work/family. Finally, we need to study how organizational actors "take up" values-driven cultural discourses and ideologies, such as neoliberalism, and integrate them into their work life.

Jeremy's Directions for CSR Research

Consistent with this broader, cultural level of analysis on organizational ethics scholarship, in general, I think we need to closely look at strategic

CSR practices to see whether and how they represent more sustained and sustainable CSR exemplars. For instance, identifying long-range business models and strategies (e.g. IBM's Smarter Planet, Verizon's Innovation Program) that mirror strategic CSR would be theoretically and practically helpful. Additionally, scholars should continue to explore recent iterations such as B Corps and firms dedicated to conscious capitalism (see Fyke et al. 2016, Fyke and Buzzanell 2013).

Second, I am fascinated by the dynamics of how societal demands affect and ultimately influence/change what companies strategize around CSR. For instance, we could further examine social media trends and map out how company CSR programs have evolved. Along similar lines, we saw earlier that a 2017 Cone Communications study demonstrated societal demands on companies to stand *up* for social issues. Academic inquiry is needed to explore the impact of these practices, for instance, via in-depth interviews and focus groups with employees working at firms known for their CSR practices to see how they measure up to such expectations around social issues. Even though access can be difficult, it potentially offers answers to important questions: How does company practice match their expectations going into the role? How do those practices affect their daily work?

Katharine's Directions for Sustainability Research

As anyone who has conducted research on sustainability can attest, further work could be done in refining the conceptualization of sustainability, similar to that of CSR. As a rather interdisciplinary concept, organizational communication scholars are fit to contribute to its conceptualization from a communicative standpoint. More broadly, I echo Mitra and Buzzanell's (2015) call for further work by organizational communication scholars in considering the organizing practices of sustainability as communicative action.

Additionally, we can further explore the practice-based approach to sustainable organizing in considering the micro-level processes of these practices (i.e. implementation and sensemaking) in everyday work (Mitra 2016, Mitra and Buzzanell 2017, 2018). Relatedly, research can continue to examine the complexities of sustainability centered on the intersection between profit, policy, and social/environmental impact.

Final Reflections

In closing, ethics, CSR, and sustainability matter in organizations. As we have shown, the bodies of research in these areas have grown over the years, offering points of distinction and fruitful overlap. If we consider *why* each matters for organization, *where* and *whom* they matter for, and *how* each might appear to us in practice, it is clear that organizational communication scholars must continue to play a big role in their future development. The stakes are too high otherwise.

Overall, as we have suggested in this chapter, ethics, CSR, and sustainability are interrelated, but distinct, realms of scholarship that provide new and important avenues for scholarship. Taken together, they represent a substantive change in how organizational communication scholars engage, critique, and create new forms of organizing. They offer us the opportunity to rethink and, in turn, remake our fundamental assumptions about what constitutes "ethics at work," as well as responsible, sustainable organizations. As such, research in ethics, CSR, and sustainability not only reminds us what organizational communication *is* but also, perhaps more importantly, motivates us towards what it *might be* in the future.

Discussion Questions

1. What are the various ways that organizational ethics could be enabled, via individual, organizational, and cultural interventions?
2. Suppose you are a leader put in charge of communicating the importance of CSR to your employees. What arguments would you draw upon to make the case?
3. What advantages, disadvantages, opportunities, and challenges do corporations have when it comes to CSR, as compared to other institutions from other sectors (e.g., nonprofits, governments, education systems)?
4. What similarities or differences/tensions do you see in the relationship between CSR and sustainability? Where do you see each of these in practice and how do you see organizations communicating their responsible business efforts?
5. Do you see organizations providing rationales for sustainability initiatives? If so, how? If not, why? Discuss the implications and importance of doing so.
6. How do you make sense of/tease out the relationships—overlaps, distinctions, tensions—between ethics, CSR, and sustainability?

References

Bartlett, J. L. 2014. "Public Relations and Corporate Social Responsibility," in Ihlen, Ø. Bartlett, J. and May, S. (eds.), *The Handbook of Communication and Corporate Social Responsibility*, Malden, MA: Wiley Blackwell, pp. 67–86.

Baumgartner, R. J. 2009. "Organizational Culture and Leaderships: Preconditions for the Development of a Sustainable Corporation," *Sustainable Development*, 17, 102–113.

Becker-Olsen, K. and Guzmán, F. 2017. "Corporate Social Responsibility in North America: Past, Present and Future," in Diehl, S. M. Karmasin, Mueller,

B. Terlutter, R. and Weder, F. (eds.), *Handbook of Integrated CSR Communication*, Switzerland: Springer, pp. 293–315.

Bowen, H. R. 1953. *Social Responsibilities of the Businessman*, New York: Harper and Row.

Bullis, C. and Ie, F. (2007) "Corporate Environmentalism," in May, S., Cheney, G. and Roper, J. (eds.), *The Debate over Corporate Social Responsibility*, New York: Oxford University Press, pp. 321–335.

Burchell, J. and Cook, J. 2006. "Confronting the 'Corporate Citizen': Shaping the Discourse of Corporate Social Responsibility," *International Journal of Sociology and Social Policy*, 26, 121–37.

Carroll, A. B. 1979. "A Three-Dimensional Conceptual Model of Corporate Performance," *Academy of Management Review*, 4, 497–505.

Chen, Y. R. and Hung-Baesecke, C. F. 2014. "Examining the Internal Aspect of Corporate Social Responsibility (CSR): Leader Behavior and Employee CSR Participation," *Communication Research Reports*, 31, 210–220.

Cheney, G. and Cloud, D. 2006. "Doing Democracy, Engaging the Material: Employee Participation and Labor Activity in an Age of Market Globalization," *Management Communication Quarterly*, 19, 501–540.

Cheney, G., Lair, D., Ritz, D. and Kendall, B. 2010. *Just a Job? Communication, Ethics, and Professional Life*, New York: Oxford University Press.

Cheney, G., May, S. K. and Munshi, D. (eds.). 2011. *The Handbook of Communication Ethics*, New York: Routledge.

Christensen, L. T., Morsing, M. and Thyssen, O. 2013. "CSR as Aspirational Talk," *Organization*, 20, 372–393.

Christensen, L. T., Morsing, M. and Cheney, G. 2008. *Corporate Communications: Convention, Complexity, and Critique*, London: SAGE.

Cloud, D. 2005. "Fighting Words: Labor and the Limits of Communication at Staley, 1993 to 1996," *Management Communication Quarterly*, 18, 509–542.

Cloud, D. 2007. "Corporate Social Responsibility as Oxymoron: Universalization and Exploitation at Boeing," in May, S., Cheney, G. and Roper, J. (eds.), *The Debate Over Corporate Social Responsibility*, Oxford: Oxford University Press, pp. 219–321.

Collins, E., Kearins, K. and Roper, J. 2005. "The Risks in Relying on Stakeholder Engagement in the Achievement of Sustainability," *Electronic Journal of Radical Organisation Theory*, 9, 81–101.

Collinson, D. 2005. "Dialectics of Leadership," *Human Relations*, 58, 1419–1492.

Cone 2017. "2017 Cone Communications CSR Study," Available from www.conecomm.com/research-blog/2017-csr-study

Conrad, C. 1993. *The Ethical Nexus*, Norwood, NJ: Ablex.

Contu, A. 2014. "Rationality and Relationality in the Process of Whistleblowing: Recasting Whistleblowing through the Readings of Antigone," *Journal of Management Inquiry*, 23, 393–406.

Cooren, F. 2001. "Translation and Articulation in the Organization of Coalitions: The Great Whale River Case," *Communication Theory*, 11, 178–200.

Deetz, S. 1992. *Democracy in an Age of Corporate Colonization*, Albany, NY: State University of New York Press.

Fairhurst, G. T., Cooren, F. and Cahill, D. J. 2002. "Discursiveness, Contradiction, and Unintended Consequences in Successive Downsizings," *Management Communication Quarterly*, 15, 501–540.

Feller, W. V. 2004. "Blue Skies, Green Industry: Corporate Environmental Reports as Utopian Narratives," in Senecah, S. L. (ed.), *The Environmental Communication Yearbook*, Mahwah: NJ: Lawrence Erlbaum, pp. 61–82.

Fulk, J. 2014. "Section VI: Communication and the Organization-Society Relationship," in Putnam, L. L. and Mumby, D. K. (eds.), *The SAGE Handbook of Organizational Communication: Advances in Theory, Research, and Methods*, Thousand Oaks, CA: SAGE, pp. 689–694

Fyke, J. P. and Buzzanell, P. M. 2013. "The Ethics of Conscious Capitalism: Wicked Problems in Leading Change and Changing Leaders," *Human Relations*, 66, 1619–1643.

Fyke, J. P., Feldner, S. B. and May, S. K. 2016. "Discourses about Righting the Business-Society Relationship," *Business and Society Review*, 121, 217–245.

Fyke, J. P., Trisler, B. and Lucas, K. 2018. "A Failure of Courageous Leadership: Sex, Embarrassment, & (Not) Speaking Up in the Penn State Sexual Abuse Scandal," in Beggan, J. K. and Allison, S. T. (eds.), *Leadership and Sexuality: Power, Principles, and Processes*, Cheltenham, UK: Edward Elgar, pp. 73–90.

Ganesh, S. and Zoller, H. M. 2014. "Organizing Transition: Principles and Tensions in Eco-Localism," in Parker, M., Cheney, G., Fournier, V. and Land, C. (eds.), *The Routledge Companion to Alternative Organization*, New York: Routledge, pp. 236–250.

Garriga, E. and Melé, D. 2004. "Corporate Social Responsibility Theories: Mapping the Territory," *Journal of Business Ethics*, 53, 51–71.

Gini, A. 2005. *Case Studies in Business Ethics (2nd ed.)*, Upper Saddle River, NJ: Prentice Hall.

Gini, A. 2000. *My Job, My Self: Work and the Creation of the Modern Individual*, New York: Routledge.

Gossett, L. M. and Kilker, J. 2006. "My Job Sucks: Examining Counter-Institutional Web Sites As Locations for Organizational Member Voice, Dissent, and Resistance," *Management Communication Quarterly*, 20, 63–90.

Hoffman, W. and Schwartz, M. 2015. "The Morality of Whistleblowing: A Commentary on Richard. T. DeGeorge," *Journal of Business Ethics*, 127, 771–781.

Ihlen, Ø. 2009. "Business and Climate Change: The Climate Response of the World's 30 Largest Corporations," *Environmental Communication*, 3, 244–262.

Ihlen, Ø. and Roper, J. 2011. "Corporate Reports on Sustainability and Sustainable Development: 'We Have Arrived,'" *Sustainable Development*, 22, 42–51.

Kassing, J. 2011. *Dissent in Organizations*, Cambridge, UK: Polity Press.

Koschmann, M. A., Kuhn, T. R. and Pfarrer, M. 2012. "A Communicative Framework of Value in Cross-Sector Partnerships," *Academy of Management Review*, 37, 332–354.

Kuhn, T. and Ashcraft, K. L. 2003. "Corporate Scandal and the Theory of the Firm: Formulating the Contributions of Organizational Communication Studies," *Management Communication Quarterly*, 17, 20–57.

Linnenluecke, M. K. and Griffiths, A. 2010. "Corporate Sustainability and Organizational Culture," *Journal of World Business*, 45, 257–366.

Livesey, S. M. 2002. "The Discourse of the Middle Ground: Citizen Shell Commits to Sustainable Development," *Management Communication Quarterly*, 15, 313–349.

Livesey, S. M. and Graham, J. 2007. "Greening of Corporations? Eco-talk and the Emerging Social Imaginary of Sustainable Development," in May, S., Cheney, G. and Roper, J. (eds.), *The Debate Over Corporate Social Responsibility*, New York: Oxford University Press, pp. 336–350.

Lutgen-Sandvik, P. 2008. "Intensive Remedial Identity Work: Responses to Workplace Bullying, Trauma, and Stigmatization," *Organization*, 15, 97–119.

May, S. K. (ed.). 2013. *Case Studies in Organizational Communication: Ethical Perspectives and Practices (2nd Edition)*, Thousand Oaks, CA: SAGE.

May, S. K., Cheney, G. and Roper, J. (eds.). 2007. *The Debate over Corporate Social Responsibility*, New York: Oxford University Press.

May, S. K. and Roper, J. 2014. "Corporate Social Responsibility and Ethics," in Putnam, L. L. and Mumby, D. K. (eds.), *The SAGE Handbook of Organizational Communication: Advances in Theory, Research, and Methods*, Thousand Oaks, CA: SAGE, pp. 767–789.

Melé, D. 2009. "Corporate Social Responsibility Theories," in Crane, A., McWilliams, A., Matten, D., Moon, J. and Siegel, D. S. (eds.), *The Oxford Handbook of Corporate Social Responsibility*, New York: Oxford University Press. pp. 47–82.

Mitra, R. 2016. "Sustainability and Sustainable Development," in Scott, C. R. and Lewis, L. (eds.), *The International Encyclopedia of Organizational Communication*, New York: John Wiley and Sons.

Mitra, R. and Buzzanell, P. M. 2015. "Introduction: Organizing/Communicating Sustainably," *Management Communication Quarterly*, 29, 130–134.

Mitra, R. and Buzzanell, P. M. 2017. "Communicative Tensions of Meaningful Work: The Case of Sustainability Practitioners," *Human Relations*, 70, 594–616.

Mitra, R. and Buzzanell, P. M. 2018. "Implementing Sustainability in Organizations: How Practitioners Discursively Position Work," *Management Communication Quarterly*, 32, 172–201.

Mitra, R., and Fyke, J. 2017. "Purpose-Driven Consultancies' Negotiation of Organizational Tensions," *Journal of Applied Communication Research*, 45, 140–159.

Montiel, I. 2008. "Corporate Social Responsibility and Corporate Sustainability: Separate Pasts, Common Futures," *Organization and Environment*, 21, 245–369.

Mory, L., Wirtz, B. W. and Göttel, V. 2017. "Corporate Social Responsibility: The Organizational View," *Journal of Management & Governance*, 21, 145–179.

Moscato, D. 2018. "Corporate Social Responsibility: Committing to Social and Environmental Impact in the Global Economy," in Laskin, A.V. (ed.), *The Handbook of Financial Communication and Investor Relations*, Malden, MA: John Wiley and Sons, pp. 221–233.

Nadesan, M. H. 2011. "Transparency and Neoliberal Logics of Corporate Economic and Social Responsibility," in Ihlen, Ø., Bartlett, J. and May, S. (eds.), *Handbook of Communication and Corporate Social Responsibility*, Boston, MA: Wiley-Blackwell, pp. 252–275.

Norton, T. 2007. "The Structuration of Public Participation: Organizing Environmental Control," *Environmental Communication*, 1, 146–170.

Novak, J. M. and Sellnow, T. L. 2009. "Reducing Organizational Risk Through Participatory Communication," *Journal of Applied Communication Research*, 37, 349–373.

O'Connor, A. and Gronewold, K. L. 2013. "Black Gold, Green Earth: An Analysis of the Petroleum Industry's CSR Environmental Sustainability Discourse," *Management Communication Quarterly*, 27, 210–236.

Paine, L. S. 2003. *Value Shift: Why Companies Must Merge Social and Financial Imperative to Achieve Superior Performance*, New York: McGraw-Hill.

Palenchar, M. J., Hocke, T. M. and Heath, R. L. 2014. "Risk Communication and Corporate Social Responsibility: The Essence of Sound Management for Risk Bearers, Generators and Arbiters," in Ihlen, Ø., Bartlett, J. and May, S. (eds.), *The Handbook of Communication and Corporate Social Responsibility*, Malden, MA: Wiley Blackwell, pp. 188–207.

Porter, M. E. and Kramer, M. R. 2006. "Strategy & Society: The Link Between Competitive Advantage and Corporate Social Responsibility," *Harvard Business Review*, 84, 77–92.

Rasche, A., Morsing, M. and Moon, J. 2017. "The Changing Role of Business in Global Society: CSR and Beyond," in Rasche, A., Morsing, M. and Moon, J. (eds.), *Corporate Social Responsibility: Strategy, Communication, Governance*, Cambridge, UK: Cambridge University Press, pp. 1–28.

Redding, C. W. 1982. "Ethics and the Study of Organizational Communication: When Will We Wake Up?" Lecture Presented to The Center for the Study of Ethics in Society. Kalamazoo, MI, Western Michigan University.

Roper, J. 2011. "Environmental Risk, Sustainability Discourses, and Public Leaders," *Public Relations Inquiry*, 1, 69–87.

Schaefer, Z., Conrad, C., Cheney, G., May, S. and Ganesh, S. 2011. "Economic Justice and Communication Ethics: Considering Multiple Points of Intersection," in Cheney, G., May, S. K. and Munshi, D. (eds.), *The Handbook of Communication Ethics*, New York: Routledge, pp. 436–456.

Schwartz, M. 2001. "The Nature of the Relationship Between Corporate Codes of Ethics and Behavior," *Journal of Business Ethics*, 32, 247–262.

Seeger, M. W. and Ulmer, R. R. 2003. "Explaining Enron: Communication and Responsible Leadership," *Management Communication Quarterly*, 17, 58–84.

Seeger, M. W., Sellnow, T. L., Ulmer, R. R. and Novak, J. 2009. "Applied Communication Ethics: A Summary and Critique of the Research Literature," in Frey, L. R. and Cissna, M. K. (eds.), *Routledge Handbook of Applied Communication Research*, New York: Routledge, pp. 290–305.

Signitzer, B., and Prexl, A. 2008. "Corporate Sustainability Communications: Aspects of Theory and Professionalization," *Journal of Public Relations Research*, 1, 1–19.

Stohl, C., and Cheney, G. 2001. "Participatory Processes/Paradoxical Practices: Communication and the Dilemmas of Organizational Democracy," *Management Communication Quarterly*, 14, 349–407.

Stohl, C. and Ganesh, S. 2014. "Generating Globalization," in Putnam, L. L. and Mumby, D. K. (eds.), *The SAGE Handbook of Organizational Communication: Advances in Theory, Research, and Methods*, Thousand Oaks, CA: SAGE, pp. 717–742.

Valente, M. 2017. "Corporate Responsibility Strategies for Sustainability," in Rasche, A., Morsing, M. and Moon, J. (eds.), *Corporate Social Responsibility: Strategy, Communication, Governance*, Cambridge, UK: Cambridge University Press, pp. 86–109.

Zorn, T. E. and Collins, E. 2007. "Is Sustainability Sustainable? Corporate Social Responsibility, Sustainable Business, and Management Fashion," in May, S., Cheney, G., and Roper, J. (eds.), *The Debate Over Corporate Social Responsibility*, Oxford, UK: Oxford University Press, pp. 405–416.

5 Identity, Identification, and Branding

George Cheney and Katie Sullivan

Persistence and Change in Organizational Identities

We always knew we were identity-challenged in the contemporary world of work, but technology and shifting boundaries as well as allegiances are making that landscape even harder to discern and navigate. Research on dispersed, virtual, and anonymous organizations and their impact on identities—both public and personal—has been going on for some time (Dwyer et al. 2018, Scott 1997, 2013). Recent information on technological development as well as changing currents in global and local linkages has greatly complicated the entire context, with wide-ranging and penetrating implications for organizations and organizing. For example, not only does the "relentless interconnectivity" predicted in the 1990s affect such things as work, roles and demands, and work–life boundaries, but it is also influencing privacy norms, individuals' sense of place, connection to the environment, and other key features of social life (Baker 2016). The very same Internet that allows freedom of expression, and rapid (and often dramatically effective) social-movement organizing has also yielded unsettling new threats to ontology and epistemology, in terms of how they are understood in scholarly investigation (Fieseler et al. 2014). We need not look far for examples of demonstrably false as well as flexible representations, stolen or hijacked identities, recasting of individuals and groups through nefarious means, or underhanded uses of technology to sway public opinion and smear reputations, which create sharper polarizations between political communities. Organizing, identity, and communication are therefore hurled into somewhat novel if not entirely new contexts.

In this chapter, we focus on identity's significance for organizational communication, while delving along the way into branding—not only as a set of specified practices but also as a major cultural and economic trend. In addition, we reference difference and diversity, which are inextricably bound up with notions of who we are at work and in other contexts, although they have not always been discussed together. We briefly discuss some primary theoretical frameworks for studying the intersections of identity, branding, and difference, and offer concrete contemporary examples to illustrate these frameworks. Finally, we discuss potential avenues for future research.

In our discussion of organizational identity, identification, diversity, and branding, we emphasize both enduring principles and upheavals in common understandings; both historical context and cultural difference; both personal and customized representations and images produced through mechanisms that are effectively out of reach of individual agency. We begin with the experiences that made us pause and spend time with not just our identities but indeed the question of identity itself.

George's Story

While in high school and college, I worked at several part-time jobs, including peddling home insulation door to door, making TV carts on a factory assembly line, selling shoes in a chain store of a nearby shopping mall—all before doing social research by interviewing newly laid-off steelworkers in my hometown of Youngstown, Ohio. Most of these jobs were means to ends rather than careers or callings in themselves. I "knew" they were temporary positions, while at the same time I was aware that the same was not the case for many of my coworkers, including in the factory.

Only the research position seemed to point toward the future, especially as I shifted my main studies from the sciences to the social sciences and humanities. Across all of these positions, I became acutely aware of the different ways people viewed and invested themselves in their roles—in other words, how identity figured into their work, hours, mental applications, and sweat. Especially curious was how some people in stores at the shopping mall became "voices" for their employers, taking pride not only in their performance but also in their very associations with the companies. I thought: "I am *not* this job." In addition to making me aware of the impacts of sudden factory closures on people's material lives, the research assistant position allowed me to see the disruptive changes in the community that dubbed itself "The Steel Valley." Bridges between individual, corporate, and community identity came into view. I could begin to see the difficulty in over-investment in a particular identity—whether for my father with his electric utility company or the larger community in terms of a single industry and associated images (as well as paychecks).

With the aid of both social-scientific and rhetorical studies late in my undergraduate years and then more intensively in graduate school at Purdue, I began to explore these issues more widely and deeply. Both rhetorical studies and social-scientific investigations—especially attitude research—were extremely helpful here in illuminating emotional, cognitive, seductive, and persuasive aspects of identity formation processes. As

I look back on those early experiences now, I realize that the basic themes have never really gone away; in fact, today they take renewed and new meanings, as the roles of class, race, gender, and other anchors of identity and markers of difference play out in dramatic ways in the U.S. economy and society. These memories are coming into even sharper relief today as we consider economic and social changes since around 1980, including the widening of the wealth gap, increased work hours, and the end of reliably long-term employment with a single organization. Identity is implicated with every one of these and other trends we discuss.

Katie's Story

I was drawn to the study of communication, identity, and difference as a way to make sense of my early work experiences in media, advertising, and marketing. Alongside many positive lessons, I learned how women's bodies are often subjected to aesthetic controls, sexualization, and de-professionalization attempts. For instance, in my early 20s, my boss told me to dye my hair blonde in order to look "more attractive" as the on-air host of a children's television program. To sell more television advertising, a manager's advice was to work on my alcohol tolerance so I could log more "happy hours" with male clients. This same manager suggested that becoming a mother was the "death" of a woman's career in sales. As a marketing professional, I was told by a VP to stay quiet unless spoken to at corporate meetings, while the VP presented my team's ideas to the board.

In addition to learning the ropes professionally, I observed how gendered identities played out, and which identities appeared to be privileged or marginalized, especially around voice and silencing. I went to graduate school motivated to ask questions about gender and identity. In particular, I was interested in the intersections between embodiment and professional identity, and the role of communication in constituting some bodies as more aligned with some work.

During graduate school at the University of Utah, and more extensively since, my interests turned to the connections between diversity, branding, and identity, and how individuals and organizations draw on the discourses and practices of branding as a means of communicating a distinct and preferred identity. Branding appears to offer some hope. For example, in the last decade there has been an increase in corporate statements publicly celebrating diversity. And yet there are reasons to be concerned that branding promotes unification and homogenization in ways that stifle organizational diversity efforts, too.

These experiences, reinterpreted both in hindsight and in terms of contemporary trends, remind us not only of the centrality of identity and diversity in the modern world but also the benefits and risks associated with certain expressions of them. This is as true at work as it is in politics and social movements. Next, we offer a brief intellectual history of identity, punctuated by key concerns and moments, to situate the concept and its associations in today's world and to widen the scope of organizational considerations of identity.

A Brief Foray into Intellectual History of Identity

Identity, Organization, and History

The first efforts at making sense of large organizations and an increasingly complex and specialized society emerged in the second half of the nineteenth century. With increased specialization, also came division, particularly as occupational classes became both more numerus and diverse (Durkheim 2014). With development of a managerial class as well as an owning class came greater distance and certain types of alienation in organizational and social structure (Marx 1983). With standardization came a certain replaceability of individuals and a new emphasis on roles within a larger framework, necessitated by the massification of offices and factories and attendant standardization (Weber 1978).

Some of the first major works on identity (Freud 1922, James 1950, Mead 1962) appeared at the same time that industrialized societies were becoming more solidified and complex. The late-nineteenth and early-twentieth century was a time of great technological and social change, including more extensive industrialization, economic upheavals, company towns, corporate growth, and antitrust responses. It was also a time of great reflection on the place of the "person" in modern ("Western") society. Scientific management became well known for the devaluation of the individual—especially individual intuition, craft, and preferences—at the same time that it promoted great benefits in terms of productivity, growth, and wealth creation.

The most famous studies in the history of work, the Hawthorne studies, are still yielding successive and diverse interpretations. While they were and still are commonly referenced as heralding a more enlightened human relations movement, more recent and sometimes critical interpretations of the field experiments emphasize gender, power, reflexivity, and the strategic use of resources by comparatively powerless employees (Gillespie 1991). Interestingly, the human relations movement both ushered in group studies within organizations (such as how peer norms shape attitudes and behaviors, including organizational identification) and reminded us of the importance of persuasion inside as well as beyond the boundaries of the organization.

As Marchand (2001) demonstrates, corporations and governmental agencies drew upon lessons from political propaganda in World War I to explore and promote different kinds of public identities. For example, AT&T portrayed, then instantiated, itself in various campaigns as a part of American community and family. Other examples abound of how organizations developed sophisticated identity and image campaigns to enlist emotional bonds (Sennett 1980), to reach local, national, and even international audiences (Cheney et al. 2014).

Bureaucracy created impersonal roles, but also systematic procedures, to put cronyism in its place; in this way, it allowed for greater diversity in organizations via merit systems and recourse to established policies and procedures in the genuine service of fairness (Sayer 1991). The implications of role definition, substantiation, and standardization for identity have therefore been two-sided—yielding greater transparency and opportunity while ultimately reducing organizational dependence upon and concern for the individual.

For three decades now, the decline of the social contract between individuals and organizations has been documented, interpreted, and bemoaned (Wartzman 2017). While we do not have the space to venture deeply into economic conditions here (see Chapter 3 for a more comprehensive account of them), it is important to mention that more precarious relations between employees and many employing organizations along with the growth in the so-called "gig economy" mean that the dynamics of organizational identification and branding have changed significantly. Moreover, this is an arena where issues of class, race, gender, and other markers of difference play out in ways that span organizational boundaries, the "inside" and the "outside" of people's experiences at work.

Contemporary research and practices underscore the connections between identity, organizing, and communication. As a field, we have known this for a long time but are now beginning to appreciate the intersections and dynamics on multiple levels (Heath et al. in press, Larson and Gill 2017). As Ashforth (2012) explains, identity is a very elastic, yet inescapable concept. There are multiple theoretical perspectives on identity in part because there are multiple concepts of identity itself in circulation in contemporary society. In the development of organizational communication research over the past 50 years, there have been post-positivist or functional explanations of identity at work, interpretive accounts, and critical assessments. For a long time, the subfield of organizational communication, leaning heavily on psychology and management, treated identity in a fairly functionalist way. From a functionalist standpoint, an individual's identification can translate into the desire and intention to better serve her or his employer. Identification with a company or other organization then implicates decision-making: premises and images held in the mind of the employee and applied at moments of choice (Tompkins and Cheney 1985).

From an interpretive standpoint, continued storytelling—or in the later language of sociology, "accounting" for one's self (Scott and Lyman 1968)—folds into what may be considered identity. Identity in this way is something that can "look at itself," "talk about itself," and "revise itself." Think of the roles this kind of feedback loop plays for individuals and groups, especially at junctures that involve ethical challenges. For example, many people will punctuate their work or career narratives with episodes, like where they were inspired by role models, their responses to challenges where they "had to do the right thing," and milestones where they "made a positive difference."

Critically speaking, how identities are shaped, constrained, and undermined involves power, often in subtle forms. For example, consider the ways the term "elite" is currently used for strategic political purposes in the news and campaigns (e.g. in the U.S. and in the European Union): it is a way of "othering" whatever group to which it is applied, even as it relies on images and experiences of hierarchical distance that may well resonate with certain voters, communities, or occupational groups. Today we have a more complete and dynamic picture of organizational identity, and at the same time are looking beyond the confines of the organization itself, both in the sense of organizing and in terms of multiple levels and spheres of identity, such as how branding plays a role in organizational identity.

Forging Links between Identity and Branding

Scholars articulate the links between identity and branding at multiple levels such as individual, occupational, and organizational (Hatch and Schultz 2003, Lair et al. 2005, McDonald and Kuhn 2016). A commonly held assumption is that organizations, occupations, and individuals use brands and engage in branding to help construct their identities and communicate to others "who they are." And yet, agreed-upon definitions of what these terms mean are elusive. Unlike the allied fields of marketing or advertising, the occupational field of "branding" lacks a coherent public message about itself (Loacker and Sullivan 2016), but instead puts forth multiple metaphors that seek to maintain the value of brands and branding processes (Müller 2017). Depending on the lens used, brands and branding can be seen as a functional business process (Kotler 2011), artifacts that assist consumers in the production of identity (Lundqvist et al. 2013), or the necessary object of critical cultural critique (Arvidsson 2005). For us, "brands" refer to a concentrated set of ideas and feelings about a product, person, nation, or other entity, while "branding" refers to "shaping what the product or organization says and does, in order to change how people think, feel, and act, in a way that creates commercial (and sometimes social) value" (Jones 2017: 23). In other words, we view branding as a set of inherently communicative activities in service of a brand.

Managerially oriented, consumer-centered, and critical-social views of brands and branding each have value, depending on the questions and tasks that scholars or practitioners address. That said, we see particular scholarly value in the latter, more critical, view articulated here that seeks to understand how brands and branding are hidden in plain sight (Mumby 2016), and function as a mechanism for the creation, maintenance, and revision of identities, implicating both employees (Brannan et al. 2015) and consumers (Arvidsson 2005). For instance, consumers might use brands to conspicuously communicate something about themselves, such as wearing Patagonia clothes to link themselves to the pro-social and pro-environment images of that company. Employees also have to navigate brands. Organizational brands assist in the construction of preferred worker's identities, as well as group affiliations or shared identities. For instance, we can "be branded" by our workplace, insomuch as we are encouraged or seduced into "living the brand" (Jeanes 2013, Vásquez et al. 2013) to express our "fit" (Kärreman and Rylander 2008), among other things.

At individual and organizational levels, one's identity can readily be marked by the branded company they keep. As such, branding encourages questions about the relationships between individual and organizational identity. This begins to bring us more in contact with the academic literature on branding and, in the popular domain, to explore the concepts of identity work, identity regulation, and what is loosely called "identity politics." In other words, while the boundaries of organizations are certainly still important in terms of membership, authority, roles, and paychecks, there is a *diffusion* of identity knowledge, attachment, and formation that transcends these boundaries.

Research on Organizational Identity, Diversity, and Branding

Here we consider themes that transcend particular programs of research and cases, such as: (1) identity and essence; (2) multiplicity and fluidity; (3) branding, diversity, and embodiment; and (4) identity crises. These themes, which are persistent, help us in considering avenues for future research and practice. They are intended both to cluster past thought and work and help point toward future investigations and applications.

Identity and the Idea of a Core, or an Essence

As we know it, individual identity, emphasizing distinctiveness over sameness, is a modern invention that can be traced to the European Renaissance, but fully blossomed in early the 1800s in public discourse (Foucault 1984, Mackenzie 1978). As both an organizing principle and a kind of social institution, modern individual identity becomes a necessary but elusive quest, not only for the individual but also for organizations, peoples, and nations. The pursuit is elusive in that the common desire is for something essential, definitive, and solid. We see tensions on every level, from the identity politics of various groups (who strive for acceptance, while also asserting specific interests and traditions) to international relations (including shame, humiliation, pride, nationalism) (Lasswell 1935). At the same time, ironically, we find a great deal of mimesis, or imitation, in organizations and institutions, just as we do in messaging within the domains of advertising, marketing, and public relations (Ganesh 2003, Lammers and Barbour 2006).

It is hard to imagine the worlds of work, advertising, and politics without regular appeals to individualism and even to "uniqueness." Consider advertising for automobiles, homes, and jeans over the decades. Today, we see individual, distinct identity emphasized in such culturally popular phrases as "entrepreneurship," "the gig economy," "self-reliance," "branding," "expression of your true self," "be yourself by being part of this special cultural crowd," and "you're on your own but . . . you're part of something bigger." The trends around uniqueness are so commonplace that they have become fodder for marketing jokes. For example, McDonald's appears to have shifted how it markets one of its products, McCafé. In 2008, the McCafé holiday campaign slogan was "Coffee as unique as you are" (Catedral-Bughao 2008). However, by 2017, the message became that McCafé was simple, and for everyone, as McCafé was playfully set up as the antithesis of "urban hipster coffee culture" (B&T 2018). In both examples, McCafé is positioned as *for* a particular type of person to identify with and, conversely, to communicate who and what these consumers should dis-identify with. In these intersections between creatives and consumers, messages are clearly designed to bolster identity as a single essence. Yet, in witnessing organizational messages shift, this case also shows that identities—in this case a corporate one—are multiple and fluid.

Multiplicity and Fluidity of Identities

Identities are multiple in at least three different senses: a person (or a group) may reference and draw upon identities that are different, disparate, or even scattered. Goffman (1959) explained back in the 1950s how a dramaturgical model of identity helps "decenter" the notion of a single, consistent, immutable self. Multiple roles may be tied to different spaces, different relationships, different formal demands of work, and as discussed at the beginning of the essay, different online communities. A person or group may have a similar role but in multiple groups (the same may be true, by analogy, for an organization). There may also be multiple identities in intersecting groups (see Burke and Stets 2009). Ultimately, as Burke (1969) explained, the rhetoric of identification is about both merger and division, as well as the ways that this is accomplished in the language of "we-ness" and "othering" by symbolic associations (e.g. and in material attachments, such as with technology).

One contribution of a more communication-centered view is the stress on fluidity and the related emphasis on narrative. The roots of this conception of identity can be traced to Nietzsche's philosophy, and the narrative construction of identity. Today, fluidity itself is often featured in expressions of individual and collective identities. Queer theory and its applications to organizational life are especially attuned to confronting what has been marginalized as strange and probing not only the fluidity of commonly presumed categories but also realizing the benefits of more inclusive approaches to identity (McDonald 2015).

Class identification, mobility, and status also relate to psychological and emotional confidence about being able to perform certain jobs, or to rub shoulders with others in certain professions. A large part of class identity involves the extent to which people feel special, assume they can "make it," or doubt they can "pass" (Mahdawi 2018).

Because of the strong tendency to want to "fix" one's own and others' identities, it is often difficult to appreciate the variety, duration, and entailments of experiences that influence what we casually refer to as our "real selves," or "who we are." In general, it's difficult for "modern" peoples to "unfix" identity because of our desire (and this was true also for pre-modern societies, though in a different way) to think of identity as either a foundation on which we stand, or a core part of us. At times this idea of identity as fixed appears to solidify privilege. For instance, leadership writers often promote authenticity (Gardner et al. 2005). In other cases, claiming authenticity, or a fixed self, emerges in response to marginalization. For example, many transgender workers experience embodied fluidity and change, while communicating a desire to live as one's "true self" (Muhr et al. 2016). This is where a communication-based perspective can be helpful to call attention to how the stories we tell (e.g. in employment interviews), or that others tell, or presume about us (Eger 2018, Wille and Derous 2017), over time become folded into our narratives.

Identity, Emotion, and (Conscious/Unconscious) Bonds

Focus on the deeply emotional aspects of identity and identity formation can be traced to Freud (1922); however, today we understand much better that identification is not just a "defense mechanism," nor should it be seen as purely "rational" or calculating. In different contexts, ranging from sports team loyalty to religious and ethnic allegiance, group bonds can powerfully affect even people who may be removed in time and space (such as identification with forebears, and future members: as in "we are all Americans" and similar national refrains).

Sennett's (1980) analysis of emotional bonds with authority brought into sharp relief the communicative aspects of these relationships and their implications for identity—in domains from therapy to the economy, to political regimes. Also consider cases under the heading of populism, where certain leaders have a knack for creating a sense among their followers that this mass messaging is exclusively "for them." The emotional dimension of these relationships transcends what has been studied as para-relationships with characters on television and other media and can actually obscure the details of shared (or, not shared) interests and policies. Consider, for example, how biographies of celebrity CEOs such as Steve Jobs, Bill Gates, Oprah Winfrey, and others attract major attention and commentary on figuring out "who they are" and why their stories compel others.

Identity, Branding, and Embodied Organizational Diversity

Organizational communication research on identity/identification and diversity/multiculturalism has grown up relatively independently but is coming together in important ways today because of ongoing cultural changes. For instance, consider diversity management and its links to branding. Critical studies of branding typically locate it as a historically homogenizing force—that is, a central driving force in branding is to create a single, unified identity and message. Yet, some view it as a double-edged sword, so that it might also increase diversity in occupations and professions (Ashcraft et al. 2012, McDonald and Kuhn 2016, Rennstam and Sullivan 2017).

In an era where brands are given more credibility in the C-suites, they also influence how an organization manages diversity and multiculturalism. For instance, many contemporary organizations seek to brand themselves as inclusive and diverse, an early exemplar being Benetton's (1980s onward) "United Colors of Benetton" campaign. While there are certainly cases in which diversity statements are mere window dressings, or package unfulfilled aspirations, there are also cases in which organizations rely on their "inclusive" brand values to justify taking a stand on diversity, particularly in global business situations. For example, in 2012, IKEA airbrushed all the women out of the Saudi Arabian version of its catalogue. Some stakeholders thought the decision was preferable, but after a swift uproar from upset consumers in and out of the company's headquarters in Sweden, IKEA apologized and claimed that the exclusion was in conflict with its values (Nylander 2012).

Bodies and other forms of materiality are also implicated in branding and diversity management and are central to professional and occupational identities (Ashcraft 2013). This includes individuals' deliberate and strategic attempts to craft identities, such as the continued interest in personal branding as both a celebrated practice and response to employment conditions (Lair et al. 2005), and the rise of bloggers who create an entrepreneurial identity online (Duffy and Hund 2015). Occupations and industries are also implicated, as many today seek to "brand" employees by trying to control their embodied and aesthetic practices in-and-outside of work—such as when an organization's promotion of fitness culture turns evangelical, akin to an employment imperative rather than a healthy suggestion (James and Zoller 2018).

Bodies and materiality, including work contexts, are also influential when we recognize how professional and occupational identities are shaped not only through the efforts of individuals or organizations but also by popular culture—with images of airline pilots, consultants, police, and care workers, to name a few (Ashcraft et al. 2012). When popular images of occupations and workers are relatively homogeneous, some occupations and work might be perceived as a perfect fit for some bodies—much more so than others, as explained by the "glass slipper" metaphor (Ashcraft 2013), which receives greater attention in Chapter 8. These explicit and implicit associations affect issues of diversity beyond popular culture, such as the organizational and occupational demographics around gender, race, class, and ability levels. Narratives and discourses may validate and celebrate certain bodies doing particular kinds of work, but they can also mark some work and bodies as less meaningful and valuable (Lucas 2011), or even as dirty or undesirable (Tracy and Scott 2005).

Materiality and identity also involve architecture, artifacts, place, and physical and online environments (e.g. Gagliardi 1990). Scholars have recently posed questions, both theoretical and practical, about the intersections between symbolic and material realms (Kuhn et al. 2017). For instance, both Albu and Etter's (2016) study of Twitter and Askay and Gossett's (2015) study of Yelp articulate how social media technologies enable organizational insiders and outsiders to "author" texts and/or create symbolic capital, which affect the organization's identity and members' identification. In some ways, organizational communication scholars are only just beginning to appreciate fully how material conditions and symbolic expressions shape, and are expressed through, one another—especially when it comes to identity.

Identity Crises for Individuals and Collectivities

The idea of an identity crisis has been popular since Fromm (1955) described it and is associated with both individual phases and passages. From a communicative standpoint, an identity crisis involves challenging messages from others and from the self, acting as something of an observer. To the extent that identities are often supported by the desire for certainty and frequently involve pride, they are often quite vulnerable. This is true for people in their roles as workers, citizens, and members of ethnic and religious groups, and other in-group/out-group identities, where the temptation to support one's own identity through denigrating another's is frequently lurking (Keen 1991).

During an identity crisis, identity is usually in flux or at least being questioned—for an individual, group, organization, industry, community, or even broader society. As Sen (2007) and others have observed, unitary or univocal identities are more prone to crises than multidimensional ones, because investment in them is so great and vulnerabilities follow. This is part of the problem for communities that become dependent on and are defined by single industries, just as it is for certain political, ethnic/racial, or religious groups that come to see themselves as inherently superior to others.

An identity crisis may be experienced by a business, a profession, an ethnic group, or an entire nation. The Danish cartoon crisis of 2005 (Rasmussen and Merkelsen 2014) demonstrates how an entire country's identity may become entangled with issues in international communication about Islam and sacredness of religious images. These processes and associations can become a life-and-death matter, such as when religious, ethnic, or political identities are threatened in the media and through face-to-face interactions.

Interestingly, the subfield of crisis communication, covered in-depth in Chapter 14, has not so much dealt with crises of identity for organizations or communities, yet these moments can be profoundly challenging. Layoffs and factory closures are obvious examples, with significant symbolic and material impacts. However, there are many other identity-centered and value-based crises in organizations, including about work, organizational, and occupational cultures. The #MeToo movement stands out as a powerful example of how a social movement that set out to tackle sexual abuses in Hollywood (and beyond) has spread to occupations and organizations around the world. The movement gained such traction and public attention that *Time* magazine named the "silence breakers"—the women who spoke out against sexual harassment and violence across different occupations and organizations—as Person of the Year (Zacharek et al. 2017), signifying how individuals in crisis can come together to question occupational and social norms.

Practical Implications

As we consider the history and narratives of identity in organizational communication research, we find that perhaps the greatest theoretical and practical need is to continue to "make strange" our assumptions about identity at work, and to look beyond customary situations for employees, managers, clients, customers, and others (for example, see Chapters 7 and 8). Identity, difference, and branding are certainly in play at every level of society today. Considering the three together better positions us to critically reflect on identity politics on global, organizational, and individual levels. For example, this set of issues may encourage us to explore political policies by nation-states, which may reinforce their racial and other identities. For instance, seemingly innocuous identities and brands such as "Pure New Zealand," or other celebrations of national distinctiveness, can give way to more nationalistic expressions—as is occurring in parts of Europe, the Middle East, South Asia, and the United States. This is partly a matter of "punctuation" of humanity, in terms of where lines are drawn; groups are defined, and legitimacy and belongingness are accorded (Benhabib and Resnik 2009). However, the 2018 rhetorical battle in the U.S. over the terms "chain migration" versus "family reunification," characterizing efforts either to restrict or allow relatives of legal immigrants to enter the country, brings identity politics into focus (Wells et al. 2015). In this set of global issues, faces and bodies become very much a part of rhetorical and political struggles, particularly as some groups attempt to assert values of homogeneity or even claims to purity. Such tensions and reactions then muddle what could be more complex debates about national immigration policies, corporate workforces, and actual roles in various economies. This is why research such as Cruz's (2014, 2017) investigations in West African markets are so valuable; these studies remind us not only that organizing patterns can be quite different from dominant modes understood even in our "alternative" literatures but also that ways of being and ways of organizing are intimately wrapped up in ethnicity, gender, and tradition, while being influenced by ideational flows that take many paths in a global society.

Identity, difference, and branding are also at play in organizations of all types. Branding practitioners and other cultural creatives play a role in creating and modifying identities, and both brands and branders have been accused of being "tone deaf" around divisive social issues. Recent examples include the Pepsi/Kendall Jenner advertisement accused of ignoring contemporary conversations around race and policing (Izadi 2017), and the Dove Campaign for Real Beauty that critics say marginalizes women of color (Astor 2017). Being tone deaf, in these cases, means that branding professionals and their clients fail to acknowledge or address a broad spectrum of conversations and concerns around human rights and inclusivity, as well as the symbolic and embodied consequences of the associations they seek to make in consumers' minds. Yet, we can envision a situation where scholars and branding practitioners work together to create inclusive campaigns, by first exploring how brands intersect with identity construction, and to the possibilities and consequences these associations permit.

Finally, the work of "making strange" our assumptions begins with all of us. At the beginning of this chapter, we reflected on how we first became interested in the study of identity, difference, and branding. By way of conclusion, we encourage scholars at every stage of their career to give themselves time to do the same. Critical reflection assists us by helping us understand the early influences that shaped our passions, and identity politics, as well as how our identities affect and are affected by our interactions with the socio-material world. Scholars can approach their reflections on identity from multiple levels, including individual, occupational, or organizational. Valentini's (2015) piece is an excellent example of how to critically reflect on occupational discourses (in this case, the author questioned the dominant idea that social media was "good" for public relations, interrogating who does public relations work and how).

On a more personal note, we see tremendous value in hearing reflections and stories from underrepresented voices in the academy. Through his vulnerability and openness around identity issues, Ferguson's (2018) recent exploration of what it means to be a Black male scholar has the potential to encourage and motivate others who, because of their race, sex, class, immigration status, or ability levels, find themselves "closeted" (McDonald 2015). Ferguson calls upon us all to continuously negotiate and renegotiate the marginalization of identities to pivot dominant narratives toward inclusion.

Discussion Questions

1. How do employees sometimes function as *ambassadors* for their organizations of employment (or not)? And how do they contribute to and respond to marketing messages by the company or agency? In other words, how are either formal organizational identities or individual identifications affirmed, challenged, subverted, and transformed?
2. How do organizational and product *brands*—and indeed, larger identities—speak to broader conversations about gender, sexuality, race, class, age, and ability? What identities, images, and texts (i.e. brands) might change attitudes toward greater inclusion and how will this suit future generations of workers or work?
3. Think of the profound ways in which *technology* is affecting identity. Identities of individuals and organizations become part of a constantly changing, sometimes expansive, and sometimes dark web of misrepresentation as well as legitimate expression. Within such a communication environment, what does a stable identity or reputation mean and how it is it maintained?
4. Of the many economic, political, and social issues that transcend national boundaries today, which do you see as affecting the ways we organize and the ways we think about ourselves as members of organizations? For example, you might consider globalization, immigration, or climate change and what they mean for organizing work?
5. What does it mean to be a citizen? A consumer? A teacher? A researcher? What images of professional academics struck you as you first saw others engaged in this line of work? What about your current image of yourself as part of a profession, say, looking ahead 5 to 10 years?

References

Albu, O. B. and Etter, M. 2016. "Hypertextuality and Social Media: A Study of the Constitutive and Paradoxical Implications of Organizational Twitter Use," *Management Communication Quarterly*, 30, 5–31.

Arvidsson, A. 2005. "Brands: A Critical Perspective," *Journal of Consumer Culture*, 5, 235–258.

Ashcraft, K. 2013. "The Glass Slipper: 'Incorporating' Occupational Identity in Management Studies," *Academy of Management Review*, 38, 6–31.

Ashcraft, K. L. Muhr, S. L. Rennstam, J. and Sullivan, K. 2012. "Professionalization as a Branding Activity: Occupational Identity and the Dialectic of Inclusivity-Exclusivity," *Gender, Work & Organization*, 19, 467–488.

Ashforth, B. 2012. *Role Transitions in Organizational Life: An Identity-Based Perspective*, New York: Routledge.

Askay, D. A. and Gossett, L. 2015. "Concealing Communities Within the Crowd: Hiding Organizational Identities and Brokering Member Identifications of the Yelp Elite Squad," *Management Communication Quarterly*, 29, 616–641.

Astor, M. 2017. [online] "Dove Drops an Ad Accused of Racism," Retrieved from www.nytimes.com/2017/10/08/business/dove-ad-racist.html [Accessed 20 Feb. 2018].

B&T Magazine. 2018. [online] "McDonald's Spoofs Hipster Coffee Culture in McCafé Campaign," Retrieved from www.bandt.com.au/advertising/mcdonalds-spoofs-hipster-coffee-culture-mccafe-campaign [Accessed 4 Nov. 2018].

Baker, D. 2016. [online] "How Disconnecting the Internet Could Help Our Identity" Retrieved from www.bbc.com/news/magazine-35895719 [Accessed 22 March 2018].

Benhabib, S. and Resnik, J. (eds). 2009. *Migrations and Mobilities*, New York: New York University Press.

Burke, K. 1969. *A Rhetoric of Motives*, Berkeley, CA: University of California Press.

Burke, P. J. and Stets, J. E. 2009. *Identity Theory*, Oxford, UK: Oxford University Press.

Catedral-Bughao, A. 2008. [online]. "McDonalds Rebrands with McCafé, Straddling Holiday Marketing with Make Your Own Snowflakes," Retrieved from http://yhadz-onlinemarketing.blogspot.com/2008/11/mcdonalds-rebrands-with-mccafe.html?q=mccafe. [Accessed 20 Feb. 2018].

Cheney, G., Christensen, L. T. and Dailey, S. 2014. "Identity, Identification and Organizational Communication," in Putnam, L. L. and Mumby, D. K. (eds.), *The SAGE Handbook of Organizational Communication*, Thousand Oaks, CA: SAGE, pp. 695–716.

Cruz, J. 2014. "Memories of Trauma and Organizing: Market Women's Susu Groups in Postconflict Liberia," *Organization*, 21, 447–462.

Cruz, J. M. 2017. "Invisibility and Visibility in Alternative Organizing: A Communicative and Cultural Model," *Management Communication Quarterly*, 31, 614–639.

Duffy, B. E. and Hund, E. 2015. ""Having It All" On Social Media: Entrepreneurial Femininity and Self-Branding Among Fashion Bloggers," *Social Media + Society*, 1, 1–11

Durkheim, E. 2014. *The Division of Labor in Society*, New York: Free Press.

Dwyer, M., Sahay, S., Scott, C. R., Dadlani, P. and McKinley, E. 2018. "Technologies of Concealment: Appropriateness, Effectiveness, and Motivations for Hiding Organizational Identity," *Western Journal of Communication*, 82, 194–216.

Eger, E. K. 2018. "Transgender Jobseekers Navigating Closeting Communication," *Management Communication Quarterly*, 32, 276–281.

Ferguson Jr., M. W. 2018. "(Re) Negotiating Organizational Socialization: Black Male Scholarship and the Closet," *Management Communication Quarterly*, 32, 282–286.

Fieseler, C., Meckel, M. and Ranzini, G. 2015. "Professional Personae: How Organizational Identification Shapes Online Identity in the Workplace," *Journal of Computer-Mediated Communication*, 20, 153–170.

Foucault, M. (1984). *The Foucault Reader*, Rabinow, P. (ed.), London: Penguin.

Freud, S. 1922. *Group Psychology and the Analysis of the Ego*, New York: Norton.

Fromm, E. 1955. *The Sane Society*, New York: Ballantine Books.

Gagliardi, P. 1990. *Symbols and Artifacts: Views of the Corporate Landscape*, Berlin: Walter de Gruyter.

Ganesh, S. 2003. "Organizational Narcissism: Technology, Legitimacy and Identity in an Indian NGO," *Management Communication Quarterly*, 16, 558–594.

Gardner, W. L., Avolio, B. J., Luthans, F., May, D. R. and Walumbwa, F. 2005. " 'Can You See the Real Me?' A Self-Based Model of Authentic Leader and Follower Development," *The Leadership Quarterly*, 16, 343–372.

Gillespie, R. 1991. *Manufacturing Knowledge: A History of the Hawthorne Experiments*, Cambridge, UK: Cambridge University Press.

Goffman, E. 1959. *The Presentation of Self in Everyday Life*, New York: Doubleday.

Heath, R. L., Cheney, G. and Ihlen, Ø. (in press). "Identification," in Ihlen, Ø. and Heath, R. (eds.) *Handbook of Organizational Rhetoric*. New York: Wiley.

Hatch, M. and Schultz, M. 2003. "Bringing the Corporation into Corporate Branding," *European Journal of Marketing*, 37, 1041–1064.

Izadi, E. 2017. [online] "A Second-By-Second Breakdown of Kendall Jenner's Unspeakably Tone-Deaf Pepsi Ad," Retrieved from www.washingtonpost.com/news/arts-and-entertainment/wp/2017/04/04/a-second-by-second-breakdown-of-kendall-jenners-unspeakably-tone-deaf-pepsi-ad/?utm_term=.b61cfd94746c [Accessed 20 Feb. 2018].

James, W. 1950. *Principles of Psychology, Vol. 1*. New York: Henry Holt.

James, E. P. and Zoller, H. M. 2018. "Resistance Training: (Re)shaping Extreme Forms of Workplace Health Promotion," *Management Communication Quarterly*, 32, 60–89.

Jeanes, E. L. 2013. "The Construction and Controlling Effect of a Moral Brand," *Scandinavian Journal of Management*, 29, 163–172.

Jones, R. 2017. *Branding: A Very Short Introduction*, Oxford, UK: Oxford University Press.

Kärreman, D. and Rylander, A. 2008. "Managing Meaning Through Branding—The Case of a Consulting Firm," *Organization Studies*, 29, 103–125.

Keen, S. 1991. *Faces of the Enemy: Reflections on the Hostile Imagination*, New York: Barnes and Noble.

Kuhn, T. R., Ashcraft, K. L. and Cooren, F. 2017. *The Work of Communication: Relational Perspectives on Working and Organizing in Contemporary Capitalism*, New York: Routledge.

Lair, D. J., Sullivan, K. and Cheney, G., 2005. "Marketization and the Recasting of the Professional Self: The Rhetoric and Ethics of Personal Branding," *Management Communication Quarterly*, 18, 307–343.

Lammers, J. C. and Barbour, J. B. 2006. "An Institutional Theory of Organizational Communication," *Communication Theory*, 16, 356–377.

Larson, G. S. and Gill, R. 2017. *Organizations and Identity*. Hoboken, NJ: John Wiley & Sons.

Loacker, B. and Sullivan, K. R. 2016. "The Liminality of Branding: Interweaving Discourses 'Making Up' a Cultural Intermediary Occupation," *Marketing Theory*, 16, 361–382.

Lasswell, H. 1965. *World Politics and Personal Insecurity*, New York: Free Press.

Lucas, K. 2011. "Blue-Collar Discourses of Workplace Dignity: Using Outgroup Comparisons to Construct Positive Identities," *Management Communication Quarterly*, 25, 353–374.

Lundqvist, A., Liljander, V., Gummerus, J. and Van Riel, A. 2013. "The Impact of Storytelling on The Consumer Brand Experience: The Case of a Firm-Originated Story," *Journal of Brand Management*, 20, 283–297.

Mackenzie, W. J. M. 1978. *Political Identity*, New York: St. Martin's.

Mahdawi, A. 2018. [online] "'Class-passing.'" Retrieved from www.theguardian.com/us-news/2018/feb/01/poor-americans-poverty-rich-class [Accessed 22 March 2018].

Marchand, R. 2001. *Creating the Corporate Soul*. Berkeley, CA: University of California Press.

Marx, K. 1983. "Preface to a Contribution to the Critique of Political Economy," in Kamenka, K. (ed.), *The Portable Karl Marx*, London: Penguin, pp. 158–161.

McDonald, J. 2015. "Organizational Communication Meets Queer Theory: Theorizing Relations of 'Difference' Differently," *Communication Theory*, 25, 310–329.

McDonald, J. and Kuhn, T. R. 2016. "Occupational Branding for Diversity: Managing Discursive Contradictions," *Journal of Applied Communication Research*, 44, 101–117.

Mead, G. H. 1962. *Mind, Self and Society*, Chicago: University of Chicago Press.

Muhr, S. L., Sullivan, K. R. and Rich, C. 2016. "Situated Transgressiveness: Exploring One Transwoman's Lived Experiences Across Three Situated Contexts," *Gender, Work & Organization*, 23, 52–70.

Müller, M. 2017. "'Brandspeak': Metaphors and the Rhetorical Construction of Internal Branding," *Organization*, 25, 42–68.

Mumby, D. K. 2016. "Organizing Beyond Organization: Branding, Discourse, and Communicative Capitalism," *Organization*, 23, 884–907.

Nylander, J. 2012. [online] "Women Erased from Saudi IKEA Catalog," Retrieved from www.swedishwire.com/business/14909-women-erased-from-saudi-ikea-catalog [Accessed 20 Feb. 2018].

Rasmussen, R. K. and Merkelsen, H. 2014. "The Risks of Nation Branding as Crisis Response: A Case Study of How the Danish Government Turned the Cartoon Crisis into a Struggle With Globalization," *Place Branding and Public Diplomacy*, 10, 230–248.

Rennstam, J. and Sullivan, K. R. 2017. "Peripheral Inclusion through Informal Silencing and Voice—A Study of LGB Officers in the Swedish Police," *Gender, Work & Organization*, 25, 177–194.

Sayer, D. 1991. *Capitalism and Modernity: An Excursus on Marx and Weber*, New York: Routledge.

Scott, C. 1997. "Identification with Multiple Targets in a Geographically Dispersed Organization," *Management Communication Quarterly*, 10, 491–522.

Scott, C. 2013. *Anonymous Agencies, Backstreet Businesses, and Covert Collectives: Rethinking Organizations in the 21st Century*, Stanford, CA: Stanford University Press.

Scott, M. B. and Lyman, S. F. 1968. "Accounts," *American Sociological Review*, 33, 46–62.

Sen, A. 2007. *Identity and Violence: The Illusion of Destiny*, New York: Norton.

Sennett, R. 1980. *Authority*, New York: Random House.

Tompkins, P. K. and Cheney, G. 1985. "Communication and Unobtrusive Control in Contemporary Organizations," in McPhee, R. D. and Tompkins, P, K. (eds.), *Organizational Communication: Traditional Themes and New Directions*. Thousand Oaks, CA: SAGE, pp. 179–210.

Tracy, S. J. and Scott, C. 2006. "Sexuality, Masculinity, and Taint Management among Firefighters and Correctional Officers: Getting Down and Dirty with 'America's Heroes' and the 'Scum of Law Enforcement', *Management Communication Quarterly*, 20, 6–38.

Valentini, C. 2015. "Is Using Social Media 'Good' for the Public Relations Profession? A Critical Reflection," *Public Relations Review*, 41, 170–177.

Vásquez, C., Sergi, V. and Cordelier, B. 2013. "From Being Branded to Doing Branding: Studying Representation Practices from a Communication-Centered Approach," *Scandinavian Journal of Management*, 29, 135–146.

Wartzman, R. 2017. *The End of Loyalty: The Rise and Fall of Good Jobs in America*, New York: Public Affairs.

Weber, M. 1978. *Economy and Society: An Outline of Interpretive Sociology (Vol. 1)*, Berkeley, CA: University of California Press.

Wells, C. C., Gill, R. and McDonald, J. 2015. " 'Us Foreigners': Intersectionality in A Scientific Organization," *Equality, Diversity and Inclusion: An International Journal*, 34, 539–553.

Wille, L. and Derous, E. 2017. "Getting the Words Right: When Wording of Job Ads Affects Ethnic Minorities' Application Decisions," *Management Communication Quarterly*, 31, 533–558.

Zacharek, S., Dockterman, E. and Edwards, H. 2017. [online] "TIME Person of the Year 2017: The Silence Breakers: The Voices That Launched a Movement," Retrieved from http://time.com/time-person-of-the-year-2017-silence-breakers/ [Accessed 21 Feb. 2018].

6 Socialization and Organizational Culture

Michael W. Kramer and Stephanie L. Dailey

As individuals who have moved, joined, and left a wide variety of organizations, as students in schools and universities, as employees in part-time and full-time jobs, and as volunteers in nonprofit community and religious organizations, it was easy for us to take a strong interest in studying how communication is critical in the success or failure of the process of socialization into an organization's culture. Having an advisor who was an expert (*The* expert?) on the subject (Fred Jablin) or a supportive advisor and committee (Keri Stephens and Karen Myers), made it easy for us each to pursue this line of research. Early success publishing in the area encouraged us to continue.

Socialization or *assimilation* refers to the process of joining, participating in, and leaving organizations (Jablin 2001, Kramer 2010). For newcomers, the socialization process involves "learning the ropes" or understanding "the way things are done around here." *Organizational culture* is typically defined as the artifacts, values, and assumptions that emerge through the communicative interactions of organizational members (Keyton 2005). If organizations were people, culture represents each organization's personality. So implicitly, the socialization process involves learning an organization's culture and then contributing to maintaining and changing it.

We both became interested in studying socialization and culture because of personal experiences joining and leaving organizations. Michael was in his third post-BA full-time teaching position within one church-based education system by the time he picked a dissertation topic; studying job transfers was of personal interest. When he became involved in community arts programs, he transitioned into studying socialization in nonprofit organizations. After working in a multinational corporation with a successful, structured internship program, Stephanie wanted to explore how internships help socialize prospective and new employees. Moreover, Stephanie's experience at this company, which boasted a unique culture and was often listed on Fortune's list of "Best Companies to Work for," sparked her interest in studying organizational culture.

In what follows, we briefly provide background on these two research areas, which are generally treated separately, before presenting an integrated perspective of socialization and culture.

Communication and Socialization and/or Assimilation

Based on formative research in the 1960s (e.g. Schein 1968) and 1970s (Van Maanen and Schein 1979), models of socialization emerged in the management literature in the 1980s to describe the process of newcomers joining organizations (e.g. Feldman 1981). Eventually, Jablin (2001) proposed a communication model of assimilation to more fully delineate the process, which includes four phases: (1) *anticipatory socialization*, the period of time when individuals consider joining particular organizations; (2) *encounter*, the onboarding process of the first days and weeks when individuals are organizational newcomers; (3) *metamorphosis*, the time when individuals no longer feel like newcomers, but rather as participating employees or members; and (4) *exit*, the time when individuals no longer are organizational participants. Scholars recognize that these phases do not represent a rigid linear process (Kramer and Miller 2014) and that membership is sometimes ambiguous, especially for volunteers (Kramer 2011). Jablin described the overall *assimilation* process as involving two simultaneous and conflicting processes. *Socialization* describes the efforts of current organizational members to influence individuals (newcomers and incumbents) to meet organizational needs while *individualization* describes the efforts of individuals to influence the organization and its members to meet their needs. Through communication organizational members influence each other in the interaction of socialization and individualization.

The terms *socialization* and *assimilation* are sometimes used interchangeably and at other times are the subject of controversy. Thus, this research area becomes more complicated to coalesce because of inconsistent use of terminology. In group literature, the overall process is considered *socialization*, involving the simultaneous interaction of *assimilation*, the efforts of current group members to influence newcomers to meet group needs, and *accommodation*, the efforts of newcomers to influence the group to meet their needs (Levine et al 2001). Other scholars criticize the use of these terms by focusing on socialization at the societal level (e.g. Clair 1996), as an individual experience (e.g. Bullis 1993) rather than as an organizational process, or as a patriarchal endeavor (e.g. Allen 1996). Due to the inconsistent usage, scholars, including Michael, have participated in rather esoteric debates of definitions and terminology that are of little practical value (e.g. Kramer and Miller 1999). Instead of continuing those debates, we now focus on broadening this line of research by exploring new topics.

Organizational Culture

Research on organizational culture developed in the 1980s as an alternative to a functional/positivist perspectives on organizations concerned primarily with objective outcomes like efficiency and profits (Putnam 1982). Derived from anthropology, the study of organizational culture focuses on how organizational members communicate through artifacts (tangible, visible objects), rituals, narratives (stories), and discourse to understand and enact a set of shared assumptions, values, and beliefs (Pacanowsky and O'Donnell-Trujillo 1983). Most managerial research or practitioners' perspectives on organizational culture (e.g. Peters and Waterman 1982) assume a unified culture that is shared by all organizational members, but our experiences suggest otherwise. For example, departmental cultures within one organization have unique characteristics that are not shared. In corporations, research and development departments are different than sales and marketing departments. At universities, engineering departments are different than communication departments.

Joanne Martin (1992) addressed this concern by developing three potential perspectives for examining organizational culture. Martin's (1992) *integrated perspective* is similar to the general definition of organizational culture. It focuses on the umbrella or unifying aspects of an organization that span across nearly the entire organization. Her *differentiated perspective* recognizes that different organizational sections develop their own artifacts, stories, and values that differentiate them from other sections. These subcultures represent islands within the organization that are separate from other islands. Subcultures might represent different departments, or upper management rather than lower-level employees, or union versus non-union employees. Her *fragmented perspective* accepts that an organization's culture includes ambiguities and shifting meanings. When clarity is achieved, it is a temporary clearing in the jungle before ambiguity returns. Supporting this perspective, studies have shown that an organization's policies on work–life balance, including maternity and/or paternity leave are often unclear and disputed (Kirby and Krone 2002, Miller et al. 1996). The different perspectives provide insight into the studying of non-traditional organizations, as well, such as farmer's markets (Hoelscher et al. 2016).

It is important to recognize that no single perspective is right or wrong, but that combining all three perspectives provides a comprehensive understanding of the culture (Martin 1992). However, some scholars argue that the multiple perspectives are problematic. For example, Keyton (2014) suggests that the multiple perspective approach assumes that all three perspectives objectively exist, rather than allowing them to emerge from an examination of the culture without such an assumption.

Scholars also disagree on the substance of culture—whether organizational culture is something the organization *has* versus something the organization *is* (Smircich 1983). Much of the popular press literature and many organizational leaders and practitioners, like organizational consultants and communication specialists, view culture as a variable—something that can be changed, controlled, or strengthened by certain organizational actions. Books by Peters and Waterman (1982) and Deal and Kennedy (1982) set the stage for this view of culture, contending that certain components, like shared values, can be used as management tools for enhancing organizational productivity and effectiveness. Although some scholars view and measure culture this way, usually through quantitative methods (Rosenfeld et al. 2004), most academic research views culture as something that the organization is. Rather than producing methods for managers to enhance culture or generalizable knowledge, this view seeks to understand how organizational members interpret, interact with, and make sense of culture, usually through interpretive methods (Dougherty and Smythe 2004).

In sum, both practitioners and scholars explore organizational culture from multiple perspectives and viewpoints. Yet, as Keyton explains, "most discoveries about culture are a byproduct of the central object of study" (2014: 564). In other words, if you go searching for research directly studying organizational culture, you may come up shorthanded. Much of our knowledge comes from understanding culture "peripherally," through other constructs like identity, leadership, and socialization. Because socialization is a key area that tells us a great deal about culture, we discuss these two areas of research jointly.

Combining Socialization and Culture

Considering socialization and organizational culture simultaneously provides several practical applications for research. In the next sections, we discuss ways that combining the two concepts can direct future research.

Anticipatory Socialization and Organizational Culture

Anticipatory socialization, the period before individuals join organizations, is divided into two processes: (1) *Anticipatory role socialization*, the process of learning about occupations or roles that might be fulfilled in various organizations; and (2) *Anticipatory organizational socialization*, the process of learning about and selecting specific organizations in which to enact those roles (Jablin 2001, Kramer 2010). Both processes implicitly include understanding of organizational culture.

Anticipatory Role Socialization

Scholars generally identify five sources for anticipatory role socialization: family, education, peers, previous experience, and media (Jablin 2001,

Kramer 2010). Scholars find that communication with family members typically has the most influence on individuals' understanding of work and career aspirations; parents encourage or discourage pursuing similar careers by their positive or negative comments about their own careers (Levine and Hoffner 2006) and children learn about work and careers through indirect and ambient communication (Buzzanell et al. 2011). Through education, individuals learn how to interact in socially responsible ways to achieve group goals through cooperation (Wentzel and Looney 2007), and also are exposed to various subjects and majors that help them select careers (Malgwi et al. 2005). Peers tend to discourage or reinforce certain career choices in adolescents (Peterson and Peters 1983), but also later in life when individuals consider career changes (Tan and Kramer 2012). Although most young adults often do not develop specific job skills in their part-time jobs that transfer to their careers because they work in retail or food services, these experiences teach adolescents to interact with supervisors and authorities (Jablin 2001). Certain factors, such as the organization's culture, have been shown to transform part-time workers' orientations toward work and build self-efficacy (Herrygers and Wieland 2017). Furthermore, when their previous experience is related to career aspirations, such as an internship in a related field, the experience can lead to greater role clarity and professional competence in future employment (Dailey 2016). Media expose individuals to occupations beyond those of their family (Hoffner, Levine and Toohey 2008), but often overrepresent some occupations (e.g. police, legal, medical professions) and provide unrealistic caricatures of them (Signorielli 2009). These sources continue to influence individuals' choices throughout their lifetime as they consider career changes and volunteer opportunities.

Such generalizations fail to consider individuals' experiences and the ways that those experiences may enable or constrain individuals' role choices. For example, factory workers' communication to their children made it easier for them to assimilate into that line of work (Gibson and Papa 2000). At the same time, parents in blue collar jobs often simultaneously encourage their children to aspire to higher-status jobs while disparaging white collar work for being elitist and not honorable and for not involving physical labor (Lucas 2011). Educational experiences also provide fragmented, limited, and often inaccurate information about occupations (Jahn and Myers 2015, Leonardi et al. 2009). Similarly, parents (Goodnow 1988), education systems (Myers et al. 2011), and media (Signorielli 2009) may reinforce racial or gendered occupational stereotypes that limit individuals' choices, which contributes to the dominance of women in education and men in STEM fields (science, technology, engineering, and math).

Taken together, these findings suggest that anticipatory role socialization creates certain expectations about the culture of organizations. Because of occupational stereotypes, certain organizations or vocations may appear to be monolithic cultures with individuals primarily of the same race, gender, and social class; some seem to be plural cultures with diversity at the organization's lower levels but not at the top; and others to be truly multicultural with diversity distributed throughout the organization (Larkey 1996). Future research can focus more directly on the ways racial, ethnic, gender, and social class are communicated during anticipatory role socialization and explore ways to change those messages. Ashcraft's (2013) "glass slipper" metaphor, which suggests that some occupations "fit" certain social identities more than others, provides an excellent theoretical stance through which additional research may explore how roles and organizational cultures are socially constructed. In addition, research should explore how anticipatory role socialization affects individuals' attitudes and commitments toward volunteering.

Practically, organizational leaders or consultants should remember that individuals often enter occupations with preconceived understandings of specific roles, which may or may not be accurate. For example, before deciding to pursue a career as an academic, Stephanie was interested in marketing and advertising. She secured a prestigious internship for a restaurant management company, and proudly reported for her first day dressed in business casual attire, expecting to brainstorm catchy slogans or conduct a competitor analysis in her professional role. To her surprise, she was asked to dress up in a pizza costume and attend a new franchise's ribbon-cutting ceremony. Through this experience, Stephanie learned that marketing and advertising careers differed from occupational depictions she had seen in the film *What Women Want*, and solidified her interest in attending graduate school to study internships and anticipatory role socialization.

Anticipatory Organizational Socialization

Whereas individuals can independently choose organizational roles to pursue, joining organizations is a mutual selection process. Incumbent organizational members recruit and select potential new members while individuals conduct reconnaissance to select organizations that seem appropriate for them (Levine et al. 2001). For employment, this shared process typically involves job interviews; volunteer settings often have a mutual selection process as well. The characteristics of effective and ineffective job interviews have been studied extensively (for a summary, see Jablin 2001).

The appropriate balance between person–job fit and person–organization fit are important aspects of the selection process (Caldwell and O'Reilly 1990). Whereas person–job fit focuses on whether individuals have specific job skills, person–organization fit focuses on whether individuals fit the organization's culture. While ideal candidates have high job and organization fit, decision makers often must choose between candidates who are higher in one than the other. The question becomes, is it better to hire someone who already shares much of the organizational culture and teach them the job or to hire someone who knows the job, but may need to be socialized into the organizational culture? Internships are a useful tool for employers, as they allow the opportunity to cultivate talent into certain organizational functions (person–job fit) and the organization's culture (person–organization fit).

Certainly, researchers and practitioners should continue to consider communication and the role of person–job and person–organization fit in hiring. In addition, organizations expend considerable effort on webpages, recruitment materials, and the selection process. Although candidates expect these depictions to be overly positive, little is known about how recruits assess an organization's culture on the basis of these presentations. As more organizations and recruiters use social media to actively and passively recruit prospective members, applicants may obtain a more differentiated perspective of the organization's culture. Also, little is known concerning how potential recruits assess their own person–job and person–organization fit and make decisions to balance the two when they receive offers. Research should explore how volunteers and individuals making job or career changes make these assessments as part of ongoing anticipatory socialization. Finally, future research should address whether person–organization fit should be assessed on the basis of the organization's integrated or differentiated culture (Martin 1992). An underlying assumption of this research is that organizational culture is shared across entire organizations.

Encounter and Organizational Culture

Newcomer experiences are the most studied part of the socialization process. Summarized elsewhere (e.g. Jablin 2001, Kramer and Miller 2014), the major research areas include the following:

1. *The nature and effect of various socialization tactics on employee satisfaction and innovation.* For example, institutionalized strategies (collective, formal, sequential, and fixed) lead to more custodial roles where newcomers adapt to the organization's needs while individual strategies (individual, informal, random, and variable) lead to more innovation and individualization (Ashforth and Saks 1996).
2. *The role of met and unmet expectations on newcomers' satisfaction and turnover.* Realistic job previews help create more appropriate expectations, while unmet expectations increase newcomers' job dissatisfaction and turnover (Wanous et al. 1992).
3. *Message content concerning the organizational culture.* For example, memorable messages are usually informal messages, such as stories

told by experienced peers, that provide keen insights into the organizational culture (Brown 1985).

4. *Information exchange* including the type (e.g. task, relational, organizational, political), sources (e.g. supervisors, peers, clients), and information-seeking strategies (Kramer and Miller 2014).

While much of this research assumes that newcomers passively receive training and information, scholars also focus on how newcomers can be proactive in their socialization. Proactive information-seeking strategies include direct and indirect communication strategies, as well as unobtrusive strategies like observation (Miller and Jablin 1991). Studies also show that newcomers proactively use communication technologies, such as internal social networking sites, to learn about cultural norms, values, and beliefs (Thom-Santelli et al. 2011). Proactive information seeking is associated with positive outcomes in a study by Ashford and colleagues (e.g. Ashford and Black 1996), but passive receipt of unsolicited information from peers and supervisors is a strong predictor of newcomer adaptation (Kramer 1993, Morrison 1993).

Current research has not explored why some individuals receive more unsolicited information than others; more studies should consider the "dark side of socialization," which might occur when newcomers adopt negative behaviors, like alcohol misuse, from incumbent members (Liu et al. 2015). In addition, proactive information seeking is not the same as individualization, the process of negotiating changes in role expectations. Further research can explore the characteristics of newcomers and the contexts that encourage newcomers to individualize or change organizations to meet their needs in employment and volunteer settings, and the communication strategies they use to achieve their goals. For example, when a theater director invited collaboration, cast members who were selected for their assertiveness developed various strategies for individualizing their parts (Kramer 2009). In practice, managers or organizational development specialists should consider how their organizations' socialization strategies are influencing newcomer role-taking, and whether new members have adequate access to various information-seeking sources.

Several scholars developed measures to study the influence of communication with supervisors and peers on newcomers' successful adjustment (e.g. Chao et al. 1994, Gailliard et al. 2010). These measures and subsequent studies assume an integrated organizational culture, such that that newcomers will receive messages that constantly reinforce a consistent, unified organizational culture. However, research suggests that newcomers often experience a differentiated culture in which subcultures are prominent. For example, new bank tellers often experienced subculture differences when they assumed their roles at branches after completing the officially sanctioned training (DiSanza 1995). During the encounter phase, rather than anticipatory socialization, newcomers develop a more complex understanding of the organization's culture that recognizes both an integrated and a differentiated culture, and culture reproduces itself through the socialization of new members (Schein 1990).

Given the popularity of studying newcomers, additional research can explore communication interactions that lead newcomers to understand both the integrated culture and subcultures. In addition to focusing on newcomer behaviors, more research could examine incumbents' role during the encounter phase. Such research may help explain the unmet expectations newcomers experience when their experiences are inconsistent with the integrated culture promoted through recruitment.

Metamorphosis and Organizational Culture

Although many practitioners' onboarding plans focus on newcomers' first 90 days, it is inappropriate to evaluate the shift from newcomer to established member on the basis of time alone, since the change is primarily based on a psychological adjustment and newcomers and incumbents may differ in their perceptions of when this transition occurs (Kramer 2011). For example, the presence of more recent newcomers may speed up the psychological transition while being the lone newcomer in a stable group may lengthen the newcomer experience. During metamorphosis, newcomers learn the organization's culture through countless organizational experiences. Here, we focus on two: interpersonal relationships and organizational change.

Interpersonal Relationships

As established members, incumbents develop various interpersonal relations. Perhaps the most important relationship is the supervisor–subordinate relationship. According to a large body of research using leader–member exchange (LMX) theory, those relationships can vary from insider/partnership relationships to outsider/overseer relationships (e.g. Graen 2003). Subordinates in high-LMX relationships (insider) receive more information, are frequently consulted on decision-making, work collaboratively, and receive career advice from their supervisors; by contrast, subordinates in low-LMX relationships primarily are included only in necessary job-related interactions (Sias 2009). As members' relationships with their managers strengthen, so does the breadth and frequency of communication between them, whereas weak leader–member relationships involve negative communicative exchanges, such as withholding information, exclusion, harsh critiques, and dirty looks (Omilion-Hodges and Baker 2017). Not surprisingly, employees in high-LMX relationships generally are more satisfied and experience more career mobility than those in low-LMX relationships (Graen and Uhl-Bien 1995). For practitioners interested in cultivating strong supervisor–subordinate relationships through communication, a diagnostic tool can gauge and improve conversational practices (Jian et al. 2014).

Similarly, incumbents develop a range of peer relationships with other members on the same organizational-hierarchical level. These relationships range from special/close peers (close or best friends who discuss work and non-work issues in depth) to collegial peers (supportive work relationships) to information peers (distant peers who primarily communicate necessary job-related information) (Sias 2009). Peers provide different levels of instrumental, informational, and emotional support (Miller et al. 2007), as well as varying amounts of solidarity, self-disclosure, and trust (Myers and Johnson 2004).

Distinct from peer relationships, organizational members also develop friendships with organizational members. Besides being voluntary, friendships are distinct from peer relationships because workplace friendships are personalistic—meaning that friends acknowledge one another as more than employees in specified organizational roles (Sias 2009). Peer relationships develop into friendships because of personal characteristics, like similar personalities, and contextual factors, such as working close to each other; newer communication channels, like email, texting, and social networking, have become important tools for maintaining workplace friendships (Sias et al. 2012). Because workplace friendships combine personal identities and coworker identities, they often experience inherent tensions (Bridge and Baxter 1992).

Newcomers and incumbents also may develop mentor relationships. A *mentor* used to be defined only as a senior person in one's department or division. Now, scholars focus more on the mentoring process rather than on positions; thus, both supervisors and peers can become mentors who help protégés develop their careers (Sias 2009). Although informal mentor relations generally are more valuable than formal mentor programs, mentor relationships of any kind typically result in more career opportunities, a better understanding of organizational issues, and more job satisfaction (Sias 2009). Nevertheless, research has shown that underrepresented minority members, particularly women of color in engineering, experience mentoring differently and in ways that do not meet certain mentees' needs and struggles (Buzzanell et al. 2015).

Individuals' supervisor, peer, and mentor relationships influence their experience of organizational culture. Those in close relationships with other organizational members have access to more information to understand organizational issues beyond their jobs (Jablin 2001). As they gain additional insight into the organizational culture, they likely begin to understand not only the integrated and differentiated aspects of an organization's culture but also its fragmented or ambiguous characteristics. For example, Martin (1992) reports a memorable story that a high-tech firm CEO told as an extraordinary example of support for an expectant mother (integrated perspective), but some employees felt the support was only offered to people of certain status and not everyone (differentiated perspective), while others thought the story made the company's culture on maternity unclear (fragmented perspective). Similarly, some organizations officially espouse very supportive family leave policies that may attract newcomers, but established employees find that "the policy exists, but you really can't use it" (Kirby and Krone 2002: 50). Established employees are more likely to have a nuanced, three-perspective understanding of organizational culture.

Organizational Change

The longer individuals remain in an organization the more likely they are to experience significant changes in its culture. Various events likely to lead to cultural changes, including leadership transitions, mergers and acquisitions, and layoffs or reduction-in-force, among others.

Organizational leadership changes often create cultural changes for organizational members. Shen and Cannella (2002) identify three possible succession plans: (1) heir apparent, where an individual is expected to build on and maintain the status quo; (2) contender successions, which may be between two candidates, one who will maintain the status quo and one who will change it; and (3) outsider successions, where an outsider is expected to bring change to the system. Whether new leaders are transformational leaders who attempt to create a new vision and culture for the organization (Tichy and Ulrich 1984) or institutional leaders who try to clarify or refine the mission (Trice and Beyer 1991), organizational artifacts, values, beliefs, or rituals change with the new leadership. Organizational-level changes occur when change involves a CEO (Garner and Peterson 2017), but subculture- or departmental-level changes occur when departmental leadership changes.

Mergers and acquisitions occur when two separate organizations merge into a single new entity. Even when the two organizations have similar cultures, minimally the artifacts (logos, business cards, etc.) and routines (operating systems and policies) must merge into a new culture. When the differences are larger, the challenges are greater. For example, in a merger of a bank and leasing company, the differences between the bank's formal communication with legalistic, written practices clashed with the informal, hand-shake practices of the leasing company (Bastien 1992). Employees who adopted the bank culture tended to have advancement opportunities while those who did not tended either to leave or remain in their positions in the leasing section of the merged company creating subcultures rather than a unified culture. By producing subcultures, mergers and acquisitions potentially foster both identification (connection) and disidentification (separation) with the new organization's culture (Pepper and Larson 2006).

An interdependent relationship exists between a reduction-in-force or layoffs and an organization's culture. Organizational and national culture influence the way in which layoff announcements are made, ranging from emotional to logical appeals (Signorielli 2009, Sisco and Yu 2010), and family communication surrounding layoffs influence individuals' resiliency (Lucas and Buzzanell 2012). A reduction-in-force affects an organization's culture. In some cases, employee layoffs violate the expectation or practice of lifetime employment. Employees who survive layoffs have changed attitudes toward the organization, sometimes experiencing survivor guilt (Brockner et al. 1993). Although supervisor communication assists in reducing the uncertainty created from a reduction-in-force, because of the potential for additional layoffs, survivors often seek employment elsewhere even if their own department did not experience reductions (Casey et al. 1997). From a fragmented perspective, areas of uncertainty and ambiguity would become particularly prominent after a reduction-in-force.

These three examples—leadership transitions, mergers and acquisitions, and reduction-in-forces—are just some of the changes that can be experienced for established employees. Changing technology (Barrett and Stephens 2017), a more diverse workforce (Kim 2017), economic and political shifts (Barrett and Dailey 2018), and environmental changes such as travel bans or climate change (Frandsen and Johansen 2011) all contribute to changing an organization's culture. The myriad of changes can affect all three perspectives of culture.

Future research can explore how interpersonal relationships assist or hinder a nuanced understanding of organizational culture during the metamorphosis phase in employment and volunteer settings. In addition, exploring how organizational members respond to official messages, by either accepting the message-senders' likely intent or modifying them or using them ironically, will provide insight into how communication creates and recreates the organizational culture (Poole et al. 1995). Adopting an intended understanding likely contributes to an integrated organizational culture, while modifying the intended meaning suggests subcultural differences and ironic understandings suggest fragmented and ambiguous aspects of the culture. Finally, examining how interpersonal relationships influence volunteers' understanding of organizational culture and responses to organizational changes deserves additional attention. For example, one study found that volunteers responded negatively to cultural changes instituted after a CEO transition and yet positive interpersonal relationships led some established volunteers to continue serving despite their dissatisfaction, but created subgroups of new and established volunteers (Kramer and Danielson 2017).

Practitioners and industry professionals should remember that communication plays a powerful role in creating and reinforcing incumbents' organizational understanding. It is through communication that members establish and sustain interpersonal relationships, as well as make sense of and respond to organizational changes. Through communication training and development, organizations can foster an environment where incumbents can learn and contribute to the changing organizational culture in positive ways.

Exit and Organizational Culture

Organizational exit is an inevitable part of the socialization process. Exit is typically divided into two types, voluntary and involuntary. Research suggests three main reasons for voluntary exit: planned exits, shocks, and gradual disenchantment (Lee et al. 1996). In planned exits, individuals exit due to some event external to the organization, such as a graduation, wedding, or spouse's retirement or transfer. Typically known in advance, these exits suggest compatibility between the individual and the organizational culture (person–organization fit). In shocks, individuals exit because of some unexpected organizational event, such as being sexually harassed or bullied, being passed over for a promotion, or experiencing a leadership change. In these cases, the individual experiences a violation of some expected organizational norm or value such that there is no longer a match between individual expectations and the organizational culture. In gradual disenchantment, what began as a positive match between the individual and the job and culture has gradually become mismatched, but for no specific event or action. Over time, the individual concludes that the job or organizational culture no longer matches the expectation created during the anticipatory and encounter phases. During the voluntary exit process, members customarily undergo three stages of exit: preannouncement, announcement of exit, and post-exit organizational sensemaking (Jablin 2001). However, some members, like those in volunteer (Kramer 2011), totalistic, and high-reliability organizations (Hinderaker 2015), experience these exit phases differently.

Involuntary exit occurs when there is a discrepancy in the person–job or person–organization fit. Although some involuntary exits are immediate, as in the case with layoffs, the dismissal process generally involves first a problem-solving breakpoint during which supervisors attempt to resolve the disparity through additional training, and a termination breakpoint when it becomes clear that the individual is not going to be able to meet the job and cultural expectations (Fairhurst et al. 1984). Essentially, involuntary exit occurs when individuals do not sufficiently adapt to an organization's culture during the socialization process in employment or voluntary settings. For example, Mars Hill, a megachurch, has expelled members who wanted to stay but did not fit the organization's culture (Garner and Peterson 2018).

The distinction between voluntary and involuntary exit is not always clear cut. Peers and supervisors may actively create an environment that encourages an employee to quit (Cox 1999). Some of those behaviors may be positive, such as suggesting individuals seem like they would be happier elsewhere, but others could be classified as bullying or harassment. Whether such turnover is voluntary or involuntary is difficult to determine.

Regardless of exit type, individuals' departures impact the organizational culture for those remaining. For example, group members often reminisce about persons who have left (Levine et al. 2001). The resulting positive or negative stories become cultural artifacts. When individuals transfer, those who remain consider the implications for their department or careers (Kramer 1989). When someone is dismissed, coworkers make sense of why the person was fired and what it says about the organization's culture (Cox and Kramer 1995). When the person who departs contributed to the unit's success, the focus may be on how to maintain its culture considering the personnel changes. When the person was detrimental to the unit, the focus may be on clarifying the unit's values and practices to avoid repeating the same problem.

Most voluntary and involuntary exit research focuses on individuals who leave (Davis and Myers 2012, Klatzke 2016). Likewise, most practitioners focus on the person(s) exiting, rather than attending to organizational survivors, who might experience confusion, guilt, or sadness. Future research on exit and culture can focus on the influence of departures on the organization's culture. When the person who leaves had a significant organizational role, the effect may be viewed as influencing the unified culture. When the person has a smaller role, the effect may be more at the department/unit level. In either case, there may be uncertainties in light of the departure. Thus, all three cultural perspectives can be used to explore how exit influences the culture.

Concluding Thoughts

Most organizational communication reference books have separate chapters on socialization/assimilation and organizational culture. Combining them provided a unique opportunity to reflect on the symbiotic relationship of the two bodies of research while expanding our understanding of each. As previously mentioned, few organizational communication scholars study culture in isolation; rather, most research provides insight into organizational cultures through other aspects of organizational communication, like sexual harassment (Dougherty and Smythe 2004) or workplace health promotions (James and Zoller 2018). This peripheral study of culture has advantages and disadvantages. For example, we gain a broader understanding of culture and how communication both enables and constrains it. Communication scholars can also adopt a variety of lenses in studying culture, which can highlight different aspects and complexities of organizational culture (Keyton 2017). At the same time, we have sacrificed some depth on the topic. To date, we lack a unifying theory of organizational culture, and new insights about culture are often a byproduct of work on another object of study (Keyton 2017).

In sum, socialization involves learning an organization's culture. However, the reality of the overly positive, unified culture presented during anticipatory socialization is replaced with a more nuanced understanding during the encounter and metamorphosis phases as individuals recognize organizational subcultures and cultural ambiguities. Exploring how communication facilitates this gradual change in understanding of organizational culture can increase theoretical and practical understandings of both socialization and organizational culture.

Discussion Questions

1. What theoretical lenses that you have encountered would be useful in studying socialization and organizational culture? In what ways could these different theories inform our understanding of the four phases of socialization in unique ways?
2. How might an organizational leader (CEO, manager, or consultant) apply the findings about anticipatory socialization and encounter to make changes in the newcomer experience in an organization? How might these changes affect the organization's culture?
3. Most socialization research focuses on how newcomers adapt to an organization's culture. In what ways might individuals or groups of individuals change an organization's culture? Consider how the changing gender, ethnic, and racial demographics of potential employees, along with generational differences, can influence an organization's culture.
4. In reflecting on your personal organizational experiences—at work, school, or in volunteer groups—how have you experienced metamorphosis? Beyond interpersonal experiences and organizational change discussed in the chapter, what experiences helped you feel like an insider? What experiences inhibited your metamorphosis?
5. What function does communication play during organizational exit? How could our understanding of organizational exit be adapted for a variety of employment and voluntary roles? How can the exit of individuals change the organization's culture?

References

Allen, B. J. 1996. "Feminist Standpoint Theory: A Black Woman's (Re)view of Organizational Socialization," *Communication Studies*, 47, 257–271.

Ashford, S. J. and Black, J. S. 1996. "Proactivity During Organizational Entry: The Role of Desire For Control," *Journal of Applied Psychology*, 81, 199–214.

Ashforth, B. E. and Saks, A. M. 1996. "Socialization Tactics: Longitudinal Effects On Newcomer Adjustment," *Academy of Management Journal*, 39, 149–178.

Barrett, A. K. and Dailey, S. 2018. "A New Normal? Competing National Cultural Discourses and Workers' Constructions of Identity and Meaningful Work in Norway," *Communication Monographs*, 85, 284–307.

Barrett, A. K. and Stephens, K. K. 2017. "The Pivotal Role of Change Appropriation in The Implementation of Health Care Technology," *Management Communication Quarterly*, 31, 163–193.

Bastien, D. T. 1992. "Change in Organizational Culture,"*Management Communication Quarterly*, 5, 403–442.

Bridge, K. and Baxter, L. A. 1992. "Blended Relationships: Friends as Work Associates," *Western Journal of Communication*, 56, 200–225.

Brockner, J., Grover, S., O'Malley, M. N., Reed, T. F. and Glynn, M. A. 1993. "Threat of Future Layoffs, Self-Esteem and Survivors' Reactions: Evidence From the Laboratory and the Field," *Strategic Management Journal*, 14, 153–166.

Brown, M. H. 1985. "That Reminds Me of a Story: Speech Action in Organizational Socialization," *Western Journal of Speech Communication*, 49, 27–42.

Bullis, C. 1993. "Organizational Socialization Research: Enabling, Constraining and Shifting Perspectives," *Communication Monographs*, 60, 10–17.

Buzzanell, P. M., Berkelaar, B. L. and Kisselburgh, L. 2011. "From the Mouths of Babes: Exploring Families' Career Socialization of Young Children in China, Lebanon, Belgium and the United States," *Journal of Family Communication*, 11, 148–164.

Buzzanell, P. M., Long, Z., Anderson, L. B., Kokini, K. and Batra, J. C. 2015. "Mentoring in Academe: A Feminist Poststructural Lens on Stories of Women Engineering Faculty of Color," *Management Communication Quarterly*, 29, 440–457.

Caldwell, D. F. and O'Reilly, C. A. 1990. "Measuring Person-Job Fit with a Profile-Comparison Process," *Journal of Applied Psychology*, 75, 648–657.

Casey, M. K., Miller, V. D. and Johnson, J. R. 1997. "Survivors' Information Seeking Following a Reduction in Workforce," *Communication Research*, 24, 755–781.

Chao, G. T., O'Leary-Kelly, A. M., Wolf, S., Klein, H. J. and Gardner, P. D. 1994. "Organizational Socialization: Its Content and Consequences," *Journal of Applied Psychology*, 79, 730–743.

Clair, R. P. 1996. "The Political Nature of the Colloquialism, 'A Real Job': Implications for Organizational Socialization," *Communication Monographs*, 63, 249–267.

Cox, S. A. 1999. "Group Communication and Employee Turnover: How Coworkers Encourage Peers to Voluntarily Exit," *Southern Communication Journal*, 64, 181–192.

Cox, S. A. and Kramer, M. W. 1995. "Communication During Employee Dismissals," *Management Communication Quarterly*, 9, 156–190.

Dailey, S. L. 2016. "What Happens Before Full-Time Employment? Internships as a Mechanism of Anticipatory Socialization," *Western Journal of Communication*, 80, 453–480.

Davis, C. W. and Myers, K. K. 2012. "Communication and Member Disengagement in Planned Organizational Exit," *Western Journal of Communication*, 76, 194–216.

Deal, T. E. and Kennedy, A. A. 1982. *Corporate Cultures: The Rites and Rituals of Corporate Life*, Reading, MA: Addison-Wesley.

DiSanza, J. R. 1995. "Bank Teller Organizational Assimilation in a System of Contradictory Practices," *Management Communication Quarterly*, 9, 191–218.

Dougherty, D. and Smythe, M. J. 2004. "Sensemaking, Organizational Culture and Sexual Harassment," *Journal of Applied Communication Research*, 32, 293–317.

Fairhurst, G. T., Green, S. G. and Snavely, B. K. 1984. "Managerial Control and Discipline: Whips and Chains," in R. N. Bostrom and B. H. Westley (eds.), *Communication Yearbook 8*. Beverly Hills, CA: SAGE, pp. 558–593.

Feldman, D. C. 1981. "The Multiple Socialization of Organization Members," *Academy of Management Review*, 6, 309–318.

Frandsen, F. and Johansen, W. 2011. "Rhetoric, Climate Change and Corporate Identity Management," *Management Communication Quarterly*, 25, 511–530.

Gailliard, B. M., Myers, K. K. and Seibold, D. R. 2010. "Organizational Assimilation: A Multidimensional Reconceptualization and Measure," *Management Communication Quarterly*, 24, 552–578.

Garner, J. T. and Peterson, B. L. 2018. "Untangling the Processes of Leaving a Member-abusive Organization," *Management Communication Quarterly*, 32, 143–171.

Gibson, M. K. and Papa, M. J. 2000. "The Mud, the Blood and the Beer Guys: Organizational Osmosis in Blue-Collar Work Groups," *Journal of Applied Communication Research*, 28, 68–88.

Goodnow, J. J. 1988. "Children's Household Work: Its Nature and Functions," *Psychological Bulletin*, 103, 5–26.

Graen, G. B. 2003. "Interpersonal Workplace Theory at the Crossroads," in Graen, G. B. (ed.), *Dealing with Diversity: LMX Leadership: The Series*, Greenwich, CT: Information Age, pp. 145–182.

Graen, G. B. and Uhl-Bien, M. 1995. "Relationship-Based Approach to Leadership: Development of Leader-Member Exchange (LMX) Theory of Leadership Over 25 Years: Applying a Multi-Level Multi-Domain Perspective," *The Leadership Quarterly*, 6, 219–247.

Herrygers, K. S. and Wieland, S. M. 2017. "Work Socialization Through Part-Time Work: Cultivating Self-Efficacy and Engagement Through Care," *Journal of Applied Communication Research*, 45, 557–575.

Hinderaker, A. 2015. "Severing Primary Ties: Exit from Totalistic Organizations," *Western Journal of Communication*, 79, 92–115.

Hoelscher, C. S., Zanin, A. C. and Kramer, M. W. 2016. "Identifying with Values: Examining Organizational Culture in Farmers Markets," *Western Journal of Communication*, 80, 481–501.

Hoffner, C. A., Levine, K. J. and Toohey, R. A. 2008. "Socialization to Work in Late Adolescence: The Role of Television and Family," *Journal of Broadcasting & Electronic Media*, 52, 282–302.

Jablin, F. M. 2001. "Organizational Entry, Assimilation and Disengagement/Exit," in Jablin, F. M. and Putnam, L. L. (eds.), *The New Handbook of Organizational Communication: Advances in Theory, Research and Methods*, Thousand Oaks, CA: SAGE, pp. 732–818.

Jahn, J. L. and Myers, K. K. 2015. "'When Will I Use This?' How Math and Science Classes Communicate Impressions of STEM Careers: Implications for Vocational Anticipatory Socialization," *Communication Studies*, 66, 218–237.

James, E. P. and Zoller, H. M. 2018. "Resistance Training: (Re)shaping Extreme Forms of Workplace Health Promotion," *Management Communication Quarterly*, 32, 60–89.

Jian, G., Shi, X. and Dalisay, F. 2014. "Leader–Member Conversational Quality: Scale Development and Validation Through Three Studies," *Management Communication Quarterly*, 28, 375–403.

Keyton, J. 2005. *Communication and Organizational Culture*. Thousand Oaks, CA: SAGE.

Keyton, J. 2014. "Organization Culture: Creating Meaning and Influence," in Putnam, L. L. and Mumby, D. K. (eds.), *The SAGE Handbook of Organizational Communication: Advances in Theory, Research and Methods*, Thousand Oaks, CA: SAGE, pp. 549–568.

Keyton, J. 2017. "Culture, Organizational," in Scott, C. R. and Lewis, L. (eds.), *The International Encyclopedia of Organizational Communication*, Malden, MA: John Wiley & Sons.

Kim, H. 2017. "Differential Impacts of Functional, Geographical and Hierarchical Diversity on Knowledge Sharing in the Midst of Organizational Change," *Management Communication Quarterly*, 32, 5–30.

Kirby, E. L. and Krone, K. J. 2002. " 'The Policy Exists But You Can't Really Use It': Communication and The Structuration of Work-Family Policies," *Journal of Applied Communication Research*, 30, 50–77.

Klatzke, S. R. 2016. "I Quit! The Process of Announcing Voluntary Organizational Exit," *Qualitative Research Reports in Communication*, 17, 44–51.

Kramer, M. W. 1989. "Communication During Intraorganization Job Transfers," *Management Communication Quarterly*, 3, 219–248.

Kramer, M. W. 1993. "Communication and Uncertainty Reduction During Job Transfers: Leaving and Joining Processes," *Communication Monographs*, 60, 178–198.

Kramer, M. W. 2009. "Role Negotiations in a Temporary Organization: Making Sense During Role Development in an Educational Theater Production," *Management Communication Quarterly*, 23, 188–217.

Kramer, M. W. 2010. *Organizational Socialization: Joining and Leaving Organizations*, Cambridge, UK: Polity.

Kramer, M. W. 2011. "Toward a Communication Model for the Socialization of Voluntary Members," *Communication Monographs*, 78, 233–255.

Kramer, M. W. and Danielson, M. A. (2017). Communication and role development for zoo volunteers: responding to role-sending, role-making, and role-remaking. *Journal of Applied Communication Research*, 45, 96–115.

Kramer, M. W. and Miller, V. D. 1999. "A Response to Criticisms of Organizational Socialization Research: In Support of Contemporary Conceptualizations of Organizational Assimilation," *Communication Monographs*, 66, 358–367.

Kramer, M. W. and Miller, V. D. 2014. "Socialization and Assimilation: Theories, Processes and Outcomes," in Putnam, L. L and Mumby, D. K. (eds.), *The SAGE Handbook of Organizational Communication*, Thousand Oaks, CA: SAGE, pp. 525–547.

Larkey, L. K. 1996. "Toward a Theory of Communicative Interactions in Culturally Diverse Workgroups," *Academy of Management Review*, 21, 463–491.

Lee, T. W., Mitchell, T. R., Wise, L. and Fireman, S. 1996. "An Unfolding Model of Voluntary Employee Turnover," *Academy of Management Journal*, 39, 5–36.

Leonardi, P. M., Jackson, M. H. and Diwan, A. 2009. "The Enactment-Externalization Dialectic: Rationalization and the Persistence of Counterproductive Technology Design Practices in Student Engineering," *Academy of Management Journal*, 52, 400–420.

Levine, J. M., Moreland, R. L. and Choi, H.-S. 2001. "Group Socialization and Newcomer Innovation," in Hogg, M. A. and Tindale, R. S. (eds.), *Blackwell Handbook of Social Psychology: Group Processes*, Oxford, UK: Blackwell, pp. 86–106.

Levine, K. J. and Hoffner, C. A. 2006. "Adolescents' Conceptions of Work," *Journal of Adolescent Research*, 21, 647–669.

Liu, S., Wang, M., Bamberger, P., Shi, J. and Bacharach, S. B. 2015. "The Dark Side of Socialization: A Longitudinal Investigation of Newcomer Alcohol Use," *Academy of Management Journal*, 58, 334–355.

Lucas, K. 2011. "Socializing Messages in Blue-Collar Families: Communicative Pathways to Social Mobility and Reproduction," *Western Journal of Communication*, 75, 95–121.

Lucas, K. and Buzzanell, P. M. 2012. "Memorable Messages of Hard Times: Constructing Short-and Long-Term Resiliencies Through Family Communication," *Journal of Family Communication*, 12, 189–208.

Malgwi, C. A., Howe, M. A. andBurnaby, P. A. 2005. "Influences on Students' Choice of College Major," *Journal of Education for Business*, 80, 275–282.

Martin, J. 1992. *Cultures in Organizations: Three Perspectives*, New York, NY: Oxford.

Miller, K. I., Considine, J. and Garner, J. 2007. "'Let Me Tell You About My Job': Exploring the Terrain of Emotion in the Workplace," *Management Communication Quarterly*, 20, 231–260.

Miller, V. D. and Jablin, F. M. 1991. "Information Seeking During Organizational Entry: Influences, Tactics and a Model of the Process," *Academy of Management Review*, 16, 92–120.

Miller, V. D., Jablin, F. M., Casey, M. K., Lamphear-Van Horn, M. and Ethington, C. 1996. "The Maternity Leave as a Role Negotiation Process," *Journal of Managerial Issues*, 8, 286–309.

Morrison, E. W. 1993. "Longitudinal Study of the Effects of Information Seeking on Newcomer Socialization," *Journal of Applied Psychology*, 78, 173–183.

Myers, K. K., Jahn, J. L. S., Gailliard, B. M. and Stoltzfus, K. 2011. "Vocational Anticipatory Socialization (VAS): A Communicative Model of Adolescents' Interests in STEM," *Management Communication Quarterly*, 25, 87–120.

Myers, S. A. and Johnson, A. D. (2004). Perceived solidarity, self-disclosure, and trust in organizational peer relationships. *Communication Research Reports*, 21, 75–83.

Omilion-Hodges, L. M. and Baker, C. R. 2017. "Communicating Leader-Member Relationship Quality: The Development of Leader Communication Exchange Scales to Measure Relationship Building and Maintenance Through the Exchange of Communication-Based Goods," *International Journal of Business Communication*, 54, 115–145.

Pacanowsky, M. E. and O'Donnell-Trujillo, N. 1983. "Organizational Communication as Cultural Performance," *Communication Monographs*, 50, 126–147.

Pepper, G. L. and Larson, G. S. 2006. "Cultural Identity Tensions in a Post-Acquisition Organization," *Journal of Applied Communication Research*, 34, 49–71.

Peters, T. J. and Waterman, R. H., Jr. 1982. *In Search of Excellence: Lessons from America's Best-Run Companies*, New York: Harper & Row.

Peterson, G. W. and Peters, D. F. 1983. "Adolescents' Construction of Social Reality: The Impact of Television and Peers," *Youth and Society*, 15, 67–85.

Poole, M. S., DeSanctis, G., Kirsh, L. and Jackson, M. 1995. "Group Decision Support Systems as Facilitators of Quality Team Efforts," in Frey, L. R. (ed.), *Innovations in Group Facilitation Techniques: Applications in Natural Settings*, Cresskill, NJ: Hampton Press, pp. 299–321.

Putnam, L. L. 1982. "Paradigms for Organizational Communication Research: An Overview and Synthesis," *Western Journal of Speech Communication*, 46, 192–206.

Rosenfeld, L. B., Richman, J. M. and May, S. K. 2004. "Information Adequacy, Job Satisfaction and Organizational Culture in a Dispersed-Network Organization," *Journal of Applied Communication Research*, 32, 28–54.

Schein, E. H. 1968. "Organizational Socialization and the Profession of Management," *Industrial Management Review*, 9, 1–16.

Schein, E. H. 1990. "Organizational Culture," *American Psychologist*, 45, 109–119.

Shen, W. and Cannella, A. A. J. 2002. "Revisiting the Performance Consequences of CEO Succession: The Impacts of Successor Type, Postsuccession Senior Executive Turnover and Departing CEO Tenure," *Academy of Management Journal*, 45, 717–733.

Sias, P. M. 2009. *Organizing Relationships: Tradition and Emerging Perspectives on Workplace Relationships*, Thousand Oaks, CA: SAGE.

Sias, P. M., Pedersen, H., Gallagher, E. B. and Kopaneva, I. 2012. "Workplace Friendship in the Electronically Connected Organization," *Human Communication Research*, 38, 253–279.

Signorielli, N. 2009. "Race and Sex in Prime Time: A Look at Occupations and Occupational Prestige," *Mass Communication & Society*, 12, 332–352.

Sisco, L. A. and Yu, N. 2010. "The Rhetoric of Chinese Layoff Memos," *Business Communication Quarterly*, 73, 326–330.

Smircich, L. 1983. "Concepts of Culture and Organizational Analysis," *Administrative Science Quarterly*, 28, 339–358.

Tan, C. L. and Kramer, M. W. 2012. "Communication and Voluntary Downward Career Changes," *Journal of Applied Communication Research*, 40, 87–106.

Thom-Santelli, J., Millen, D. R. and Gergle, D. 2011. "Organizational Acculturation and Social Networking," *Proceedings of the ACM 2011 Conference on Computer Supported Cooperative Work*, Hangzhou, China: ACM.

Tichy, N. M. and Ulrich, D. O. 1984. "SMR Forum: The Leadership Challenge— A Call for the Transformational Leader," *Sloan Management Review*, 26, 59.

Trice, H. M. and Beyer, J. M. 1991. "Cultural Leadership in Organizations," *Organization Science*, 2, 149–169.

Van Maanen, J. and Schein, E. G. 1979. "Toward a Theory of Organizational Socialization," in Staw, B. M. (ed.), *Research in Organizational Behavior*, Greenwich, CT: JAI, pp. 209–264.

Wanous, J. P., Poland, T. D., Premack, S. L. and Davis, K. S. 1992. "The Effects of Met Expectations on Newcomer Attitudes and Behaviors: A Review and Meta-Analysis," *Journal of Applied Psychology*, 77, 288–297.

Wentzel, K. R. and Looney, L. 2007. "Socialization in School Settings," in Grusec, J. E. and Hastings, P. D. (eds.), *Handbook of Socialization: Theory and Research*, New York: Guilford, pp. 382–403.

7 Gender and Sexuality

Jessica A. Pauly and Patrice M. Buzzanell

Our Stories

We begin this chapter with some commonalities that we both have experienced, beginning first with Jess and then adding Patrice.

Jess

Experiences, thoughts, and identities pertaining to gender and sexuality have caused me to question and (re)consider many moments in life. While I have formally studied gender since returning to graduate school, in some respects I (we all, for that matter) have "studied" gender our entire lives. I have vivid memories of gendered interactions since I was a little girl, but more recently a few prime examples stand out: men looking at my husband when responding to a question I asked; feeling completely inept and uneasy when walking into a car repair shop full of hard working men; and being told I should "hit my dad up for money" when attempting to negotiate salary with the HR director at one of my first jobs. These experiences add to my curiosity about gender and how it operates in our social reality.

To complicate things, I also identify as Catholic, which creates nuance on the topic of sexuality for me. Growing up in parochial school, I was under the impression that sexuality is something that is taboo and sin-inducing. We wore uniforms, in part, to avoid issues of showing too much skin, or wearing inappropriate clothing. School dances were always carefully chaperoned by watchful administrators, teachers, and parents, making sure to remind us to keep 6 inches of space between us and our dance partners; or, as it was often demanded, "Make room for the Holy Spirit!" Much of this talk encouraged a kind of fear inside of me. I was already a fairly well-mannered kid, afraid to break rules or disappoint my parents. What I was learning about my body, my sexuality, and expectations of me as a Catholic girl made me feel as if I shouldn't have desires at all, and to recognize that interests in boys (because girls could only have interests in boys) could quickly lead to sin.

Gender and sexuality become ever present, and take on new meaning, in motherhood. While writing this chapter, my 1-year-old baby became sick with the stomach flu. My physical and emotional response to her illness was nothing short of visceral. This, coupled with her bodily experience—how she responded to this sudden sickness that she had never before known—results in a prime example of how bodies can be unpredictable, and similarly, how our expressions of desire and emotion, in relation to bodily functions, are also often temperamental. I'm sure my baby desired to feel better, and I felt the same for her; we both felt sad and frustrated by our lack of control of the situation. Such is the nature of sexuality and gender; ever in flux and somewhat unpredictable, but nonetheless present everywhere we go.

I bring all of this past experience and understanding with me as I enter this chapter. We now turn to Patrice's story.

Patrice

It was fascinating for me to read Jess's opening. I knew that we were both Catholic and attended parochial school, but I didn't know how much our stories would overlap. I, too, attended parochial schools. For 12 years, I participated in the enriched academic program that meant taking Latin, French, and advanced courses in math, physics, chemistry, biology, and English. I also minored in art and took the required religion classes that, in high school, incorporated philosophy, mythologies of Christ-like figures in world religions ancient and contemporary, archaeological and anthropological bases for religions, and discussions of papal encyclicals, including the one on birth control, read in Latin. We also had sessions in "religion" class where we could ask any question we wanted, which typically were about sex and where our lay male instructor brought in artificial birth control so that we could see, touch, and ask questions about it. Our English classes included controversial novels plus reading Beowulf and Chaucer in the most recent understandings of Old and Middle English. Our learning was cognitive and embodied in sounds and performance; our hearts and spirituality were stretched as we were encouraged to seek out other religions to challenge ourselves and defend our choices. And yet I remained very naïve about sexuality. Like Jess, I felt and learned the taboos and binaries—in/appropriate, un/Catholic, un/disciplined, censored/uncensored, il/legal, public/private, mind/body, sacred/profane. I too felt the paradoxes and wasn't equipped to navigate the tensions. There were sins and not-sins; there were different categories of sin; there were workarounds for sin. For example, one was supposed to attend Sunday Mass. But one could arrive during the Gospel and leave right after receiving Communion—and be "covered" (i.e. Mass would "count"; no sin this week!). Likewise, one had to think about and learn workarounds and rules for sexuality. How did one remain "good" Catholic girls and women—seemingly linked to purity, marriage, and childbearing/childrearing with a strange asexual twist— and still acknowledge the erotic, hormonal changes and desires, as well as awakenings to sexual relationships? Attending sometimes bawdy Irish Catholic and Italian Catholic gatherings, along with the Russian Orthodox ceremonies with rich materialities that made up my heritage, displayed sensualities, pleasures, and interactions that seemed to contrast markedly with the parochial school teachings and comments (often) by nuns about bodies, purity, and routes to Heaven. I still feel intellectually enriched and eternally grateful to my parents' sacrifices to enable me to have such a fine education and upbringing. I feel like I skim across sexualities despite my rich life with a partner and six birth children and despite my scholarship on pregnancy in the workplace and parental leave policies, practices, and ethics.

Our openings show that we found our ways into this subject as white, cisgendered, heterosexual, middle-class, Catholic women. We both experience sexualities as tensions that pose dilemmas and contradict ideologies of rational–legal bureaucracies. We both see sexualizing organizational communication not only as an opportunity to embrace and enrich theory, personal lives, and career, but also to develop policy, structures, and practices that foreground the both/and in human nature. The crux of the matter is how. As we move into our overview of research, we retain our personal vantage points and tensions to question scholarship and popular media on sexuality and gender.

Review of Scholarship on Sexuality and Gender

The emergence of gender and sexuality research within organizational communication studies is a result of enhanced interest in gender and organizing literature over the course of the past 35 years. In 1983, Hearn and Parkin illuminated the neglected area that is gender and organizations, highlighting sexuality as a byproduct of gender worth considering within organizational spaces. This attention paved the way for additional work that is beyond the scope of our chapter, though notable contributions from our field of organizational communication include Buzzanell (2000) and Ashcraft and Mumby (2004). Scholarship on sexuality and gender has greatly evolved since the 1990s to recognize how ambivalence, tensions, stigma, curiosity, attraction, stereotyping, and upbringing can surface when considering current scholarship such as that on transgender job seekers (Eger 2018) and legal sex work (Blithe et al. 2019).

This chapter discusses the emergence of sexuality and gender in interdisciplinary organizational and organizational communication scholarship that moved from writing sexualities into theory and research (beyond commentary on the dangers of sexual attractions in the workplace) to more complex and nuanced understandings of the ways sexualities are implicated in and/or drive expectations, treatment, and performance of self and others as well as standard practices, policies, and structures. We admit that our overview does not cover all topics but only some prominent tension-centered areas. We begin with conceptualizing sexuality and gender, and then move into exploring dialectics of control and resistance. In doing so, we disrupt organizational communication through sexualities and gendered identities.

Conceptualizing Sexuality and Gender

At its basis, sexuality is about interest, expressions, doing sex, as well as understanding ourselves as sexual beings. Folded into human sexuality are gender, sexual orientation, and social or normative aspects. Although seemingly straightforward, conceptualizations are messy as a result of their socially and historically constructed natures and the multiple and overlapping ways in which both sexualities and gender are framed colloquially and in scholarship as outcome (gender-sexuality difference), performance (doing of gender-sexuality), text-conversation dialectic (organizing), and social text (discourse) (see Ashcraft 2004), with a fifth frame called communication as discursive-material evolution added by Ashcraft and Harris (2014). This complicated multilayered nature makes it difficult to pin down how sexuality and gender are defined today. In this section, we define sexuality, gender, and some main ways organizational scholars have categorized distinctions.

Sexuality is an elusive term (Burrell and Hearn 1989), and yet, a "primal part of human identity" (Allen 2011: 133). It defies simple definitions because of its relation to the physical, biological, physiological, emotional, spiritual, and other aspects of personal and organizational life. Sexuality is linked to desire (Burrell and Hearn 1989), and often considered a private matter; yet, because of its political nature, involving action and power (Hearn and Parkin 1995), sexuality is associated with organizing. Although always inherent in organizational life and organizing processes and structures (Acker 1990), with increasing attention to difference (e.g. gender, race, ethnicity, disability, sexual-social orientation, class, nationality) sexuality requires renewed attention to whose interests are embedded in and drive organizing. That is, whose sexuality is controlled, in whose interests, for what purposes, and with what everyday individual, relational, organizational, societal, and global consequences?

Like sexuality, gender, too, is politicized. While contemporary research takes a more nuanced and nonbinary approach, gender is traditionally conceived of as a social category assigned at birth, based on an individual's biological sex that traditionally is polarized (i.e. male and female). However, what gender means and how one should live as a gendered being is a learned process (West and Zimmerman 1987). Subtle and not-so-subtle messages about "doing gender" (in)appropriately teach us how to behave in masculine and feminine ways appropriate to our backgrounds and to the contexts in which we live and work. Effectively, gendered identities emerge in social situations and are used to explain social arrangements as well as support basic divisions of society (West and Zimmerman 1987). In recognizing the outcome-oriented, socially constructed or performative, and political nature of gender, we acknowledge that gender has consequences for our wellbeing and our organizational experiences.

Gender is fundamental to the ways we structure our personal life, organizations, and societies (i.e. text-conversation dialectic [organizing], and social text [discourse] frames). For instance, gender inequality persists globally and in every sector despite policies and laws (Örtenblad et al. 2017). Gender inequality is manifest in differential treatment and outcomes. Men typically earn more money than women for doing the same work, and men experience fewer health issues as compared to women (Arendt and Buzzanell 2017). Men typically do less house work regardless of employment, class, and other differences, with "profound influences of [such] unpaid work on women's lives" and profound privileges in men's lives (Jung and O'Brien, 2017). These examples relate to the social, communicative nature of what it means to be a man or woman.

In categorizing the distinctions between sexuality and gender, Burrell and Hearn (1989) offered four ways of conceptualizing these areas— biological essences, outcomes of social roles, fundamental political categories, or communicative practices and discourses of power—similar to Ashcraft's (2004) frames. This foundational set of approaches enabled scholars to engage in interdisciplinary dialogue. While recent work has begun problematizing sexuality and gender (e.g. Compton and Dougherty 2017), Brewis, Tyler, and Mills (2014: 303) note, "sexuality remains a relatively marginal topic in mainstream organization studies" (see also Hearn and Parkin, 1995, Ward and Winstanley 2003). In organizational communication scholarship, sexuality is embedded explicitly and implicitly in multilevel analyses centering on sexuality as the "social expression of, and relations to bodily desires, real or imagined, by or for others or for oneself, together with the related bodily states and experiences" (Hearn and Parkin 1995: 58). Moreover, as Allen (2011: 129) suggests, "sexuality is always an absent presence." Given the complex nature of sexuality and gender, we expand on Brewis, Tyler, and Mills' (2014: 306) depiction of sexuality as a "dialectical . . . site of control and resistance." Consistent with this scholarship and our opening remarks, we discuss key tensions, contradictions, and dilemmas within the overarching dialectic of control and resistance.

Exploring Dialectics of Control and Resistance

There are numerous ways of explicating power in organizational communication but a recurrent theme within this work is dialectics of control and resistance whereby one process is seen as productive for and/ or embedded in and co-constitutive of the other (Mumby 2005). In this section, we first discuss this dialectic as being manifest in the ways in which women are disciplined and positioned historically, discursively, and materially as deviant from the norm in workplaces. Second, we examine the ideal worker ideology as asexual and contrastive to sexuality, particularly women's sexuality and romance in the workplace. Third, we discuss specific occupations marked by sexuality and how members constitute their membership. In other words, we organize this section by workplace, ideal worker and membership, and occupations and career, spanning micro, meso, and macro discourses in each section on control and resistance.

Workplace

First, as a result of men dominating the workplace for centuries, and women being relegated to the home, women as a group are disciplined and positioned as deviant in numerous ways in workplaces, resulting in such processes as unequal divisions of labor, career processes and outcomes, and overall well-being (Arendt and Buzzanell 2017, Jung and O'Brien 2017). Whereas organizations may attempt to control sexuality in the workplace through policies and rules, employees may actively construct sexuality as forms of resistance. Ultimately, the relationship between organization and sexuality is inherently paradoxical, (re)generating new understandings of workplace roles and relationships, the embodied worker, and so forth.

Over the course of history, strong notions of the two sexes constructed men to be in the public eye, engaged in production and politics, while women were left to the private world of childrearing and housekeeping (Allen 2011). Such became the foundation for understanding modern gendered differences between men and women, and notions of where/ how issues of sexuality belonged. The development of sex-based differences and how they inform understandings of "men's work" and "women's work" resulted in gendered organizational logic that is inherently flawed and generally favors male workers over women workers (Acker 1990). By turning attention to the "purportedly gender-neutral policies and practices in maintaining occupational sex segregation and gender inequality in organizations" (Britton 1997: 814) gendered organizational logic illuminated the firmly established, problematic foundation of organizations—and organizational control—still present today.

This gendered organizational logic influences organizational policies and practices, which can be used to construct or dictate appropriate and inappropriate ways to express sexuality within the workplace. Dress codes, sexual harassment policies, and rules or regulations about dating coworkers are all ways in which organizations can control or discipline sexuality and sexual behavior (Allen 2011). Yet, just as organizations attempt to construct sexuality, organizations are also constructed by sexuality. For instance, the use of makeup can be understood as one strategy women use within the workplace to disguise or reinforce their sexuality. Some women may wear makeup to avoid being labeled as lesbian, or as a means of personal empowerment (Allen 2011). Consequently, makeup use can reproduce presumed gender differences between men and women (and even between groups of women), and thus, contribute to inequalities in the workplace (Dellinger and Williams 1997).

Burrell and Hearn (1989: 25) offer another understanding of the relationship between organizations and sexuality: "organization sexuality," indicating an interwoven, paradoxical relationship wherein "the very actions of organizing and being organized may carry a sexual cachet—be, in some sense, sexual." Examples of the boss–secretary, now supervisor–assistant, relationship (e.g. *Mad Men*; see D'Enbeau and Buzzanell 2014), or the doctor–nurse relationship convey the kind of sexual dynamics at play in organization sexuality. Central to this conceptual understanding is the role of power, which subsequently is a strong factor in cases of sexual harassment in the workplace; workplace power dynamics can materialize in ways that encourage un/welcomed attraction between colleagues (Bargh et al. 1995). In these ways, organization sexuality is considered problematic, wrapped up in mechanisms of control and resistance.

Ideal Worker and Membership

Second, the ideal worker is asexual, acontextual, majority in race, privileged in class, able bodied, career oriented, and socially attuned to professional networking actions and sites (Acker 1990, Buzzanell 2018). In this section we discuss ideal worker norms and understandings. The resulting pressure on women means fewer children, casual relationships, and not being taken seriously in career when attractiveness/their sexuality is used for organizational purposes.

Notions of the ideal worker stem from the classical approach to management, recognizing the man who "would appear to almost lose physical presence, or be a mere disembodied bearer of role, in effect part of a machine system" (Hearn and Parkin 1995: 19). By focusing entirely on one's task within the workforce, the ideal worker is free from issues of sexuality and gender, and the organization maintains complete control of its worker. Such an ideology, constructed with men in mind, challenges the inherent embodiment of women's sexuality. Indeed, women's bodies are recognized as the primary problem within organizational contexts because of possible pregnancy, menstruation, and emotions. As Trethewey (1999: 445) explains, the female body is perceived as a workplace liability, and as such, women go to great lengths "to keep the body in check, to prevent leaks, in short, to discipline and control the body" (see also Acker 1990).

Not only are women's bodies problematic, but relationships between bodies—sexual harassment, romantic relationships, and pregnant employees—can be considered disruptions of work or productivity, at best, or a potential legal issue, at worst. Workplace sexual harassment is common among women who work outside of the home yet generally underreported within organizations (Clair 1993). Romance within the workplace has grown as there is an increased number of women in the workforce, spending more time with colleagues at work. Romance is, in part, a result of the attractive woman worker whose sexual attractiveness deems her worthy of success within the organization (Buzzanell 2001) and yet, must also be carefully controlled and strictly professional (Trethewey 1999). Pregnancy becomes an issue of sexuality in the workplace, by virtue of women workers. Arrangements for maternity leave—if it is an option, how much time off is allowed, who takes over during this time—can disorder workplace processes and change the nature of interpersonal dynamics within the workplace, especially if the pregnancy is not viewed as normative (e.g. woman with disabilities, see Buzzanell 2003).

In an effort to achieve the ideal worker norm and commit to career, some women put off relationships and families in order to privilege career goals. Knight and Wiedmaier (2015: 159) studied casual sexual involvement and occupational pursuits of young adults and discovered individuals are not just delaying relationships for the purpose of a career, but rather "de-investing in romantic partnerships so as to enable complete devotion to professional activities." Such endeavors support the notions of the ideal worker norm by focusing on self and maintaining complete control of their future plans. Yet, by indefinitely delaying (serious) romantic relationships and families, women risk sacrificing their personal life for a career that may or may not pan out.

While women's bodies are deemed unfit and problematic for the organizational workspace, men's bodies inform norms for organizational processes. For instance, the military and the world of sports—two male-dominated industries—are often used as key metaphors for communicating organizational success (Acker 1990). As such, the ideal worker has taken on a masculine sexuality that dominates workplace discourse and culture, further marginalizing women's realities as inappropriate for organizational spaces. Women workers who refuse to sacrifice personal interests for organizational success have turned to part-time work, remote work, telework, and alternative work (e.g. farming, baking) as a means of negotiating their workplace identity (Stone 2007, Wilhoit 2014).

Occupations and Career

Occupations and career/leadership remain heavily sexualized. We select some obvious examples but note that more women are in service occupations—waiting on people, caregiving in health care settings—servicing clients and customers. Traditional leadership as aligned with career advancement has sexual imagery in its linear upward imagery and language of decisiveness, strength, control, and direction.

Considering all that has been said about the historical development of gendered organizational logic, it should be no surprise to find certain professions are thought to be feminine or masculine in nature, creating cultural practices or norms that may cause certain individuals to feel uncomfortable or unwelcomed. Generally speaking, career fields centering on manual labor, aggression, competition, authority, and safety—stereotypically masculine traits—are considered men's domain while those focused on service, ethics of care, and emotions—stereotypically feminine traits—are assumed women's work (e.g. pilots, see Ashcraft and Mumby 2004). For instance, the nursing profession is thought to be a career field for individuals with stereotypically feminine characteristics. As a result, men who are nurses are often thought to be gay, and even experience questions about their sexuality (Clair 1994, Harding 2007). Similarly, law enforcement is stereotypically a masculine occupation, causing gay and lesbian officers to feel excluded, and sometimes be subjected to sexist behavior within their work lives (Miller et al. 2003). Such issues may not only deter individuals from considering careers in these lines of work, but also actively sexualize the worker and reframe (and increase status and prestige) of occupations as more applicable to men rather than women (e.g. masculinization of airline pilots, Ashcraft and Mumby 2004).

Despite the gendered nature of a particular occupation, the performance of sexuality within the job can inform common understandings of careers. Tracy and Scott (2006) studied identity construction of two "dirty" occupations, firefighters and correctional officers, and found that while both careers are masculine in nature, the performance of sexuality creates drastic differences. Firefighters are discursively depicted as hypermasculine heroes and are celebrated publicly, while correctional officers are viewed as cruel babysitters whose work is solitary. Once again, the public/private in addition to gender norms inform depictions of sexuality in profession. Sullivan (2014) also sexualizes and desexualizes the materalities—sites, bodies, and objects—of a particular occupation, namely, massage therapists. Noting the contradictory control-resistance dynamics in different occupations, Sullivan (2014: 347) writes: "Teachers, doctors or social workers might rely on being above suspicion and therefore purposively disavow sexuality. Other occupations such as bartenders, flight attendants or consultants might selectively employ sexuality to receive benefits without calling into suspicion their professional identities."

In a more obvious example of sexuality as evident in occupations, Blithe et al. (2019) provide an in-depth account of the legal prostitution in Nevada. These brothels are similar to but different from other covert work occupations with comparable policies, structures, work–life considerations, and other organizational processes. On the individual level, the stories of these women's reasons for embarking upon, staying in, and (in a few cases) leaving their occupations portray their choices within the context of their lives. On the meso or organizational level, Blithe et al. (2019) recount the differences among houses, policies, rewards, and leadership. On the macro level, discussions about societal notions about stigma, appropriate women's work, work–life considerations, and other issues play against neoliberal backdrops. What makes this work both significant and distinctive is the way in which Blithe and colleagues normalize an occupation for readers who most likely have kept (or pretended to keep) sexualities of this nature at arm's length. Moreover, exploration of living and working spaces coupled with these women prostitutes' stories and embodied labor paradoxically calls attention to and makes invisible/normal sexuality and gender.

Disrupting Organizational Communication Through Sexualities and Gendered Identities

Until now we have reviewed gender and sexuality with regard to organizations, particularly from a heteronormative approach. Considering it on the basis of gendered organizational logic, the workplace—and organizing, more generally speaking—is a process founded in a binary understanding of gender. Despite good intentions to deconstruct the gender binary and promote gender equality in organizations or institutions, occupations, industries, and sectors globally, it seems incredibly difficult to break down (Örtenblad et al. 2017) and theorize without binaries (McDonald 2013). Enter nonbinary bodies, who attempt to navigate the heteronormative practices and processes of organizational life. In this section we review how LGBTQ individuals approach and engage the organizational workplace, and the resulting challenges they face in the process.

Individuals who do not fit into the gender binary face a host of nuanced issues in comparison to men and women when it comes to the organization. Transgender jobseekers face employment struggles and discrimination as they attempt to navigate disclosure of their identities while securing employment (Connell 2010, Eger 2018). As Connell (2010) argues, trans people practice "doing transgender" through various strategies that attempt to solve the disconnection they experience between sex, gender, and sex category. Some transgender individuals choose to remain "stealth," meaning "they (do) not identify themselves as transgender, nor (are) they (at least to their knowledge) 'read' as transgender by their coworkers and clientele" (Connell 2010: 39). Others may engage "closeting communication" which extends the closet metaphor to explain the communication process of navigating disclosure of trans peoples' various identities (Eger 2018). From this perspective the navigation process is seen as an ongoing social experience wherein individuals determine when/if/how to reveal information about their sexuality. Others, still, utilize the act of silence, which can be an effective tool in the construction of transgender identity—or minority sexual identity—in the workplace. Used as a means of self-protection, censorship, or otherwise, the power of silence is dynamic and charged with resistance (Ward and Winstanley 2003). Such conceptions of communication processes about and around transgender individuals' experience is important considering not all transgender persons transgress similarly, nor consistently across contexts (Muhr et al. 2016). In other words, this process may be multilayered and textured by material realities and interpersonal relationships (O'Shea 2018).

Adding to the complexity of transitioning during/after the job search, trans individuals may experience new access to power (if they transitioned to men), or the loss of power (if they transitioned to women) as a result of their new gender identity (Connell 2010). No matter the changes, understandings of workplace identity tend to remain firmly grounded in the gender binary; colleagues' experience of a transsexual's open workplace transition requires renegotiation of gender and sexuality, which oftentimes upholds heteronormativity and sexism. Despite the frustration this may cause for transgender workers, "a vulnerable population economically (they) must balance political desires to shake up gender with job security" (Schilt and Connell 2007: 616). What this suggests is the dominant heteronormative culture within the workplace constrains possibilities for gender expression. Muhr et al. (2016: 67) recognize the significance of such situated contexts as they pertain to transgender bodies, allowing space for "pushing our understandings of transgression to value its multiplicity and contradictoriness, especially when grounded in lived, material life" (see also Cavalcante 2016).

Situated contexts extend to workplace social events, and discursive constructions of family life for LGBTQ employees who may feel excluded or anxious as a result of heteronormativity in the workplace. For instance, workplace social events, operating as occasions to communicate sexual orientation, can be problematic for LGBTQ employees who feel pressure to bring a partner of the opposite sex (Dixon 2013). Similarly, single and childless LGBTQ employees may experience being "othered" in the workplace as a result of not fitting in to common conceptions and understandings of the traditional family structure (Dixon and Dougherty 2014). Both instances underscore the expectation involved in contributing to or supporting hegemonic heteronormative discourse within the workplace.

Ultimately, the contemporary workplace is a situated context not very supportive or encouraging of individuals who do not fit in the gender binary. Sexuality is not an issue related to the workplace, though when it must be addressed it is recognized as heteronormative sexuality. Such is the challenge for LGBTQ individuals, who disrupt normative patterns of organizing, requiring a (re)negotiation of interpersonal power dynamics and sexualities in the organization (Compton and Dougherty 2017). Discursive and material realities of the heteronormative workplace construct a space where LGBTQ individuals do not fit, and as a result, they are left to navigate their uncertainty alone. Organizational norms pressure LGBTQ individuals to conform to the gender binary, or remain silent, so as to maintain "work as usual" (Williams et al. 2009). Many strategies to resist or push back on this heteronormative culture exist, though LGBTQ individuals are warned to proceed with caution because of their vulnerable position (Schilt and Connell 2007).

Practical Applications of this Research

We take the idea of practical application to be both an inclusion of our own personal and practical ways of understanding, doing, and valuing sexualities and gender and as an effort to draw from research to develop strategies for practice.

Integration of Practical and Expert Knowledge for Application

We return to our own experiences and integrate research into these recollections, ambivalences, and confusions about sexualities and gender.

Patrice

I remember when I was reading about pregnancy at work and thinking that this is an HR issue to ensure the health and well-being of a particular workforce segment. It seemed like a straightforward process—pregnancy is part of everyday life so what's the big deal?

Then I started reading. That's when I learned about the "organizational taboos concerning the voluntary sexual behavior of women," the gendered power relations regarding sexualized employees ("pregnant female employee upsets the sexual status quo in an organization. She is sexually active."), and the forbidden even incestuous associations of workplace pregnancy with sex (e.g. Martin 1990: 349). I knew that sex could lead to pregnancy. One cannot have six children and not know that. But the idea that people look at pregnant employees and think "Oh, we know what you've been doing" or "Why wasn't I the one getting sex?" ("Sex is happening and the high-ranking male employee is getting none of it," [Martin 1990: 349]) is really creepy. And the whole notion that it's taboo in the workplace seemed ridiculous. I know that the taboo is related to the sexualities that we presumably repress in organizational life, but it seemed as though adults could simply acknowledge that we are fully human rather than behaving as though there is something secretive.

Some things have stood out to me. One is the maternity leave piece I wrote about the woman who had disabilities and was pregnant (Buzzanell 2003). People actually asked her how she became pregnant—she laughed when she recounted the episode in the interview, because it's the least of the stupid things people have said to her over the years, and because she had a perfect comeback.[1] But the laughter made me wonder how we educate people to treat others respectfully as fully human, regardless of abilities, sexualities, longing, attraction, pleasure, and other processes.

Jess

I recognize much of our orientations to sexuality and gender are based on and wrapped up in dominant cultural ways of thinking and understanding life. Western culture encourages women to see our sexuality as some kind of weapon that can paralyze men with desire and therefore, must be carefully wielded (e.g. D'Enbeau and Buzzanell 2014). We see the consequences of this way of thinking playing out in our everyday lives. For instance, in the United States many women conceal breastfeeding in public (I know that I did) because breasts are sexual in nature (and stigmatized as a result). Not only is this perspective on women's sexuality insulting and harmful, but it also shames and blames women for their sexuality.

Research to Practice

Efforts to correct gendered inequality in institutions have resulted in equal opportunity laws, Affirmative Action, hiring quotas and goals, and diversity trainings (Örtenblad et al. 2017). Yet, we do not seem to have reframed sexualities as dialectic processes and contradictory structures that offer opportunities to create workplaces that embrace humanity in its fullness.

The primary practice that our research calls us to apply is dialogue. Our review of literature suggests that we ought to spend more time conceptualizing sexualities, interrogating dilemmas, and seeking avenues for disrupting commonsense ideas and prescriptions to manage sexualities in the workplace, in membership, and in occupations and careers. Only then might we see the range of sexualities across the lifespan. Only then might we envision older Americans in nursing homes as adults with sexual identities rather than infantilized clients. Only then might we acknowledge the class, race, ethnic, and other bases of reproductive technology and surrogacy use (David 2016).

Future Directions for Organizational Communication Researchers

As we take a look back at our chapter, scholars' and practitioners' shifting conceptualizations, ways of handling sexuality and gender in practice and in policy, and trends in popular media and scholarship point to exciting directions in which organizational communication can inform and be informed by interdisciplinary research. Here, we outline four particular directions scholars might consider in their efforts to build on and expand understandings of organization, gender, and sexuality.

First, sexuality and gender are continuously being contested in the workplace, in ideal worker imagery, in occupations and career, and in the disruptions and reintegrations that mark organizing and organizational life. It has only been in the last several decades that sexual harassment was named and is now prominent again in media and everyday conversation. It was not that long ago that nonheterosexual relationships and queer or transgender identities were closeted from family, friends, and coworkers (although many nonheterosexual relationships continue to be closeted in organizational settings and beyond). It was not that long ago that there were no policies for parental leave, flexibility, lactation, and accommodations for posttraumatic stress attributable to gendered violence. The present seems full of possibilities because of the tensions in and conversations about these issues as organizational and societal members try to find adequate responses to current events and inequalities in their everyday lives. How, where, and why these shifts and tensions occur in productive, or positive, ways for particular groups of women and men can provide aspirational examples of transformation (e.g. network feminism that utilizes the multivocality and affordances of the global technological world, Fotopoulou 2016). Our chapter asserts that one basis for inequality and source for equality is the control-resistance dynamic in sexuality and gender.

Recent media headlines over the course of 2017 and 2018 indicate just how problematic "silence on sexuality" (Burrell and Hearn 1989) can be. The #MeToo movement, the "Times Up!" movement, and the Harvey Weinstein scandal unearthing a myriad of accounts illustrates the dark and serious issue of sexual harassment in the United States, just as organizational communication studies taking tension-centered lenses utilizing difference and commonality provide new insights into sexual violence on U.S. campuses (D'Enbeau 2017, Harris 2017). Recognition of sexuality as a real and significant issue should continue to be a top priority in research.

Second, while scholarship is lacking on the topic of sexuality and organizations, this phenomenon is undeniably challenging to study, not to mention measure. Burrell and Hearn (1989: 13) explain sexuality is "an inherently subtle and qualitative issue, and it is not possible to measure 'it,' even if one rashly assumes 'it' to be a singular, universal feature of human existence." Sexuality is a process; it is ever in flux, changing and shifting. As McDonald (2013: 138) writes in his autoethnographic account of his experience shifting identities during the course of his research project: "My narrative complicates the widely accepted idea that researchers should disclose their social identities to participants when they enter the field through declarations such as 'I am straight.'" Considering the difficulty involved in measuring, and thereby, accounting for sexuality in the workplace, future scholarship—perhaps guided by queer theory—should consider how best to make sense of this phenomenon within organizations.

To capture sexuality and gender as discursive and material, we suggest continuation of the feminist, postcolonial, poststructural, and/or ethnographic work in these areas (e.g. Sullivan 2014) but add that incorporation of constitutive approaches would aid understandings through examinations of human and nonhuman agency in control-resistance dialectics and spaces. Moreover, Blithe et al. (2019) make a compelling case that legal prostitution operates in similar ways to other industries despite the societal stigma and everyday designations of sex workers' labor as dirty work. They accomplish this goal of making sexuality very visible through use of mixed methods—autoethnographic, thematic, narrative, photo elicitation, participant observation field notes, and other data and analyses—that lay the groundwork for greater understanding of, respect for, and change on behalf of sex workers while also differentiating them from those victimized by sex trafficking.

Third, most approach sexuality as dilemmas, dialectical in nature: as either–or, wicked–normal, irrational–rational. But sexualities and our understandings and enactments of them are constantly socially (re)constructed, context based, and fraught with contradiction, ambivalence, and ambiguity. Attempting to define and establish boundaries, deemed necessary in Western organizational life because of rational-legal bureaucratic notions and prominence of particular kinds of organizations, is challenging at best. We do not talk as much about family firms and entrepreneurships. Often discussions are multilevel—namely, about the perceptions, doing, organizing, norms, and conversations should be broader in this sense, recognizing the complex possibilities beyond the dialectical perspective, and integrate nontraditional organizations as legitimate sites of gender performance and organization sexuality. Moreover, the seemingly problematic nature of sexuality should be embraced as a means of theorizing beyond material and discursive constraints of the organizational workplace.

Finally, even as individuals' understandings of their own and others' sexuality change, the gendered nature of organization and organizing has not. Organizations, occupations, policies, and their processes remain masculine and sexualized such that dominant members exert disproportional power and control, often normalizing violence against women and people of color. Research delving into how sexualities have been erased or desexualized and how violence has been constituted as normative in particular contexts can increase understandings of the complexities of human experience.

In closing, sexuality is a key site for contradiction, ambiguity, and ambivalence; it brings together discursive and material; it highlights embodied nature of human interaction. Sexuality complicates the productivity and reality of the organization, but also multiplies the possibilities for the embodied nature of work and worker identity. These tensions call for greater attention by organizational communication scholars.

Discussion Questions

1. If sexuality in the workplace is seen as problematic, then what does healthy organizational sexuality look like? How can organizations encourage or support (appropriate/healthy) sexuality in the workplace?
2. What about sexuality and talk about sexuality makes you uncomfortable? Why?
3. What would change in the workplace if the ideal worker became constructed as a worker with sexualities and interests other than work and career success?
4. Consider how the #MeToo and "Times Up!" movements conceptualize gender in the workplace and in society. How effective are these broad-based public strategies?

Note

1. "Julianna" (pseudonym) said, "I even had people say how did it happen? . . . I then went on to describe the birds and the bees" and that coworkers "drooled, their mouths hung open. They were aghast because of my very obvious physical handicap that it was even possible for me to be pregnant let alone for them to figure out how it had happened" (Buzzanell 2003: 59).

References

Acker, J. 1990. "Hierarchies, Jobs, Bodies: A Theory of Gendered Organizations," *Gender & Society*, 4, 139–158.
Allen, B. J. 2011. *Difference Matters: Communicating Social Identity* (2nd ed.). Long Grove, IL: Waveland.
Arendt, C. and Buzzanell, P. M. 2017. "Gender Equality in the United States." in Örtenblad, R., Marling, R. and Vasiljević, S. (eds.), *Gender Equality in a Global Perspective*, New York: Routledge, pp. 177–197.

Ashcraft, K. L. 2004. "Gender, Discourse, and Organization: Framing a Shifting Relationship," in Grant, D., Hardy, C., Oswick, C. and Putnam, L. L. (eds.), *Handbook of Organizational Discourse*, London, UK: SAGE, pp. 275–298.

Ashcraft, K. L. and Harris, K. L. 2014. "'Meaning That Matters': An Organizational Communication Perspective on Gender, Discourse, and Materiality," in Kumra, S., Simpson, R. and Burke, R. (eds.), *The Oxford Handbook of Gender in Organizations*, New York: Oxford University Press, pp. 130–150.

Ashcraft, K. L. and Mumby, D. K. 2004. *Reworking Gender: A Feminist Communicology of Organization*, Thousand Oaks, CA: SAGE.

Bargh, J., Raymond, P., Pryor, J. and Strack, F. 1995. "Attractiveness of the Underling: An Automatic Power◊Sex Association and its Consequences for Sexual Harassment and Aggression," *Journal of Personality and Social Psychology*, 68, 768–781.

Blithe, S., Wolfe, A. and Mohr, B. 2019. *Sex and Stigma: Stories of Everyday Life in Nevada's Legal Brothels*. New York: NYU Press.

Brewis, J., Tyler, M. and Mills, A. 2014. "Sexuality and Organizational Analysis—30 Years On: Editorial Introduction," *Organization*, 21, 305–311.

Britton, D. M. 1997. "Gendered Organizational Logic: Policy and Practice in Men's and Women's Prisons," *Gender & Society*, 11, 796–818.

Burrell, G. and Hearn, J. 1989. "The Sexuality of Organization," in Hearn, J., Sheppard, D., Tancred-Sheriff, P. and Burrell, G. (eds.), *The Sexuality of Organization*, London: SAGE, pp. 1–28.

Buzzanell, P. M. (ed.). 2000. *Rethinking Organizational and Managerial Communication from Feminist Perspectives*, Thousand Oaks, CA: SAGE.

Buzzanell, P. M. 2001. "Gendered Practices in the Contemporary Workplace," *Management Communication Quarterly*, 14, 517–537.

Buzzanell, P. M. 2003. "A Feminist Standpoint Analysis of Maternity and Maternity Leave for Women with Disabilities," *Women & Language*, 26(2), 53–65.

Buzzanell, P. M. 2018. "Legitimizing and Transforming the Closet/Closeting," *Management Communication Quarterly*, 32, 297–300.

Cavalcante, A. 2016. "'I Did It All Online:' Transgender Identity and the Management of Everyday Life," *Critical Studies in Media Communication*, 33, 109–122.

Clair, R. P. 1994. "Resistance and Oppression as a Self-Contained Opposite: An Organizational Communication Analysis of One Man's Story of Sexual Harassment." *Western Journal of Communication*, 58, 235–262.

Clair, R. P. 1993. "The Use of Framing Devices to Sequester Organizational Narratives: Hegemony and Harassment," *Communication Monographs*, 60, 113–136.

Compton, C. A. and Dougherty, D. S. 2017. "Organizing Sexuality: Silencing and the Push–Pull Process of Co-Sexuality in the Workplace," *Journal of Communication*, 67, 874–896.

Connell, C. 2010. "Doing, Undoing, or Redoing Gender? Learning from the Workplace Experiences of Transpeople," *Gender & Society*, 24(1), 31–55.

David, M. 2016. *Mama's Gun: Black Maternal Figures and the Politics of Transgression*, Columbus, OH: Ohio University Press.

Dellinger, K. and Williams, C. 1997. "Makeup at Work: Negotiating Appearance Rules in the Workplace," *Gender & Society*, 11, 151–177.

D'Enbeau, S. 2017. "Unpacking the Dimensions of Organizational Tension: The Case of Sexual Violence Response and Prevention among College Students," *Journal of Applied Communication Research*, 45, 237–255.

D'Enbeau, S. and Buzzanell, P. M. 2014. "The Erotic Heroine and the Politics of Gender at Work: A Feminist Reading of *Mad Men*'s Joan Harris," in Jones, N., Bajac Carter, M. and Batchelor, B. (eds.), *Heroines of Film and Television: Portrayals in Popular Culture*, Lanham, MD: Rowan & Littlefield, pp. 3–16.

Dixon, J. 2013. "Uneasy Recreation: "Workplace Social Events as Problematic Sites for Communicating Sexual Orientation," *The Florida Communication Journal*, 63–71.

Dixon, J., and Dougherty, D. S. 2014. "A Language Convergence/Meaning Divergence Analysis Exploring How LGBTQ and Single Employees Manage Traditional Family Expectations in the Workplace," *Journal of Applied Communication Research*, 42, 1–19.

Eger, E. K. 2018. "Transgender Jobseekers Navigating Closeting Communication," *Management Communication Quarterly*, 32, 276–281.

Fotopoulou, A. 2016. "Digital and Networked by Default? Women's Organisations and the Social Imaginary of Networked Feminism," *New Media & Society*, 18, 989–1005.

Harding, T. 2007. "The Construction of Men Who are Nurses as Gay," *Journal of Advanced Nursing*, 60, 636–644.

Harris, K. 2017. "Re-Situating Organizational Knowledge: Violence, Intersectionality and the Privilege of Partial Perspective, *Human Relations*, 70, 263–285.

Hearn, J. and Parkin, W. 1983. "Gender and Organizations: A Selective Review and a Critique of a Neglected Area, *Organization Studies*, 4, 219–242.

Hearn, J. and Parkin, W. 1995. *"Sex" at "Work": The Power and Paradox of Organisation Sexuality* (revised ed.). New York: St. Martin's Press.

Jung, A-K. and O'Brien, K. (2017). "The Profound Influence of Unpaid Work on Women's Lives: An Overview and Future Directions," *The Journal of Career Development*. Advance online publication.

Knight, K. and Wiedmaier, B. 2015. "Emerging Adults' Casual Sexual Involvements and the Ideal Worker Norm," in Martinez, A. R and Miller, L. J. (eds.), *Gender in a Transitional Era*, Lanham, MD: Lexington, pp. 151–165.

Martin, J. 1990. "Deconstructing Organizational Taboos: The Suppression of Gender Conflict in Organizations," *Organization Science*, 1, 339–357.

McDonald, J. 2013. "Coming Out in the Field: A Queer Reflexive Account of Shifting Researcher Identity," *Management Learning*, 44, 127–143.

Miller, S. L., Forest, K. and Jurik, N. 2003. "Diversity in Blue: Lesbian and Gay Police Officers in a Masculine Occupation," *Men and Masculinities*, 5, 355–385.

Muhr, S. L., Sullivan, K. and Rich, C. 2016. "Situated Transgressiveness: Exploring One Transwoman's Lived Experiences Across Three Situated Contexts," *Gender, Work & Organization*, 23, 52–70.

Mumby, D. K. 2005. "Theorizing Resistance in Organization Studies," *Management Communication Quarterly*, 19, 19–44.

Örtenblad, A., Marling, R. and Vasiljević, S. 2017. *Gender Equality in a Global Perspective*, New York: Routledge.

O'Shea, S. C. 2018. "This Girl's Life: An Autoethnography," *Organization*, 25(1), 3–20.

Schilt, K. and Connell, C. 2007. "Do Workplace Gender Transitions Make Gender Trouble?" *Gender, Work and Organization*, 14, 596–618.

Sullivan, K. 2014. With(out) Pleasure: Desexualization, Gender and Sexuality at Work," *Organization*, 21, 346–364.

Stone, P. 2007. *Opting Out? Why Women Really Quit Careers and Head Home*, Los Angeles, CA: University of California Press.

Tracy, S. J. and Scott, C. 2006. "Sexuality, Masculinity, and Taint Management Among Firefighters and Correctional Officers: Getting Down and Dirty with 'America's Heroes' and the 'Scum of Law Enforcement,'," *Management Communication Quarterly*, 20, 6–38.

Trethewey, A. 1999. "Disciplined Bodies: Women's Embodied Identities at Work," *Organization Studies*, 20, 423–450.

Ward, J. and Winstanley, D. 2003. "The Absent Presence: Negative Space within Discourse and the Construction of Minority Sexual Identity in the Workplace," *Human Relations*, 56, 1255–1280.

Williams, C., Giuffre, P. and Dellinger, K. 2009. "The Gay-Friendly Closet," *Sexuality Research & Social Policy*, 6, 29–45.

West, C. and Zimmerman, D.H. 1987. "Doing Gender," *Gender & Society*, 1, 125–151.

Wilhoit, E. 2014. "Opting Out (Without Kids): Understanding Non-Mothers' Workplace Exit in Popular Autobiographies," *Gender, Work & Organization*, 21, 260–272.

8 Difference, Diversity, and Inclusion

Patricia S. Parker and Jamie McDonald

Understanding difference in organizational communication requires attention to both *organizing* and *organization* (Cooren and Fairhurst 2009, Fairhurst and Putnam 2004). As such, we begin this chapter on difference, diversity, and inclusion with stories that show both how difference has mattered in our lives and how difference is a central organizing feature of society, both within and beyond the bounds of organizations. We share our stories in the spirit of critical reflexivity, a complex concept that we see as crucial to all scholarship, regardless of method. From our perspective, to engage in critical reflexivity during the research process entails, at a minimum, thinking critically about why we do the research that we do, how we shape different aspects of the research process, and who stands to gain from this research (Cunliffe 2003).

Although we believe that critical reflexivity is an integral part of the research process, we do not suggest that it requires "coming out" about everything to readers and exposing all of our vulnerabilities (Harris and Fortney 2017). In our cases, the stories that we share show how aspects of our scholarship are informed by many of our personal experiences, but they should not be taken as an exhaustive account of the ways in which our scholarship and personal experiences are intertwined.

Our Stories

Pat's Story[1]

The most important questions about difference, diversity, and inclusion first emerged through my experience with school desegregation in the U.S. Deep South as a third grader. In 1966 I was among several African American students who integrated the Atkins, Arkansas Elementary and Junior High School—the White school. In a plan for gradual integration, a few African American students had enrolled in the high school 2 years earlier, and one of my brothers and two of my sisters had been among them. My memory of the intense emotional climate of that time is firmly entrenched in my mind because of the tragic death of my 16-year-old third cousin who had gone missing on a warm April evening in 1964. My parents and others had gathered at the two-room segregated Black school to discuss the planned integration. There was some controversy in the Black community as to whether it was safe to send the children to the White school. The reports that some White people in the town were vowing that their children "would never attend school with niggers," naturally created uneasiness and apprehension. However, most parents, including my own, felt it imperative to support the planned integration. The meeting was interrupted by someone bringing news that my cousin, Pete, was missing and that his clothes had been discovered on the banks of a nearby pond where he frequently went swimming. It was a White neighbor who used his fishing boat to assist in the search for Pete's body and subsequently dove into the pond to bring his body to shore where his parents, those who had been at the school meeting, and other townsfolk, both Black and White, stood in silent shock. In that moment the community stood together not as people divided by racial politics, but as a community connected at a profound level of humanity, understanding and compassion.

At 5 years old, I was in bed by the time my parents returned home that night. I learned of Pete's death from an older sister who awakened me as she whispered the news through her tears. In my memory of that time, the thoughts of my cousin Pete's untimely and accidental death, and the transition from my neighborhood school to the White School, trigger the same feelings of loss, uncertainty, and apprehension.

Three years later, during my first days at the White school, came the opportunity to begin working through those emotions in context. When someone came to the door of my third-grade classroom, pointing, counting, and announcing to my teacher, "Okay, you have two," I knew they were referring to my Blackness and that of the other African American third-grader in the room. And when my new White friend followed the advice of her old White friend that she shouldn't play with me, it seemed obvious that they, too, were referring to my Blackness. The confusion and hurt I felt in response to those events were real, but yet undefined. Somehow, I sensed at age eight that these (in retrospect) seemingly mundane events were signals for what this strange place represented for me: "outsider, object, Black." Yet those signals stood in such sharp contrast to what I experienced in my own familiar 8-year old world. That world was one in which I had begun to think of my family and my community as a wonderful collection of personalities; where I had come to view myself as "special" as I competed with my 12 brothers and sisters for the attention of my parents and siblings. Most of all, I had come to see life as being filled with hope and infinite possibilities. There was a sense among many of the families in my community that this generation of children would soar to new heights of achievement, and they did everything they could to ensure that their children had educational opportunities, no matter what the sacrifices.

So, in my 8-year-old mind, I had the knowledge of my concrete, lived experience grounded in life with my family and my community. And I had the reality of some intense negative emotional responses I was experiencing as I interacted with the teachers and students at the White school. Those two realities stood in stark contradiction. Out of necessity, I worked through those contradictions by developing a set of premises for which I was the reference point. I began with the answers—I *knew* who I was—the strangers in my new world had to learn who I was; and from their interactions, they obviously did not have a clue. From that personal truth, I developed a posture of perpetual questioning based on the fundamental premise that in experiencing the world, it is possible, and perhaps even probable that a particular social context will be in contradiction to my concrete experience. It is up to me to determine the salience of my concrete experience in the situation. But always, my experience gives me the vision to see the contradiction, the gaps, the unstated assumptions that make a particular social context "work" to fulfill a particular ideology or interest.

It was not until I began my doctoral work, some 20 years later, that I began to understand my early schooling and subsequent experiences within predominantly White Colleges and Universities in terms of post-modern and poststructural philosophies (Deleuze and Guattari 1987, Foucault 1995), critical organizational communication theories (Deetz 1982), and Black feminisms (Allen 1996, Collins 1991, Crenshaw 1989). These lenses helped me to understand those institutions and the larger communication landscape not as gender and race neutral, but as interactive spaces shaped by gendered, raced, and classed discourses (Parker 2005). I became interested in unmasking the negotiated organizational spaces where the structure of opportunity for everyone, including Black girls and women, is enacted in the everyday conversations among its participants (Parker 2003). I argued that in the case of African American women, these discourses are part of the larger racial, gender, and class politics informed by the reproduction of negative stereotyping of African American women in literature and film, the news media, and television "reality" shows and sitcoms (Parker 2005). These negative stereotypes inform discursive frames that influence perceptions of African American women in everyday interactions, for example, in the academy, such as those that occur among faculty, students, and administrators, in classrooms, meeting rooms, and informal interactions. It is in the context of these everyday communicative encounters, informed by an analysis of how discursive power circulates throughout them, that the potential for transformation is palpable.

From my perspective, the aim of organizational communication scholarship on difference, diversity, and inclusion is not to provide a prescription for how to navigate particular contexts, but to unmask the ways in which the politics of race, gender, class, sexuality, and other discursive frames alternate as figure and ground in everyday social encounters. It is an unending process that, for me, is a project aimed at creating opportunities for people across contexts to see their accountability for creating a society grounded in commitments to fairness, democracy, equity and inclusion (Parker 2014, Parker et al. 2017).

Jamie's Story

My first experiences with difference, diversity, and inclusion took place in a very different setting than Pat's. Whereas Pat's story shows how race was a painfully salient aspect of growing up in the Deep South during the era of desegregation, this was not the case in the small Canadian town where I grew up, where there was little in the way of any type of diversity. In fact, the first time I was ever asked to reflect on my race was when I was 20 years old at a happy hour organized by my student association in Montréal.

"De quelle race es-tu?" a fellow student asked me. Translation: "What race are you?"

I will always remember the shock I felt when I was asked that question so nonchalantly. Interestingly, I felt then—and still do—that her question was more directed at my cultural identity than my racial identity, as we both appeared to be what would be considered "White". But at that point in my life I had never thought of myself as White—or even as having a race at all. To talk about race, I thought at the time, was racist. That was before I had learned of whiteness studies and the problematic assumptions underlying those thoughts (Ashcraft and Allen 2003).

Instead of answering her question by referring to my racial phenotype, I explained my cultural identities and upbringing: that I grew up in a small town in southwestern Ontario, Canada; that I have a French-Canadian mother from Québec and an English-Canadian father from Ontario; and that I identify with Québécois culture.

The question about race marked me as "different" and shows that my Québécois identity is not taken for granted; rather, it is something that must be accomplished through communication. It is also something that can be—and has been—contested by others. Does the fact that my mother was born in Québec, that I lived there for many years, that I'm close to my extended Québécois family, and that I identify with Québécois culture even as I now live in Texas mean that I can legitimately claim a Québécois cultural identity? Some believe so. But can I really be Québécois if only one of my parents is French-Canadian and I don't have what would be considered a typical Québécois accent when I speak French? Others don't believe so, as I am not what some call "Québécois de souche"; that is, "pure blood Québécois". As we see here, the question of who is and can be "Québécois" is inherently political and subjective, as is the question of who is or can be considered to be "White".

A few years after the incident at the happy hour, pursuing my master's degree in Communication at the Université de Montréal and my doctoral degree at the University of Colorado Boulder provided me with theoretical lenses that have helped me make sense of that experience and many others. In particular, postmodern conceptions of identity have helped me better understand the ways in which my cultural identities are fleeting, fragmented, and contested. I was also drawn very much to queer theory, which we discuss later in this chapter, because of how it resonates with the ways in which I've experienced my gender and sexual identities. For instance, I rarely see myself represented in generalized claims about "men," and have thus sought to deconstruct such claims through the lens of queer theory in some of my work (McDonald 2016). Moreover, queer theory has helped me better understand the fluid and shifting nature of my sexual identity over the course of my life, which I have written about in what started as a comprehensive exam question and culminated in an award-winning article in *Management Learning* (McDonald 2013).

Further engagement with queer theory has recently led me to problematizing the closet (Harris and McDonald 2018), a concept that has been central to my life and that we also elaborate on later in this chapter. For me, the closet has been experienced in relation to a whole host of identities and experiences. In regard to sexuality, I have experienced the closet as both someone who identifies as gay and as someone who has identified as straight. That is, there are times when I have been presumed by others to be gay when I really identified as straight and other times where I have been presumed to be straight when I actually identified as gay. Moreover, as a Canadian who now lives in the U.S. and who speaks English with an accent that is commonly interpreted as American, I have experienced the closet in relation to both my national identity and the multiple visa statuses that I held before being granted legal permanent residency in 2017. This has forced me to negotiate when, how, and if to come out as an immigrant in certain interactions, such as during job interviews or when people come to my door and ask if I would like to register to vote.

Ultimately, what I have learned from understanding my own experiences through the lens of queer theory over the years is that difference matters in ways that stable identity categories cannot always explain. This realization is what led me to develop an anti-categorical approach to difference that is rooted in queer theory (McDonald 2015). Importantly, this approach to difference is political in that it explicitly challenges the normative discourses that construct certain forms of difference as the taken-for-granted norm and anything else as deviant. My hope is that as we continue to interrogate and disrupt these normative discourses, we can work towards building organizations that are inclusive of difference in all of its forms.

Tracing the Historical Trajectory of Difference Scholarship

The stories of our personal routes to difference studies are, in some ways, revealing of the historical trajectory of difference scholarship in organizational communication studies. Our stories are a reflection of our positionalities as scholars from marginalized identity groups and they are also instructive for what they reveal about the field via the lens of the intergenerational span of our respective careers. The self-identified indigenous scholar Linda Tuhwai Smith (1999, 2007) has written extensively about the urgent and unsettled questions that indigenous scholars encounter in the academy, such as feeling the need to write in a way that is informed by, and informing of, indigenous experiences, and yet having to face resistance to advance such scholarship. Jamie, as an early career scholar, is writing at a time when critical scholarship on race, queer theory, and decolonizing methodologies are well on their way to becoming part of the mainstream in our field. On the other hand, Pat entered the field at a time when these were areas that represented "new ground." Yet, she was bolstered by the work of scholars such as Brenda J. Allen in organizational communication and Ella Bell and Stella Nkomo in management studies who were leading the way forward with groundbreaking research published in mainstream journals (Allen 1996, Bell 1990, Nkomo 1992). This in turn influenced other scholars, eventually creating a space for more groundbreaking work.

In the sections that follow, as we trace the historical trajectory of scholarship in this area, we invite you to imagine choice points where the work of difference, diversity, and inclusion might have followed an alternative trajectory, as well as places where we might begin to write-back to that history in transformative ways.

Functionalist Origins

During the first decades of the 20th century, the field of organizational communication emerged as a robust area of social science research. Influenced by advances in cognate fields of management and industrial psychology, the study of "difference" in those early days focused on the managerial control of difference and was unquestioning about the nomenclature and assumptions of positivism (Tompkins and Wanca-Thibault 2001). Consistent with variable-analytic and functionalist approaches, the focus was almost always reliant upon "an objective means of measuring the operation and consequences of an organizational communication system" (Tompkins 1967: 17–18). What is advanced in the early era of the field is an understanding of difference as an enduring feature of organizational life, but with an emphasis on managerial control and reification of the status quo. The primary concerns were with worker productivity, motivation, and processes that contributed to the smooth flow of workplace operations and the erasure of difference that might impede those operations. Noticeably missing was a critical analysis of how power circulates via communicative processes to produce, sustain, and transform difference.

The Interpretive and Critical Turns

As discussed in earlier chapters, the field of organizational communication went through an interpretive turn in the 1980s, which broke with earlier functionalist approaches and spurred research that focused on the communicative processes through which organizational actors create meanings, cultures, and identities (Putnam and Pacanowsky 1983). By the early 1990s, the field was also going through a critical turn with increased scholarship devoted to explaining how power dynamics shape meanings, cultures, identities, and other organizational phenomena (Deetz 1992, Mumby 1993). With the interpretive and critical turns in the field, research on difference, diversity, and inclusion progressed from early top-down functionalist approaches to the current focus on bottom-up and emergent interpretive/critical/materialist frameworks (for a comprehensive review, see Parker et al. 2017). As such, key theoretical frameworks and questions guiding current issues now focus on how power circulates via communicative processes to produce, sustain, and transform difference. Within these frameworks, difference is conceptualized as a social construction that refers to how individuals differ from each other in socially significant ways, including along the lines of gender, race, class, sexuality, and ability (Allen 2011, McDonald 2015).

The turn to the field's current focus on how power relations are embedded into difference has laid the groundwork for advancing more complex approaches that make visible the multiple and interlocking systems of political, social, and cultural making. These approaches are in line with the principles of intersectionality, a concept originally developed by legal scholar Kimberlé Crenshaw (1991) to refer to the ways in which multiple forms of oppression are experienced simultaneously rather than independently. In particular, she pointed to a case in which women of color were simultaneously discriminated against on the basis of both gender and racial oppression. In this case, the experiences of these women were shaped not by gender or race alone, but by both at the same time, and thus at the intersection of both gender and race. Although Crenshaw (1991) focused on the intersections of gender and race in her original articulation of the concept, she also noted the importance of referring to additional intersections that highlight discrimination on the basis of multiple forms of difference. In this regard, Holvino (2010) suggests that intersectional research should simultaneously attend to intersections related to gender, race, class, sexuality, and nation. Importantly, she also posits that studies of intersectionality should attend to how intersections of difference simultaneously shape both everyday organizational interactions and broader structures and ideologies. However, one of the challenges of adopting intersectional frameworks in empirical studies continues to be foregrounding particular identities and shared experiences without essentializing them and thereby negating the complexities and nuances of the intersections at stake (Harris 2015, McDonald 2015, Parker 2014).

Feminist frameworks have been central to advancing the study of difference through the lens of intersectionality. Critical/interpretive and postmodern/poststructural feminist research about difference, diversity, and inclusion focuses on communicative practices that help to construct knowledge about dominant conceptions related to difference, as well as organizational actors' diverse identities. Feminist scholarship following critical/interpretive approaches has been fundamental to studies of communicating difference and organizing. Importantly, feminists of color have critiqued the narrow focus on gender as a broad category of difference, championing intersectionality and calling on scholars to examine additional constructions (Parker and Ogilvie 1996). Allen's (1996, 1998, 2011) work in this area, which draws from feminist standpoint theory and Black feminist thought, has been particularly influential in fostering research that examines how multiple forms of difference "matter"; that is, how they act as figure and ground to influence everyday communicative experiences. Indeed, race was largely absent in organizational communication scholarship prior to her work that showed how existing research was limited by its neglect of race (Allen 1996, 1998, 2000). By neglecting race, prior scholarship had problematically assumed whiteness as an unspoken, invisible, and universal norm—a phenomenon vividly documented in Ashcraft and Allen's (2003) critical analysis of major organizational communication textbooks at the time.

Postmodern/poststructuralist feminist studies in organizational communication conceptualize gender as fluid, contingent upon dominant belief systems, sometimes contradictory, and related to current dominant constructions of femininity and masculinity (Mumby 1996). Thus, rather than viewing gender and difference as stable, binary categories, postmodern/poststructural approaches deconstruct the very notion of categories of difference (McDonald 2015). Through this deconstruction, postmodern/poststructuralist feminist studies examine how we come to *appear* different—despite the arbitrariness of identity categories and the meanings embedded into them (Ashcraft 2014). Some postmodern/poststructuralist feminist research about power and discourse also explores dialectical relationships between control and resistance to illustrate complexities of identity constructions and interactions.

Recent Developments

Today, difference scholarship is flourishing in organizational communication. Over the past decade, the field has seen the publication of several books devoted to difference and organizing (e.g. Allen 2011, Mumby 2011b), as well as the first chapter devoted to difference and organizing in an organizational communication handbook (Parker 2014). Moreover, difference scholarship continues to populate the field's most esteemed disciplinary and interdisciplinary journals (Alvarez et al. 2015, Compton and Dougherty 2017, Eger 2018, Harris 2013, 2017, McDonald 2015, Mease 2016). While a comprehensive review of this research is outside of the purview of this chapter, we note a common trend in these studies: a constitutive view of communication. That is, communication is increasingly viewed as constituting both difference and work itself.

Viewing communication as constitutive of both difference *and* work enables us to examine the how particular meanings of difference are intertwined with meanings of work. In this regard, Ashcraft (2011) has argued that work is understood and known through difference; that is, through the gendered and raced bodies with which certain types of work are associated. Rather than focusing on questions of difference *at* work, she offers an alternative question for difference scholars to explore: "How does difference play into the organization of work in the first place?" (Ashcraft 2011: 8). This question presupposes that difference is a constitutive feature of organizing and that organizing processes cannot be fully understood without attending to difference (Mumby 2011a).

In order to theorize difference as a constitutive feature of work and organizing, Ashcraft (2013) has proposed the metaphor of the glass slipper. Just as slippers are made for particular feet but not others, she argues that work is—strategically and discursively—made for people who embody particular configurations of difference. For instance, a wealth of interdisciplinary research has shown how certain jobs (e.g. accountants, pilots, doctors) have historically been cast as within the purview of particular groups of people (e.g. White men) and outside of the purview of others (e.g. women and people of color) in order for the practitioners of these occupations to make claims regarding the value and importance of their work (Ashcraft 2007, Ashcraft and Mumby 2004, Ensmenger 2010, Kerfoot 2002, Kirkham and Loft 1993, Witz 1992). Investigating discourses about work, occupations, and difference thus enables us to examine how certain lines of work become associated with particular bodies, as well as how organizations may seek to challenge these discourses by branding currently segregated occupations (e.g. computing and information technology) as inclusive and diverse (McDonald and Kuhn 2016).

Underexplored Frameworks and Future Directions

Looking forward, we offer the following future directions for difference scholarship in organizational communication: (1) examining underexplored intersections of difference; (2) exploring the closet metaphor; and (3) engaging more with underexplored and nontraditional theoretical frameworks, such as queer theory and postcolonial theory.

Examining Underexplored Intersections of Difference

One way of advancing difference scholarship is examining intersections of difference that have received less attention to date. Although intersectionality has long been recognized as a framework to examine the interlocking nature of multiple forms of difference, most existing empirical research that attends to intersectionality has foregrounded the intersections of gender and race (McDonald 2015). Given that gender and race are intertwined with extremely powerful systems of domination (Allen 2007), future difference research must continue to attend to these dynamics. However, there are many socially significant forms of difference that intersect with gender and race and that organizational communication researchers have been slow to explore, including, but not limited to, class, disability, nationality, citizenship status, and native language. By foregrounding these additional intersections of difference and more, we will be able to better understand the complexities and nuances of the ways in which difference shapes organizational experiences and is related to systems of privilege, domination, and oppression—which is a crucial step towards building more inclusive organizations that break down these systems.

Exploring the Closet Metaphor

Recently, organizational communication researchers have begun to explore difference through the metaphor of the closet. Although the closet is most often associated with the concealing of nonnormative sexual identities, Harris and McDonald (2018) have suggested that it can be extended to all invisible forms of difference that are subject to stigma and that require confirmation to be revealed. For instance, a special forum in *Management Communication Quarterly* on "Queering the Closet at Work" has shown how the closet metaphor can shed light on a multitude of forms of difference that shape organizational experiences and are intertwined with power and privilege, including nonnormative family structures and relationship orientations (Dixon 2018), gender identities (Eger 2018), communities of origin (Ferguson 2018), citizenship statuses (McDonald 2018), and lifestyle and health choices (Romo 2018). In this sense, the closet can draw our attention to intersections of difference that have traditionally been unexplored.

Examining the closet is consistent with the performative approach to difference that is espoused by queer theory, which we discuss in the following section.

Engaging with Queer Theory

Queer theory is a dynamic and heterogeneous body of thought that has a strong presence in communication studies but that has only recently begun to be explored by scholars of organizational communication (Harris and McDonald 2018). Drawing heavily from the work of scholars such as Judith Butler (1990), Eve Sedgwick (1990), and Michael Warner (1999), queer theory conceptualizes difference in a fluid way and as it relates to the broad concept of (hetero)normativity. As such, rather than take the existence of identity categories such as gender and sexuality for granted, queer theory examines the normative processes through which such categories are constituted. In this regard, Butler's notion of gender performativity suggests that identity categories come into existence through the performative reenactment of the normative practices associated with particular identities such as "women" and "gay" (Butler 1990). Rather than basing political claims on categories of difference, queer theory also espouses an antinormative political stance; that is, a politics of absolute recognition and celebration of difference in all of its forms (Cohen 2005, Parker 2001).

There are many ways in which queer theory can help extend difference research in organizational communication. By adopting a queer theoretical framework, we can attend to the ways in which organizations are not only inequality regimes (e.g. Acker 2006) but also normative regimes that seek to suppress difference and assimilate members into organizational cultures (Lee et al. 2008, McDonald 2015). Queer theory's anti-categorical stance toward difference and intersectionality enables us to examine intersections of difference beyond traditional categories, and thus identify coalitions between people who are very different from each other, but who share the position of being cast as nonnormative in some way (Cohen 2005, McDonald 2015).

Engaging with Postcolonial Theory

In addition to queer theory, postcolonial theory offers a helpful framework that organizational communication scholars can further explore to examine relations of difference. Although a significant body of postcolonial scholarship can be found in management and organization studies circles, organizational communication has been slower to engage with this framework (Broadfoot and Munshi 2014).

Postcolonial theory refers to a broad, heterogeneous, and interdisciplinary body of thought that is associated with the work of scholars such as Franz Fanon (1967), Edward Said (1978, 1993), and Gayatri Spivak (1988, 1999). Postcolonial scholarship is primarily concerned with examining the ways in which macro structures of power and domination that arise from historical and geopolitical arrangements shape contemporary social relations and knowledge production (Shome and Hegde 2002). An important goal of postcolonial scholarship is to debunk Western-centric assumptions and seek social change by "challenging universalization, invoking local specificities, and problematizing the politics of knowledge production" (Pal and Buzzanell 2013: 216). Similarly, Grimes and Parker (2009) call for decolonizing organizational communication as a priority for the field.

Broadfoot and Munshi (2007) have drawn from postcolonial theory to critique the field's tendencies to rely on Eurocentric constructions, as well as the unquestioned sovereignty of Western logics in research and other disciplinary practices. They suggest that postcolonial approaches can enable organizational communication scholars to challenge the U.S. centrism and insularism of much of the field's scholarship. They identify three commitments of postcolonial organizational scholarship, each of which has a deconstructive element that challenges dominant understandings and a reconstructive element that offers new possibilities (Broadfoot and Munshi 2014).

The first postcolonial commitment is to disrupt and reimagine organizing space(s). In this regard, Broadfoot and Munshi (2014) suggest that organizational communication research has largely been confined to North American contexts and Western theoretical frameworks, as if North American organizations and Western thought represented some type of universal norm. Adopting a postcolonial theoretical stance entails examining organizing outside of hegemonic Western contexts, such as Indian call centers (Pal and Buzzanell 2008, 2013) and grassroots organizations in postconflict Liberia (Cruz 2014, 2015, 2017b). Moreover, Grimes and Parker (2009) call for scholars to focus on organizational communication as a "decolonizing project" and, as such, suggest that listening to and sharing the stories of those who are marginalized and colonized within the U.S.-European center is consistent with postcolonial work.

The second postcolonial commitment that Broadfoot and Munshi (2014) identify is resisting colonial discourse and rethinking organizing practices. As such, postcolonial work enables us to identify the Western-centric assumptions that are embedded into scholarship on topics such as career success (Hanchey and Berkelaar 2015), dirty work (Cruz 2015), and resistance (Pal and Buzzanell 2013), as well as to advance alternative understandings of these phenomena.

Lastly, Broadfoot and Munshi (2014) suggest that conducting postcolonial scholarship requires a commitment to questioning the dominant means through which we organize knowledge, and being open to alternative ways of representing knowledge. In this regard, Cruz's (2017a) poetic account of the experiences of her multiple identities—Brown, immigrant, female, and professor—offers an exemplar of how it is possible to present scholarly knowledge in nontraditional ways.

Practical Applications

Difference, diversity, and inclusion are topics that matter to everyone. As Buzzanell (Buzzanell 2018: 298) wrote in response to the recent *Management Communication Quarterly* forum on the closet, "the realization that everyone at some point in the lifespan might engage in closeting because of some non-normative characteristic, identity, or behavior makes this Forum applicable to all." Moreover, U.S. workplaces have never been so diverse and they are poised to continue to become even more so over the next several decades (Lieber 2008). Given this context, organizational communication scholarship on difference, diversity, and inclusion has important implications for practice. Indeed, we believe that one of the main goals of scholarship in this area should be to help ensure that as organizations become more diverse, they also become more inclusive of difference.

When considering the practical applications of research on difference, diversity, and inclusion, it is important to note that the word *diversity* has increasingly taken on a functionalist and managerial connotation, as is especially evident in discourse on "diversity management" (Tomlinson and Schwabenland 2010). In diversity management discourse, the words *equality* and *inclusion* seldom appear, as the focus is not explicitly on fostering greater equality or inclusion. Rather, the focus is on recognizing and valuing diversity for the avowed purpose of improving organizational performance and helping organizations become more competitive (Noon 2007, Özbilgin and Tatli 2011). This philosophy, commonly referred to as "the business case for diversity," has been critiqued on numerous grounds. For instance, emphasizing diversity can cause the goals of equality and inclusion to become overlooked since the term diversity does not necessarily invoke a commitment to action for social justice (Ahmed 2007). Moreover, Noon (2007) argues that the business case is fatally flawed because it could be interpreted as implying that if it were profitable, discrimination could be justified on economic grounds. Furthermore, he argues that the business case for diversity views diverse bodies as mere resources that can be used to achieve organizational ends, thereby circumventing what Kalonaityte (2010: 33) calls "the ethical and human side of workplace diversity."

Although we critique the business case for diversity for the reasons listed previously, research on diversity consultants has shown that it may not be advisable to dismiss it altogether. For instance, Mease (2016: 64) argues that tensions between business case arguments and equality arguments are a "constitutive feature of diversity work" that diversity consultants negotiate in everyday interactions. In line with this claim, Ahmed's (2007) study of diversity consultants at Australian universities demonstrates that either business case or equality arguments can be used strategically depending upon the audience and context. Drawing from her work, we suggest that what is most important is that either business case or equality arguments are used reflexively by diversity consultants and other organizational members. That is, it is crucial to reflect on why particular types of arguments are being used, why they are being made, what political implications they have, and who stands to benefit from any given diversity initiative.

Another important tension that is constitutive of the work of diversity consultants consists in operationalizing diversity; that is, "delineating what groups diversity work should focus on" (Mease 2016: 68). This tension becomes particularly visible when diversity work is viewed through the lens of queer theory (Bendl et al. 2008, Bendl and Hofmann 2015). From this perspective, diversity management discourse does not just represent subjects, but actively constitutes them by hailing particular individuals as the "subjects of diversity" (Just and Christiansen 2012: 321). Thus, diversity management discourse functions to mark certain subjects as diverse and "different" from the norm, which inadvertently reifies the normative subject against which the diverse subject is cast (Bendl et al. 2008). Moreover, diversity management discourse can reify binary and stable notions of identity by assuming inherent differences between the social groups that are delineated. As such, diverse subjects can become tokens that are expected to represent the entire group to which they are hailed as belonging, whereas normative subjects are seen as representing only themselves (Gist and Hode 2017). We thus believe that diversity consultants must be reflexive about the political implications of casting certain groups within the purview of diversity management. Drawing from Just and Christiansen (2012: 331), we also suggest that diversity management discourse should "address the subjects of diversity in ways that are less productive of closure" and invite individuals to enact difference in ways that do not conform to preexisting stereotypes.

As a final practical application, we invite readers to imagine what an ideal workplace would look like for everyone. Buzzanell (2018: 298) offers this depiction of the ideal workplace, which we find particularly compelling: "A workplace in which people can be authentic about identities and behaviors important to them and/or the group to which they identify as members." We would add that the ideal workplace would be a participative space, where people throughout the organization are attuned to how power circulates to create inequities with regard to difference. Pat has coined the term *intersectional leadership* to describe critically self-reflexive organizational members, who develop the capacity to "see" inequitably derived difference and create innovative and adaptive ways of organizing for equity and inclusion (Parker 2017).

Ideal workplaces like the one we have imagined do not just naturally exist. Indeed, all organizations are communicated into existence and (re)constituted through everyday communication practices (Brummans et al. 2014). As such, we challenge us all to communicate in ways that create organizations—including our own academic departments—that invite inclusiveness, openness, difference, and compassion.

Discussion Questions

1. What are your philosophical assumptions about difference? To what extent should categories of difference be taken-for-granted or viewed as discursive constructions?
2. What are the challenges of operationalizing intersectionality in empirical studies? What are some ways to address these challenges?
3. What is your take on the so-called "business case for diversity"? How can the business case for diversity be reconciled with commitments to equality, inclusion, and social justice?
4. How can organizational communication research on difference, diversity, and inclusion help us build more just and equitable organizations?
5. What does the ideal workplace look like to you? What are the challenges of creating this ideal workplace and what communication practices could help create it?

Note

1. A version of this story appears in: Parker, P. S. 2009. ""Always at Risk?: African American Women Faculty, Graduate Students, and Undergraduates,"" in Cleveland, D. (Ed.), *When Minorities Are Strongly Encouraged to Apply: Diversity and Affirmative Action in Higher Education*, New York, NY: Peter Lang, pp. 119–134.

References

Acker, J. 2006. "Inequality Regimes: Gender, Class, and Race in Organizations," *Gender & Society*, 20, 441–464.

Ahmed, S. 2007. "The Language of Diversity," *Ethnic and Racial Studies*, 30, 235–256.

Allen, B. J. 1996. "Feminist Standpoint Theory: A Black Woman's (Re)View of Organizational Socialization," *Communication Studies*, 47, 257–271.

Allen, B. J. 1998. "Black Womanhood and Feminist Standpoints," *Management Communication Quarterly*, 11, 575–586.

Allen, B. J. 2000. " 'Learning the Ropes': A Black Feminist Standpoint Analysis," in Buzzanell, P. M. (ed.) *Rethinking Organizational and Managerial Communication from Feminist Perspectives*, Thousand Oaks, CA: SAGE, pp. 177–208.

Allen, B. J. 2007. "Theorizing Race and Communication," *Communication Monographs*, 74, 259–264.

Allen, B. J. 2011. *Difference Matters: Communicating Social Identity*, Long Grove, IL: Waveland.

Alvarez, W., Bauer, J. C. and Eger, E. K. 2015. "(Making a) Difference in the Organizational Communication Undergraduate Course," *Management Communication Quarterly*, 29, 302–308.

Ashcraft, K. L. 2007. "Appreciating the 'Work' of Discourse: Occupational Identity and Difference as Organizing Mechanisms in the Case of Commercial Airline Pilots," *Discourse & Communication*, 1, 9–36.

Ashcraft, K. L. 2011. "Knowing Work through the Communication of Difference: A Revised Agenda for Difference Studies," in Mumby, D. K. (ed.), *Reframing Difference in Organizational Communication Studies: Research, Pedagogy, Practice*, Thousand Oaks, CA: SAGE, pp. 3–29.

Ashcraft, K. L. 2013. "The Glass Slipper: 'Incorporating' Occupational Identity in Management Studies," *Academy of Management Review*, 38, 6–31.

Ashcraft, K. L. 2014. "Feminist Theory," in Putnam, L. L. and Mumby, D. K. (eds.), *The SAGE Handbook of Organizational Communication: Advances in Theory, Research, and Methods*, Thousand Oaks, CA: SAGE, pp. 127–150.

Ashcraft, K. L. and Allen, B. J. 2003. "The Racial Foundation of Organizational Communication," *Communication Theory*, 13, 5–38.

Ashcraft, K. L. and Mumby, D. K. 2004. *Reworking Gender: A Feminist Communicology of Organization*, Thousand Oaks, CA: SAGE.

Bell, E. L. 1990. "The Bicultural Life Experience of Career-Oriented Black Women," *Journal of Organizational Behavior*, 11, 459–477.

Bendl, R., Fleischmann, A. and Walenta, C. 2008. "Diversity Management Discourse Meets Queer Theory," *Gender in Management*, 23, 382–394.

Bendl, R. and Hofmann, R. 2015. "Queer Perspectives Fuelling Diversity Management Discourse: Theoretical and Empirical-Based Reflections," in Bendl, R., Bleijenbergh, I., Henttonen, E. and Mills, A. J. (eds.), *The Oxford Handbook of Diversity in Organizations*, Oxford, UK: Oxford University Press, pp. 195–217.

Broadfoot, K. J. and Munshi, D. 2007. "Diverse Voices and Alternative Rationalities: Imagining Forms of Postcolonial Organizational Communication," *Management Communication Quarterly*, 21, 249–267.

Broadfoot, K. J. and Munshi, D. 2014. "Postcolonial Approaches," in Putnam, L. L. and Mumby, D. K. (eds.), *The SAGE Handbook of Organizational Communication: Advances in Theory, Research, and Methods*, Thousand Oaks, CA: SAGE, pp. 151–172.

Brummans, B. H. J. M., Cooren, F., Robichaud, D. and Taylor, J. R. 2014. "Approaches to the Communicative Constitution of Organizations," in Putnam, L. L. and Mumby, D. K. (eds.), *The SAGE Handbook of Organizational Communication: Advances in Theory, Research, and Methods*, Thousand Oaks, CA: SAGE, pp. 173–194.

Butler, J. 1990. *Gender Trouble: Feminism and the Subversion of Identity*, New York: Routledge.

Buzzanell, P. M. 2018. "Legitimizing and Transforming the Closet/Closeting," *Management Communication Quarterly*, 32, 297–300.

Cohen, C. J. 2005. "Punks, Bulldaggers, and Welfare Queens: The Radical Potential of Queer Politics?," in Johnson, E. P. and Henderon, M. G. (eds.), *Black Queer Studies: A Critical Anthology*, Durham, NC: Duke University Press, pp. 21–51.

Collins, P. H. 1991. *Black Feminist Thought: Knowledge, Consciousness, and the Politics of Empowerment*, New York: Routledge.

Compton, C. A. and Dougherty, D. S. 2017. "Organizing Sexuality: Silencing and the Push–Pull Process of Co-Sexuality in the Workplace," *Journal of Communication, 67,* 874–896.

Cooren, F. and Fairhurst, G. T. 2009. "Dislocation and Stabilization: How to Scale up from Interactions to Organizations," in Putnam, L. L. and Fairhurst, G. T. (eds.), *Building Theories of Organization: The Constitutive Role of Communication,* New York: Routledge, pp. 117–152.

Crenshaw, K. W. 1989. "Demarginalizing the Intersection of Race and Sex: A Black Feminist Critique of Antidiscrimination Doctrine, Feminist Theory and Antiracist Politics," *University of Chicago Legal Forum,* 139–167.

Crenshaw, K. W. 1991. "Mapping the Margins: Intersectionality, Identity Politics, and Violence against Women of Color," *Stanford Law Review, 43,* 1241–1299.

Cruz, J. M. 2014. "Memories of Trauma and Organizing: Market Women's Susu Groups in Postconflict Liberia," *Organization, 21,* 447–462.

Cruz, J. M. 2015. "Dirty Work at the Intersections of Gender, Class, and Nation: Liberian Market Women in Post-Conflict Times," *Women's Studies in Communication, 38,* 421–439.

Cruz, J. M. 2017a. "Brown Body of Knowledge: A Tale of Erasure," *Cultural Studies ↔ Critical Methodologies, 18.*

Cruz, J. M. 2017b. "Invisibility and Visibility in Alternative Organizing: A Communicative and Cultural Model," *Management Communication Quarterly, 31,* 614–639.

Cunliffe, A. L. 2003. "Reflexive Inquiry in Organizational Research: Questions and Possibilities," *Human Relations, 56,* 983–1003.

Deetz, S. A. 1982. "Critical Interpretive Research in Organizational Communication," *Western Journal of Speech Communication, 46,* 131–149.

Deetz, S. A. 1992. *Democracy in an Age of Corporate Colonization: Developments in Communication and the Politics of Everyday Life,* Albany, NY: State University of New York.

Deleuze, G. and Guattari, F. l. 1987. *A Thousand Plateaus: Capitalism and Schizophrenia,* Minneapolis, MN: University of Minnesota Press.

Dixon, J. 2018. "Looking Out from the Family Closet: Discourse Dependence and Queer Family Identity in Workplace Conversation," *Management Communication Quarterly, 32,* 271–275.

Eger, E. K. 2018. "Transgender Jobseekers Navigating Closeting Communication," *Management Communication Quarterly, 32,* 276–281.

Ensmenger, N. L. 2010. "Making Programming Masculine," in Misa, T. J. (ed.), *Gender Codes: Why Women Are Leaving Computing,* Hoboken, NJ: Wiley, pp. 115–141.

Fairhurst, G. T. and Putnam, L. L. 2004. "Organizations as Discursive Constructions," *Communication Theory, 14,* 5–26.

Fanon, F. 1967. *Black Skin, White Masks,* New York: Grove Press.

Ferguson, M. W. 2018. "(Re)Negotiating Organizational Socialization: Black Male Scholarship and the Closet," *Management Communication Quarterly, 32,* 282–286.

Foucault, M. 1995. *Discipline and Punish: The Birth of the Prison,* New York: Vintage.

Gist, A. N. and Hode, M. G. 2017. "Race and Organizing," in Lewis, L. K. and Scott, C. R. (eds.), *International Encyclopedia of Organizational Communication,* Malden, MA: Wiley-Blackwell.

Grimes, D. S. and Parker, P. S. 2009. "Imagining Organizational Communication as a Decolonizing Project: In Conversation with Broadfoot, Munshi, Mumby, and Stohl " *Management Communication Quarterly, 22,* 502–511.

Hanchey, J. N. and Berkelaar, B. L. 2015. "Context Matters: Examining Discourses of Career Success in Tanzania," *Management Communication Quarterly, 29,* 411–439.

Harris, K. L. 2013. "Show Them a Good Time: Organizing the Intersections of Sexual Violence," *Management Communication Quarterly, 27,* 568–595.

Harris, K. L. 2015. "Reflexive Voicing: A Communicative Approach to Intersectional Writing," *Qualitative Research, 16,* 111–127.

Harris, K. L. 2017. "Re-Situating Organizational Knowledge: Violence, Intersectionality and the Privilege of Partial Perspective," *Human Relations, 70,* 263–285.

Harris, K. L. and Fortney, J. M. 2017. "Performing Reflexive Caring: Rethinking Reflexivity through Trauma and Disability," *Text and Performance Quarterly, 37,* 20–34.

Harris, K. L. and McDonald, J. 2018. "Introduction: Queering the 'Closet' at Work," *Management Communication Quarterly, 32,* 265–270.

Holvino, E. 2010. "Intersections: The Simultaneity of Race, Gender and Class in Organization Studies," *Gender, Work & Organization, 17,* 248–277.

Just, S. N. and Christiansen, T. J. 2012. "Doing Diversity: Text-Audience Agency and Rhetorical Alternatives," *Communication Theory, 22,* 319–337.

Kalonaityte, V. 2010. "The Case of Vanishing Borders: Theorizing Diversity Management as Internal Border Control," *Organization, 17,* 31–52.

Kerfoot, D. 2002. "Managing the 'Professional' Man," in Dent, M. and Whitehead, S. M. (eds.), *Managing Professional Identities: Knowledge, Performativity and the 'New' Professional,* London: Routledge, pp. 81–95.

Kirkham, L. M. and Loft, A. 1993. "Gender and the Construction of the Professional Accountant," *Accounting, Organizations and Society, 18,* 507–558.

Lee, H., Learmonth, M. and Harding, N. 2008. "Queer(Y)Ing Public Administration," *Public Administration, 86,* 149–167.

Lieber, L. 2008. "Changing Demographics Will Require Changing the Way We Do Business," *Employment Relations Today, 35,* 91–96.

McDonald, J. 2013. "Coming out in the Field: A Queer Reflexive Account of Shifting Researcher Identity," *Management Learning, 44,* 127–143.

McDonald, J. 2015. "Organizational Communication Meets Queer Theory: Theorizing Relations of 'Difference' Differently," *Communication Theory, 25,* 310–329.

McDonald, J. 2016. "Expanding Queer Reflexivity: The Closet as a Guiding Metaphor for Reflexive Practice," *Management Learning, 47,* 391–406.

McDonald, J. 2018. "Negotiating the "Closet" in U.S. Academia: Foreign Scholars on the Job Market," *Management Communication Quarterly, 32,* 287–291.

McDonald, J. and Kuhn, T. R. 2016. "Occupational Branding for Diversity: Managing Discursive Contradictions," *Journal of Applied Communication Research, 44,* 101–117.

Mease, J. J. 2016. "Embracing Discursive Paradox: Consultants Navigating the Constitutive Tensions of Diversity Work," *Management Communication Quarterly, 30,* 59–83.

Mumby, D. K. 1993. "Critical Organizational Communication Studies: The Next 10 Years," *Communication Monographs*, 60, 18–25.

Mumby, D. K. 1996. "Feminism, Postmodernism, and Organizational Communication Studies: A Critical Reading," *Management Communication Quarterly*, 9, 259–295.

Mumby, D. K. 2011a. "Organizing Difference: An Introduction," in Mumby, D. K. (ed.) *Reframing Difference in Organizational Communication Studies: Research, Pedagogy, Practice*, Thousand Oaks, CA: SAGE, pp. vii–xiii.

Mumby, D. K. (ed.) 2011b. *Reframing Difference in Organizational Communication Studies: Research, Pedagogy, Practice*, Thousand Oaks, CA: SAGE.

Nkomo, S. M. 1992. "The Emperor Has No Clothes: Rewriting "Race in Organizations"," *Academy of Management Review*, 17, 487–513.

Noon, M. 2007. "The Fatal Flaws of Diversity and the Business Case for Ethnic Minorities," *Work, Employment and Society*, 21, 773–784.

Özbilgin, M. and Tatli, A. 2011. "Mapping out the Field of Equality and Diversity: Rise of Individualism and Voluntarism," *Human Relations*, 64, 1229–1253.

Pal, M. and Buzzanell, P. M. 2008. "The Indian Call Center Experience: A Case Study in Changing Discourses of Identity, Identification, and Career in a Global Context," *Journal of Business Communication*, 45, 31–60.

Pal, M. and Buzzanell, P. M. 2013. "Breaking the Myth of Indian Call Centers: A Postcolonial Analysis of Resistance," *Communication Monographs*, 80, 199–219.

Parker, M. 2001. "Fucking Management: Queer, Theory and Reflexivity," *Ephemera*, 1, 36–53.

Parker, P. S. 2003. "Control, Resistance, and Empowerment in Raced, Gendered, and Classed Work Contexts: The Case of African American Women," *Annals of the International Communication Association*, 27, 257–291.

Parker, P. S. 2005. *Race, Gender, and Leadership: Re-Envisioning Organizational Leadership from the Perspectives of African American Women Executives*, Mahwah, NJ: Lawrence Erlbaum.

Parker, P. S. 2014. "Difference and Organizing," in Putnam, L. L. and Mumby, D. K. (eds.), *The SAGE Handbook of Organizational Communication: Advances in Theory, Research, and Methods*, Thousand Oaks, CA: SAGE, pp. 619–643.

Parker, P. S. 2017. "From Managing Diversity to Intersectional Leadership," Paper presented at the annual meeting of the *National Communication Association*, Dallas, TX.

Parker, P. S., Jiang, J., McCluney, C. L. and Rabelo, V. C. 2017. "Race, Gender, Class, and Sexuality," in Nussbaum, J. F. (ed.), *Oxford Research Encyclopedia of Communication*, Oxford, UK: Oxford University Press.

Parker, P. S. and Ogilvie, D. 1996. "Gender, Culture, and Leadership: Toward a Culturally Distinct Model of African-American Women Executives' Leadership Strategies," *The Leadership Quarterly*, 7, 189–214.

Putnam, L. L. and Pacanowsky, M. E. (eds.) 1983. *Communication and Organizations, an Interpretive Approach*, Beverly Hills, CA: SAGE.

Romo, L. K. 2018. "Coming out as a Non-Drinker at Work," *Management Communication Quarterly*, 32, 292–296.

Said, E. W. 1978. *Orientalism*, New York: Vintage Books.

Said, E. W. 1993. *Culture and Imperialism*, New York: Vintage Books.

Sedgwick, E. K. 1990. *Epistemology of the Closet*, Berkeley, CA: University of California Press.

Shome, R. and Hegde, R. S. 2002. "Postcolonial Approaches to Communication: Charting the Terrain, Engaging the Intersections," *Communication Theory*, 12, 249–270.

Smith, L. T. 1999. *Decolonizing Methodologies: Research and Indigenous Peoples*, London: Zed Books.

Smith, L. T. 2007. "On Tricky Ground," in Denzin, N. K. and Lincoln, Y. S. (eds.), *The Landscape of Qualitative Research*, 3rd ed, Thousand Oaks, CA: SAGE, pp. 113–144.

Spivak, G. C. 1988. "Can the Subaltern Speak?," in Nelson, C. and Grossberg, E. (eds.), *Marxism and the Interpretation of Culture*, Urbana, IL: University of Illinois Press, pp. 271–313.

Spivak, G. C. 1999. *A Critique of Postcolonial Reason: Toward a History of the Vanishing Present*, Cambridge, MA: Harvard University Press.

Tomlinson, F. and Schwabenland, C. 2010. "Reconciling Competing Discourses of Diversity? The Uk Non-Profit Sector between Social Justice and the Business Case," *Organization*, 17, 101–121.

Tompkins, P. K. 1967. Organizational Communication: A State-of-the-Art Review. *Marshall Space Flight Center Conference on Organizational Communication*, Detroit, MI.

Tompkins, P. K. and Wanca-Thibault, M. 2001. "Organizational Communication: Prelude and Prospects," in Jablin, F. and Putnam, L. L. (eds.), *The New Handbook of Organizational Communication: Advances in Theory, Research, and Methods*, Thousand Oaks, CA: SAGE, pp. xvii–xxxi.

Warner, M. 1999. *The Trouble with Normal: Sex, Politics, and the Ethics of Queer Life*, New York: The Free Press.

Witz, A. 1992. *Professions and Patriarchy*, London: Routledge.

9 Emotion and Relationships in the Workplace

Sarah J. Tracy and Shawna Malvini Redden

Personal Reflections

Sarah's Journey

I gulped in several breaths of warm evening air from the penthouse suite balcony. It felt good to escape the air conditioning and drama inside. Gazing toward the glowing lights several miles away, I imagined the Friday night West Los Angeles scene—beautiful people enjoying the beginning of their weekend. My watch read 8:12 p.m. I needed to get my face back together before returning to my current reality: working late, *again*, in a toxic environment, under deadline.

My boss had made it clear: if I wanted to succeed, not only did my public relations writing need to be impeccable but I also needed to get used to working long hours and towing the line. Further, I had to conveniently look away from coworkers frequently glossing over ethical missteps. One of my senior colleagues called it "dancing." I called it making things up. I was 22 years old and absolutely miserable.

Just 6 months earlier, I had been so hopeful and happy. I was serving as guest relations coordinator at my beloved alma mater and had just landed this coveted public relations agency position during the recession of 1993. Sure, I was only making $21,000 a year, but at least someone offered me a job. What's more, it was for a public relations agency specializing in socially responsible businesses. What could be better?

My university coursework had trained me to write strategic plans, interact with corporate executives, and craft meaningful community events. The actualities of my job stood in sharp contrast: 60-hour work weeks, a demeaning boss, forced cheerfulness, endless faxing, and unrealistic deadlines. I was burned out, exhausted, devastated.

And so, on that penthouse balcony that summer night, I made myself a promise. I would go to graduate school and make it my mission to somehow help organizations be nicer places to work. And I would get myself the hell out of that "socially responsible" public relations agency.

One year later, I was a doctoral student at the University of Colorado-Boulder. Three classes there fundamentally impacted my research trajectory: organizational identification and control by Philip Tompkins, organizational ethics by George Cheney, and emotion and communication by Sally Planalp. For class projects, I learned everything I could about organizational burnout, wrote a case study on the ethical problems of basing public relations on corporate social responsibility, and was introduced to the research of Arlie Hochschild (1983), a sociologist whose writing style, savvy, and interest in emotional labor shaped my career.

Also during this time, my language and social interaction professor Karen Tracy (no relation) took me under her wing to study interactions between citizens and emergency 911 call takers. She was interested in how conversational particulars resulted in calls that were especially rude (K. Tracy and Tracy 1998), whereas I was intrigued by the ways call takers managed their emotion when dealing with especially frightening, humorous, or irritating calls (S. Tracy and Tracy 1998).

Two years later, I took a break from my Ph.D. coursework to work on the "Radiant Sun" cruise ship. For 229 days straight, I danced the macarena, chit-chatted, called bingo, told stupid jokes, and mostly kept a smile plastered on my face. I took notes and recorded interviews with the idea that I should analyze the emotional labor on the ship when I returned to graduate school. To my excitement, Stanley Deetz started working at CU-Boulder during my year away, and his mentorship helped me critically analyze emotional control in the closed and surveilled environment of the cruise ship (Tracy 2000).

Deetz's (1998) critical organizational standpoint informed my dissertation and early career studies of correctional officers' burnout and problematic emotional construction (Tracy 2004). I paid attention to how officers communicatively managed the monotonous, often degrading, and sporadically dangerous work of being "babysitters" and "glorified flight attendants" for convicted felons (Tracy 2005).

Along the way, I designed and taught one of the first communication courses focused on emotion and organizing. Until that time, with few exceptions, emotion and organization scholars basically ignored one another. To make my point on the first day of class, I asked my students to scan the index of the *Handbook of Communication and Emotion* (Andersen and Guerrero 1998) for the word "organization" and the *Handbook of Organizational Communication* (Jablin et al. 1987) for the word "emotion." Each word was missing from the other book's index.

Clearly, there was work to be done. Over the next few years, I introduced students to the small but growing scholarship on emotion and organizing. My first doctoral advisee, Pamela Lutgen-Sandvik (2003) wrote her semester-paper-turned-publication on workplace emotional abuse, and from there, we partnered on several studies related to workplace bullying (e.g. Lutgen-Sandvik et al. 2007). This work attracted attention from the media, international bullying scholars, and the organizational communication discipline like nothing I'd written before. However, the process of qualitatively studying workplace bullying coupled with my past research on burnout and emotional labor was itself emotionally exhausting, and I yearned for something a bit more uplifting.

All this time, I had focused on one guiding notion: if I can describe and analyze the *problems* of emotion in the workplace, then I could help solve these problems and make workplaces nicer places to be. However, focusing on the emotional *problems* was only half-baked. Studying burnout, emotional labor, and bullying certainly gave names to bad behavior. However, it did not create prosocial emotions in their place.

For organizations to be places where generosity, exuberance, compassion, and healthy relationships thrive, I realized that attention was sorely needed for studying desired and especially humane workplace emotional conditions. Along with colleagues, over the last few years I have turned attention to compassion and organizational communication (e.g. Clark and Tracy 2016, Tracy and Huffman 2017, Way and Tracy 2012) and developed new classes such as "Communication and the Art of Happiness" and "Organizational Emotions and Well-being." I'm indebted to the doctoral students who have collaborated and written emotion and organizational communication related dissertations along the way[1], including this chapter's coauthor, Shawna Malvini Redden.

Shawna's Journey

I found myself studying emotion and organizing somewhat by accident while in line at the airport. At the time, I traveled frequently between my apartment in Tempe where I was studying at Arizona State University's doctoral program and my home in Sacramento where my husband and dog lived. Although I was supposed to be investigating spirituality and workplace relationships, my declared research interests, I couldn't help but notice how weird people acted in airport lines.

In security, I'd see people huffing and puffing, sometimes literally, as if this anxious behavior might help them get through the line faster even if there were still 15 people ahead of them. I noticed people who would act twitchy and nervous while interacting with Transportation Security Administration (TSA) officers, but then once they got to the gate area, they would relax. I realized how much anxiety I experienced when I got caught with "contraband" and had my corkscrew/cheese knife contraption confiscated, my bag searched, and my body patted down. It initially shocked me how I'd never really noticed the feelings flying all over the airport before.

It's no surprise to me that my airport line epiphanies started to take shape at the same time I took Sarah's qualitative methods seminar and began honing my craft as an ethnographer, or as I describe to my students, a professional people-watcher. It also helped that access to my planned research context—a hospital system—fell through at the last minute, and I could fully devote myself to understanding the emotional experience of the airport.

Since then, I've immersed myself in thinking about how emotions influence organizational settings, especially between people and groups, as emotions become shared and evolve in cycles (Hareli and Rafaeli 2008, Scarduzio and Tracy 2015). I'm also deeply interested in the relationships between emotion, power, and identity. In the airport, I noticed that passengers were required to perform a particular type of emotion work that wasn't accounted for in the literature. I call these "emotional taxes" for the way certain emotional fronts have to be "paid" during compulsory interactions (see Malvini Redden 2013). I was especially concerned that certain people—namely people of color and those with differing physical abilities—had to perform more difficult emotion work due to their identities. My friend and colleague Jennifer Scarduzio and I have continued thinking about the relationships between intersecting identities and emotion work for organizational members and patrons alike (Malvini Redden and Scarduzio 2017). We hope our work helps organizations craft policies and practices that make emotion work less difficult.

An Overview of Emotion and Relationships at Work

Work is inherently emotional. Flight attendants calm nervous flyers, waiters smile, teachers inspire, police officers encounter scared citizens, and border patrol agents navigate the tensions of upholding the law while being compassionate to suffering border crossers (Rivera and Tracy 2012). However, only in the last 25 years have organizational scholars treated seriously the role of emotion at work. Before that time, emotion was traditionally written out of organizational studies and considered antithetical to rational organizational goals focused on productivity (Kramer and Hess 2002). In this worldview, emotions were either ignored or measured as variables of job satisfaction, morale, or commitment.

In the last three decades, scholarship examining emotion formation, expression, and control in the workplace has become mainstream in fields including organizational communication, management, sociology, and psychology. Emergent work feelings—which are experienced, shaped, shared, and interpreted through communication—are an integral part of relational interaction at work (Riforgiate and Komarova 2017).

While much organizational research is still influenced by discourses of rationality, "bounded emotionality" is an "alternative mode of organizing in which nurturance, caring, community, supportiveness, and interrelatedness are fused with individual responsibility to shape organizational experiences" (Mumby and Putnam 1992: 474). From this vantage, emotion in organizations functions not as a commodity to be controlled; rather, feelings are integral to the workplace. Indeed, emotional display, empathy, and emotional intelligence (Salovey and Mayer 1990) are not the opposite of rationality or cognition (Planalp 1999), but function as key parts of good leadership and effective organizing.

Emotion work touches an entire range of occupations including boundary spanners, like receptionists; emotional believers, including hospice workers who really have faith in their work; emotional elicitors, like stand-up comics; resilience builders, such as military sergeants who toughen up their employees; orchestrators who motivate feelings in others; coolers and soothers who ease upset clients; guides and seekers who inspire (or brainwash) followers; moral emoters, such as activists who provoke outrage; and utility players who engage in toxin management and mood shifting (Waldron 2012). In these jobs, we see how emotion can manifest in emotional displays required as part of the job (something called "emotional labor"); emotional reactions that stem from the job, such as stress, engagement, or compassion; emotion related to coworker interactions and relationships, including loyalty or betrayal; and emotions brought to work from home or nonwork spaces (Waldron 2012). Each of these arenas can include positive or negative emotion, and each influences organizational processes in specific ways.

For instance, moral emotions such as guilt and shame can help people make sense of difficult work situations and aid ethical decision-making (Rivera and Tracy 2014). Emotion strengthens workplace relationships (Lutgen-Sandvik et al. 2011), raises awareness (Waldron 2012), ignites transformation (Krone and Dougherty 2015), and can lead to a variety of preferred organizational outcomes (Barsade and Gibson 2007). At the same time, many organizational problems are emotional in nature, such as dissonance between authentic feeling and emotional display (Tracy 2005), stress (Boren and Veksler 2015), burnout (Maslach et al. 2001), incivility (Kassing and Waldron 2014), and workplace bullying (Lutgen-Sandvik and Tracy 2012). However, seemingly "negative" emotions can have positive outcomes. Case in point: sarcasm and intimidation can actually function to increase collaboration and camaraderie among employees (Scarduzio and Malvini Redden 2015). For instance, TSA officers and courtroom employees describe using sarcasm to discipline and make fun of patrons in ways that build a sense of "us versus them" togetherness for employees who work "in the trenches" together.

It's easy to think about emotion and issues connected to organizational well-being as concerns of the individual (Ganesh and McAllum 2010). However, emotion is inherently relational, constituted via collective interaction (Malvini Redden 2013) and cycles of reciprocal influence (Hareli and Rafaeli 2008). For example, Scarduzio and Tracy (2015) demonstrate how different organizational actors' emotional displays influence others and serve important sensemaking functions in municipal courtrooms.

Courtroom bailiffs buffer emotions between judges and defendants, and the emotional displays of judges "give sense" to defendants in the courtrooms. Likewise, in her study of sexual violence on universities campuses, Harris (2013) shows that while individual feelings and experiences of violence are often foregrounded in discussions of sexual violence, violence is an element of the organizational process.

With the complex nature of emotional processes in mind, we now turn to some important research themes related to emotion in organizations.

Control and Commodification of Emotion at Work

Arlie Hochschild (1983) coined the terms "emotion management," which refers to personal control over feelings, and "emotional labor," which describes the commodification of employees' emotion for organizational use. Hochschild investigated the experiences of flight attendants and bill collectors to understand how labor is not solely about physical productivity but also includes the production and performance of organizationally prescribed emotions. For instance, flight attendants are paid to perform safety duties and provide in-flight comfort, but also to smile at rude customers or hide their fear during flight safety issues.

Subsequent scholarship has focused on the difficulties and negative consequences related to performing emotional labor, such as stress and burnout, which we discuss in the following sections. Some look at the degree to which employees internalize organizational discourses and how that influences their emotional performances. "Surface acting" refers to when people force themselves to show a certain emotion even if they do not feel it (Hochschild 1983), such as performing "service with a smile" to rude customers. On the other hand, "deep acting" involves both feeling and demonstrating the displayed emotion, whether naturally or through reframing.

When employees feel the emotion they are expressing, this is "emotional harmony," whereas emotive dissonance is a mismatch between felt and expressed emotion—whether that entails emotional amplification, suppression, or masking. Emotive dissonance is associated with negative consequences, such as tension and strain (Ashforth and Humphrey 1993) and reduced immune function (Conrad and Witte 1994). The more employees feel they must "fake it in bad faith"—or generate inauthentic emotions when they do not agree with the mandated emotional labor—the greater the negative consequences, such as burnout (Rafaeli and Sutton 1987), depression and cynicism (Ashforth and Humphrey 1993). Employees can also engage in emotional deviance (Rafaeli and Sutton 1987) by expressing an emotion that violates the prescribed emotional performance. This happens when a judge giggles in response to a misbehaving defendant rather than being stoic or disciplinary. Employees who have a lot of power (like judges) have more privilege to deviate from organizational expression rules than do lower-power employees (like restaurant servers). Indeed, Scarduzio (2011) has shown how judges frequently drop their prescribed neutral expression to show irritation or make jokes at defendants' expense.

The consequences of emotional performances also vary as the complexity of those performances increases. Sometimes employees are required to perform conflicting emotions, like when correctional officers have to care for inmates and demonstrate vulnerability while simultaneously maintaining authority and demonstrating detachment (Tracy 2004) or when TSA officers must demonstrate intimidation and professionalism at the same time (Malvini Redden and Scarduzio 2017). In these situations of paradox, employees may experience even greater stress and burnout, especially if organizational processes limit their ability to cultivate a preferred identity or express themselves in desired ways (Tracy 2004).

Doing emotional labor is especially difficult when its performance conflicts with employees' preferred identities. This is the case with border patrol agents who largely care for a population of stigmatized, undocumented immigrants and manage interactions with a public that views border patrol suspiciously (Rivera 2015). On the one hand, agents are criticized for being too masculine and stoic, while on the other hand, they are demeaned when engaging in the feminized work of being too caring and compassionate. "Emotional taint" is characterized by emotion work that is viewed by others as "inappropriate (not fitting the situation), excessive (too much or too little emotion required for the situation), or vulnerable (causing the person to subject themselves to "difficult" feelings)" (Rivera 2015: 218). In such cases, the difficulty of the work is not as much about faking emotion as it is about creating distance from the emotionally tainted part of the job. A case in point: women who work in legal brothels distance themselves from an identity that some perceive as socially undesirable but align themselves with nonstigmatized aspects of the industry (Wolfe and Blithe 2015).

While much research considers emotional labor in stigmatized or low-prestige occupations, a recent thread of scholarship explores the ways that emotional labor operates in professional and high-prestige contexts, including with airline pilots (Fraher 2017) and health-care executives (Urasadettan and Burellier 2017). Recent work also considers the intersections of emotional management with identity categories, such as race, class, and gender. Malvini Redden and Scarduzio (2017) coined the term "hidden taint" to describe the unexpected emotion work and power dynamics that emerge when identities categories are foregrounded—for instance when employees scrutinize patrons on the basis of their race or class or when customers sexualize encounters and emphasize gender differences with employees.

Thinking about how emotional labor is a complex social process and not just an individual experience moves scholarship in interesting directions. Emotion management can help groups and families function better. For instance, public safety employees manage their own emotions as well as those of their family members, something Bochantin (2017) refers to as "humorous bilateral emotional labor" (HBEL). Humor allows employees to make light of dangerous work activities and ease the tension of worrying family members. At the same time, emotion management also highlights problematic organizational practices, as when customers in low-power positions are made to pay "emotional taxes" like suppressing irritation in order to navigate compulsory interactions (Malvini Redden 2013).

In summary, emotional labor takes different forms depending on the job. Some key implications of this line of research include: (1) low-status employees, women in particular, are expected to perform more emotional labor than high-status employees, and do not enjoy the "status shield" (Hoschschild 1983) that protects men from the associated difficulties of emotional labor; (2) employees experience emotional labor as more difficult when they feel they are faking inauthentic emotions for an unworthy purpose, when working with stigmatized populations, and when their emotional performance threatens a preferred identity; and (3) over time, expressing organizationally prescribed emotions can lead to disconnection from one's own spontaneous emotional experience and generate serious consequences. Indeed, one of the potential results of emotional labor is burnout.

Burnout

Stress and burnout are associated with working too hard and too much, managing conflicting expectations, or toiling away at demeaning tasks that do not engage employees' core interests and skills. In contrast, when employees do work they find meaningful, have regular breaks, enjoy supportive interactions, and are given opportunities to talk about their emotional stressors, they are likely to be much more engaged and productive at work (Tracy 2017).

Stress is the difference between worker satisfaction (represented by individual need fulfillment) and the realities of an employee's day-to-day work (Tracy 2009). Burnout is a result of that stress and is marked by emotional exhaustion, depersonalization, cynicism, and decreased personal accomplishment or sense of efficacy (Maslach et al. 2001). Burnout is especially common in human service workers who interact with suffering clients. Social workers, correctional officers, and many governmental workers must manage and reframe the negative emotions of others, something called toxin management (Frost 1999). Employees who interact with suffering clients can manage burnout, in part, through showing empathetic concern but not swaying to the polar extremes of emotional contagion (which involves feeling parallel negative emotion) or complete depersonalization and aloofness (Miller et al. 1988).

Employees who enjoy strong relationships and feelings of identification with peers, workgroups, and supervisors are better able to avoid burnout and the negative results of stress (Maslach and Leiter 1997). Indeed, when employees feel restricted in talking with their support network about stressful or overwhelming things at work, they are likely to experience communicatively restricted organization stress (CROS) and its associated negative outcomes, such as poor organizational climate, reduced productivity, and increased emotional and physical exhaustion (Boren and Veksler 2015). However, not all supportive interaction at work is created equal. Co-rumination, or excessive negative talk about an issue, is linked to increasing levels of stress and burnout, in part because it forecloses consideration of possible solutions (Boren 2014). Furthermore, identification with the work group is more important than identification with the organization for reducing burnout (Lammers et al. 2013).

Other recent organizational communication research related to burnout includes considerations of communication technology, work-life balance, and the downsides of identifying or having too much passion for work. Hours of work-related use of communication technology outside of regular work hours contributes to perceptions of work–life conflict, and perceptions of work-life conflict predict job burnout and job satisfaction (Wright et al. 2014). And despite the importance of engagement at work, when passion and emotional labor meet, this can lead to burnout, as is the case with nonprofit employees who really believe in the value of their work but feel challenged in accomplishing it (Eschenfelder 2012).

Abusive Workplace Interactions

"Workplace bullying" refers to "persistent verbal and nonverbal aggression at work that include personal attacks, social ostracism, and a multitude of other painful messages and hostile interactions" (Lutgen-Sandvik 2006: 406). Unfortunately, workplace bullying is all too common with up to 35% of employees bullied sometime during their work history and 11% currently witnessing coworkers being bullied (Workplace Bullying Institute 2010). Whereas healthy workplace environments encourage authentic and constructive conflict about work tasks and processes, destructive and abusive emotional interactions focus on the person involved and can range from a series of microaggressions and incivilities to ritualized hazing and violent abuse.

Bullying is characterized by several factors, including repetition, duration of 6 months or more, escalation, significant physical or psychological harm, power disparity between the bully and target, and the target perceiving that the bully purposefully intends to abuse (Lugen-Sandvik and Tracy 2012). So, what does bullying look and feel like? Targets talk about bullying as if it is akin to a nightmare, torture, imprisonment, child abuse, or being tricked by a devil (Tracy et al. 2006). If you were watching a movie of workplace bullying in action, you might see whispering, eye rolls, name-calling, insults, gossip, sneering, and threats. It can also involve the silent treatment, withholding needed information, or refusing to acknowledge a coworker's presence or ideas. Abuse is even more common among minorities or immigrant professionals who face microaggressions related to their ethnicity, culture, or other demographic category (Razzante et al. in press). In such cases, employees deal with abuse by creating alternative selves in some cases and taking ownership or blaming themselves in others (Shenoy-Packer 2015).

Unlike everyday organizational conflict, bullying is quite difficult to disrupt or ameliorate. Bullying persists in part due to macro-level discourses that penalize "thin-skinned" employees, while glorifying tough bosses and linking harassment to increased productivity. All too often, workplace policies intentionally or unintentionally condone abusive behavior (Keashly and Jagatic 2003), as human resource (HR) personnel interpret policies in a variety of unpredictable ways (Cowan 2011). Indeed, in over 70% of cases, bullying targets feel that upper management was complicit in the abuse, by taking no action or making the situation worse (Namie and Lutgen-Sandvik 2010). This is of little surprise when we consider that most workplace bullies are supervisors, and when targets seek help from above, they are stymied by HR professionals who see bullying as a direct manager's responsibility rather than a structural issue for which they are responsible (Cowan 2012). Rather than seeing malicious bullying, some HR personnel simply see competitive behavior, and they must be convinced that the perpetrator is creating an objectively hostile work environment—as evidenced, for example, from reports by bystanders (Cowan 2012).

Bullying is also exacerbated by the fact that targets of abuse often have difficulty articulating their plight. Tye-Williams and Krone (2015) found that the most common type of narrative told by targets of workplace bullying is one of chaos. Such stories highlight targets' loss, isolation, and lack of social support from peers and suggest that coworkers are as likely to ignore or participate in the bullying than to stop it. Unfortunately, these fragmented narratives are much more common than factual reports or quest narratives that frame bullying as a difficult but resolvable journey. Although bystanders feel guilty when they see their coworkers being abused, they are often even more scared of escalating the situation and triggering abusive attention toward themselves (Tracy, Lutgen-Sandvik and Alberts 2006). When coworkers do try to help, they sometimes give simplistic advice, such as telling the target to simply leave their job, fight back, or ignore it (Tye-Williams and Krone 2017).

Unfortunately, organizational exit from emotionally abusive workplaces is fraught with tension and fear of threats and discipline, especially when employees are highly identified and socially intertwined (Garner and Peterson 2018). Coworkers can help targets feel better by reinforcing targets' preferred identity (e.g. as a valued coworker) (Lutgen-Sandvik 2008), engaging in collective fantasies of revenge (Tye-Williams and Krone 2015) or conversationally pivoting when they hear an employee being unfairly critiqued (Foss and Foss 2011). Such communicative moves can help targets reframe the situation, feel connected to others, and may even halt some of the bad behavior.

Cultivating Prosocial Emotions in the Workplace

Although a significant amount of scholarship focuses on the repercussions of negative emotions in organizations—how to prevent or resolve burnout, what to do about workplace bullies, and how to deal with difficult emotional labor requirements—increasingly, researchers are analyzing affirmative and prosocial emotions. Of particular interest are emotional processes related to cultivating humor, affirmation, compassion, and resilience in organizations.

Humor provides much more than comic relief at work. Organizational members use humor to manage stress and uncertainty while making sense of job expectations, organizational culture, and organizational affiliations. Humor can enhance job satisfaction, relieve tension, provide ingroup solidarity, help employees to make sense of complex or incongruous work, and reduce burnout and job stress (Tracy, Myers and Scott 2006). Furthermore, through humor, organizational members identify with the organization and co-construct organizational norms and expectations (Heiss and Carmack 2012). For instance, while airport security might not seem like a very funny place, Malvini Redden observed TSA officers joking with passengers. Instead of shouting out reminders about going through the advanced imaging, one officer intoned, "One shoe, two shoes, red shoes, blue shoes, laptops, flip flops, they all must come off!" and playfully reframed a boring task for his and passengers' amusement. However, humor should be used carefully because it can also function to separate workers from one another, trivialize important issues, or simplify complex organizational problems.

Caring interactions at work dramatically influence people's experience of organizations whether they are employees or patrons. Affirming positive behavior can help create healthy organizational cultures, whether through overt public or private praise, formal acknowledgment, or using body language to indicate approval (Bowes-Sperry and O'Leary-Kelly 2005). Likewise, organizations that foster "high-quality interpersonal connections" involving trust, respect, play, and collaboration (Dutton 2003) are more likely to have employees who feel safe at work and cultures that are learning focused and resilient (Carmelli et al. 2009). When work includes regular positive emotional experiences, people are more likely to feel important, included, and inspired (Lutgen-Sandvik et al. 2011).

Compassion is an important emotional process in organizations (Miller 2007) that has three primary components: (1) recognizing, which involves "understanding and applying meaning to others' verbal and nonverbal communicative cues," including context and subtext; (2) relating, which includes "identifying with, feeling for, and communicatively connecting with another to enable sharing of emotions, values, and decisions"; and (3) reacting, by "communicating in ways that are seen . . . as compassionate" (Way and Tracy 2012: 307). Fostering compassion in organizations can improve organizational relationships, customer service, productivity, and reputation, and can be fostered through transformational leadership (Men 2014). In his study of homeless young adults, Huffman (2017) found that "embodied aboutness"—or the process of making one's body about the other via physical presence, acts of service, and nonverbal immediacy—is especially compassionate. This type of calming and "I'm in it with you" presence is particularly salient in explosive or dangerous situations, as was the case when a front-desk bookkeeper compassionately talked down a would-be school shooter (Tracy and Huffman 2017).

Employees inevitably face challenges at work. How they cope is a testament to their resilience. Psychologically speaking, resilience is considered to be the ability to bounce back and recover after a crisis, disruption, or set-back, often through the foregrounding of positive emotions, such as hopefulness (Richardson 2002). A communication lens emphasizes that resilience isn't simply a personal trait but rather a social process that is "fundamentally grounded in messages, d/Discourse, and narrative" (Buzzanell 2010: 2). In the face of significant challenges, resilient people cultivate normalcy, create "affirming identity anchors," maintain social ties, creatively reframe the situation, and emphasize positive emotions (Buzzanell 2010). Importantly, a communicative focus on resilience accommodates negative feelings. When trauma or challenges happen, those things are often painful and difficult. Cultivating resilience doesn't pretend otherwise but rather focuses on productive action. Organizing for mindfulness can help organizational members build resilience in times of challenge and an orientation of "non-attachment" has the potential to transform challenging organizational situations into opportunities for compassion and wisdom (Brummans and Hwang 2010).

Many of the prosocial ways of being discussed in this section relate to the concept of emotional intelligence (EI), a combination of several capabilities: emotional self-awareness, emotional self-regulation, motivating oneself and others, and recognizing and empathizing with the emotions of others (Salovey and Mayer 1990). Most of the EI research stems from the fields of psychology and management, and has spurred big business, popular press books, TED Talks, and Harvard Business Review (2015) special issues. Meanwhile, the concept has undergone significant critique in three main areas, including controversy about its definition and distinction from other concepts, ways to measure EI, and skepticism about the significance of EI for preferred outcomes like productivity and creativity (Murphy 2014).

Conclusion and Future Directions

In this chapter, we have traced our own journeys of studying emotion at work and reviewed four central areas of research related to emotion and organizational communication: (1) the commodification and control of work feeling, (2) burnout and stress, (3) abusive workplace interactions, and (4) prosocial emotions at work. We close with some questions and issues that should spur additional research.

First, although organizational communication burnout research peaked in the 1990s, several areas are ripe for continued exploration. These include bolstering the current dominance of quantitative studies with qualitative case analyses of what burnout looks in time and space, and narrative studies that ask how more current terms—fear of missing out (FOMO) or decision fatigue—are more apropos areas of stress in organizations than depersonalization and emotional exhaustion. Further, in line with the goal of cultivating prosocial emotion rather than just decreasing problematic emotions, researchers should consider examining the opposite of burnout: organizational engagement (Tracy 2009, 2017). Studying positive deviants of organizational activities that bring energy and meaning to work holds promise not only for combating burnout but also for moving toward organizational flourishing.

Second, although many of facets of emotional intelligence are closely connected to topics of concern by communication scholars (e.g. compassion, resilience, mindfulness), there is scant communication research focusing squarely on emotional intelligence. This may be due to the concept's association with using emotions as a means to profit or productivity ends (Dougherty and Krone 2002). Despite these critiques, the concept and related ideas like "emotional agility" (David 2016) continue to thrive in interdisciplinary conversations about creating healthy, happy, creative, and humane organizations. Communication scholars could usefully contribute this conversation, not only to critique the EI concept but also to transform it. Indeed, communication scholars are well poised to highlight how discourse and interaction are vital for identifying and perceiving emotion, developing trust and vulnerable connection, and framing emotions in a way that serves relevant parties.

Relatedly, workplace bullying research could be extended by examining surprising spaces of workplace kindness, flourishing, and joy. Certainly, all too many organizations employ jerks, and some workplaces cultivate stressful and competitive environments. However, workplaces can also cultivate especially moral, heroic, and affirming behaviors.

Although communication scholars have dipped their toe into studying positive interactions and prosocial emotions, there is much unchartered territory in examining courage, generosity, passion, playfulness, connection, engagement, and micro-affirmations in organizations. Furthermore, organizational communication scholars could usefully partner with interpersonal researchers to study the ways that these emotions are talked into being through mindful workplace practices, interactions, policies, and leadership.

Fourth, most of the emotion and organizing research reported in this chapter is related to face-to-face interaction. Given that organizations are increasingly connected via various types of communication technology, future research could valuably explore the way emotion issues occur differently due to employees' reliance on email, video conferencing, text messaging, and social media. Interpersonal and health communication scholars have already examined cyberbullying (Brody and Vangelisti 2016, Danielson and Emmers-Sommer 2017). On the one hand, employees' increasing reliance on technology may result in increased depersonalization, bullying, and abuse. On the other hand, technology might provide a useful emotional buffer between suffering clients and exhausted employees. What's more, technologies such as Skype and Zoom also have the potential to bring employees closer together to foster empathy and connection.

Finally, organizational communication research on emotion, like most scholarly work, is primarily epistemological in nature. In other words, the research analyzes topics of study with the primary goal of leaving readers *knowing more about* a topic. Especially with a turn toward studying prosocial emotions, we encourage researchers to consider ways to leave readers and learners "being" the emotions at hand—something that Tracy and her colleagues have called an OPPT-in approach (Tracy and Donovan 2018). OPPT-in stands for ontological, phenomenological, phronetic, transformative. Such an approach suggests ways that scholarship, through its form and delivery, may trigger humane craft practice and practical wisdom (Flyvbjerg 2001). This may be accomplished through thick, performative representations in which readers see and feel themselves as part of the action, experiential and transformative pedagogical activities, and scholarship that motivates reflection, discovery, and practice of desired ways of being.

Discussion Questions

1. What are the opportunities and constraints of researching emotional problems in the workplace (bullying, burnout, and toxic relationships) as compared to studying the emotional issues we may want to cultivate (compassion, resilience, or generosity)? What are the potential upsides and downsides to each? Which appeals more to you and why?

2. In what ways have you engaged in emotional labor? Did you feel forced or did you do it by choice? Which emotions are easiest to portray? Using concepts from the reading, analyze why you think you felt the emotional labor activities were easy or difficult. What are the ethical implications of asking employees to amplify, suppress, or mask their emotional communication in the workplace?
3. How might organizations unwittingly encourage or condone emotional abuse in the form of microaggressions, harassment, or bullying? What can or should coworkers do when they witness this type of organizational behavior?
4. What types of challenge or setbacks have you faced at work? How did you cope? Did you use humor? Did other people show you compassion? How have you helped others? In what ways is resilience a communicative construction?

Note

1. An incomplete list of former doctoral students who have contributed to Sarah's scholarship and thinking related to emotion and organizations include Lou Clark, Emily Cripe, Elizabeth Eger, Timothy Huffman, Pamela Lutgen-Sandvik, Jessica Kamrath, Karen Kroman Myers, Shawna Malvini Redden, Robert Razzante, Sarah Riforgiate, Kendra Rivera, Jennifer Scarduzio, Clifton Scott, Sophia Town, Amy Way, and Debbie Way.

References

Andersen, P. A. and Guerrero, L. K. (eds.) 1998. *Handbook of Communication and Emotion: Research, Theory, Applications, and Contexts*, San Diego, CA: Academic Press.

Ashforth, B. E. and Humphrey, R. H. 1993. "Emotional Labor in Service Roles: The Influence of Identity," *Academy of Management Review*, 18, 88–115.

Barsade, S. G. and Gibson, C. B. 2007. "Why Does Affect Matter in Organizations?" *Academy of Management Perspectives*, 21, 36–59.

Bochantin, J. E. 2017. "'Ambulance Thieves, Clowns, and Naked Grandfathers' How PSEs and Their Families Use Humorous Communication as a Sensemaking Device," *Management Communication Quarterly*, 31, 278–296.

Boren, J. P. 2014. "The Relationships between Co-Rumination, Social Support, Stress, and Burnout among Working Adults," *Management Communication Quarterly*, 28, 3–25.

Boren, J. P. and Veksler, A. E. 2015. "Communicatively Restricted Organizational Stress (CROS) I: Conceptualization and Overview," *Management Communication Quarterly*, 29, 28–55.

Bowes-Sperry, L. and O'Leary-Kelly, A. M. 2005. "To Act or Not to Act: The Dilemma Faced by Sexual Harassment Observers," *Academy of Management Review*, 30, 288–306.

Brody, N. and Vangelisti, A. L. 2016. "Bystander Intervention in Cyberbullying," *Communication Monographs*, 83, 94–119.

170   *Tracy and Malvini Redden*

Brummans, B. H. and Hwang, J. M. 2010. "Tzu Chi's Organizing for a Compassionate World: Insights into the Communicative Praxis of a Buddhist Organization," *Journal of International and Intercultural Communication*, 3, 136–163.
Buzzanell, P. M. 2010. "Resilience: Talking, Resisting, and Imagining New Normalcies into Being," *Journal of Communication*, 60, 1–14.
Carmeli, A., Brueller, D. and Dutton, J. E. 2009. "Learning Behaviours in the Workplace: The Role of High-Quality Interpersonal Relationships and Psychological Safety," *Systems Research and Behavioral Science*, 26, 81–98.
Clark, L. and Tracy, S. J. 2016. "Grieving Adolescents Co-perform Compassion as They Stop in the Name of Love!: A Qualitative Study of Collective Compassion at Comfort Zone Camp," Paper presented at the annual meeting of the *National Communication Association*, Philadelphia, PA.
Conrad, C. and Witte, K. 1994. "Is Emotional Expression Repression Oppression? Myths of Organizational Affective Regulation," *Annals of the International Communication Association*, 17, 417–428.
Cowan, R. L. 2011. "'Yes, We Have an Anti-Bullying Policy, but . . .' HR Professionals' Understandings and Experiences with Workplace Bullying Policy," *Communication Studies*, 62, 307–327.
Cowan, R. L. 2012. "It's Complicated: Defining Workplace Bullying from the Human Resource Professional's Perspective," *Management Communication Quarterly*, 26, 377–403.
Danielson, C. M. and Emmers-Sommer, T. M. 2017. "'She Stopped Me from Killing Myself': Bullied Bloggers' Coping Behaviors and Support Sources," *Health Communication*, 32, 977–986.
David, S. 2016. *Emotional Agility: Get Unstuck, Embrace Change, and Thrive in Work and Life*, New York: Penguin Random House.
Deetz, S. 1998. "Discursive Formations, Strategized Subordination and Self-Surveillance," in McKinley, A. and Starkey, K. (eds.), *Foucault, Management and Organizational Theory*, London: SAGE, pp. 151–172.
Dougherty, D. S. and Krone, K. J. 2002. "Emotional Intelligence as Organizational Communication: An Examination of the Construct," *Annals of the International Communication Association*, 26, 202–229.
Dutton, J. E. 2003. *Energize Your Workplace: How to Create and Sustain High-Quality Connections at Work*, San Francisco, CA: John Wiley & Sons.
Eschenfelder, B. 2012. "Exploring the Nature of Nonprofit Work Through Emotional Labor," *Management Communication Quarterly*, 26, 173–178.
Flyvbjerg, B. 2001. *Making Social Science Matter: Why Social Inquiry Fails and How It Can Succeed Again*, New York: Cambridge University Press.
Foss, S. K. and Foss, K. A. 2011. *Inviting Transformation: Presentational Skills for a Changing World*, Long Grove, IL: Waveland Press.
Fraher, A. L. 2017. "Invisibilised Dirty Work: The Multiple Realities of US Airline Pilots' Work," *Culture and Organization*, 23, 131–148.
Frost, P. J. 1999. "Why Compassion Counts!" *Journal of Management Inquiry*, 8, 127–133.
Ganesh, S. and McAllum, K. 2010. "Well-Being as Discourse: Potentials and Problems for Studies of Organizing and Health Inequalities," *Management Communication Quarterly*, 24, 491–498.
Garner, J. T. and Peterson, B. L. 2018. "Untangling the Processes of Leaving a Member-Abusive Organization," *Management Communication Quarterly*, 32, 143–171.

Hareli, S. and Rafaeli, A. 2008. "Emotion Cycles: On the Social Influence of Emotion in Organizations," *Research in Organizational Behavior, 28,* 35–59.

Harris, K. L. 2013. "Show Them a Good Time: Organizing the Intersections of Sexual Violence," *Management Communication Quarterly, 27,* 568–595.

Harvard Business Review. 2015. *HBR's 10 Must Reads on Emotional Intelligence,* Boston, MA: Harvard Business Review Press.

Heiss, S. N. and Carmack, H. J. 2012. "Knock, Knock; Who's There? Making Sense of Organizational Entrance Through Humor," *Management Communication Quarterly, 26,* 106–132.

Hochschild, A R. 1983. *The Managed Heart: Commercialization of Human Feeling,* Berkeley, CA: University of California Press.

Huffman, T. P. 2017. "Compassionate Communication, Embodied Aboutness, and Homeless Young Adults," *Western Journal of Communication, 81,* 149–167.

Jablin, F. M., Putnam, L. L., Roberts, K. H. and Porter, L. W. (eds.) 1987. *Handbook of Organizational Communication,* Newbury Park, CA: SAGE.

Kassing, J. and Waldron, V. R. 2014. "Incivility, Destructive Workplace Behavior, and Bullying," in Putnam, L. L. and Mumby, D. K. (eds.), *The SAGE Handbook of Organizational Communication,* Thousand Oaks, CA: SAGE, pp. 643–664.

Keashly, L. and Jagatic, K. 2003. "By Any Other Name: American Perspectives on Workplace Bullying," in Einarsen, S., Hoel, H. and Cooper, C. L. (eds.), *Bullying and Emotional Abuse in the Workplace: International Perspectives in Research and Practice,* London: Taylor and Francis, pp. 31–61

Kramer, M. W. and Hess, J. A. 2002. "Communication Rules for the Display of Emotions in Organizational Settings," *Management Communication Quarterly, 16,* 66–80.

Krone, K. J. and Dougherty, D. J. 2015. "From Emotional Labor to Critical Emotional Agency," *Electronic Journal of Communication, 25.*

Lammers, J. C., Atouba, Y. L. and Carlson, E. J. 2013. "Which Identities Matter? A Mixed-Method Study of Group, Organizational, and Professional Identities and Their Relationship to Burnout," *Management Communication Quarterly, 27,* 503–536.

Lutgen-Sandvik, P. 2003. "The Communicative Cycle of Employee Emotional Abuse: Generation and Regeneration of Workplace Mistreatment," *Management Communication Quarterly, 16,* 471–501.

Lutgen-Sandvik, P. 2006. "Take This Job and . . .: Quitting and Other Forms of Resistance to Workplace Bullying," *Communication Monographs, 73,* 406–433.

Lutgen-Sandvik, P. 2008. "Intensive Remedial Identity Work: Responses to Workplace Bullying Trauma and Stigmatization," *Organization, 15,* 97–119.

Lutgen-Sandvik, P., Riforgiate S. and Fletcher, C. 2011. "Work as a Source of Positive Emotional Experiences and the Discourses Informing Positive Assessment," *Western Journal of Communication, 75,* 2–27.

Lutgen-Sandvik, P. and Tracy, S. J. 2012. "Answering Five Key Questions About Workplace Bullying: How Communication Scholarship Provides Thought Leadership for Transforming Abuse at Work," *Management Communication Quarterly, 26,* 3–47.

Lutgen-Sandvik, P., Tracy, S. J. and Alberts, J. K. 2007. "Burned by Bullying in the American Workplace: Prevalence, Perception, Degree, and Impact," *Journal of Management Studies, 44,* 837–862.

Malvini Redden, S. 2013. "How Lines Organize Compulsory Interaction, Emotion Management, and 'Emotional Taxes': The Implications of Passenger Emotion and Expression in Airport Security Lines," *Management Communication Quarterly*, 27, 121–149.

Malvini Redden, S. and Scarduzio, J. A. 2017. "A Different Type of Dirty Work: Hidden Taint, Intersectionality, and Emotion Management in Bureaucratic Organizations," *Communication Monographs*, 85, 224–244.

Maslach, C. and Leiter, M. P. 1997. *The Truth About Burnout*, San Francisco, CA: Jossey-Bass.

Maslach, C., Schaufeli, W. B. and Leiter, M. P. 2001. "Job Burnout," *Annual Review of Psychology*, 52, 397–422.

Men, L. R. 2014. "Strategic Internal Communication: Transformational Leadership, Communication Channels, and Employee Satisfaction," *Management Communication Quarterly*, 28, 264–284.

Miller, K. 2007. "Compassionate Communication in the Workplace: Exploring Processes of Noticing, Connecting, and Responding," *Journal of Applied Communication Research*, 35, 223–245.

Miller, K. I., Stiff, J. B. and Ellis, B. H. 1988. "Communication and Empathy as Precursors to Burnout Among Human Service Workers," *Communication Monographs*, 55, 250–265.

Mumby, D. K. and Putnam, L. L. 1992. "The Politics of Emotion: A Feminist Reading of Bounded Rationality," *Academy of Management Review*, 17, 465–486.

Murphy, K. R. (ed.) 2014. *A Critique of Emotional Intelligence: What Are the Problems and How Can They Be Fixed?* New York: Routledge.

Namie, G. and Lutgen-Sandvik, P. E. 2010. "Active and Passive Accomplices: The Communal Character of Workplace Bullying," *International Journal of Communication*, 4, 343–373.

Planalp, S. 1999. *Communicating Emotion*, New York: Cambridge University Press.

Rafaeli, A. and Sutton, R. I. 1987. Expression of Emotion as Part of the Work Role," *Academy of Management Review*, 12, 23–37.

Razzante, R., J., Tracy, S. J. and Orbe, M. P. In Press. "How Dominant Group Members Can Transform Workplace Bullying," in West, R. and Beck, C. (eds.), *Routledge Handbook of Communication and Bullying*, London: Routledge.

Richardson, G. E. 2002. "The Metatheory of Resilience and Resiliency," *Journal of Clinical Psychology*, 58, 307–321.

Riforgiate, S. E. and Komarova, M. 2017. "Emotion at Work," in Scott, C. R. & Lewis, L. K. (eds.), *International Encyclopedia of Organizational Communication*, Chichester, UK: Wiley-Blackwell.

Rivera, K. D. 2015. "Emotional Taint: Making Sense of Emotional Dirty Work at the US Border Patrol," *Management Communication Quarterly*, 29, 198–228.

Rivera, K. D. and Tracy, S. J. 2012. "Arresting the American Dream: Patrolling the Borders of Compassion and Enforcement," in May, S. (ed.), *Case Studies in Organizational Communication: Ethical Perspectives and Practices*, 2nd ed. Thousand Oaks, CA: SAGE, pp. 271–284.

Rivera, K. D. and Tracy, S. J. 2014. "Embodying Emotional Dirty Work: A Messy Text of Patrolling the Border," *Qualitative Research in Organizations and Management*, 9, 201–222.

Salovey, P. and Mayer, J. D., 1990. "Emotional Intelligence," *Imagination, Cognition and Personality*, 9, 185–211.

Scarduzio, J. A. 2011. "Maintaining Order Through Deviance? The Emotional Deviance, Power, and Professional Work of Municipal Court Judges," *Management Communication Quarterly*, 25, 283–310.

Scarduzio, J. A. and Malvini Redden, S. 2015. "The Positive Outcomes of Negative Emotional Displays: A Multi-Level Analysis of Emotion in Bureaucratic Work," *Electronic Journal of Communication*, 25.

Scarduzio, J. A. and Tracy, S. J. 2015. "Sensegiving and Sensebreaking Via Emotion Cycles and Emotional Buffering: How Collective Communication Creates Order in the Courtroom," *Management Communication Quarterly*, 29, 331–357.

Shenoy-Packer, S. 2015. "Immigrant Professionals, Microaggressions, and Critical Sensemaking in the US Workplace," *Management Communication Quarterly*, 29, 257–275.

Tracy, S. J. 2000. "Becoming a Character for Commerce: Emotion Labor, Self-Subordination and Discursive Construction of Identity in a Total Institution," *Management Communication Quarterly*, 14, 90–128.

Tracy, S. J. 2004. "The Construction of Correctional Officers: Layers of Emotionality Behind Bars," *Qualitative Inquiry*, 10, 509–533.

Tracy, S. J. 2005. "Locking Up Emotion: Moving Beyond Dissonance for Understanding Emotion Labor Discomfort," *Communication Monographs*, 72, 261–283.

Tracy, S. J. 2009. "Managing Burnout and Moving Toward Employee Engagement: A Critical Literature Review and Communicative Approach Toward Reinvigorating the Study of Stress at Work," in Lutgen-Sandvik, P. and Davenport Sypher, B. (eds.), *The Destructive Side of Organizational Communication: Processes, Consequences and Constructive Ways of Organizing*, New York: Routledge, pp. 77–98.

Tracy, S. J. 2017. "Burnout in Organizational Communication," in Scott, C. R. and Lewis, L. K. (eds.) *International Encyclopedia of Organizational Communication*, Chichester, UK: Wiley-Blackwell.

Riforgiate, S. E. and Komarova, M. 2017. "Emotion at Work," in Scott, C. R. and Lewis, L. K. (eds.), *International Encyclopedia of Organizational Communication*, Chichester, UK: Wiley-Blackwell.

Tracy, S. J. and Donovan, M. C. J. 2018. "Moving from Practical Application to Expert Craft Practice in Organizational Communication: A Review of the Past and OPPT-Ing into the Future," in Salem, P. J. and Timmerman, E. (eds.), *Transformative Practices and Research in Organizational Communication*, Hershey, PA: IGI Global, pp. 202–220.

Tracy, S. J. and Huffman, T. P. 2017. "Compassion in the Face of Terror: A Case Study of Recognizing Suffering, Co-Creating Hope, and Developing Trust in a Would-Be School Shooting," *Communication Monographs*, 84, 30–53.

Tracy, S. J., Lutgen-Sandvik, P. and Alberts, J. K. 2006. "Nightmares, Demons, and Slaves: Exploring the Painful Metaphors of Workplace Bullying," *Management Communication Quarterly*, 20, 148–185.

Tracy, S., Myers, K. K. and Scott, C. W. 2006. "Cracking Jokes and Crafting Selves: Sensemaking and Identity Management among Human Service Workers," *Communication Monographs*, 73, 283–308.

Tracy, K. and Tracy, S. J. 1998. "Rudeness at 911: Reconceptualizing Face and Face Attack," *Human Communication Research*, 25, 225–251.

Tracy, S. J. and Tracy, K. 1998. "Emotion Labor at 911: A Case Study and Theoretical Critique," *Journal of Applied Communication Research*, 26, 390–411.

Tye-Williams, S. and Krone, K. J. 2015. "Chaos, Reports, and Quests: Narrative Agency and Co-Workers in Stories of Workplace Bullying," *Management Communication Quarterly*, 29, 3–27.

Tye-Williams, S. and Krone, K. J. 2017. "Identifying and Re-Imagining the Paradox of Workplace Bullying Advice," *Journal of Applied Communication Research*, 45, 218–235.

Urasadettan, J. and Burellier, F. 2017. "Appropriation Process of Dirty Work: Focus on Health Executives in a Medical Services Restructuring," *Journal of Organizational Change Management*, 30, 569–583.

Waldron, V. R. 2012. *Communicating Emotion at Work*, Malden, MA: Polity Press.

Way, D. and Tracy, S. J. 2012. "Conceptualizing Compassion as Recognizing, Relating and (Re)Acting: An Ethnographic Study of Compassionate Communication at Hospice," *Communication Monographs*, 79, 292–315.

Wolfe, A. W. and Blithe, S. J. 2015. "Managing Image in a Core-Stigmatized Organization: Concealment and Revelation in Nevada's Legal Brothels," *Management Communication Quarterly*, 29, 539–563.

Workplace Bullying Institute. 2010. Results of the 2010 and 2007 WBI U.S. Workplace Bullying Survey [Accessed 10 February 2017]. Retrieved from www.workplacebullying.org/wbiresearch/2010-wbi-national-survey/

Wright, K. B., Abendschein, B., Wombacher, K., O'Connor, M., Hoffman, M., Dempsey, M. . . . and Shelton, A. 2014. "Work-related Communication Technology Use Outside of Regular Work Hours and Work Life Conflict: The Influence of Communication Technologies on Perceived Work Life Conflict, Burnout, Job Satisfaction, and Turnover Intentions," *Management Communication Quarterly*, 28, 507–530.

10 Group Decision-Making and Collaboration

Jennifer Ervin and Joann Keyton

In this chapter, we focus on decision making and collaboration in small groups. Throughout, we point readers to relevant resources such as book chapters and recent reviews of the group and organizational communication literature that addresses decision-making and collaborative processes. To provide some context, we use the first sections to define small group communication and discuss major underlying assumptions that influence our approach to understanding decision making and collaboration in organizational groups. Following that, we describe the history of, current trends in, and future directions for research in this domain.

Decision-making and collaboration processes are central to groups across industries. As just a few examples, project teams are creating and producing software, health-care teams are making treatment decisions, senior management teams are developing financial and operational goals for their organizations, and citizen groups are working in their local governments and nonprofits to secure services for their citizens. Although context does matter, the communicative processes that manifest as group members collaborate and make decisions can be quite similar across levels and circumstances. For instance, in this chapter we do not distinguish between the terms *group* and *team*. These labels are artifacts of context (e.g. softball team, sales team, marketing group, technical support group); seldom do these labels, by themselves, distinguish the type of communication processes members enact. And while decision-making and collaboration are studied by group scholars in anthropology, economics, education, engineering, history, information systems, medicine, nursing, organizational behavior, philosophy, psychology, political science, public health, and sociology, this review focuses on understanding whether and how groups as a context influence the creation of symbols, the exchange of messages, and the meanings members create. Focusing on these symbolic exchanges allow us to make claims about what members say and do to create shared meaning during group discussions.

Group Communication

The way we characterize groups, and assumptions we make about them, provide some context and scope conditions for this chapter. For example, group communication scholars define *groups* as three or more individuals who identify as members of a group, and who work together to accomplish a shared task or achieve some other type of superordinate goal. Doing so allows us to distinguish small groups from interpersonal (i.e. dyadic) communication contexts, both in the number of relationships being negotiated and the ways that member relations facilitate and sometimes constrain communication in fundamentally different ways (see Moreland 2010). The introduction of a third person sets up the opportunity for coalitions to form and for members to engage in hidden communication. Such subgrouping creates an imbalance of power that can only occur between three or more people.

We choose not to set an upper limit on what constitutes a group, but group size does have important implications for processes and outcomes. For example, larger groups are able to expand the pool of skills and talents available to the group. Yet, increased size can produce diminishing returns—bigger is not always better (Bettenhausen 1991, Hare 1982, Wheelan and Mckeage 1993). More members can increase problems with coordination and motivation. Members of larger groups also tend to become dissatisfied, feel less cohesive with one another, and perceive less identification with the group. This is likely related to participation disparities and diminishing opportunities for each member to talk. These logistical problems often hinder group work. The best way to capitalize on larger groups is to make sure each member (a) is attentive to establishing relationships among other members, (b) agrees with other members about group goals, and (c) has a clearly defined role and is held accountable for activity associated with that role.

This chapter focuses on collaboration in decision-making groups. We do, however, acknowledge that not all groups make decisions. Groups sometimes convene to fulfill or enhance people's social, educational, problem-solving, or consulting needs and capabilities. In contrast, *decision-making groups are typically expected to discuss task-relevant information while selecting a course of action, ideally talking through the available options and influencing each other along the way.* Embedded in this statement are two additional assumptions that require a bit of explication. First, interaction drives group decision making; second, disagreement is central to group decision-making processes and outcomes.

As detailed in the 2009 colloquy in *Human Communication Research*, researchers have debated whether and how individual members behave in *grouplike* ways. Knowing our backgrounds as Communication scholars, it is probably of no surprise where we stand on this issue—that interaction helps create and sustains groups. As articulated by Bonito and Sanders (2011: 4), group discussion is "the basis for there being a group effort at all rather than independent individual efforts." By extension, our position is that *interaction is fundamental to group decision making*. It is true that communication sometimes has a disruptive influence on decision-making groups by contributing to members' acceptance of inaccurate or irrelevant information, or preventing members from fully considering the issue(s) at hand (Gouran and Hirokawa 1983, Stasser and Titus 2003). However, these potential costs are offset by important benefits. Group discussion allows members to retrieve, share, summarize, and sometimes generate new information (Bonito 2007, Ervin et al. 2017, Meyers 1989, Propp 1997). Interaction also shapes group-member relations as far as recognizing and utilizing member skills and expertise, role negation, and emotion expression and regulation (Bonito et al. 2017, Bonner et al. 2002, Johnson et al. 2016, Keyton 1999, Keyton and Beck 2010, Keyton and Springston 1990, Lehmann-Willenbrock and Allen 2014).

The other assumption is that *disagreement is central to group decision-making processes and outcomes*. Decision-making groups will typically begin discussion by polling members' opinions and decision preferences, irrespective of whether they were instructed to, and often times even when they are told not to. Agreement at the outset of discussion tends to suppress deliberation and information evaluation, which often leads to suboptimal decision making (Janis 1972, Schulz-Hardt et al. 2000, Schweiger et al. 1986). An underlying reason for this observation is that group members sometimes falsely believe that consensus implies correctness. However, scholars have demonstrated that preference diversity tends to increase information exchanges (Boster and Mayer 1984, De Dreu et al. 2008, McGrath 1991, Meyers and Seibold 1990, Postmes et al. 2001). In such cases, disagreement enables groups to make higher-quality decision that members feel confident in, satisfied with, and committed to (Nijstad and Kaps 2008, Schulz-Hardt et al. 2002), but only when members avoid becoming hostile with one another and refrain from other forms of verbal aggression (Anderson and Martin 1999).

Collaboration in Decision-Making Groups

Group members can communicate without collaborating, but they cannot collaborate without communicating. To clarify, collaboration is about creating new knowledge and shared understanding as groups work together interdependently to achieve some collective goal. It is also important to note that not all tasks require collaboration. For example, eureka-type tasks can be solved by a single group member who is motivated and able to communicate the correct solution to members who are willing to listen. Creation and innovation tasks, on the other hand, require that groups work in a non-summative fashion by accepting and embracing mutual influence. The core issue is that task characteristics affect whether and to what extent members need to communicate and collaborate when making decisions (Laughlin 1999, McGrath 1984).

Decision Making and Collaboration in Organizations

Communication serves many functions in the corporate world, ranging from individual-level processes such the development and perpetuation of professional identity and efficacy beliefs, to macro-level processes such as the creation and support of organizational missions. In light of these complexities, it is of no surprise that communication skills and the ability to work in teams continue to be among the top, if not most, desired attributes in employees.

In the *International Encyclopedia of Organizational Communication*, Reimer, Russell, and Roland (2017) highlighted several other ways that organizations, as a context, influence group dynamics. The organizational context creates additional complexity as groups are often embedded (i.e. they are connected to other teams; teams are the organizing structure of an organization), cross-functional (i.e. work groups are often composed of members from different functional backgrounds), and/or self-managing (i.e. members are task interdependent and collectively responsible for regulating work execution and outcomes). This type of organizational complexity coupled with problem complexity also lead to groups comprised of members from several organizations (see Keyton et al. 2008).

In the *Harvard Business Review*, Cross, Rebele, and Grant (2016) outlined barriers and facilitators of collaboration in organizations. While many managers and employees spend more than half of their time collaborating, only a very small percentage are doing so effectively. Unfortunately, it is common for the most successful collaborators to quickly become overburdened by requests for informational, social, and personal resources, thereby reducing workplace satisfaction and performance. A related issue is that people are rarely intrinsically motivated to collaborate; they are often, by nature, competing to gain recognition and advance their own career goals. Therefore, it is important to incentivize people to collaborate, while also reserving collaboration for tasks and projects that cannot be successfully completed without it. As we describe in greater detail later in this chapter, much of the current work in this domain focuses on conditions where technology facilitates or prevents effective collaboration as groups make decisions within and across organizations.

To summarize thus far, we define *small group communication* as the study of symbolic message use in the creation of shared meaning among three or more individuals. We established that interaction and disagreement significantly influence group decision making. We also describe collaboration as a valuable and unique attribute of groups, but warn that its use should be limited to decision-making tasks that require it.

Historical Trends in Group Decision-Making and Communication Scholarship

In this section, we discuss five lines of research that have had a considerable impact on our current understanding of communication processes in decision-making groups. Each takes a slightly different approach to understanding how members influence one another during group discussion. We first review scholarship on information use and influence processes. Following that, we discuss group polarization and the hidden profile information-sharing paradigm. We also discuss groupthink and its effects on decision-making interactions. We close this section with the functional theory of group decision making.

Information and Influence

Interaction facilitates influence processes among members of decision-making groups. Of particular interest is whether, when, and to what extent people influence and are influenced by others. Most famously Asch (1951), Deutsch and Gerard (1955), Kelman (1953), Sherif (1935), and later Milgram (1963), Moscovici (1976), and Zimbardo (1973) made the distinction between two types of influence processes and outcomes. Informational influence occurs when group members accept others' knowledge as evidence about reality, whereas normative influence takes place when social rewards are offered or threatened to induce some kind of cognitive or behavioral change. Informational influence tends to be associated with private acceptance and long term attitudinal or behavioral changes. Normative influence is associated with temporary public acceptance of a position or action that is only maintained in the presence of other group members. There are several noteworthy reviews on the associations between influence, information, and group decision making. We point readers to Propp's (1999) chapter in *The Handbook of Group Communication, Theory, and Research*, in which she synthesizes relevant research to put forth a model describing how group members engage in collective information processing. She also identifies a number of key factors that facilitate or inhibit this process, including group size and composition, task characteristics, and information load and redundancy. For a more general review, the handbook also contains a chapter by Meyers and Brashers (1999), who categorize and compare prevailing perspectives on group argument, influence, and decision-making. For those interested in social influence and compliance, we refer readers to reviews by Pavitt (1993, 2014) and Sisaye (2005), and Wood et al.'s (1994) meta-analysis.

Group Polarization and the Hidden Profile

A fundamental issue for group scholars is to identify the ways in which individual members' pre-discussion preferences, attitudes, and arguments map onto group outcomes. Researchers have been perplexed by the inability to consistently predict what group members say and do during decision-making interactions; groups sometimes make riskier or more cautious decisions than what individual members' positions would suggest (e.g. Moscovici and Zavalloni 1969, Myers and Lamm 1976, Stoner 1961). Now commonly referred to as *group polarization*, this scholarly focus was rather short-lived (Isenberg 1986). One major criticism was that polarization might be a statistical artifact of relying too heavily on group means without considering the distribution of individual members' actual attitudes, opinions, and knowledge. Nevertheless, this phenomenon inspired a host of new theories and methods for evaluating how information influences group deliberation and decision-making processes.

One of the most prolific areas of group decision-making research to come out of the polarization literature is the hidden profile information-sharing paradigm (HPIP). Since its inception (Stasser and Titus 1985), this paradigm has produced hundreds of studies on thousands of groups (for reviews and meta-analyses, see Lu et al. 2012; Reimer et al. 2010). The paradigm gets its name from a particular type of task—the hidden profile, where information is distributed so that some data is known to (i.e. shared by) all group members, whereas other information is unique to a minority or single member. Most studies within the HPIP are designed such that novel or unique information must be known or integrated by group members to identify the correct solution from a predetermined set of decision alternatives. For example, Hollingshead (1996) had participants discuss and select the best financial investment among three potential businesses. If group members contributed and evaluated unique information regarding one company's new product development and marketing strategies, they should be able to identify it as the superior choice. She found that groups engaged in higher-quality deliberation and were more likely to solve the hidden profile when members interacted face-to-face and were instructed to rank order the alternatives rather than simply select the best decision solution.

By and large, groups working on hidden profile tasks perform poorly, in part because members tend to favor shared information that does little in the way of solving the hidden profile. Two underlying reasons for the preoccupation with shared information are related to limitations imposed by the task itself. First, HPIP researchers provide greater amounts of shared information that, by definition, are redundant across members, thus increasing the likelihood that members will contribute it to discussion more frequently than unique information (Stasser 1992). Wittenbaum,

Hubbell, and Zuckerman (1999) put forth a second explanation that shared information is mutually enhancing in that it can be validated by others, allowing group members to establish a common ground, whereas unique information does not and cannot elicit the same level of perceived validity or utility. For a discussion of these and other limitations of the HPIP, see Wittenbaum, Hollingshead, and Botero (2004).

Despite its shortcomings, several key findings from the HPIP extend to groups working on other types of decision-making tasks. In particular, data suggest separating information exchanges from decision-making discussions by suppressing group members' need to poll preferences at the outset of discussion. Doing so enables groups to more objectively pool and consider their relevant informational resources prior to making a decision. To clarify, we do not expect group members to share all of the information made available to them. Rather, the hope is that groups deliberate long enough to make satisficing decisions using what they deem to be a sufficient amount of information. The major concern is that information sharing tends to be biased. Rather than sharing all of the information at their disposal, members favor and contribute to discussion evidence that is supportive of their own position. Stating preferences at the outset of discussion enhances this tendency, which is sometimes referred to as the preference consistency bias.

Groupthink

While influence, polarization, and HPIP researchers are primarily interested in what group members say during decision-making discussions, groupthink focuses more on what group members withhold. To date, groupthink remains one of the most intuitively appealing explanations for why "good" groups sometimes make "bad" decisions. Janis (1972) proposed eight reasons why members may fail to mention information during group discussion, leading the group to engage in faulty decision-making processes. They are as follows:

1. The illusion of invulnerability: The optimistic belief that together members are able to make sound, rational decisions, leading them to ignore warning signs to the contrary.
2. Collective rationalization: Ignoring or discounting negative information that contradicts the positions held by a majority of group members.
3. Belief in inherent morality: Ignoring or failing to appreciate ethical or moral implications of a given course of action.
4. Stereotyping: The inability to recognize heterogeneity among the group and those likely to be affected by the group's decision.
5. Self-censorship: Members avoid voicing fears, concerns, or doubts regarding the majority's position.

6. Mind guards: Members will suppress the questioning of the majority's position.
7. Illusion of unanimity: The belief that those who do not express their opinions or concerns are supportive of the majority's position.
8. Direct pressure: Members will rely on normative influence to convince dissenters to support the majority's position.

There are a number of historic cases where groupthink resulted in fiascos, including the Bay of Pigs, Pearl Harbor, the United States' involvement in the Viet Nam War, Watergate, and the Challenger Space Shuttle disaster (Esser 1998, Hirokawa et al. 1988). These studies found that groupthink is also perpetuated by ambiguous language use and ineffective persuasive attempts among group members. To avoid faulty communication processes associated with groupthink, the most widely cited recommendation is to assign one or more members to take on the role of devil's advocate, who is responsible for questioning the quality of group deliberation throughout the decision-making process.

Functional Theory of Group Decision Making

Finally, we highlight the functional theory of group decision making (e.g. Gouran and Hirokawa 1983, Gouran et al. 1993, Hirokawa 1980), as it is arguably the most popular prescriptive approach outlining the steps necessary for groups to make effective decisions. This theory assumes that groups make decisions to solve certain problems. Therefore, groups need to analyze the context in which a problem occurs, including its urgency and the consequences for not solving the problem (i.e. not rendering a decision). Additionally, groups need to establish evaluative criteria for decision solutions. For example, group members might identify parameters for the greatest number of costs and least benefits allowable in feasible solutions. Groups should also generate a reasonable number of alternatives that might sufficiently solve the problem at hand. This step aligns nicely with other perspectives, including the HPIP, brainstorming (Osborn 1957), the nominal group technique (Delbecq and Van de Ven 1971), and reflective thinking (Dewey 1933), which all emphasize the need to objectively share and evaluate task-relevant information and realistic courses of action prior to rendering a group decision. More specifically, groups should reach a final decision by applying the evaluative criteria to possible decision solutions, focusing on the pros and cons of each. Hirokawa and others were agnostic to the rank or order in which these steps should be followed. Meta-analytic findings suggest that assessing the negative repercussions of potential solutions is the most predictive of effective group decision making (Orlitzky and Hirokawa 2001).

Together these lines of research reveal a number of challenges that potentially hinder a group's ability to make effective decisions. Further, these lines of research are examples of how the discipline places a premium on the ways in which communication (and sometimes its breakdowns) influence a group's decision-making processes.

Practical Applications in Current Research Trends

There are a number of new, exciting lines of research being pursued by group communication scholars. We focus on diversity and technology use, as they are inherently tied to organizational functioning.

Decision Making in Diverse Teams

There are many ways for groups to be diverse. For a thorough review, see "Organizational Diversity Processes" in Miller's (2015) *Organizational Communication: Approaches and Processes*. The current trend for research in this domain is identifying ways to either maximize the benefits of diversity in groups, such as an increased variety of knowledge and skills, or suppress its negative effects like high levels of conflict and animosity through diversity management. Regarding the nature of diversity, Harrison and Klein (2007) distinguished between surface-level and deep-level diversity. Surface-level cues are (relatively) recognizable traits such as sex, gender, age, or race. Deep-level cues represent a person's core values, knowledge, perspectives, and attitudes. While surface-level cues are observable, deep-level characteristics can only be revealed or identified through communication. Collectively, data suggest that demographic variables alone do little to consistently affect group decision-making discussions and outcomes (Horwitz and Horwitz 2007, Oetzel et al. 2007, Stalh et al. 2010). This is likely attributable to the fact that communication processes such as conflict management (e.g. Adair et al. 2017), uncertainty reduction (Dayan et al. 2017), and the creation and adaption of efficacy beliefs (Hoever et al. 2017) moderate the relationship between surface-level diversity and decision-making performance.

It has become increasingly common to evaluate the combined effect of both surface- and deep-level cues. One challenge is that different types of diversity have heterogeneous effects on group communication processes, which also vary by task characteristics such as decision difficulty, informational requirements, discussion time, and trust and efficacy beliefs (Guillaume et al. 2017). Despite these differences, the general consensus seems to be that organizational commitment to diversity motivates members to engage in more open and inclusive discussions, which fosters perspective taking, understanding, and the ability to appreciate how each individual member can contribute to shared goals (e.g. Barak et al. 2016, Ellemers and Rink 2016, Peters et al. 2010). Importantly, all other things being equal, groups that value diversity tend to outperform groups that do not (Harrison and Klein 2007). Considering the social and legal implications of workplace diversity, we expect that this will remain a popular domain for interdisciplinary research.

Using Communication Technology to Make Group Decisions

There are ongoing efforts to understand how the proliferation of technology in our everyday lives influences the way that people communicate. While still a relatively new field, studies of technology use in groups date back to the mid-1980s. For the most part, our approaches to evaluating groups engaging in computer mediated communication (CMC groups) have remained the same. Researchers typically either examine CMC groups with similar theories and concepts derived from groups that interact face-to-face (FtF groups) or make direct comparisons between CMC and FtF groups (Gilson et al. 2015, Shen et al. 2015). Data overwhelmingly suggest that FtF groups are more efficient and effective at making decisions (Purvanova 2014), although there is some evidence to suggest that differences might be limited to temporary and ad hoc groups, with weaker or nonsignificant effects being observed in more fully developed and longer standing groups (Ortiz de Guinea et al. 2012, Walther 2002).

This line of work has flourished as organizations increasingly rely on groups who communicate through various channels. Yet, a fundamental question remains unanswered: Do CMC groups communicate in comparable ways to FtF groups? Take, for example, Corman and Kuhn's (2005) study, in which participants read a transcript of actual group discussion, or a fictitious jury deliberation with speaking turns randomly generated by a computer. Findings revealed that people are worse than chance at correctly identifying the source of the transcripts. This is in part because group interaction does not proceed as smoothly or orderly as we think it does. Rather FtF deliberation among group members includes interruptions, swift topic shifts, and many instances where members begin and then quickly abandon lines of thought within and across speaking turns. That is, group communication can be a bit messy as members negotiate the tension between sharing and obtaining floor space. We have no doubt that groups using richer mediums such as video-conferencing software interact in similar ways to FtF groups. However, these types of interactions are quite different than what takes place over leaner mediums (e.g. email, chat rooms) where communication is asynchronous, or when members might never have or will never meet FtF, as seen in virtual groups whose members are geographically dispersed and only communicate and *exist* through electronic media (Hertel et al. 2005, Walther 1992).

Unfortunately, current theories do not sufficiently account for differences across communication mediums, group types, or task characteristics with varied levels of decision difficulty and information-sharing requirements (Håkonsson et al. 2016, Marlow et al. 2017, Schaubroeck and Yu 2017). The current work on organizational collaboration seeks to fulfill these knowledge gaps. We want to point readers to Nikoi and Boateng's (2013) *Collaborative Communication Processes and Decision Making in Organizations* and Strode (2016) for more in depth discussions on collaboration technology and how different platforms can solve (but sometimes also create) problems for decision-making groups. As theorists and researchers continue to grapple with these issues, we want to emphasize the need to study *actual* communication among group members as it takes place *in situ*, in ad hoc, naturally occurring, and ongoing groups. We discuss this issue in greater detail in the next section.

Future Research Directions

We have two recommendations for future group communication scholars interested in decision making and collaboration. The first recommendation relates to methods and designs for studying groups in organizations. The second pertains to comparisons made across groups.

We are concerned about losing sight of what it means to examine communication phenomena in decision-making groups from a quantitative perspective. Admittedly, studying groups is time, labor, and resource-intensive. Researchers are also faced with a host of logistical problems, including the difficulty in gaining access to naturally occurring groups that will allow their interactions to be documented or recorded. When these opportunities arise, Joann recommends taking time to develop a relationship with the person(s) who invited or approved the data collection, as that person serves the vital role in linking researchers to other participants. That relationship also serves as testimony to the researcher's credentials and integrity. These relationships may also lead to other data collection opportunities. Others risk ecological validity by trying to convince participants to come to a lab and engage in ad hoc group discussions with strangers.

Both of us find it necessary to schedule six participants to a laboratory session to ensure that at least three (the minimum number of participants for a group) will show up. In an hour session, several brief interactions among the ad hoc groups can be recorded. However, within the research session, time must be allocated for participants to adjust to the laboratory environment (or having the researcher present) and to orient themselves with one another. Because of issues related to statistical power, most studies need to contain at least 20 groups; due to scheduling challenges, data collection for a study of 30 to 50 groups can take up to a year.

We are often asked if observing a group causes its members to behave differently. Generally, our observing becomes benign; after a few minutes group members forget that researchers are there. Researchers should never make direct eye contact with participants and never sit at the table with participants. Rather, researchers should sit as far away from the discussion as possible (at the corners, rather than sides or ends of the room). Once group meetings have convened, the discussion data needs to be transcribed. The alternative is to set up a virtual environment in which participants' interaction by text serves as the data, which comes with its own set of potential limitations (see more as follows). For each research project, researchers and research assistants must be trained to reliably unitize and code the transcripts; this step is unique to each data collection. After the discussion data has been coded, researchers must conduct sophisticated analyses that account for non-independence among group members (see Ervin and Bonito 2014, Bonito et al. 2016). It is a grueling but necessary process that pays off with incredibly rich data (as compared to perceptual data gathered by questionnaire). We refer readers to the 2010 special issue of *Small Group Research* as it demonstrates how five analytic approaches can be applied to the same interaction (i.e. the jury deliberations for *Ohio v. Ducic*) to support varied claims about communication processes during decision-making discussions. The point is that the strongest claims about group decision making are derived from studies of actual communication phenomena at both the individual- and group-levels of analysis. Innovative techniques, such as machine learning, will soon enable even greater possibilities for applying or generating new coding schemes. Keeping the bona fide group perspective (Putnam and Stohl 1990, 1996) in mind when designing research questions and studies will help communication scholars remain grounded in their discipline's traditions and at the same time offer conclusions about group members' interaction that communication scholars are uniquely prepared to provide.

Our second recommendation is for researchers to remain vigilant when making comparisons across groups and studies. This is particularly salient for future research that examines technology use in groups. Are CMC and FtF groups truly comparable? For instance, researchers might place participants in an online chat group with members that they know very little about. After some predetermined amount of time to interact and make a decision, the group disbands. This design allows researchers to evaluate the ways that chatroom members shared information, expressed disagreement, and claimed leadership, for example. However, members tend to have little to no investment in the task, which fundamentally influences the way they approach interaction and each other. An important question is whether and how studies on virtual ad hoc interactions can provide greater insight into organizational group decision making.

In addition to the points raised here, we encourage those interested in group and team interaction to consult several recent online encyclopedia entries (e.g. Drury-Grogan 2017, Frey 2008, Gouran 2008, Hirokawa 2008, Pavitt 2008, Reimer et al. 2017) and this handbook review chapter

(Seibold et al. 2014). These review articles and chapter will help the next generation of communication scholars learn about the theoretical traditions, research methodologies, and nuances of studying group decision-making and collaboration.

Discussion Questions

1. Reflecting on groups you've been in, how did the communication of other group members influence you? How did your communication influence them?
2. How do the five key concepts presented in this chapter (influence, polarization, HPIP, groupthink, and the functional perspective) align with your experiences in groups?
3. How are different types of decision-making groups (e.g. creative or decision-making, work-related, or life-related) similar to and different from one another? In what ways are these similarities or differences meaningful?
4. You're asked to give advice to a group or team. After reading this chapter, what three ideas or concepts would you present to them? Why?
5. You are given the task to design a study of group communication, group decision-making, and collaboration. What are some key issues and/or variables that ought to be considered for each of these concepts? What are some key questions you might hypothesize about regarding the relationship among these concepts and their underlying variables? Now, draw a visual illustrating the relationship(s) among these three concepts and their underlying variables.

References

Adair, W. L., Liang, L. H. and Hideg, I. 2017. "Buffering Against the Detrimental Effects of Demographic Faultlines: The Curious Case of Intragroup Conflict in Small Work Groups," *Negotiation and Conflict Management, 10*, 28–45.
Anderson, C. M. and Martin, M. M. 1999. "The Relationship of Argumentativeness and Verbal Aggressiveness to Cohesion, Consensus, and Satisfaction in Small Groups," *Communication Reports, 12*, 21–31.
Asch, M. J. 1951. "Nondirective Teaching in Psychology: An Experimental Study," *Psychological Monographs: General and Applied, 65*, 1–24.
Barak, M. E., Lizano, E. L., Kim, A., Duan, L., Rhee, M. K., Hsiao, H. Y. and Brimhall, K. C. 2016. "The Promise of Diversity Management for Climate of Inclusion: A State-of-the-Art Review and Meta-Analysis," *Human Service Organizations: Management, Leadership and Governance, 40*, 305–333.
Bettenhausen, K. L. 1991. "Five Years of Groups Research: What We Have Learned and What Needs to be Addressed," *Journal of Management, 17*, 345–381.

Bonito, J. A. 2007. "A Local Model of Information Sharing in Small Groups," *Communication Theory*, 17, 252–280.

Bonito, J. A., Ervin, J. N., and Staggs, S. M. 2016. "Estimation and Application of the Latent Group Model," *Group Dynamics: Theory, Research, and Practice*, 20, 126–143.

Bonito, J. A., Keyton, J. and Ervin, J. N. 2017. "Role-Related Participation in Product Design Teams: Individual-and Group-Level Trends," *Communication Research*, 44, 263–286.

Bonito, J. A. and Sanders, R. E. 2011. "The Existential Center of Small Groups: Member's Conduct and Interaction," *Small Group Research*, 42, 343–358.

Bonner, B. L., Baumann, M. R. and Dalal, R. S. 2002. "The Effects of Member Expertise on Group Decision-Making and Performance," *Organizational Behavior and Human Decision Processes*, 88, 719–736.

Boster, F. J. and Mayer, M. 1984. "Choice Shifts: Argument Qualities or Social Comparisons," *Annals of the International Communication Association*, 8, 393–410.

Corman, S. R. and Kuhn, T. K. 2005. "The Detectability of Socio-Egocentric Group Speech: A Quasi-Turing Test. *Communication Monographs*, 72, 117–143.

Cross, R., Rebele, R. and Grant, A. 2016. "Collaborative Overload," *Harvard Business Review*, 94, 74–79.

Dayan, M., Ozer, M. and Almazrouei, H. 2017. "The Role of Functional and Demographic Diversity on New Product Creativity and the Moderating Impact of Project Uncertainty," *Industrial Marketing Management*, 61, 144–154.

De Dreu, C. K., Nijstad, B. A. and van Knippenberg, D. 2008. "Motivated Information Processing in Group Judgment and Decision Making," *Personality and Social Psychology Review*, 12, 22–49.

Delbecq, A. L. and Van de Ven, A. H. 1971. "A Group Process Model for Problem Identification and Program Planning," *The Journal of Applied Behavioral Science*, 7, 466–492.

Deutsch, M. and Gerard, H. B. 1955. "A Study of Normative and Informational Social Influences upon Individual Judgment," *The Journal of Abnormal and Social Psychology*, 51, 629–636.

Dewey, J. 1933. *How We Think: A Restatement of the Relation of Reflective Thinking to the Educative Process*, Washington, DC: DC Heath and Company.

Drury-Grogan, M. L. 2017. "Decision Making Processes in Organizations," in Scott, C.R. and Lewis, L. (eds.), *The International Encyclopedia of Organizational Communication*, 1st ed. Hoboken, NJ: John Wiley & Sons.

Ellemers, N. and Rink, F. 2016. "Diversity in Work Groups," *Current Opinion in Psychology*, 11, 49–53.

Ervin, J. N., Bonito, J. A. and Keyton, J. 2017. "Convergence of Intrapersonal and Interpersonal Processes across Group Meetings," *Communication Monographs*, 84, 200–220.

Ervin, J. N. and Bonito, J. A. 2014. "A Review and Critique of Partner Effect Research in Small Groups," *Small Group Research*, 45, 603–632.

Esser, J. K. 1998. "Alive and Well After 25 years: A Review of Groupthink Research," *Organizational Behavior and Human Decision Processes*, 73, 116–141.

Frey, L. R. 2008. "Group Communication," in Donsbach, W. (ed.), *The International Encyclopedia of Communication*, Hoboken, NJ: Blackwell.

Gilson, L. L., Maynard, M. T., Jones Young, N. C., Vartiainen, M. and Hakonen, M. 2015. "Virtual Teams Research: 10 Years, 10 Themes, and 10 Opportunities," *Journal of Management*, *41*, 1313–1337.

Gouran, D. S. 2008. "The Functional Theory of Group Decision-Making," in Donsbach, W. (ed.), *The International Encyclopedia of Communication*, Hoboken, NJ: Blackwell.

Gouran, D. S. and Hirokawa, R. Y. 1983. "The Role of Communication in Decision-Making Groups: A Functional Perspective," *Communications in Transition*, *21*, 168–185.

Gouran, D. S., Hirokawa, R. Y., Julian, K. M. and Leatham, G. B. 1993. "The Evolution and Current Status of the Functional Perspective on Communication in Decision-Making and Problem-Solving Groups," *Annals of the International Communication Association*, *16*, 573–600.

Guillaume, Y. R., Dawson, J. F., Otaye-Ebede, L., Woods, S. A. and West, M. A. 2017. "Harnessing Demographic Differences in Organizations: What Moderates the Effects of Workplace Diversity?" *Journal of Organizational Behavior*, *38*, 276–303.

Håkonsson, D. D. Obel, B., Eskildsen, J. K. and Burton, R. M. 2016. "On Cooperative Behavior in Distributed Teams: The Influence of Organizational Design, Media Richness, Social Interaction, and Interaction Adaptation," *Frontiers in Psychology*, *7*, 692–703.

Hare, A. P., 1982. *Creativity in Small Groups*. Thousand Oaks, CA: SAGE.

Harrison, D. A. and Klein, K. J. 2007. "What's the Difference? Diversity Constructs as Separation, Variety, or Disparity in Organizations," *Academy of Management Review*, *32*, 1199–1228.

Hertel, G., Geister, S. and Konradt, U. 2005. "Managing Virtual Teams: A Review of Current Empirical Research," *Human Resource Management Review*, *15*, 69–95.

Hirokawa, R. Y., 1980. "A Comparative Analysis of Communication Patterns within Effective and Ineffective Decision-Making Groups," *Communications Monographs*, *47*, 312–321.

Hirokawa, R. Y. 2008. "Group Communication and Problem-Solving," in Donsbach, W. (ed.), *The International Encyclopedia of Communication*, Hoboken, NJ: Blackwell.

Hirokawa, R. Y., Gouran, D. S., and Martz, A. E. 1988. "Understanding the Sources of Faulty Group Decision Making: A Lesson from the Challenger Disaster," *Small Group Research*, *19*, 411–433.

Hoever, I. J., Zhou, J., and van Knippenberg, D. 2017. "Different Strokes for Different Teams: The Contingent Effects of Positive and Negative Feedback on the Creativity of Informationally Homogeneous and Diverse Teams," *Academy of Management*. Advance online publication.

Hollingshead, A. B. 1996. "Information Suppression and Status Persistence in Group Decision Making: The Effect of Communication Media," *Human Communication Research*, *23*, 193–219.

Horwitz, S. K. and Horwitz, I. B. 2007. "The Effects of Team Diversity on Team Outcomes: A Meta-Analytic Review of Team Demography," *Journal of Management*, *33*, 987–1015.

Isenberg, D. J. 1986. "Group Polarization: A Critical Review and Meta-Analysis," *Journal of Personality and Social Psychology*, *50*, 210–222.

Janis, I. 1972. *Victims of Groupthink*, New York: Houghton Mifflin.

Johnson, G. F., Black, L. W., and Knobloch, K. R. 2017. "Citizens' Initiative Review Process: Mediating Emotions, Promoting Productive Deliberation," *Policy and Politics*, 45, 431–447.

Kelman, H. C. 1953. "Attitude Change as a Function of Response Restriction," *Human Relations*, 6, 185–214.

Keyton, J. 1999. "Relational Communication in Groups," in Frey, L. R., Gouran, D. S. and Poole, M. S. (eds.), *The Handbook of Group Communication Theory and Research*, Thousand Oaks, CA: SAGE, pp. 192–222.

Keyton, J. 2017. "Collaboration," in Scott, C.R. and Lewis, L. (eds.), *The International Encyclopedia of Organizational Communication*, Hoboken, NJ: John Wiley & Sons.

Ketyon, J. and Beck, S. J. 2010. "Examining Laughter Functionality in Jury Deliberations," *Small Group Research*, 41, 386–407.

Keyton, J., Ford, D. J. and Smith, F. I. 2008. "A Meso-Level Communicative Model of Interorganizational Collaboration," *Communication Theory*, 18, 376–406.

Keyton, J. and Springston, J. 1990. "Redefining Cohesiveness in Groups," *Small Group Research*, 21, 234–254.

Laughlin, P. R. 1999. "Collective Induction: Twelve Postulates," *Organizational Behavior and Human Decision Processes*, 80, 50–69.

Lehmann-Willenbrock, N. K. and Allen, J. A. 2014. "How Fun Are Your Meetings? Investigating the Relationship between Humor Patterns in Team Interactions and Team Performance," *Journal of Applied Psychology*, 99, 1278–1287.

Lu, L., Yuan, Y. C. and McLeod, P. L. 2012. "Twenty-Five Years of Hidden Profiles in Group Decision Making: A Meta-Analysis," *Personality and Social Psychology Review*, 16, 54–75.

McGrath, J. E. 1984. *Groups: Interaction and Performance*, Englewood Cliffs, NJ: Prentice-Hall.

McGrath, J. E. 1991. "Time, Interaction, and Performance (TIP): A Theory of Groups," *Small Group Research*, 22, 147–174.

Marlow, S. L., Lacerenza, C. N. and Salas, E. 2017. "Communication in Virtual Teams: A Conceptual Framework and Research Agenda," *Human Resource Management Review*, 27, 575–589.

Meyers, R. A. 1989. "Testing Persuasive Argument Theory's Predictor Model: Alternative Interactional Accounts of Group Argument and Influence," *Communication Monographs*, 56, 112–132.

Meyers, R. A. and Brashers, D. 1999. "Influence Processes in Group Interaction," in Frey L. R., Gouran, D. S. and Poole, M. S. (eds.), *The Handbook of Group Communication Theory and Research*, Thousand Oaks, CA: SAGE, pp. 288–312.

Meyers, R. A. and Seibold, D. R. 1990. "Perspectives on Group Argument: A Critical Review of Persuasive Arguments Theory and an Alternative Structurational View," in Anderson, J. (ed.), *Communication Yearbook*, Newbury Park, CA: SAGE, pp. 268–302.

Milgram, S. 1963. "Behavioral Study of Obedience," *The Journal of Abnormal and Social Psychology*, 67, 371–378.

Moreland, R. L. 2010. "Are Dyads Really Groups?" *Small Group Research*, 41, 251–267.

Moscovici, S. 1976. *Society Against Nature: The Emergence of Human Societies*, Atlantic Highlands, NJ: Humanities Press.

Miller, K. 2015. *Organizational Communication: Approaches and Processes*, 7th ed. Issaquah, WA: Cengage Learning.

Moscovici, S. and Zavalloni, M. 1969. "The Group as a Polarizer of Attitudes," *Journal of Personality and Social Psychology, 12*, 125–135.

Myers, D. G. and Lamm, H. 1976. "The Group Polarization Phenomenon," *Psychological Bulletin, 83*, 602–627.

Nijstad, B. A. and Kaps, S. C. 2008. "Taking the Easy Way Out: Preference Diversity, Decision Strategies, and Decision Refusal in Groups," *Journal of Personality and Social Psychology, 94*, 860–870.

Nikoi, E. and Boetang, K. 2013. *Collaborative Communication Processes and Decision Making in Organizations*, Hershey, PA: IGI Global.

Oetzel, J., Dhar, S. and Kirschbaum, K. 2007. "Intercultural Conflict from a Multilevel Perspective: Trends, Possibilities, and Future Directions," *Journal of Intercultural Communication Research, 36*, 183–204.

Orlitzky, M. and Hirokawa, R. Y. 2001. "To Err is Human, To Correct for It Divine: A Meta-Analysis of Research Testing the Functional Theory of Group Decision-Making Effectiveness," *Small Group Research, 32*, 313–341.

Ortiz de Guinea, A., Webster, J. and Staples, S. 2012. "A Meta-Analysis of the Consequences of Virtualness on Team Functioning," *Information and Management, 49*, 301–308.

Osborn, A. F. 1957. *Applied Imagination*, New York: Scribner.

Pavitt, C. 1993. "Does Communication Matter in Social Influence during Small Group Discussion? Five positions," *Communication Studies, 44*, 216–227.

Pavitt, C. 2014. "An Interactive Input–Process–Output Model of Social Influence in Decision-Making Groups," *Small Group Research, 45*, 704–730.

Pavitt, C. 2008. "Group Communication and Social Influence," in Donsbach, W. (ed.), *The International Encyclopedia of Communication*, Hoboken, NJ: Blackwell.

Peters, K., Morton, T. A., and Haslam, S. A. 2010. "Communication Silos and Social Identity Complexity in Organizations," in Giles, H., Ried, S. A., and Harwood, J. (eds.), *The Dynamics of Intergroup Communication*, New York: Peter Lang, pp. 221–234.

Postmes, T., Spears, R. and Cihangir, S. 2001. "Quality of Decision Making and Group Norms," *Journal of Personality and Social Psychology, 80*, 918–930.

Propp, K. M. 1997. "Information Utilization in Small Group Decision Making: A Study of the Evaluative Interaction Model," *Small Group Research, 28*, 424–453.

Propp, K. M. 1999. "Collective Information Processing in Groups," in Frey L. R., Gouran, D. S. and Poole, M. S. (eds.), *The Handbook of Group Communication Theory and Research*, 1st ed. Thousand Oaks, CA: SAGE, pp. 225–250.

Purvanova, R. K. 2014. "Face-to-Face Versus Virtual Teams: What Have We Really Learned?" *The Psychologist-Manager Journal, 17*, 2–29.

Putnam, L. L. and Stohl, C. 1990. "Bona Fide Groups: A Reconceptualization of Groups in Context," *Communication Studies, 41*, 248–265.

Putnam, L. L. and Stohl, C. 1996. "Bona Fide Groups: An Alternative Perspective for Communication and Small Group Decision Making," in Hirokawa, R. Y.

and Poole, M. S. (eds.), *Communication and Group Decision Making*, 2nd ed., Thousand Oaks, CA: SAGE, pp. 147–178.

Reimer, T., Reimer, A. and Czienskowski, U. 2010. "Decision-Making Groups Attenuate the Discussion Bias in Favor of Shared Information: A Meta-Analysis," *Communication Monographs*, 77, 121–142.

Reimer, T., Russell, T. and Roland, C. 2017. "Groups and Teams in Organizations," in Scott, C. R. and Lewis, L. (ed.), *The International Encyclopedia of Organizational Communication*, Hoboken, NJ: John Wiley & Sons.

Schaubroeck, J. M. and Yu, A. 2017. "When Does Virtuality Help or Hinder Teams? Core Team Characteristics as Contingency Factors," *Human Resource Management Review*, 27, 635–647.

Schulz-Hardt, S., Frey, D., Lüthgens, C. and Moscovici, S. 2000. "Biased Information Search in Group Decision Making," *Journal of Personality and Social Psychology*, 78, 655–669.

Schulz-Hardt, S., Jochims, M. and Frey, D. 2002. "Productive Conflict in Group Decision Making: Genuine and Contrived Dissent as Strategies to Counteract Biased Information Seeking," *Organizational Behavior and Human Decision Processes*, 88, 563–586.

Schweiger, D. M., Sandberg, W. R. and Ragan, J. W. 1986. "Group Approaches for Improving Strategic Decision Making: A Comparative Analysis of Dialectical Inquiry, Devil's Advocacy, and Consensus," *Academy of Management Journal*, 29, 51–71.

Seibold, D. R., Hollingshead, A. B., and Yoon, K. 2014. "Embedded Teams and Embedding Organizations," in Putnam, L. L. and Mumby, D. (eds.), *The SAGE Handbook of Organizational Communication*, Thousand Oaks, CA; SAGE, pp. 327–350.

Shen, Z., Lyytinen, K. and Yoo, Y. 2015. "Time and Information Technology in Teams: A Review of Empirical Research and Future Research Directions," *European Journal of Information Systems*, 24, 492–518.

Sherif, M. 1935. "A Study of Some Social Factors in Perception," *Archives of Psychology*, 27, 5–16.

Sisaye, S. 2005. "Management Control Systems and Organizational Development: New Directions for Managing Work Teams," *Leadership & Organization Development Journal*, 26, 51–61.

Stahl, G. K., Maznevski, M. L., Voigt, A., and Jonsen, K. 2010. "Unraveling the Effects of Cultural Diversity in Teams: A Meta-Analysis of Research on Multicultural Work Groups," *Journal of International Business Studies*, 41, 690–709.

Stasser, G. 1992. "Information Salience and the Discovery of Hidden Profiles By Decision-Making Groups: A 'Thought Experiment,'" *Organizational Behavior and Human Decision Processes*, 52, 156–181.

Stasser, G. and Titus, W. 1985. "Pooling of Unshared Information in Group Decision Making: Biased Information Sampling during Discussion," *Journal of Personality and Social Psychology*, 48, 1467–1478.

Stasser, G. and Titus, W. 2003. "Hidden Profiles: A Brief History," *Psychological Inquiry*, 14, 304–313.

Stoner, J. A. F. 1961. *A Comparison of Individual and Group Decisions Involving Risk*, Doctoral dissertation, Massachusetts Institute of Technology, Cambridge, MA.

Strode, D. E. 2016. "A Dependency Taxonomy for Agile Software Development Programs," *Information Systems Frontiers*, *18*, 23–46.

Walther, J. B. 1992. "Interpersonal Effects in Computer-Mediated Interaction: A Relational Perspective," *Communication Research*, *19*, 52–90.

Walther, J. B. 2002. "Time Effects in Computer-Mediated Groups: Past, Present, and Future," in Hinds, P. J. and Iesler, K.S. (eds.), *Distributed Work*, 1st ed., Cambridge, MA: MIT Press, pp. 235–257.

Wheelan, S. A. and Mckeage, R. L. 1993. "Developmental Patterns in Small and Large Groups," *Small Group Research*, *24*, 60–83.

Wittenbaum, G. M., Hollingshead, A. B. and Botero, I. C. 2004. "From Cooperative to Motivated Information Sharing in Groups: Moving beyond the Hidden Profile Paradigm," *Communication Monographs*, *71*, 286–310.

Wittenbaum, G. M., Hubbell, A. P. and Zuckerman, C. 1999. "Mutual Enhancement: Toward An Understanding of the Collective Preference for Shared Information," *Journal of Personality and Social Psychology*, *77*, 967–978.

Wood, W., Lundgren, S., Ouellette, J. A., Busceme, S. and Blackstone, T. 1994. "Minority Influence: A Meta-Analytic Review of Social Influence Processes," *Psychological Bulletin*, *115*, 323–345.

Zimbardo, P. G. 1973. "On the Ethics of Intervention in Human Psychological Research: With Special Reference to the Stanford Prison Experiment," *Cognition*, *2*, 243–256.

11 Leadership

Guowei Jian and Gail T. Fairhurst

Guowei: As I reflected on the path I had taken to organizational communication research, three names came to mind: Gail Fairhurst, Stanley Deetz, and Kevin Barge, whom I regard as my intellectual mentors and whose work inspired me in different ways. First, I had the good fortune of studying under the advice of Fairhurst and Deetz during my graduate training. Fairhurst's seminal work on discursive leadership ignited my interest and laid down a conceptual foundation; Deetz introduced me to continental philosophies and their applications to understanding managerial control; Barge's work on dialogue and practice lent me another rich perspective. Their important contributions to a communicative understanding of leadership will become clear in the remainder of this chapter.

Gail: Thank you, Guowei! As I reflected on my path into leadership, I fondly remember the late Fred Jablin. He spent his career trying to give some communicative life to leadership psychology, the dominant perspective on leadership in the field of management and the starting place for most organizational communication research. Like Fred, I have always spanned the boundaries between the fields of communication and management, and throughout my career, I have consistently been struck by the impoverished view of communication that dominated leadership studies. Early on, communication was strictly a transmission, which lent itself to study via surveys and 7-point scales and where issues of meaning and power were easily elided. Today, the field of management has certainly changed, although I sometimes feel that U.S. leadership studies hasn't quite gotten the memo. Interestingly, some communication scholars avoid the topic of leadership either because it is well worn; it has that transmissional/psychological/survey history; or they are unaware that multiple lenses, including a critical lens, can and should be applied to the study of leadership. But regardless of dispositions or trends, there is just no getting away from the fact that communication is not ancillary but foundational to leadership, leadership is foundational to a society constantly on the move, and communication scholars are uniquely suited to addressing this phenomenon.

Leadership has been a thriving research field. A quick search on Google Scholar with the keyword "leadership" resulted in 3.78 million hits, out of which 1.5 million were dated after year 2000. A search on the global serials directory Ulrichsweb™ returned with 82 active, peer-reviewed scholarly journals devoted to the topic of leadership, which are published in wide-ranging fields from business and management to education, medicine, and engineering. For practitioners, the term "leadership" is ubiquitous in contemporary organizational life, appearing in corporate newsletters, employee handbooks, performance evaluations, training manuals, annual reports, and executive speeches. For everyone as a consumer and citizen, public accounts that attribute organizational success or failure to leadership have become a familiar narrative in the form of news reports, political punditry, and organizational lore.

The subject's ever-growing popularity begs the question: What is leadership? Although a seemingly simple question, typically involving asymmetric influence and goal-directed activity, the answer to it is much more complex. You may have heard the refrain that "there are almost as many different definitions of leadership as there are people who have tried to define it" (Northouse 2016: 2). In this chapter, we do not pretend to have found a universal definition of leadership or attempt to introduce our own. Instead, we treat definitions as ways of seeing, each of which reveals distinct features of leadership and may enable different practices. Thus, our goal in this chapter is to chart the terrain of leadership as a social scientific subject by showing how scholars define and study leadership in various fashions, how leadership theories and research inform practice, and what are the directions for future research. Given the vast expanse of this field and the limited space allowed here, we focus our review on ways in which communication has contributed to its understanding. In addition, in line with the purpose of this book, we limit our purview to organizational contexts, thus excluding areas such as politics, community development, and social movements, although we acknowledge the contextual boundaries are porous and often blurred.

To organize our review, we adapted a conceptual framework used by Deetz (1996) to describe the various research orientations in organization studies. The framework summarizes research approaches in four types of social scientific discourse: normative, interpretive, critical, and dialogic. Each discourse represents a unique type of language game that researchers engage in thinking, studying, and writing about leadership. It is less about which discourse gets it right than seeing the differences that make a difference in meeting organizational challenges. Just like different lenses, each discourse draws our attention to, and constitutes, leadership in distinct ways. Therefore, the four discourses shouldn't be taken as rigid categorizations but to "aid attention to meaningful differences and similarities" (Deetz 2001: 11) among various orientations. In the following, we present the four research discourses and their associated communication scholarship on leadership.

Leadership as an Objective Phenomenon

It can be argued that normative leadership discourse, in comparison to others, has the longest history, consists of the most extensive literature in volume, and has been the most influential in affecting the laymen's view of leadership. Normative studies typically treat leadership as a naturally existing object. Researchers follow a variable-analytic approach, similar to that in the physical sciences, by breaking an object into parts and properties and attempting to define them and identify the regularity in their relationships. The goals are to describe, predict, and control the phenomenon and its associated variables. Thus, leadership theories in normative discourse tend to take the form of law like propositions of causal relationships between leadership properties and their antecedents and outcomes. To test theories, studies often employ quantitative methods, such as surveys and experiments.

Within normative discourse, leadership theories have relied on the assumption that organizations, like large, complex objects, are multi-leveled and comprised of small and large units. As a result, theories tend to locate leadership in a certain analytical unit ranging from individuals and dyads to teams and organizational networks. Let us start with theories that are anchored in individuals, which constitute the largest body of normative leadership research. The overarching conceptual question is, to what extent do individual differences make a difference in leadership emergence and effectiveness?

Leader-Centric Theories

In this stream of research, communication is commonly treated as a state-like individual property in the form of speech characteristics and oral and written communication skills, which moderately correlate with leadership effectiveness (Hoffman et al. 2011). In research that focuses on what a leader does, scholars identify and categorize specific behaviors that predict leadership outcomes. Although taxonomies and theories in this tradition abound, Behrendt et al. (2017) argue that task- and relations-oriented behaviors are two meta-categories at the root of many behavior-based leadership research. Task-oriented behaviors include enhancing understanding, strengthening motivation, and facilitating implementation, while relations-oriented behaviors consist of fostering coordination, promoting cooperation, and activating resources (Behrendt et al. 2017). Arguably, the behaviors in these categories are either clearly communicative in nature or must be accomplished in part through communication.

One example of behavioral leadership theory is transformational leadership (Bass and Avolio 1993, Burns 1978), which has garnered significant scholarly attention in recent decades. Unlike earlier behavioral theories that attend solely to leader behavior, transformational leadership takes into consideration follower and group processes, such as follower self-concept, motivational needs, and collective identity (Conger 1999), although the primary agency of leadership is still located in leaders. This theory emphasizes the leader's role in formulating and articulating visions and missions and motivating followers to generate transformative change. However, the theory is ambiguous about underlying communicative processes and behaviors.

Within leader-centric studies, the association between gender and leadership has remained a constant theme for decades. One of the persistent questions is, does gender make a difference in leadership performance? Meta-analyses over the years (e.g. Eagly 1995, Gipson et al. 2017) found no clear evidence for gender difference in leadership performance across contexts, although differences emerged when moderating factors were considered. For example, women leaders were perceived less effective in roles that were defined in more masculine terms. Role congruity theory helps explain this result by arguing that the incongruity between gender role expectations and leader role requirements leads to gender bias and disadvantages women's position in organizations (Eagly and Karau 2002).

Follower-Centric Theories

In contrast to the leader-centric approaches discussed previously is the development of follower-centric perspectives, which question the romanticized, heroic role of leaders and recognize and theorize followers as (co) producers of leadership (Meindl 1995, Uhl-Bien, et al. 2014). Representative of this approach are implicit leadership theories (ILTs), which theorize leadership through followers' cognitive information–processing processes in forming leadership perceptions (Lord and Maher 1991). Specifically, followers hold leadership prototypes (i.e. a general standard) and their perceptions of leadership form through matching individual features and attribution reasoning. Leaders who match followers' implicit leadership prototype tend to be rated higher in performance, although such effects may be moderated by many contextual factors (Junker & van Dick 2014).

Leader–Member Exchange (LMX)

Unlike leader- and follower-centric theories, LMX conceptualizes leadership from the perspective of relational development between a leader and his or her followers. This theory postulates that the dyadic relationship quality between a leader and his/her followers could range from high to low. Leaders in higher quality relationships offer more time, support, challenging tasks, decision latitude, and autonomy to followers in exchange for higher commitment and loyalty and greater work contributions (Graen and Uhl-Bien 1995). An LMX relationship develops over time through a role-making process in which leaders only form high-quality relationships with a selected few in a workgroup (Graen and Uhl-Bien 1995). LMX theory has generated a vast body of literature that continues to expand. Research has examined a wide range of antecedents of LMX (e.g. characteristics of leaders and followers) and outcomes (e.g. follower performance) (Dulebohn et al. 2012, Martin et al. 2016). In general, higher-quality LMX is associated with more positive individual and organizational outcomes.

Because of LMX's focus on relational exchange, communication scholars have made meaningful contributions to normative LMX research. For instance, researchers have examined the association of LMX with many facets of organizational communication, such as upward influence (Olufowote et al. 2005) and coworker exchange (Omilion-Hodges and Baker 2013). Methodologically, researchers have developed new measurement instruments to better examine communicative processes, such as a leader-member conversational quality scale (Jian et al. 2014).

Shared Leadership

In recent years, *leadership in the plural* has been gaining a lot of momentum (Denis et al. 2012). Distinct from the unitary or dyadic views discussed previously, *leadership in the plural* conceptualizes leadership as a collective phenomenon and has appeared in the literature under various labels, for example, shared, collective, collaborative, integrative, or distributed leadership. Within normative discourse, *leadership in the plural* is often referred to as "shared leadership," defined as "a dynamic, interactive influence process among individuals in groups for which the objective is to lead one another to the achievement of group or organizational goals or both" (Pearce and Conger 2003: 1). Empirical research in teams and work groups, such as virtual teams (Eisenberg et al. 2016), suggests hierarchical leaders, support structures, and cultural values are significant antecedents to shared leadership, producing positive individual and collective outcomes (Wassenaar and Pearce 2016).

As reviewed thus far, social and behavioral psychological theories dominate normative leadership discourse (Fairhurst 2007). The field is wide open for the development of communication-based normative leadership theories or those that can integrate communicative and psychological processes and constructs.

Leadership as an Interpretive Accomplishment

Interpretive leadership discourse differs from normative leadership discourse in three fundamental ways. First, leadership is socially constructed; in other words, it is a coproduced, relational accomplishment performed in and through social interaction (Fairhurst and Uhl-Bien 2012). It eschews a view of individuals with strong inner motors, as in normative discourse. Second, while normative discourse holds that the essence of leadership lies in the qualities of the leader or aspects of the context, interpretivists believe that leadership is in the eye of the beholder. If people make different leadership attributions, interpretive discourse wants to know how these differences came about and coexist. Third, interpretive discourse adopts a meaning-centered view of human communication, while normative discourse is either heavily transmissional or views leaders as the primary symbolizing agents. For interpretivists, leaders and followers are comanagers of meaning, a key assumption that—if taken seriously in the research process—helps us understand leadership apart from a hierarchical designation (Holm and Fairhurst 2018). Leadership, unlike management, may shift and distribute itself among any organizational members who collaborate (Denis et al. 2012). By untying leadership from authority relationships, leadership can be seen as influential acts of organizing and advancing the task apart from hierarchical role. The interpretive lens has several research streams that include sensemaking and framing; aesthetics; and influential acts of human and material organizing.

Sensemaking and Framing

Sensemaking, which involves the assignment of meaning for "the situation here and now," is a primary generator of action (Drazin et al. 1999). It is what followers expect of leaders, particularly when uncertainty exists, and it becomes a means by which leadership attributions form when one is able to make sense of the world in ways that others cannot.

There are a host of terms for leadership actors' meanings for people and situations that include frames, enactments, schemas, and cognitive maps. Frames and framing are heavily used concepts, where the former are cognitive meaning structures and the latter designates a communication process (Fairhurst 2011). "Sensemaking" and "sensegiving" have similarly been distinguished on these grounds in leadership contexts (Gioia and Chittipeddi 1991).

Fairhurst (2011) wrote about framing as the *sine qua non* of effective leadership. Through framing, leadership actors create realities to which they must then respond. In the ambiguity of "the situation here and now," the opportunity to emerge as a leader occurs when an actor makes sense of the world in ways that connects with others. Indeed, it can also spell a leader's downfall, as studies on the "failure framing" strategies of leaders attempting to deflect responsibility in major scandals have shown (Craig and Amernic 2004, Liu 2010).

However, the study of identity is also tied to leadership sensemaking and framing because, as individuals or collectives, we also often ask ourselves, "Who am I in this context? Who are we?" When interpretive scholars study leadership sensemaking, they want to know how, through framing, leaders and followers introduce, understand, or adopt a new organizational change initiative (Foldy et al. 2008, Stensaker and Falkenberg 2007). They may want to contrast framing by multiple stakeholders to reveal how frames conflict and coincide (Lewis 2011). Finally, they may want to understand how leaders and followers try to reconfigure new individual and/or collective selves from within a change initiative; such identity framing may signal how much they identify with the change and thus likely to adopt it (Alvesson and Spicer 2011, Sonenshein 2010).

Aesthetics

What do we mean by aesthetics? According to Riley (1988: 82), charisma and vision, concepts from normative discourse that drive the business of organizations, also invoke the art form of leadership. Analysts thus attune themselves to issues of style, meaning, and drama. We see this in work on "social poetics" for managers involving a "precognitive understanding in which poetic images and gestures provoke a response as we feel the rhythm, resonance, and reverberation of speech and sound" (Cunliffe 2002: 134). Hansen, Ropo, and Sauer (2007) likewise cast aesthetics as felt meaning, tacit knowing, and emotions integral to leading and following. Analysts might therefore study the ways in which discourses, narratives, storytelling, metaphors, or other language forms contribute to authentic and emotionally impactful performances that win leadership attributions (Ladkin 2008).

Beyond words, symbols, and emotions, however, aesthetics increasingly focuses on leaders' and followers' bodies, including gendered bodies. Interpretivists criticize normativists for too much reliance on the cognitive and symbolic to the neglect of body possibilities (Sinclair 2005); for example, Johansson, Tienari, and Valtonen (2017) argue that healthy, fit and athletic bodies are instrumental to the construction of contemporary managerial identities. Even ephemeral leadership qualities like *presence* takes on new meaning when bodies and artifacts are considered (Fairhurst and Cooren 2009).

Influential Acts of Human and Material Organizing

This category studies leadership-as-it-happens in key interactional moments. It focuses upon influential moves, turning points, or passage points in social and socio-material interaction in which collective action is made possible and leadership attributions follow. Grounded in action, the organization is thus cast as in a constant state of becoming (Fairhurst and Putnam 2004).

For example, Holm and Fairhurst (2018) studied the relationship between shared and hierarchical leadership in a Danish municipality vis-à-vis the study of authoring and resistance authoring patterns over time. They highlighted the ambiguity of this space by focusing on the ways in which the hierarchical leader made his presence known by setting expectations at the start of team meetings and configuring both figurative and concrete (intranet) texts as they concluded; the meetings themselves, however, were highly participative. This combination of discourse and (the materiality of) texts required interrogating leadership attributions, the outcomes of which involved requests, from team members, for specifically timed control moves by the hierarchical leader to guarantee the success of shared leadership.

Several "grounded in action" studies focus on influential acts of organizing to mobilize collectives (e.g. to advance discussions, facilitate consensus, spur decision making, create collective identities, win commitments, or reinforce obligations) (Larsson and Lundholm 2013, Wodak et al. 2011), define LMX relationships (Fairhurst 1993, Fairhurst and Chandler 1989), or create and diffuse organizational strategy (Liu and Maitlis 2014, Sorsa et al. 2014).

To summarize, interpretive discourse seeks to understand leadership-as-it-happens, how it is socially constructed in and through language, communication and, increasingly, materiality. Such scholars are taking to heart Grint's (1997: 17) wry observation that, "naked, friendless, money-less, and technology-less leaders are unlikely to prove persuasive."

Leadership as a Form of Power and Control

When leadership is conceived as a form of power and control, this is otherwise known as a critical discourse lens because it draws from such continental philosophies as critical theory and poststructuralism. Critical discourse shares many of the same sensibilities of interpretive discourse, but goes a step further by foregrounding leadership as a form of power and control. Most interpretive researchers leave open the possibility of power and control until leadership actors themselves make it relevant to the context under study (e.g. Boden 1994).

One such critical perspective is critical management studies (CMS), whose focus is on power and the politics of meaning (Cunliffe 2009). In this perspective, leadership and its study are often the subject of criticism. For example, Marxist or neo-Marxist perspectives focus on leadership as a form of control that privileges elites such as managers, owners, or shareholders (Deetz 1992, Willmott 1997). They elide the term "leadership" altogether, or cast it as a form of domination, citing the privileging of managerial interests by normativists and, in particular, the business press around which an entire industry has developed to commodify leadership. Postcolonial leadership studies, another CMS concern, critique the dominance of Western views of leadership in a global business context (Hall 2010, Said 1993). Here the subject of critique is the undue influence of the United States in normalizing leadership for global contexts subject to widely varying conditions. The goal is to strike down the presumption of universal standards. Poststructuralist studies, a final CMS concern, have been the most prolific generator of research on leadership, specifically in the areas of denaturalization and dialectics, on which we now elaborate.

Denaturalization

The term itself refers to that which appears "natural" or "the way things are" (Fournier and Grey 2000). The focus is on discourse, or language systems, texts, and ways of thinking, speaking, and behaving, as well as institutionalized structures, social practices, or techniques of power regulating what is normal or appears natural (Cunliffe 2009: 25). Much of this work is influenced by Foucault's (1995/1975, 1983) sociological conception of power, which is a more encompassing form of power than what we have seen in normative or interpretive discourses. His writings show us how leaders, not just followers, are passive receptors of meaning (i.e. cultural products), as much as they are managers of meaning (Fairhurst 2007). The latter, of course, is a pillar of charismatic and transformational leadership theory in normative leadership discourse.

Specifically, Foucault inspired work by Fairhurst and colleagues (Fairhurst 2007, Fairhurst et al. 2011) who portrayed "discursive leadership" at the intersection of little "d" language practices in social interaction, such as sequencing moves, category use, narratives, and so on, with big "D" Discourses, as socio-historical systems of thought. They studied the ways in which Foucault's (1990) examination and confessional technologies of power operated within executive coaching Discourses to discipline yet normalize alpha males as senior leaders to the exclusion of female leaders. Subtly, such Discourses reinforced, "think leadership, think male."

Indeed, issues of gender and race are key concerns in critical and poststructuralist approaches. Here, communication is often a site of struggle in which various articulations of the "body that leads" (and, by implication, the "body that follows") is a negotiated product of various human and nonhuman (e.g. uniforms, regalia, technology, and so on) agencies

(Ashcraft et al. 2009, Kuhn et al. 2017). The leader's body is not reduced to a fixed independent variable, as normativists conceive it, but literally "takes shape" in communication itself. By doing so, such enactments (re) produce gendered norms, structures, and outcomes that frequently privilege white males. Parker (2005), for example, wrote about race neutrality in U.S. leadership studies, finding that Black women leaders were subjugated through unquestioned assumptions about superiority and inferiority of raced and gendered bodies. They were excluded from the site or sources of knowledge production and ultimately controlled by silencing the vocal.

Alvesson and Sveningsson (2003) argued that normative leadership researchers have also made leadership into something special when it often gets lost amidst the everyday aspects of work. They adopt CMS scholars' traditional suspicion of (popular Discourses of) leadership as a mechanism of domination (Hardy and Clegg 1996) and overly reductionist (Cunliffe 2009). Kelly (2008), however, responded by arguing that they lacked an understanding of constructionist thinking: If leaders, followers, or any other constituencies are using the term "leadership," the power and influence-oriented language games they are playing deserve study, although they may share only a family resemblance. In effect, there is no right and final definition of leadership, which normative discourse seeks out. Interpretivists want to understand the variety and how they come to exist, while critical leadership discourse casts each as an exercise in power.

More generally, several scholars have suggested a number of compatibilities between a critical agenda and the study of leadership, which has led Collinson (2014) to solidify critical leadership studies (CLS) as an area of study. One such area within CMS, and now CLS, concerns the dialectics of leadership to which we now turn.

Leadership Dialectics

Because of Foucault's notion that power and resistance are inseparable, many CMS scholars argue against treating them as a simple binary (i.e. privileging one or the other) because they can be conceived more complexly by treating them as co-occurring (Fleming and Spicer 2008, Mumby 2005). In leadership situations, they may fold into each other, operate at more than one level, or mask each other's effects. Tensions like control and resistance thus often take on paradoxical qualities, which lead scholars to treat the intertwined relationship as one of struggle.

Structuration theory is useful here because Giddens (1979, 1984) conceives of organizations as marked by an "antagonism of opposites" and the "dialectic of control," where the less powerful inevitably exert a measure of control over the powerful. For example, Jian (2007) used a structuration lens to study the unintended consequences of a planned organizational change. Demonstrating the dialectic of control through conflictual relationships between a variety of management and employee groups, organizational leaders needed to shift from monologues to dialogues to more substantively ground the organizational change and minimize unplanned outcomes.

More generally, Collinson (2005: 1427) has written about the dialectics of leadership by suggesting that leadership is "discursive, dialectical, contested, and contradictory." He argued that leadership is marked by three dialectics: control/resistance, dissent/consent, and men/women—to which Zoller and Fairhurst (2007) added fixed/fluid meaning potentials, overt/covert behavior, and reason/emotion to show how leadership emerges, sans hierarchical position, when these dialectics are well managed. However, with the study of tension, contradiction, dialectics, and paradox rising more generally in the fields of management and communication (Putnam et al. 2016, Schad et al. 2016), a growing number of studies are applying them to leadership/management contexts (e.g. Gibbs 2009, Sheep et al. 2017).

To summarize, issues of power and materiality are central in critical leadership discourse. The interests of multiple stakeholders are privileged over management's, the politics of meaning are a central concern, and binaries are to be avoided to focus instead on the struggle between power and resistance in an attempt to conceive of both in more complex terms. The dialectics of leadership are ongoing concerns, especially as they multiply and impact one another.

Leadership as Dialogue and Practice

Dialogic leadership discourse differentiates itself by a relational ontology, an emphasis on dialogic and reflexive practices, and a leadership ethics grounded in communicative terms. First, a relational ontology argues that our being is defined by a multitude of relationships, our experience is intersubjective (Shotter 2008), and "the emotions, pleasure, and pain that we long-held as part of our private body are in fact manifestations of relationship" (Gergen 2009: 2416). Leadership theories based on a relational ontology do not just pay attention to the relational dynamic between leaders and members, as in LMX; rather, leadership is conceptualized as "a way of being-in-relation-to-others" (Cunliffe and Eriksen 2011: 1430).

Building on the relational ontology is a preoccupation with dialogue and conversation as the central forms of leadership practice. Scholars have drawn inspirations from dialogic theorists, such as Buber (1970), Bahktin (1981, 1984), and Bohm (1996), with the aim of generating leadership theories designed to create practical alternatives for action. Leadership dialogue encourages relational reflexivity (Barge 2004). Instead of being a cognitive, intellectual exercise, "relational reflexivity refers" to the dialogic practice of inviting "others to participate in conversation and make sense of situations in new ways" (Barge 2004: 92) and "a way of connecting with others in conversations" (71). In the face of wicked problems that are intractable and have no known solutions (Grint 2005), dialogic leadership is especially valued because of the power of dialogue in generating creative solutions and new meanings (van Loon and van Dijk 2015).

Several dialogic leadership theories have emerged in recent years. For example, building on a systemic constructionist theory of leadership (Barge and Fairhurst 2008), Barge (2014) proposed *pivotal leadership* to capture the conversational flow and reflexive practices that constitute leadership in an evolving organizational context. Leadership emerges from embodied conversational practices (e.g. designing, layering, and sequencing conversations) that can create change in relationship, task, identity, and context. Guided by four tenets, "collectiveness, concurrency, collaboration, and compassion," Raelin (2012: 9–11) suggested viewing leadership as *leaderful practice*, by which employees or community members all "[participate] in leadership not only collectively but concurrently" through dialogue and deliberation.

Furthermore, the dialogic perspective has inspired scholars to challenge and re-constitute some conventional leader-centric theories. For instance, "authentic leadership" originated from an individualist ontology and was defined as individual leader's capacity to develop heightened self-awareness and self-regulation that leads to authentic behavior (George 2015). Questioning heroic, leader-centric thinking, dialogists (e.g. Hanold 2017) argue that authenticity is a product of dialogue and an embodied experience that occurs in a relationship between individuals who share power. Authenticity is re-conceptualized as "an *orientation* whereby we allow ourselves to integrate 'others and othernesses' into our own way of being and thinking" (Hanold 2017: 456; italics in the original). Mitra's (2013) reworking of transformational leadership offers another example. Rather than a tidy predictive model, leadership transformations are found in the messy and fluid sequences of communicative action/re-action and outcomes between leaders and participants in social change. In particular, drawing upon CCO research (see Chapter 2), Mitra (2013: 401) identifies "naming of identities, processes, and concepts through dialogue" as a transformative, communicative practice with contingent outcomes.

Finally, dialogic discourse is explicit in its ethical concern with leadership. Rather than treating ethics as a set of personal virtues possessed by heroic leaders, dialogic leadership theories ground ethics in relational and interactional terms. Specifically, answerability (Bakhtin 1990, 1993) and responsibility (Levinas 1969) in dialogue form the basis of an ethical relationship between leaders and members (Lollar 2013). Cunliffe and Eriksen (2011: 1439) propose the term "relational integrity" as a guideline for leadership, which means *"to be responsive, responsible and accountable to others in our everyday interactions with them"* (italics in the original).

In summary, dialogic discourse foregrounds leadership as a way of relating to others through dialogic practice. Leadership emerges in the artful management of conversation and dialogue that brings about new possibilities, drives organizational and relational change, and advances tasks. Although dialogic studies are limited by, among other things, insufficient attention to power and authority, its practical orientation holds growing appeal to communication scholars and practitioners alike.

Future Directions

Our review has drawn a sketch of the burgeoning landscape of leadership research, which holds abundant opportunities for future development. Here we would like to highlight a few areas where organizational communication scholars are well positioned to make significant contributions. First, recent developments on *leadership in the plural* (Denis et al. 2012) have raised more questions than answers. For example, how does power function in communication and discourse that enables or hinders collective leadership? How do formal authority structures interact with the emergence of shared leadership?

Second, we need leadership research that can adequately address the role of materiality, including nonhuman actants. More specifically, considering how communication technologies imbricate with human actions in the process of organizing, how does leadership emerge and function in human-material networks? How do we configure materiality in leadership dialogue?

Third, many organizations are facing increasing dialectical tensions and paradoxes as the pace of change quickens to produce more turbulent environments. How should leaders educate and help their people in recognizing and managing these tensions? Is training in paradoxical thinking, a both/and approach to resolving opposing poles (Smith and Lewis 2011), enough? What role should leaders play in helping their people understand that for many, such tensions and paradoxes are the new normal?

Finally, how does ethics, grounded in dialogue, enable and link to the morality of organizational decisions that could have consequential impact on society and their stakeholders? We believe that answering these challenging questions would require cross-fertilization among the four discourses as well as innovation both conceptual and methodological.

Practical Applications

By this point, if you're in a leadership position in your workplace or community or aspire to be a leader, you must be wondering how leadership research can inform practice. To address this question, let's apply the four discursive orientations one more time.

First, normative leadership research allows practitioners to measure, predict, and control leadership behavior and its related outcomes. For example, knowing the predictive effect of communication skills on leadership effectiveness informs leadership selection, assessment, and development. Second, taking an insider's view amidst change and action, interpretive leadership studies reveal influential moves, turning points, or passage points in social interaction. They provide leadership actors with contextually rich information and assist them in deciding how and where to intervene in a complex situation. Third, by revealing the contested, value-laden nature of leadership processes, critical leadership studies challenge practitioners to be reflective on the dialectical functioning of power and the legitimacy of authority. The literature also lends voice to those who organize to resist repression and challenge injustice. Finally, dialogic leadership studies are squarely aimed at improving communicative practice of leadership. For example, to enact dialogic leadership ethics, Cunliffe and Eriksen (2011) suggest creating opportunities for surfacing tensions in relationships and being responsive to differences in conversations. Barge and Fairhurst (2008) propose value commitments of communication to guide leadership conversations.

To conclude, communication as a practical discipline holds great promise in enriching both the scholarly dialogue on, and everyday practice of, leadership. We hope that our comparison and contrast between the discursive orientations have effectively demonstrated the plurality and vibrancy of leadership research and its relevance to practice.

Discussion Questions

1. Please identify a few empirical leadership studies and explain which discursive orientation(s) each study takes. How is "communication" defined differently across these studies explicitly or implicitly? How is the discursive orientation related to their definition of communication? How could we further each study based on such cross-discourse comparison?

2. How do you see the relationship between the four discourses of leadership research? Are they incommensurable, contradictory, or complementary? Why? Please use examples to explain and support your arguments.

3. Think of an organization you are working for or affiliated with right now. Which leadership theories in this chapter resonate with your leadership experience, and why? To what extent, and how, do you think these theories can guide positive change in your organization?

References

Alvesson, M. and Spicer, A. 2011. *Metaphors We Lead By: Understanding Leadership in The Real World*, London: Routledge.

Alvesson, M. and Sveningsson, S. 2003. "The Great Disappearing Act: Difficulties in Doing 'Leadership'," *Leadership Quarterly, 14*, 359–381.

Ashcraft, K. L., Kuhn, T. and Cooren, F. 2009. "Constitutional Amendments: 'Materializing' Organizational Communication," *Academy of Management Annals, 3*(1), 1–64.

Bakhtin, M. M. 1981. "Discourse in the Novel," in Holquist, M. (ed.), *The Dialogic Imagination: Four Essays by Bakhtin, M. M.* (Emerson, C. and Holquist, M.), Austin, TX: University of Texas Press, 259–422.

Bakhtin, M. M. 1984. *Problems of Dostoevsky's Poetics*, (Emerson, C.), Minneapolis, MN: University of Minnesota Press.

Bakhtin, M. M. 1990. *Art and Answerability: Early Philosophical Essays*, in Holquist, M. and Liapunov, V. (eds.) (Liapunov, V. and Brostrom, K. Trans.), Austin, TX: University of Texas Press.

Bakhtin, M. M. 1993. *Toward a Philosophy of the Act*, in Liapunov, V. and Holquist, M. (eds.), Austin, TX: University of Texas Press.

Barge, J. K. 2004. "Reflexivity and Managerial Practice," *Communication Monographs, 71*, 70–96.

Barge, J. K. 2014. "Pivotal Leadership and the Art of Conversation," *Leadership, 10*, 56–78.

Barge, J. K. and Fairhurst, G. T. 2008. "Living Leadership: A Systemic Constructionist Approach," *Leadership, 4*, 227–251.

Bass, B. M., and Avolio, B. J. 1993. *Improving Organizational Effectiveness Through Transformational Leadership*, Thousand Oaks, CA: SAGE.

Behrendt, P., Matz, S., and Göritz, A. S. 2017. "An Integrative Model of Leadership Behavior," *Leadership Quarterly, 28*, 229–244.

Boden, D. 1994. *The Business of Talk: Organizations in Action*, Cambridge, UK: Polity Press.

Bohm, D. 1996. *On Dialogue*, New York: Routledge.

Buber, M. 1970. *I and Thou* (Kaufman, W. Trans.), New York: Charles Scribner and Sons.

Burns, J. M. 1978. *Leadership*, New York: Harper & Row.

Collinson, D. L. 2005. "Dialectics of Leadership," *Human Relations, 58*, 1419–1442.

Collinson, D. L. 2014. "Dichotomies, Dialectics and Dilemmas: New Directions for Critical Leadership Studies," *Leadership, 10*, 36–55.

Conger, J. A. 1999. "Charismatic and Transformational Leadership in Organizations: An Insider's Perspective on These Developing Streams of Research," *Leadership Quarterly, 10*, 145–179.

Craig, R. J. and Amernic, J. H. 2004. "Enron Discourse: The Rhetoric of a Resilient Capitalism," *Critical Perspective on Accounting, 15*, 813–851.

Cunliffe, A. L. 2002. "Social Poetics as Management Inquiry: A Dialogical Approach," *Journal of Management Inquiry, 11*, 128–146.

Cunliffe, A. L. 2009. *A Very Short, Fairly Interesting and Reasonably Cheap Book about Management*, Thousand Oaks, CA: SAGE.

Cunliffe, A. L. and Eriksen, M. 2011. "Relational Leadership," *Human Relations, 64*, 1425–1449.

Denis, J-L., Langley, A. and Sergi, V. 2012. "Leadership in the Plural," *The Academy of Management Annals, 6*, 211–283.

Deetz, S. A. 1992. *Democracy in an Age of Corporate Colonization: Developments in Communication and the Politics of Everyday Life*, New York: State University of New York Press.

Deetz, S. A. 1996. "Describing Differences in Approaches to Organization Science: Rethinking Burrell and Morgan and Their Legacy," *Organization Science, 7*, 190–207.

Deetz, S. A. 2001. "Conceptual Foundations," in Jablin, F. M. and Putnam, L. L. (eds.), *The New Handbook of Organizational Communication: Advances in Theory, Research, and Methods*, Thousand Oaks, CA: SAGE, pp. 3–46.

Drazin, R., Glynn, M. A. and Kazanjian, R. K. 1999. "Multilevel Theorizing about Creativity in Organizations: A Sensemaking Perspective," *Academy of Management Review, 24*, 286–307.

Dulebohn, J. H., Bommer, W. H., Liden, R. C., Brouer, R. L. and Ferris, G. R. 2012. "A Meta-Analysis of Antecedents and Consequences of Leader-Member Exchange: Integrating the Past with an Eye toward the Future," *Journal of Management, 38*, 1715–1759.

Eagly, A. H. and Karau, S. J. 2002. "Role Congruity Theory of Prejudice toward Female Leaders," *Psychological Review, 109*, 573–598.

Eagly, A. H., Karau, S. J. and Makhijani, M. G. 1995. "Gender and the Effectiveness of Leaders: A Meta-Analysis," *Psychological Bulletin, 117*, 125–145.

Eisenberg, J., Gibbs, J. and Erhardt, N. 2016. "The Role of Vertical and Shared Leadership in Virtual Team Collaboration," in Graham, C. (ed.), *Strategic Management and Leadership for Systems Development in Virtual Spaces*, Hershey, PA: Business Science Reference, pp. 22–42.

Fairhurst, G. T. 1993. "The Leader-Member Exchange Patterns of Women Leaders in Industry," *Communication Monographs, 60*, 1–31.

Fairhurst, G. T. 2007. *Discursive Leadership: In Conversation with Leadership Psychology*, Thousand Oaks, CA: SAGE.

Fairhurst, G. T. 2011. *The Power of Framing: Challenging the Language of Leadership*, San Francisco, CA: Jossey Bass.

Fairhurst, G. T. and Cooren, F. 2009. "Leadership as the Hybrid Production of Presence(s)," *Leadership, 5*, 469–490.

Fairhurst, G. T. and Chandler, T. A. 1989. "Social Structure in Leader-Member Interaction," *Communication Monographs, 56*, 215–239.

Fairhurst, G. T., Church, M., Hagen, D. E. and Levi, J. T. 2011. "Whither Female Leaders? Executive Coaching and the Alpha Male Syndrome," in Mumby, D. (ed.), *Reframing Difference in Organizational Communication Studies: Research, Pedagogy, and Practice*, Thousand Oaks, CA: SAGE, pp. 77–100.

Fairhurst, G. T. and Putnam, L. L. 2004. "Organizations as Discursive Constructions," *Communication Theory, 14*, 1–22.

Fairhurst, G. T. and Uhl-Bien, M. 2012. "Organizational Discourse Analysis (ODA): Examining Leadership as a Relational Process," *Leadership Quarterly, 23*, 1043–1062.

Fleming, P. and Spicer, A. 2008. "Beyond Power and Resistance: New Approaches to Organizational Politics," *Management Communication Quarterly, 21*, 301–309.

Foldy, E. G., Goldman, L. and Ospina, S. (2008) "Sensegiving and the Role of Cognitive Shifts in the Work of Leadership," *Leadership Quarterly*, 19, 514–529.

Foucault, M. 1983. "The Subject and Power," in Dreyfus, H. L. and Rabinow, P. (eds.), *Michel Foucault: Beyond Structuralism and Hermeneutics*, Chicago: Chicago University Press, pp. 208–226.

Foucault, M. 1990. *The History of Sexuality: Volume 1*, New York: Vintage/ Random House.

Foucault, M. 1995/1975. *Discipline and Punish*, New York: Vintage/Random House. Fournier, V. and Grey, C. 2000. "At the Critical Moment: Conditions and Prospects for Critical Management Studies," *Human Relations*, 53, 7–32.

George, B. 2015. *Discover Your True North* (Expanded and updated edition), Hoboken, NJ: John Wiley & Sons.

Gergen, K. 2009. *Relational Being: Beyond Self and Community*, New York: Oxford University Press.

Gibbs, J. 2009. "Dialectics in a Global Software Team: Negotiating Tensions across Time, Space, and Culture," *Human Relations*, 62, 905–935.

Giddens, A. 1979. *Central Problems in Social Theory*, Berkeley: University of California Press.

Giddens, A.1984. *The Constitution of Society*, Berkeley: University of California Press.

Gioia, D. A. and Chittipeddi, K. 1991. "Sensemaking and Sensegiving in Strategic Change Initiation," *Strategic Management Journal*, 12, 433–448.

Gipson, A. N., Pfaff, D. L., Mendelsohn, D. B., Catenacci, L. T. and Burk, W. W. 2017. "Women and Leadership: Selection, Development, Leadership Style, and Performance," *Journal of Applied Behavioral Science*, 53, 32–65.

Graen, G. B. and Uhl-Bien, M. 1995. "Relationship-Based Approach to Leadership: Development of Leader-Member Exchange (LMX) Theory of Leadership Over 25 Years: Applying a Multi-Level Multi-Domain Perspective," *Leadership Quarterly*, 6, 219–247.

Grint, K. 1997. *Leadership: Classical, Contemporary, and Critical Approaches*, Oxford, UK: Oxford University Press.

Grint, K. 2005. "Problems, Problems, Problems: The Social Construction of 'Leadership'," *Human Relations*, 58, 1467–1494.

Hall, M. 2010. "Constructions of Leadership at the Intersection of Discourse, Power, and Culture: Jamaican Managers' Narratives of Leading in a Postcolonial Cultural Context," *Management Communication Quarterly*, 20, 1–32.

Hanold, M. 2017. "Toward a New Approach to Authentic Leadership: The Practice of Embodied Dialogical 'Thinking' and the Promise of Shared Power," *Advances in Developing Human Resources*, 19, 454–466.

Hansen, H., Ropo, A. and Sauer, E. 2007. "Aesthetic Leadership," *Leadership Quarterly*, 18, 544–560.

Hardy, C. and Clegg, S. R. 1996. "Some Dare Call it Power," in Clegg, S. R., Hardy, C., and Nord, W. R. (eds.), *Handbook of Organization Studies*, London: SAGE, pp. 622–641.

Hoffman, B. J., Woehr, D. J., Maldagen-Youngjohn, R. and Lyons, B. D. 2011. "Great Man or Great Myth? A Quantitative Review of the Relationship between Individual Differences and Leader Effectiveness," *Journal of Occupational and Organizational Psychology*, 84, 347–381.

Holm, F. and Fairhurst, G. T. 2018. "Configuring Shared and Hierarchical Leadership through Authoring," *Human Relations*, 71, 692–721.

Jian, G. 2007. "Unpacking Unintended Consequences in Planned Organizational Change: A Process Model," *Management Communication Quarterly*, 21, 5–28.

Jian, G., Shi, X. and Dalisay, F. 2014. "Leader-Member Conversational Quality: Scale Development and Validation through Three Studies," *Management Communication Quarterly*, 28, 375–403.

Johansson, J., Tienari, J. and Valtonen, A. 2017. "The Body, Identity and Gender in Managerial Athleticism," *Human Relations*, 70, 1141–1167.

Junker, N. M. and van Dick, R. 2014. "Implicit Theories in Organizational Settings: A Systematic Review and Research Agenda of Implicit Leadership and Followership Theories," *Leadership Quarterly*, 25, 1154–1173.

Kelly, S. 2008. "Leadership: A Categorical Mistake?" *Human Relations*, 61, 763–782.

Kuhn, T., Ashcraft, K. L. and Cooren, F. 2017. *The Work of Communication: Relational Perspectives on Working and Organizing in Contemporary Capitalism*, New York: Routledge.

Ladkin, D. 2008. "Leading Beautifully: How Mastery, Congruence and Purpose Create the Aesthetic of Embodied Leadership Practice," *Leadership Quarterly*, 19, 31–41.

Larsson, M. and Lundholm, S. E. 2013. "Talking Work in a Bank: A Study of Organizing Properties of Leadership in Work Interactions," *Human Relations*, 66, 1101–1129.

Levinas, E. 1969. *Totality and Infinity* (Lingis, A. Trans.), Pittsburgh, PA: Duquesne University Press.

Lewis, L. K. 2011. *Organizational Change: Creating Change through Strategic Communication*, New York: Wiley-Blackwell.

Liu, H. 2010. "When Leaders Fail: A Typology of Failures and Framing Strategies," *Management Communication Quarterly*, 24, 232–259.

Liu, F. and Maitlis, S. 2014. "Emotional Dynamics and Strategizing Processes: A Study of Strategic Conversations in Top Team Meetings," *Journal of Management Studies*, 51, 202–234.

Lollar, K. 2013. "Dialogic Ethics: Leadership and the Face of the Other," *Journal of the Association for Communication Administration*, 32, 15–26.

Lord, R. G. and Maher, K. J. 1991. *Leadership and Information Processing: Linking Perceptions and Performance*, Boston: Unwin Hyman.

Martin, R., Guillaume, Y., Thomas, G., Lee, A. and Epitropaki, O. 2016. "Leader-Member Exchange (LMX) and Performance: A Meta-Analytic Review," *Personnel Psychology*, 69, 67–121.

Meindl, J. R. 1995. "The Romance of Leadership as a Follower-Centric Theory: A Social Constructionist Approach," *Leadership Quarterly*, 6, 329–341.

Mitra, R. 2013. "From Transformational Leadership to Leadership Transformations: A Critical Dialogic Perspective," *Communication Theory*, 23, 395–416.

Mumby, D. K. 2005. "Theorizing Resistance in Organization Studies: A Dialectical Approach," *Management Communication Quarterly*, 19, 19–44.

Northouse, P. G. 2016. *Leadership: Theory and Practice* (7th ed.), Thousand Oaks, CA: SAGE.

Olufowote, J. O., Miller, V. D. and Wilson, S. R. 2005. "The Interactive Effects of Role Change Goals and Relational Exchanges on Employee Upward Influence Tactics," *Management Communication Quarterly, 18,* 385–403.

Omilion-Hodges, L. M. and Baker, C. R. 2013. "Contextualizing LMX within the Workgroup: The Effects of LMX and Justice on Relationship Quality and Resource Sharing among Peers," *Leadership Quarterly, 24,* 935–951.

Parker, P. S. 2005. *Race, Gender, and Leadership,* Mahwah, NJ: Lawrence Erlbaum.

Pearce, C. L. and Conger, J. A. (eds.) 2003. *Shared Leadership: Reframing the Hows and Whys of Leadership,* Thousand Oaks, CA: SAGE.

Putnam, L. L., Fairhurst, G. T. and Banghart, S. G. 2016. "Contradictions, Dialectics, and Paradoxes in Organizations: A Constitutive Approach," *Academy of Management Annals, 10,* 65–172.

Raelin, J. A. 2012. "Dialogue and Deliberation as Expressions of Democratic Leadership in Participatory Organizational Change," *Journal of Organizational Change Management, 25,* 7–23.

Riley, P. 1988. "The Merger of Macro and Micro Levels of Leadership," in Hunt, J. G., Baglia, B. R., Dachler, H. P. and Schriesheim, C. A. (eds.), *Emerging Leadership Vistas,* Lexington, MA: Lexington Books, pp. 80–83.

Said, E. W. 1993. *Culture and Imperialism,* New York: Knopf.

Schad, J., Lewis, M., Raisch, S. and Smith, W. 2016. "Paradox Research in Management Science: Looking Back to Move Forward," *Academy of Management Annals, 10,* 5–64.

Sheep, M. L., Fairhurst, G. T. and Khazanchi, S. 2017. "Knots in the Discourse of Innovation: Investigating Multiple Tensions in a Reacquired Spin-Off," *Organization Studies, 38,* 463–488.

Shotter, J. 2008. *Conversational Realities Revisited: Life, Language, Body and World.* Chagrin Falls, OH: Taos Institute Publications.

Sinclair, A. 2005. "Body Possibilities in Leadership," *Leadership, 1,* 387–406.

Smith, W. K. and Lewis, M. W. 2011. "Toward a Theory of Paradox: A Dynamic Equilibrium Model of Organizing," *Academy of Management Review, 36,* 381–403.

Sonenshein, S. 2010. "We're Changing—or Are We? Untangling the Role of Progressive, Regressive, and Stability Narratives during Strategic Change Implementation," *Academy of Management Journal, 53,* 477–512.

Sorsa, V., Palli, P. and Mikkola, P. 2014. "Appropriating the Words of Strategy in Performance Appraisal Interviews," *Management Communication Quarterly, 28,* 56–83.

Stensaker, I. and Falkenberg, J. 2007. "Making Sense of Different Responses to Corporate Change," *Human Relations, 60,* 137–77.

Uhl-Bien, M., Riggio, R. E., Lowe, K. B. and Carsten, M. K. 2014. "Followership Theory: A Review and Research Agenda," *Leadership Quarterly, 25,* 83–104.

van Loon, R. and van Dijk, G. 2015. "Dialogic Leadership: Dialogue as Condition Zero," *Journal of Leadership, Accountability, and Ethics, 12,* 62–75.

Wassenaar, C. L. and Pearce, C. L. 2016. "The Nature of Shared Leadership," in Hickman, G. H. (ed.), *Leading Organizations: Perspectives for a New Era* (3rd ed.), Thousand Oaks, CA: SAGE, pp. 177–196.

Willmott, H. 1997. "Rethinking Management and Managerial Work: Capitalism, Control, and Subjectivity," *Human Relations, 50,* 1329–1359.

Wodak, R., Kwon, W. and Clarke, I. 2011. "'Getting People on Board': Discursive Leadership for Consensus Building in Team Meetings," *Discourse & Society*, 22, 592–616.

Zoller, H. M. and Fairhurst, G. T. 2007. "Resistance as Leadership: A Critical, Discursive Perspective," *Human Relations*, 60, 1331–1360.

12 Change and Change Management

Laurie Lewis and Surabhi Sahay

Change is a prominent, complex, and consequential process in organizational activity. Change is often necessary to solve problems, adjust to new environmental demands, address injustices, revitalize energy of participants, maintain competitiveness, and to please key stakeholders. Without change, organizations would eventually become obsolete through failure to adapt to changing demands of environments, stakeholders, and circumstances. *Organizational change* is a term used both to describe something introduced as new to an organization, and the processes involved in bringing new ideas into practice. Even though organizational activity is made up of processes and thus is always in motion and always changing (Zorn et al. 1999) change scholars typically focus on disrupted periods during which specific practices, objects, or ways of doing are altered or brought into practice as something unfamiliar.

Change is consequential for individuals within and around organizations. We refer to these individuals as stakeholders. Stakeholders include employees, community members, customers and clients, suppliers, affiliated groups and organizations, governmental and regulatory agencies, professional associations, as well as collaborative and competitive organizations within a shared industry or sector, among many others. Stakes of these individuals/groups may include financial, environmental, physical, and symbolic goods (e.g. status, attention). The consequences of change for these stakeholders derive both from the new thing that is introduced (e.g. adopted new technologies, policies, procedures, processes, arrangements, and structures) and from the process of changing. During change there is likely to be disruption of routines, rewards, expertise, status, security, familiarity, relationships, and physical surroundings, and increased demands on cognitive, physical, and emotional capacities. Further, changes rarely occur as singular events and organizations tend to be implementing multiple changes simultaneously.

Scholars generally distinguish between planned and unplanned change. Unplanned change is often a focus of organizational sociologists who are interested in "natural" or evolutionary change that occurs as organizations and organizational environments. Examples of unplanned changes include those due to uncontrollable forces (e.g. fire burns down plant, governmental shutdown of production) or emergent processes and interactions in the organization (e.g. drift in practices, changing demographics of workforce, erosion of skills, shift in cultural acceptance of organization's products and services). Some scholars have termed unplanned change as continuous change, deeming it by nature to be ongoing, evolving, and cumulative. Alternatively, planned changes are those that are purposefully designed and selected by organizational decision-makers. Scholars have examined changes of large scope including mergers, cultural transformation, reorganizations, as well as introduction of technologies, production methodologies, employee programs, process improvements, and policies requiring, proscribing or forbidding behaviors among many others.

Implementation is a term used to describe the activities and processes employed to translate a specific change into ongoing practices and routines in an organization. Implementers are those individuals in organizations charged with bringing a change initiative into practice through a myriad of activities. These activities include alteration of work processes, work roles, reporting relationships, reward systems and feedback and appraisal mechanisms. They might also include installing new equipment or processes and creation of supportive infrastructure (e.g. training manuals, helpdesks, and incentive programs). A key set of activities will relate to the communication with stakeholders that provide information, updates, requests for input, and measurement of outcomes.

Our interest in organizational change started early for both of us. In our graduate school studies, organizational change become a fascinating topic that launched our research programs. In the next sections we detail our own stories of how we entered into this research; overview important themes in current research; project future directions for this area; and briefly highlight important applied implications.

Our Stories

Laurie's Story

My scholarly interest in organizational change began during my master's program. In a course on program evaluation taught by David Seibold at the University of Illinois, my fellow students and I undertook a research project that sought to assist a large food manufacturing plant with assessing a major change initiative. Our experiences in assessing that change led to development of a theoretical model and case study which Dave and I later published in *Academy of Management Review* (Lewis and Seibold 1993). As Dave and I reflected on the case, it was clear that the talk between stakeholders (e.g. employees, groups within the company, supervisors, leaders) made all the difference in how the innovation was thought of, how it was acted upon, and its level of acceptance within the company. That experience taught me the power of communication in organizations. I realized that sensemaking and social influence made a huge difference in how the change program was understood and how various employee groups influenced its use through talking about it in certain ways.

Later in my career, I undertook a 4-year project with Craig Scott and Scott D'Urso. We initiated the Collaborative Technologies for Organizations Serving the Homeless (C-TOSH) project during which we played roles as researchers and implementers. We secured in-kind donations and other support to provide new technologies and collaborative software to a set of homeless service providers in Austin, Texas. Our tasks included garnering the interest and cooperation of a wide variety of organizational leaders and other stakeholders, installing hardware, providing training and tech support, and monitoring the reactions to and use of the new resources over time. We learned a great deal from this longitudinal project (Scott et al. 2009, Scott et al. 2010). It further enriched my understanding of how change processes work, and added a perspective that demonstrated how networks of professionals can play a role in influencing adoption and use of a change.

Upon my move to Rutgers University, I launched a book project to coalesce what I had learned to that point in my career (Lewis 2011). This book revised a model of communication and change that I had published in *Communication Theory* (Lewis 2007). For me, this was a statement piece that helped me to claim the intellectual ground I had developed over a young career to that point. A book project enables the author to get beyond the specifics of any given data set or research project to ponder what he or she really thinks about a topic. I assembled what I thought was the scope of research evidence pertinent to organizational change.

In my current work, I have refocused my efforts at understanding what I've come to believe is a key communication activity that determines many change outcomes: soliciting input. In my work in recent years, I've come to appreciate the dynamics surrounding implementers' solicitation of stakeholders' (especially employee) opinions, concerns, views, and perspectives about change and change processes. Engaging stakeholders throughout a change process is a critical activity for implementers and leaders. What is especially exciting about a career as a scholar is the ability to learn and then refocus one's work throughout one's career. This has certainly been the case with me as my journey in understanding and explaining organizational change has shifted over time.

Surabhi's Story

My interest in change management research really took off during my pursuit of the master's degree at Rutgers University. The first course

I took as a graduate student was on interorganizational relationships taught by Laurie. Following that experience, I worked on projects with Laurie and she eventually became my advisor for my doctoral studies. My focus highlighted my interest in grassroots-level dialogue. This topic was very close to my heart, as I had grown up observing stakeholder dialogues regarding policy development and modifications at home. I was always fascinated by the way these initiatives were designed, keeping in mind the culture and prevalent bureaucratic arrangements of the place.

My first big qualitative research project was to ask feedback providers about their perspectives regarding input solicitation (Sahay and Lewis 2016). The study found that individuals provided feedback for various reasons such as to appease the management, promote one's political goals, and as helpers of management even when the managers were not perceived as having power to alter the course of the change. The study found that tenure in the organization, level of comfort with management, and feedback loop also shaped perceptions regarding input solicitation.

During my doctoral program I made connections between literature on change management and anonymity, distortion, uncertainty reduction, deception to name a few. Much of this credit goes to working with my team, headed by Craig Scott, where we conducted a study to understand perceptions of the public regarding hidden organizations that conceal themselves and their members (Dwyer et al. 2018, Sahay et al. 2017). As I progressed in the program, my interest was caught by the "communication as design" perspective (Aakhus and Jackson 2014, Aakhus and Bzdak 2015, Aakhus and Laureij 2012), which offered me a useful means of approaching input solicitation. Kevin Barge and Josh Barbour also provided insights regarding collective designs that further shaped my ideas around this (Barbour et al. 2017).

In my subsequent projects, I interviewed senior level executives of big corporations in order to understand their take on input solicitation (Sahay and Lewis 2016) and also conducted a study with change management consultants to understand their perspectives on how input solicitation should be conducted and the value it has for organizations. My dissertation took on the context of nursing work (Sahay 2017). This was a population that has significant value for healthcare, but is often ignored and lacks power. Through my network, I was able to locate hospitals that would allow me to conduct research with them, although it was definitely a challenge to find a hospital that would open its doors to a researcher who was trying to study concepts related to voice and resistance during an organizational change. I was able to collect insightful data and also learned much about organizational support and negotiations from the process. I conducted a mixed methods study that explored the perspectives of nurses regarding a much debated change. A key finding of my research suggested that designs of input solicitation influenced the pathway of the change. This was indeed a critical learning experience, which also made me determined to pursue more research on organizational change in the healthcare context. Currently, I am further exploring how voice and input are shaped by programs that claim to empower stakeholders, and if they add or influence the designs of solicitation and the input.

Current Research Trends

Organizational change scholarship spans diverse disciplines, where the focus usually tends to be on how leaders manage the change. Change is often viewed as a sign of progress and innovation that is critical for organizational sustainability. Management goals and implementation strategies are at the forefront of these studies, where leaders and implementers garner support for change in order to reach desired change goals (Aladwani 2001, Beer and Nohria 2000, Bordia et al. 2004). Far less attention has been paid to the stakes and strategies of other stakeholders who react and respond to the change.

New trends in scholarship critique this orientation and argue that while change provides various opportunities, it also comes with downsides (Lewis 2011, Zorn et al. 1999). Change is often equated with organizational development that can help capitalize available resources and maybe even fix dysfunctional problems in the organization. Often overlooked are the concerns and unintended consequences of fatigue that can arise in this culture of constant change. Stressors that influence stakeholder involvement and reactions are now receiving some attention. The following review highlights trends and shifts in research about organizational change. In general, current research places more focus on dynamic models of communication while highlighting stakeholder involvement, framing, participation, and emotionality.

Dynamic Model of Communication

One of the earliest attempts to model processes related to organizational change in communication include Rogers' (1995) work, wherein he identified the critical concepts of agenda setting, matching, redefining and restructuring (reinvention), clarifying, and routinizing. Rogers' work inspired scholars from different disciplines to study the life cycle of technologies, which helped generate works focused on education and learning (Less 2003), ICT use in community engagement (Wenger et al. 2009), and organizational management (Zakaria and Yusof 2001), among others.

In another core theoretical development, Van de Ven and Poole (1995) describe four change motors in an effort to explain change processes. In that chapter, the authors describe how change can be triggered. Poole and Van de Ven (2004) suggest that these four processes are distinguishable in terms of the degree to which change is premised on the actions of a single or of multiple entities, and whether change events are presupposed or emerging as the change process unfolds. These four motors are:

- **Life cycle:** Change progresses are conducted through a sequence of stages. Frameworks like the Unfreeze-Change-Freeze model (Lewin 1947) that follows a sequential pattern of change is based on this idea of life cycle, where each stage is prescribed and follow the previous one.
- **Teleological:** Here, change is socially constructed by the people involved, and goals are created, implemented, evaluated and modified in the process.
- **Dialectical:** Organizations are made up of several entities that pave way for tensions, paradoxes, and confrontations. Change therefore is viewed to be a result of conflicts and tensions that arise between entities, and is deep-rooted in Marxist values where thesis and antithesis clash/connect to formulate a new synthesis.
- **Evolutionary:** Here change is viewed as a result of struggle for resources that sustain the organization. Repetitive cycles of variation, selection and retention dictate organizational change, just as it dictates the evolutionary cycle.

More recent trends are driven by the dynamic nature of communication and relationships. Lewis (2011), in her comprehensive stakeholder model of change, focuses on change as a context within which organizational constituencies, or stakeholders, can make their stakes known in hopes of legitimizing their position. Her use of stakeholder theory highlights the dynamic nature of communication in change processes. This dynamic positioning has extended the traditional hub-and-spokes stakeholder perspective—wherein the organization sits in the middle of a network of individual and isolated stakeholders. The new conceptualization highlights the relationships stakeholders share, not only with their focal organization, but most importantly with each other. With those relationships comes much potential for creating and executing influence over change process. According to Lewis, stakeholders are strategic about their participation during change and they also occupy multiple informal roles during change. They might be opinion leaders (i.e. individuals who have an influence on others), connectors (i.e. individuals who bring people together), counselors (i.e. individuals who provide support to others) and journalists (i.e. individuals who collect information and offer their interpretation).

Stakeholders' strategic actions may be directed from various goals, which can range from an idea to defeat the change, to gaining resources, to garnering support for the change. Stakeholders might spread rumors, distort information upwards, highlight positives, launder negative information, and/or feign ignorance to further those goals. This model brings to light the fluid and complex process of the complicated organizational environment during change.

Information During Change

Information may be perceived as an invaluable resource during organizational change, and it is often the most prized and contested resource. Unequal access to information and different interpretations make organizational change a contested terrain. In the past, information was often portrayed as a possession of implementers and upper-level decision-makers (Larkin and Larkin 1994). Some studies have even suggested that employees prefer receiving their information from direct supervisors and support the idea that information exchange must remain within the organizational hierarchy (Hargie and Tourish 2000). The management was responsible for disseminating any type of information to its members. In that conceptualization, employees and other stakeholders were perceived as mere receivers of information, lacking deeper understanding for the change. Employees (and other non-leader stakeholders) were rarely considered to possess the ability to assess change-related information or alternatives, therefore positioning implementers as the key holders and disseminators of information. For instance, in a research study we conducted (Sahay and Lewis 2016), implementers perceived the lower-level employees to be narrowly focused with limited understanding of the big picture.

Change scholars suggest that information is often disseminated with the intention to reduce uncertainty during change (Bordia et al. 2004). Individuals may react to uncertainty related to ambiguous organizational positioning or operation, or regarding job or status instability in the organization. It is common during change for stakeholders to experience uncertainty regarding the details of the change and the implication the change has for them—their daily routines, position in the organization, or policies they must observe. Honesty, trustworthiness, information sharing, and participation may reduce this uncertain state. Uncertain states are often viewed as a challenge that need to be resolved, and is often tackled using information dissemination strategies in the organization. However, too much information, contradictory information, or information that is indecipherable and difficult to comprehend may add to uncertainty.

Bordia et al. (2004) found that involving employees early on in the change effort through participative decision making is a helpful strategy to decrease uncertainty. Scholars have argued that uncertainty is not only reduced through formal information dissemination channels, but that stakeholders also share information with each other (Kramer 1993). Grapevine communication, informal discussions, and peer mentoring, among other methods, can help resolve uncertainties regarding tasks, roles, and relationships. Kramer, in his longitudinal study on socialization during job transfers, found that requests for information from peers increased as uncertainties regarding supervisors or task roles increased. In these situations, individuals banked on more informal sources of information instead of extending the requests to supervisors directly. This highlights the importance of stakeholder involvement in change that breaks away from the top-down information dissemination schema and pays attention to information sharing between stakeholders.

Framing Change

Another part of coping with information and uncertainty during change concerns the way change is framed by stakeholders. Change scholars argue that change and change process are interpreted through different frames used by stakeholders (Lewis 2011). According to Fairhurst (2010), frames are structured ways of thinking where leaders can gain control of the situation. Like a literal "picture frame," framing is a means to bracket important points of focus and eliminate other elements from view or consideration. Leaders find framing opportunities and use communication to address issues to one's advantage. Furthermore, framing helps leaders connect with their audience by using, elaborating on or eliminating meanings ascribed to circumstances or events. During change, framing helps highlight certain aspects of the process or goals while underscoring or obscuring others. Fyke and Buzzanell (2013) found that leaders used specific language to position themselves discursively. In another study, Whittle, Suhomlinova and Muller (2010) identified the "funnel of interests" phenomenon in which change agents created specific lenses of interpreting and reinterpreting the change in order to realign the change to the recipient's interest.

Dewulf et al. (2009) categorized two types of frames—cognitive or mental frames and interactional frames that are a result of dynamic processes of ongoing interaction. Interactional frames are created when stakeholders interact with one another and make collective sense of the situation. Together they categorize and arrange ambiguous events in meaningful ways. Framing and retrospective sensemaking help stakeholders communicate with one another and interpret the change. These are the conversations where people figure out "what is going on here?", "what does this mean?", and "why is this happening?" This perspective views change as contextually enacted and created through communication between stakeholders. For instance, Leonardi (2009), in his study concerning technology implementation and sensemaking, argued that employees interpret technologies by assessing their functional value and through interactions with other users.

Stakeholders interact with each other and with technologies available to them to make sense of the situation. This is a shift from the traditional assumption that views stakeholders as passive audiences or mere receptors of information, and suggests that stakeholders perceive information in different ways and are deliberative in framing their messages that helps support their perspectives. They elaborate on or eliminate meanings associated with change events. Stakeholders are active audiences who negotiate and manage their stakes through different frames.

Stakeholder Participation and Input Solicitation

Much previous work suggests that asking for opinions, feedback, and reactions in organizations can empower stakeholders (Lines 2004, Monge and Miller 1988, Stohl and Cheney 2001). Scholars and practitioners agree on the value of stakeholder participation during change as an involvement strategy that can remediate resistance, develop trust and support, and empower employees. Management scholars argue that readiness to change can be created through early solicitation as that helps employees cope with resistance (Armenakis et al. 1993). Such early conversations can promote openness, where stakeholders can discuss and understand the need for the change. According to Armenakis et al. (1993), stakeholders must believe that (a) change is necessary for the organization, (b) the particular proposed change is the correct one for them, (c) the organization is capable of implementing the change, and (d) opinion leaders are committed to the change. These beliefs can help increase the readiness or the commitment employees feel towards their organization and the change.

As discussed earlier, information in organizations is shared among stakeholders and this collective sensemaking matters because it defines the trajectory of the change. Input solicitation is a strategic mechanism used by organizations to solicit feedback from its non-managerial stakeholders. While research suggests that organizations tend to favor downward dissemination of information over participatory methods, input might still be solicited for various reasons, even if it is not always genuine (Lewis 2011, Lewis and Russ 2012). Some implementers may use input solicitation merely to suggest that they are welcoming of feedback, while others might actually use that input as a resource for the organization. The motivations to solicit input varies and may be directed at improving the change, monitoring organization, gaining compliance, clarifying orders, or mollifying those who are upset to name a few. For example, in their research on popular press books on change management, Lewis, Schmisseur, Stephens, and Weir (2006) found that participation was a recommended means of gaining compliance.

Scholars have started to acknowledge several gaps in this literature regarding limited guidance on how implementers can invite, gather, and analyze input (Lewis et al. 2006). We have very little understanding about the type of pressures implementers face to listen to or ignore input. Sahay (2017) aimed to understand this gap regarding how input solicitation is designed and the implications and consequences such designs have for stakeholders. She found that the quality of input provided by stakeholders depended upon their level of comfort with the solicitor, comfort with the space where input was solicited, as well as how informed the providers felt. These factors influenced how hesitant employees felt and the degree to which input providers would be candid in what they shared. Furthermore, Sahay found that distortion and suppression of candor started at the lowest levels of the organization because (a) change was perceived to be a result of deliberation of only a small group of decision-makers, and (b) the means of soliciting input signaled a lack of genuine interest in input of lower-level stakeholders.

Lewis and Russ (2012) conducted a study in which they interviewed human resource professionals charged with collecting input during change in their organizations. Interviewees reported different strategies used for collecting and using stakeholder input. The findings suggest that implementers often attempt to justify dismissing as much feedback and as many providers as possible, to narrow down the feedback to more positive and more doable suggestions. Negative input is generally avoided and carriers of such input are oftentimes stereotyped as whiners, complainers, or as inflexible. Implementers tend to welcome input from those who are perceived as embracing the change. Those charged with collecting feedback are often under significant pressure to ensure the successful implementation of the original change.

There are various design decisions that require attention when structuring and offering input solicitation. For instance, Lewis (2011) argues that participation itself may be of varied types, including direct or indirect/representative, voluntary or involuntary, and formal or informal. Other decisions may include timing, setting, anonymous access, choice of facilitator, and previous attempts at solicitation, to name a few. These dimensions of input solicitation will likely influence how individuals participate in the process. A noteworthy example here is the study conducted by Barge et al. (2008). Barge and colleagues collected data on a multi-stakeholder initiative and identified three dualities related to who should have voice. The duality of inclusion–exclusion surfaced as a design challenge and was specific to participation. This study elaborated the conflict faced by implementers when including different stakeholders in different phases of the change because who got invited to the table and at which phase was critical for the organization.

Stakeholder involvement is a critical aspect of successful change management. Although it is more commonplace for organizations provide formal mechanisms to their stakeholders to provide input and comment on change and change processes, there is evidence of wide variation in the sincerity of those soliciting input. Further, the design features of input solicitation are thus far quite underexplored. Recently, researchers have identified this gap and have begun to make strides in identifying and explaining design choices for participation as well as the implications and consequences these designs have for organizations and stakeholders.

Stakeholder Emotionality: Complex Responses to Change

Various terms are used to describe individual reactions to change, but they are found in disparate bodies of literature and often without any clear distinction: *readiness, resistance, withdrawal, cynicism, commitment, openness, acceptance, support, coping,* and *adjustment* are a few of these words that are used to define individual expressions and responses by change management scholars (e.g. Armenakis et al. 2007, George and Jones 2001, Herscovitch and Meyer 2002, Martin et al. 2005, Oreg 2006, Stanley et al. 2005). Stakeholder responses are usually measured in terms of valence. For instance, resistance and cynicism have negative valence, while commitment has a positive valence. Management scholars have argued that employee responses should not be solely measured on valence and that activation (e.g. activated emotions such as anger may trigger an active behavior such as voice) is critical in understanding these responses (Oreg et al. 2018). There is a greater push in management towards understanding emotionality in the workplace and to examine complex affective relationships (Brief and Weiss 2002, Miller 2002).

Resistance in general is viewed negatively by organizations. The term *resistance* itself is drawn from a metaphorical understanding of physical force that moves in the opposite direction and thus tries to maintain the status quo. The idea of overcoming resistance to change was first discussed in the 1940s and since then, resistors often have been stereotyped as dysfunctional, problematic, and sometimes irrational. Lewis (2011) argues that resistance can manifest in various ways and may be situated on a continuum with subtle forms (e.g. merely asking questions or seeking support) at one end and more forceful forms (e.g. protesting) at another. Resistance is often perceived by management as a problem that needs to be quelled. The focus of the implementers is then placed on alleviating this dysfunctional state through communication. These communicative responses often include altering or discrediting their views, coercing them into silence, or negotiation of minimal levels of acceptable cooperation (Sahay 2017).

Increasingly change scholars argue that resistance will be a given during organizational change and can never be fully curbed. Scholars discuss different ways by which resistance and negative feelings towards the organization might be mitigated. For instance, Van der Voet and Vermeeren (2017) found that change management practices such as management support can mitigate the negative effects of job-related attitude and improve organizational commitment. Furthermore, this study also distinguished between commitment and work engagement, where commitment to the organization is defined by the identification one feels with their particular organization, whereas engagement is the positive fulfilling work-related state of mind. In reflection, this suggests that people might be committed to their organization and still not feel engaged. Resistance might crop up even when individuals feel strongly for their organization and it does not always surface as a negative reaction against the organization or the change, but as a strategy to improve the negative work-related experiences.

Some scholars have suggested the importance of viewing resistance as a resource for the organization, even if it is motivated by self-interest, because the information may still be accurate and may raise valid concerns for the organization (Piderit 2000). Oreg et al. (2018) found that the negative assumptions surrounding resistance are simplistic and incorrect. Even negative active responses or resistance can facilitate change in the long run because they can help clarify problems with the change.

Communication research has explored multiple forms of resistance, as was seen in Chapter 3. Resistance to change can take the form of both peer-focused dissent (i.e. to voice concerns to those close to us but lack the power to change the change) and upward dissent (i.e. targeted to those in the organization who have power). Peer-focused dissent may be more prevalent in places that label input providers as troublemakers or cynics and has negative consequences for them. Lack of trust can generate this sense of cynicism that leads to long-term pessimism. Relatedly, breaches in expectations for procedural fairness from past experiences can be an outcome of negative cycles of poor communication (Korsgaard et al. 2002). These breaches may result in higher turnover and distrust for the organization. Furthermore, management plays an important role in mitigating the adverse effects of social atmosphere through supervisory informational justice in the initial phase of the change (De Ruiter et al. 2017). In the discourse tradition, resistance is viewed as a result of changes to the structures and modified goals of individuals (Heracleus and Barrett 2001). Resistance may also be compared to counter-resistance, which develops from an impulse to resist the resistance, therefore neutralizing it (Kärreman and Alvesson 2009).

Overall, it may be said that there is little attention paid to emotionality in change management studies, which usually lumps employee reactions into two broad categories—one in which employees support the change such as commitment and openness and one in which employees are viewed as problematic for the change, such as resistors and cynics. A recent shift in scholarship suggests that employee reactions, even the negative ones, can prove to be beneficial for the organization. Also, resistance and commitment are made of a range of reactions, which does not necessarily tell us that an employee is committed or resistant towards their organization. Employees can be committed to their organizations and yet be resistant to a particular change and vice versa.

Future Research Directions

Communication scholars have a long-standing and rising interest in the study of organizational change. Change is a growing topic in communication publications, at disciplinary conferences, and in courses at every level of instruction. Communication scholarship on change management can be found in numerous journals and conferences in other disciplines as well. It is clear that organizational scientists across disciplines have concluded that communication plays a pivotal role in the creation, adoption, and implementation of change. There are a number of areas for future research and theory-building that would be productive paths for scholars to pursue.

First, it would be beneficial for change scholars to take more notice of stakeholders other than managers and employees, and exploring change from multiple perspectives. Far too much of past scholarship has focused on managerial-centric approaches which highlights stakes, goals, and outcomes of leaders and managers. When we have expanded the perspective of our research to include others it has often been limited to consideration of paid employees within the organization undergoing change. Thus, the vast majority of our scholarship has depicted the interplay in perspectives of managers and their employees as they sort out what change will be, how it will progress, and how they will respond to one another.

In selecting this focus, we forego examination of myriad other impacted stakeholders. For example, scant research has focused on exploring experiences of clients, customers, consumers of organizational products and outcomes that result from change programs. The external receivers of change processes and innovation experience uncertainty and disruption and must grapple with new practices. For instance, changes in product labeling necessitates much adjustment on the part of consumers. Communication scholars could certainly explore the ways in which industry, expert, advocacy organizations, and government agencies communicate about labeling. What are the strategies that consumers use to sort out what labels to believe and which to ignore/question? How do consumers interact with grocers, commercial advertisement, advocacy campaigns, media presentations, cultural discourse as they interpret product labeling?

In a larger sense, focus on this category of stakeholders would provide insight into ways in which collective consumer response to organizational change may alter the course of those changes. This can span a range of concerns including product change (e.g. consumers' negative reactions to "New Coke,"); confusion about organizational policies (e.g.

policy on the Affordable Care Act); or demands for change (e.g. protests of stores opening on Thanksgiving in the United States). There is much potential for communication scholars to explore how communication by and to wide sets of stakeholders regarding organizational change gives rise to various outcomes and consequences.

In a second area for future research, scholars can and should increase attention to the study of communication as it unfolds in real time and in natural interaction. Since the early 2000s, scholars in management and communication fields have increasingly focused on the accounts of change stakeholders about their experiences with change and the ways in which they create accounts of change processes. This scholarship has thus far tended to focus on sensemaking about change in a moment-in-time. That is, researchers often ask informants for their opinions/perspectives on change and may ask them to explain how they arrived at that conclusion. What this approach leaves out is a mapping of how opinions and perspectives evolve through multiple conversations, experiences, and persuasive interactions. We have seen few attempts in research to examine how perspectives, attitudes, reactions, and strategies move and shift over time. This gap in our current research creates opportunity for future research that would yield insights into how individuals and groups of stakeholders come to hold views on change programs through evolving reflection, interaction, and the sharing of information and opinions with other stakeholders. Exploration of unfolding communication during a change process encourages scholars to describe and develop explanations of how stakeholders persuade and influence each other. Future research should identify how change implementers and opinion leaders within these stakeholder networks sometimes conflict with each other.

In a third area for future research, it will be useful for change scholars to reconsider their understanding of the concept of resistance. Thus far, scholars have tended to consider resistance to change as a "problem" in need of a solution. Communication scholarship has too often focused on messaging around change that can negate or reduce resistance to change on the part of stakeholders' whose cooperation is needed to move change processes along. This tendency in our scholarship limits our efforts to understand stakeholders' reactions to change in light of the frameworks of sensemaking, dissent, voice, and counter-narratives.

In future research, scholars' reframing of "reactions to change" as a process of sensemaking and sensegiving could provide new theoretical explanations for how change processes take shape. As communication among stakeholders occurs, the contours and reality of any give change are created in interaction. Our understandings become our realities. The social influence that takes place among implementers, opinion leaders, and sets of stakeholders foments a sense of the change and its goals, downsides, advantages, advocates, detractors, beneficiaries, successes and failures. By investigating the emergent understanding of change and

228 Lewis and Sahay

change processes, scholars can come to better account for the outcomes of change for all those who are affected. Avoidance of privileging the managerial goals over goals of other stakeholders is another important piece of this approach. It will be important for researchers to examine a variety of intentions and stakes as they approach reactions to a change program. Treating organizations as places with multiple competing stakes and varying perspectives enables a sophisticated understanding of how sense is made of any given change. With such an approach, we avoid the overly simplistic depiction of managerial intention and resistors' disruption as the two sides of a single conversation. We might even want to engage in research to explore what makes resistance to change most effective!

Practical Implications

Change scholarship has produced some cautionary notes if not useful guidelines for practice. Our research has helped us to question assumptions including the core belief that change is also necessary or always a marker of a successful organization. Both internal and external environments must be monitored and evaluated to make critical decisions about the need for change and the direction that change should take. Further, there are cautionary notes for implementers as they consider how they interact with stakeholders during change processes. Decisions about how to involve various stakeholders (employees, customers, and others) in change planning and assessment is complex. Research suggests communication must be planned in advance and with stakeholders' stakes in mind. Timing of and channels used to solicit input, as well as creation of a feedback loop have been found to be important choices that signal to employees an authenticity of intention (Sahay 2017, Sahay and Lewis 2016). On the other hand, if input solicitation is perceived to be a method to ferret out "resistors," it may lead to conflict, polarization, and politicization within the organization. Stakeholders will likely evaluate personal risks and try to protect themselves, which will often result in laundered versions of input (Sahay 2017). The result of poor involvement and listening is likely to yield useless input or, in the worst case, foster mistrust and negativity among stakeholders. On the other hand, in organizations where efforts to involve stakeholders early, often, and with genuine intent to make use of perspectives, wisdom, and experience, the likely results are to build trust and avoid unnecessary conflict surrounding change programs.

Conclusion

We started this chapter by stating that change is a prominent, complex, and consequential process. Hopefully, our review of theory and research has underscored that claim. There is much yet to learn about organizational change from a communication perspective. How stakeholders engage with leaders and sponsors of change, and how communication plays a role in strategy, influences unfolding paths of change, and bolsters or challenges leaders' preferences for change are all critical directions for investigation. It will be important for scholars to further our understanding of how communication may be used strategically to benefit the operational health of organizations and promote the stakes of stakeholders. We hope that future research in this area will promote a multi-stakeholder approach embracing a diverse set of perspectives on change. Organizational change will certainly always be a part of the landscape of organizational experience and has major implications for how all of us experience our work lives and our other contacts with organizations. Thus, it is critical to explain, and ultimately apply, what we learn in order to improve organizational change practices.

Discussion Questions

1. Do you think that it is important for organizations to constantly change in order to sustain themselves? Why or why not? Can you provide some examples of either situation?
2. How would you define a successful change implementation? From whose perspective would we be gauging "success" and how might this definition from a different stakeholder's perspective?
3. What are some forms of resistance to organizational change? In what ways is resistance good for organizations? For stakeholders? What makes resistance effective?
4. What are some of the skills required to effectively gather input about a change process? What is most likely to encourage candid and useful input to be provided?

References

Aakhus, M. and Bzdak, M. 2015. "Stakeholder Engagement as Communication Design Practice," *Journal of Public Affairs*, 15, 188–200.
Aakhus, M. and Jackson, S. (eds.). 2014. Design and Communication [Special Issue]. *Journal of Applied Communication Research*, 42.
Aakhus, M. and Laureij, L. V. 2012. "Activity, Materiality, and Creative Struggle in the Communicative Constitution of Organizing: Two Cases of Communication Design Practice," *Language and Dialogue*, 2, 41–59.
Aladwani, A. M. 2001. "Change Management Strategies for Successful ERP Implementation," *Business Process Management Journal*, 7, 266–275.
Armenakis, A. A., Bernerth, J. B., Pitts, J. P. and Walker, H. J. 2007. "Organizational Change Recipients' Beliefs Scale: Development of an Assessment Instrument," *The Journal of Applied Behavioral Science*, 43, 481–505.

Armenakis, A. A., Harris, S. G. and Mossholder, K. W. 1993. "Creating Readiness for Organizational Change," *Human Relations*, 46, 681–703.

Barbour, J. B., Ballard, D. I., Barge, J. K. and Gill, R. 2017. "Making Time/Making Temporality for Engaged Scholarship," *Journal of Applied Communication Research*, 45, 365–380.

Barge, J., Lee, M., Maddux, K., Nabring, R. and Townsend, B. 2008. "Managing Dualities in Planned Change Initiatives," *Journal of Applied Communication Research*, 36, 364–390.

Beer, M. and Nohria, N. 2000. "Cracking the Code of Change," *HBR's 10 Must Reads on Change*, 78, 133–141.

Bordia, P., Hobman, E., Jones, E., Gallois, C. and Callan, V.J. 2004. "Uncertainty during Organizational Change: Types, Consequences, and Management Strategies," *Journal of Business and Psychology*, 18, 507–532.

Brief, A. P. and Weiss, H. M. 2002. "Organizational Behavior: Affect in the Workplace," *Annual Review of Psychology*, 53, 279–307.

De Ruiter, M., Schalk, R., Schaveling, J. and Van Gelder, D. 2017. "Psychological Contract Breach in the Anticipatory Stage of Change: Employee Responses and the Moderating Role of Supervisory Informational Justice," *The Journal of Applied Behavioral Science*, 53, 66–88.

Dewulf, A., Gray, B., Putnam, L. L., Lewicki, R., Aarts, N., Bouwen, R. and Van Woerkum, C. 2009. "Disentangling Approaches to Framing in Conflict and Negotiation Research: A Meta-paradigmatic Perspective," *Human Relations*, 62, 155–193.

Dwyer, M., Sahay, S., Scott, C. R., Dadlani, P. and McKinley, E. 2018. "Technologies of Concealment: Appropriateness, Effectiveness, and Motivations for Hiding Organizational Identity," *Western Journal of Communication*, 82, 194–216.

Fairhurst, G. T. 2010. *The Power of Framing: Creating the Language of Leadership* (Vol. 290). John Wiley & Sons.

Fyke, J. P. and Buzzanell, P. M. 2013. "The Ethics of Conscious Capitalism: Wicked Problems in Leading Change and Changing Leaders," *Human Relations*, 66, 1619–1643.

George, J. M. and Jones, G. R. 2001. "Towards a Process Model of Individual Change in Organizations," *Human Relations*, 54, 419–444.

Hargie, O. and Tourish, D. 2000. "Charting Communication Performance in a Healthcare Organization," in Hargie, O. and Tourish, D. (eds.), *Handbook of Communication Audits for Organizations*, London: Routledge, pp. 195–209.

Heracleous, L. and Barrett, M. 2001. "Organizational Change as Discourse: Communicative Actions and Deep Structures in the Context of Information Technology Implementation," *Academy of Management Journal*, 44, 755–778.

Herscovitch, L. and Meyer, J. P. 2002. "Commitment to Organizational Change: Extension of a Three-Component Model," *Journal of Applied Psychology*, 87, 474–487.

Kärreman, D. and Alvesson, M. 2009. "Resisting Resistance: Counter-Resistance, Consent and Compliance in a Consultancy Firm," *Human Relations*, 62, 1115–1144.

Korsgaard, M. A., Sapienza, H. J. and Schweiger, D. M. 2002. "Beaten before Begun: The Role of Procedural Justice in Planning Change," *Journal of Management*, 28, 497–516.

Kramer, M. W. 1993. "Communication and Uncertainty Reduction during Job Transfers: Leaving and Joining Processes," *Communications Monographs*, 60, 178–198.

Larkin, T. J. and Larkin, S. 1994. *Communicating Change: How to Win Employee Support for New Business Directions*, New York: McGraw-Hill.

Leonardi, P. M. 2009. "Why Do People Reject New Technologies and Stymie Organizational Changes of Which they are in Favor? Exploring Misalignments between Social Interactions and Materiality," *Human Communication Research*, 35, 407–441.

Less, K. H. 2003. "Faculty Adoption of Computer Technology for Instruction in the North Carolina Community College System," Doctoral Dissertation, East Tennessee State University, Johnson City, TN.

Lewin, K. 1947. "Frontiers in Group Dynamics: Concept, Method and Reality in Social Science; Social Equilibria and Social Change," *Human Relations*, 1, 5–41.

Lewis, L. K. 2007. "An Organizational Stakeholder Model of Change Implementation Communication," *Communication Theory*, 17, 176–204.

Lewis, L. K. 2011. *Organizational Change: Creating Change through Strategic Communication*, Chichester, UK: Wiley-Blackwell.

Lewis, L. K. and Russ, T. L. 2012. "Soliciting and Using Input during Organizational Change Initiatives: What Are Practitioners Doing?" *Management Communication Quarterly*, 26, 267–294.

Lewis, L. K., Schmisseur, A. M., Stephens, K. K. and Weir, K. E. 2006. "Advice on Communicating during Organizational Change: The Content of Popular Press Books," *The Journal of Business Communication*, 43, 113–137.

Lewis, L. K. and Seibold, D. R. 1993. "Innovation Modification during Intraorganizational Adoption," *Academy of Management Review*, 18, 322–354.

Lines, R. 2004. "Influence of Participation in Strategic Change: Resistance, Organizational Commitment and Change Goal Achievement," *Journal of Change Management*, 4, 193–215.

Martin, A. J., Jones, E. S. and Callan, V. J. 2005. "The Role of Psychological Climate in Facilitating Employee Adjustment during Organizational Change," *European Journal of Work and Organizational Psychology*, 14, 263–289.

Miller, K. 2002. "The Experience of Emotion in the Workplace: Professing in the Midst of Tragedy," *Management Communication Quarterly*, 15, 571–600.

Monge, P. R. and Miller, K. I. 1988. "Communication Processes in Participative Systems," in Goldhaber, G.M. (ed.), *Handbook of Organizational Communication*, New York: Ablex, pp. 213–230

Oreg, S. 2006. "Personality, Context, and Resistance to Organizational Change," *European Journal of Work and Organizational Psychology*, 15, 73–101.

Oreg, S., Bartunek, J. M., Lee, G. and Do, B. 2018. "An Affect-Based Model of Recipients' Responses to Organizational Change Events," *Academy of Management Review*, 43, 65–86.

Piderit, S. K. 2000. "Rethinking Resistance and Recognizing Ambivalence: A Multidimensional View of Attitudes toward An Organizational Change," *Academy of Management Review*, 25, 783–794.

Poole, M. S. and Van de Ven, A. H. (eds.). 2004. *Handbook of Organizational Change and Innovation*, Oxford, UK: Oxford University Press.

Rogers Everett, M. 1995. *Diffusion of Innovations*, New York: Simon and Schuster.

Sahay, S. 2017. "Communicative Designs for Input Solicitation during Organizational Change: Implications for Providers' Communicative Perceptions and Decisions," Doctoral Thesis, Rutgers University, New Brunswick, NJ.

Sahay, S. Dwyer, M. Scott, C. R. Dadlani, P. and McKinley, E. 2017. "Organizations in Hiding: Appropriateness, Effectiveness, and Motivations for Concealment. *The Electronic Journal of Communication, 27.*

Sahay, S. and Lewis, L. K. 2016. "Perspectives on Soliciting and Providing Input During Organizational Change: The Provider, the Executive, and the Consultant," Paper presented at the annual meeting of the National Communication Association, Philadelphia, PA.

Scott, C. R., Lewis, L. K. and D'Urso, S. C. 2010. "Getting on the 'E' List: Email List Use in a Community of Service Provider Organizations for People Experiencing Homelessness," in Shedletsky, L. and Aitken, J.E. (eds.), *Cases on Online Discussion and Interaction: Experiences and Outcomes,*" Hershey, PA: IGI-Global, pp. 334–350.

Scott, C. R., Lewis, L. K., Davis, J. D. and D'Urso, S. C. 2009. "Finding a Home for Communication Technologies," In Keyton, J. and Shockley-Zalabak, P. (eds.), *Case Studies for Organizational Communication: Understanding Communication Processes* (2nd ed.), New York: Oxford University Press, pp. 83–88.

Stanley, D. J. Meyer, J. P. and Topolnytsky, L. 2005. "Employee Cynicism and Resistance to Organizational Change," *Journal of Business and Psychology, 19,* 429–459.

Stohl, C. and Cheney, G. 2001. "Participatory Processes/Paradoxical Practices: Communication and the Dilemmas of Organizational Democracy," *Management Communication Quarterly, 14,* 349–407.

Van de Ven, A. H. and Poole, M. S. 1995. "Explaining Development and Change in Organizations," *Academy of Management Review, 20,* 510–540.

Van der Voet, J. and Vermeeren, B. 2017. "Change Management in Hard Times: Can Change Management Mitigate the Negative Relationship between Cutbacks and the Organizational Commitment and Work Engagement of Public Sector Employees?" *The American Review of Public Administration, 47,* 230–252.

Wenger, E., White, N. and Smith, J.D. 2009. *Digital Habitats: Stewarding Technology for Communities,* Portland, OR: CPsquare.

Whittle, A., Suhomlinova, O. and Mueller, F. 2010. "Funnel of Interests: The Discursive Translation of Organizational Change," *The Journal of Applied Behavioral Science, 46,* 16–37.

Zakaria, N. and Yusof, S. A. M. 2001. "The Role of Human and Organizational Culture in the Context of Technological Change," in *Change Management and the New Industrial Revolution, 2001. IEMC '01 Proceedings,* IEEE., pp. 83–87.

Zorn, T. E., Christensen, L. T. and Cheney, G. 1999. *Constant Change and Flexibility: Do We Really Want Constant Change?* San Francisco, CA: Berrett-Koehler.

13 Networks and Technology

William C. Barley and Marshall Scott Poole

Digital technologies afford access to networks of people and information at a scale well beyond those accessible to generations past. A recent poll from the Pew Research Center found that 68% of adults in the U.S. are on Facebook and most of these users visit the site multiple times every day (Pew Research Center 2018). We use platforms like this to maintain an awareness of friends who we have not seen in person for years. We no longer have to wonder about things—we can simply type a query into a web browser on our phone and scratch our mental itch within seconds. And now our problem is not too little, but too much information—and sorting out accurate from fake information. When we need a job, we can log in to a platform like LinkedIn to publicize our expertise and to identify potential employers. The technologies in our lives have clearly become intertwined with structures of our social networks. Yet this relationship is a comparatively novel phenomenon.

Traditionally, the study of social networks was distinct from the study of technology. When Scott started studying teams, the idea of combining study of technology and networks was a novel and intriguing possibility. He was fascinated by the ways that new information and communication technologies (ICTs) might allow teams to overcome their biases to make better decisions. His fascination with technology, however, was hindered by the fact that most organizations did not yet have access to things like the Internet or even email. He and his collaborators had to develop prototypes and test them in the lab to examine whether and how these new types of computerized tools might impact group processes (DeSanctis et al. 2008). Many organizational scholars initially balked at the notion that a researcher in their field would study computers and human behavior, as the study of technology was largely considered a domain for computer scientists and engineers.

Will had his first contact with academia only a little over a decade after Scott's early works on ICTs were published, but his experiences were markedly different. Although he has vestigial memories of a time before the Internet, he was in college when a friend convinced him to make an account on a webpage made by some students at Harvard. The page was called "The Facebook" and his friends assured him it was way cooler than MySpace. By the time Will realized he was fascinated by the processes by which individuals share knowledge in organizations, it seemed laughable to study how social networks operated *without* considering the role that information and communication technologies played in enabling group processes.

This chapter explores this dramatic shift by examining the co-evolution of research on technology and networks in organizational communication over the past two decades. Organizational communication has a long tradition of adopting a network perspective to understand the structure and behavior of organizations (for a history, see Monge and Contractor 2003). It was also one of the earliest fields to acknowledge how important communication technologies would become to organizations (Rice 1984, Fulk and Steinfield 1990). We begin by introducing readers to the network perspective on organizational communication, and by discussing what we mean by "technology." Then, we turn to research on technology and on social networks, to examine how advances in each of these areas have influenced the other.

Basic Concepts

The Network Perspective

"Network" is an abstract term referring to a set of nodes interconnected by links. Nodes can be any type of entity, such as people, organizations, or machines. Linkages between the nodes (also called "ties" or "edges") constitute the network. There are a wide variety of linkages between nodes, including communication, liking, authority over, and dependency. Each type of linkage creates a different type of network, for example, a communication network, an affiliation network, or a workflow network. Figure 13.1 shows an example of an interpersonal communication network in a small organization.

The network perspective emphasizes the effects of interconnections, and so it offers a different explanation of behavior than do traditional viewpoints that emphasize the individual. Rather than explaining an actor's behavior as a product of individual personality traits, motivations, attitudes, and the like, a network approach argues that behavior is influenced by the actors' position in her or his network. What seems to be Nguyen's innate beliefs and attitudes, for example, may in fact be shaped by her connections to Jack, Milly, and Dontrelle. These ties allow Jack, Milly, and Dontrelle to route information to Nguyen and to transmit normative messages that may influence Nguyen's subsequent behavior. Over time, these influences contribute to Nguyen's beliefs, attitudes, and motivations. We must consider the entire network to understand Nguyen's attitudes, including the direct effects of those she is connected

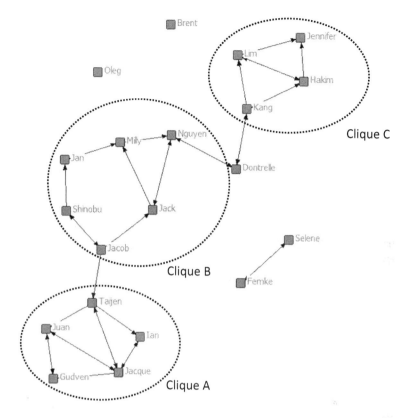

Figure 13.1 Example of an Interpersonal Communication Network in a Small Organization

to and the "indirect" effects of others in the network who influence Jack, Lim, and Dontrelle.

Properties of Networks

Scholars have developed a number of measures to capture the complexity of networks. One type of measure describes *characteristics of the ties* between actors in a network, such as their *strength* (how frequently the tie is used and on the intensity of the relationship). Ties also vary in terms of *direction*, whether the link goes one way (e.g. Jack may identify Milly as a friend, but Milly may not feel the same about Jack) or is reciprocated. Two actors are linked *indirectly* when they are connected by another actor (e.g. Shinobu links Jan and Jacob in a one-step link). A final characteristic of links is their *multiplexity*. Two actors are connected with a *uniplex* link when they have a single type of link, for example, liking or authority, and the tie is multiplex if they share more than one type of like (e.g. liking, giving advice to, and trust).

A second measure describes characteristics of the nodes in the network. *Degree* refers to the number of direct links with other actors that an actor has. These links can either be in-coming (*in-degree links*) or outgoing (*out-degree links*), and each actor can be described in terms of how many in-degree links versus how many out-degree links he/she has. Nguyen has three in-degree links and two out-degree links. This enables us to assess the relative *prestige* (also called "preference") of an actor; actors are higher in prestige to the extent that they have more in-degree than out-degree links. *Centrality* refers to the extent to which an actor is central to the network. An actor with high centrality is positioned so they can reach other actors in the network through relatively few steps. *Cliques* (also called "clusters" or "groups") are sets of highly interconnected members. There are three cliques in Figure 13.1.

Another set of measures characterize the role that individuals play in the network. A *star* is an actor who is highly central in the network (e.g. Nguyen or Jack). A *liaison* (e.g. Dontrelle) is a member who connects two or more cliques who would not otherwise be connected, but is not a member of either clique. By contrast, a *bridge* is a member of one clique who connects it to another clique (e.g. Jacob). An *isolate* (e.g. Oleg) is an actor with no or relatively few links to others in the network. While we may think of isolates as undesirable network roles, a person or dyad may be isolated for good reasons, such as working at different times than the others in the network.

Brokerage is another important network role. It refers to the degree to which actors have the potential to connect groups of people who are not presently connected. Jan, Hakim, and Ian all have high brokerage potential in Figure 13.1. If any of them formed a tie with each other they would bring large numbers of actors in the network closer to one another. Engaging in brokerage has been shown to give actors power in the network (Stephens et al. 2009).

A third type of network measure describes the network itself. The *size* of a network refers to the number of actors who make up the network. The network in Figure 13.1 is small compared to the Internet, which is perhaps the largest human network (networks of insects and fungi in the soil, by comparison, are much larger in size then any human network!). Networks also vary in the *density* of their connections, which is defined as the number of actual links in the network compared to the total number of possible links if everyone node was connected. The density of the network in Figure 13.1 is 0.095 (36 observed ties divided by 390 possible ties in a 20-node network), which means this network is relatively sparsely connected. A related property is *reachability* (also called "connectivity"), which refers to the extent to which actors in the network are linked by direct or indirect ties. A network with low reachability is broken up into separate islands, whereas in one with high reachability, every actor can potentially connect to every other one, even if only through a long indirect multi-step path. Finally, *centralization* of the network refers to the degree to which one or a few actors control the network.

Factors and Processes that Shape Networks

A number of network theories have been advanced and Monge and Contractor (2003) grouped these into eleven major families. We will focus on two of the many topics addressed by these theories: (1) explanations for network link formation, maintenance, and dissolution (which we will call "reticulation"); and (2) common network processes and their effects on actors and on the network as a whole.

One of the most influential factors affecting the reticulation process is the actor's *interests*, either the actors' self-interests or collective interests, such as when a community works together to recover from a disaster. One important type of interest is an *exchange* relationship, in which actors exchange things of value, such as friendship or advice. Another common factor leading to link formation is *propinquity*: actors who are physically close are more likely to form links. Another common explanation for reticulation is *homophily*: actors tend to seek out those like themselves on some dimension, such as age, gender, or occupation ("birds of a feather flock together). Finally, reticulation occurs through *brokerage*, as previously mentioned.

Actor beliefs and characteristics also affect reticulation. Actors' perceptions of who is central (and therefore important) in a network can lead them to try to link up with central others (Kilduff and Brass 2010). Actors' attitudes toward "networking" also affect reticulation. Kuwabara, Hildebrand, and Zou (2018) argue that actors who believe they can actively shape their social relationships will engage in networking more enthusiastically than actors who believe social structure is relatively fixed and stratified according to status. Actors who believe social relations are fixed tend to have networks that are smaller, less dense, and less diverse than actors who hold a more malleable view of the social world and are more engaged in networking.

In addition to reticulation, other social processes shape the network. *Reciprocity*, the tendency of actors to reciprocate links once someone connects with them, tends to foster stronger ties over time, and also to lead to multiplex ties. *Transitivity* is the tendency for two actors who share a common connection to also link with each other (forming triangles like Milly, Jack, and Nguyen in Figure 13.1). Transitivity has been explained as a function of the need for psychological balance, whereby a person tries to sustain consistency among her or his ties (Krackhardt and Kilduff 1999), but it may also occur simply because when two actors are connected to the same third-party, they are more likely to come into contact with that third actor (Lee and Monge 2011). Finally, *preferential attachment* happens when nodes that have a lot of in-degree links attract more and more links over time. In this "rich get richer" scenario, a few nodes become highly central to the network.

These processes lead to constant change in the links of the network, but if we consider which links are predominately maintained over a long period of time, we can define overall structures for networks. In a *core-periphery* network there is one large central cluster of highly connected actors which sends links out to peripheral members not as tightly connected to the core. A *clustered* network structure is one in which there are several highly connected clusters that are only loosely connected to each other.

Technology

When we use the term "technology" in this chapter, we are referring not only to physical artifacts (e.g. computers, communications networks made of cables and routers, machine tools) and software but also to the actors carrying out work processes and interactions with these artifacts. Technologies are "sociomaterial systems" in that their impacts depend on how they are used and incorporated into work, and this depends on how human actors interpret and use them (Leonardi 2012). This is clear for technologies like email or social media which require human participation to work, but it also applies to largely automated technologies like machine tools or document routing systems, because their design and use depend on human agents being "in the loop" at decisive points.

This chapter focuses primarily on information and communication technologies (ICTs), because they have wrought the largest social changes over past twenty years. A few ICTs used by organizations include email, phone, teleconferencing, instant messaging, webpages, social networking sites (e.g. Facebook, LinkedIn), wikis, blogs, microblogs (e.g. Twitter or Yammer), team support systems (e.g. Slack), shared file systems (e.g. Dropbox), and office automation and workflow management tools (e.g. WorkForce). Although large organizations, private, governmental, and nonprofit, get much of the attention for ICT use, smaller organizations have increasingly utilized ICTs as services such bookkeeping, legal advice, and customer/client contact have grown.

A useful way to understand the sociomaterial system of ICTs is in the distinction between features offered by ICTs and the affordances users perceive in these features (Treem and Leonardi 2012). *Features* are the designed capabilities that ICTs have (e.g. the ability to enter and summarize data and to make complex calculations in a spreadsheet). *Affordances* are the possible ways that the features of an ICT can fit into a specific context of use. Users can appropriate the affordances of their technologies in considerably different ways. For example, most users of spreadsheets perceive them as useful for data organization; however, only those comfortable with learning some programming and might perceive macros for complex calculations as an affordance of the spreadsheet. Users appropriate those affordances of the ICT that are useful to them, and since each user, group of users, and organization is different, the same ICT can be used in very different ways across different users, groups, and organizations. The fact that affordances must be *perceived* before a user appropriates them places communication processes at the center of understanding ICTs, as user interactions often mediate which appropriations users often take up in their work (Norman 1999).

ICTs are complex systems, and so their effects are sometimes unanticipated. Kiesler and Sproull (1991) distinguished *first-order effects*, the intended effects of a technology from *second-order effects*, which are its unanticipated consequences. First-order effects are generally planned and pertain to the immediate affordances of the technology for users. Second-order effects are often social and political in nature and cannot be planned; they are unanticipated and often occur gradually over time. For example, a first order effect of the Internet is to make communication much easier and faster and to connect businesses to customers. One second-order effect of the Internet has been to create political divisions by facilitating contacts among like-minded people of all stripes (e.g. right-wing hate groups, animal activists, hobbyists), which many analysts say has resulted in fragmentation of politics and an increase in incivility.

Conceptualizing the Dynamic Relationship between Network and Technology Theories

Until a decade or so ago, most network research in the social sciences focused on networks of humans. As networking technologies have become more ubiquitous and more powerful, however, there has been an increasing focus on what Shumate and Contractor (2014) call "multidimensional networks," which include humans, documents, organizations, and machines as nodes in the same network. Focusing on multidimensional networks is valuable because it allows us to take content and context of the network into account. For example, if we map out communication networks among people in an office and also map the network of who uses which office machines in the network, we have more context to see how workflow influences communication.

Shumate and Contractor (2014) discuss a second way in which technological networks shape organizational communication networks. The technical infrastructure that underlies organizational networks both enables new connections and constrains and limits communication. For example, if an organization installs a rigid "firewall" that prevents the passing of files by its members to others outside the organization, this may hamper collaborations between members of the organization and outside consultants. The Internet itself enables amazing new connections, but it also has built-in limitations to its technology that constrain what can be done (e.g. in the current incarnation of the web, links do not have memory of their histories, so we can't trace how they have been changed over time). Internet policies also constrain users (e.g. as net neutrality rules are suspended, some websites might get more bandwidth than others and gain an advantage in speed).

In the remainder of this chapter we will discuss how the literatures on networks and technology have influenced each other. Studies of networks and technology largely form a duality, or relationship where two distinct phenomena mutually influence one another, so that advances in each area have had dramatic consequences for the other. Table 13.1 displays these impacts in four quadrants, each containing a research question illuminating a different aspect of the duality of social networks and technology. We see two different types of impacts associated with the shifting sociotechnical landscape: phenomenological impacts and epistemological impacts. Phenomenological impacts involve shifts in the qualities of an object of study as a phenomenon observed in the real world. In the case of the network-technology relationship, these impacts concern how shifts in technology have impacted the actual structures of organizational networks, and vice-versa. Epistemological impacts, on the other hand, involve changes to the ways that we study a phenomenon. In the case of network-technology relationship, these impacts involve how advances in technology have influenced how we study social networks, and vice versa. In the following pages, we consider each of the four questions to give a sense of the "state-of-the art" in each quadrant.

Table 13.1 Conceptual Framework for the Review

	Phenomenological Impacts	*Epistemological Impacts*
Impacts of Technology on Social Networks	Q1. How has the shifting nature of technology affected the nature of social networks?	Q2. How has the shifting nature of technology affected how we *study* social networks?
Impacts of Social Network Analysis on Technology	Q4: How has our growing understanding of social networks affected the technological landscape?	Q3: How has our growing understanding of social networks affected how we *study* the technological landscape?

Q1: How has the shifting nature of technology affected the nature of social networks?

Organizations have increasingly deployed networked ICTs to coordinate work, to manage knowledge, and to build cohesive organizations and interorganizational alliances. An influential study by Monge, Fulk, Kalman, Flanagin, Parnassa, and Rumsey (1998) identified two affordances ICTs have for organizational networks: (1) *connectivity*, the ability of actors, groups, and organizations to directly communicate with one another through the ICT; and (2) *communality*, access to a commonly available pool of information by actors, groups, and organizations.

The connectivity that ICTs provide can greatly increase information flow through organizational networks. It also affects who connects with whom. "Mediated propinquity," analogous to physical propinquity, is correlated with reticulation. It is in part a function of how easily two actors can communicate with each other, but it is also a function of the skill with which actors communicate via the network, which affects their perceived "nearness" (Walther and Bazarova 2008).

Communality, the creation of a common information and knowledge resource, offers organizations the capability for knowledge management at a previously unprecedented level. Organizations have tried to implement knowledge management systems since the advent of filing cabinets and some, such as Xerox, famously developed systems that enabled workers to store records of problems they encountered and their solutions for other workers to consult. Building these knowledge networks "manually," however, required so much effort that they were difficult keep up to date. The advent of enterprise social media (ESM: social networking sites, wikis, blogs, microblogs, and social tagging systems) is sparking a revolution in knowledge management.

Going beyond these two basic affordances of ICTs, Treem and Leonardi (2012: 150) identify four affordances of ESM that fundamentally change the nature of organizational networking: (1) *visibility*, which affords users the ability "to make their behaviors, knowledge, preferences, and communication network connections that were once invisible (or at least very hard to see) visible to others;" (2) *persistence*, which preserves information and interactions over time; (3) *editability*, the ability to consciously plan presentation of self and information so it has maximum advantage; and (4) *association*, the ability to show the connections of users to one another and to information and accomplishments. These affordances influence reticulation by giving actors information about others they would not ordinarily have and thus encouraging (and discouraging in some instances) the formation of links. Through these and other affordances, networking technologies have had a number of impacts on organizational processes, both positive and negative.

Knowledge Management

Organizations are more effective if they have a capacity to take advantage of their employee's expertise. This is often challenging because employees are either unaware of "who knows what" in their organization, or they lack the ability to access experts (Brandon and Hollingshead 2004), which reduces their ability to improve and leads to duplication of work (Faraj and Sproull 2000). Network technologies, such as ticketing systems, knowledge-sharing platforms, and ESM, increase awareness of and access to experts (Yuan et al. 2007). These tools often take advantage of affordances of visibility to allow members to become aware of their peers' expertise and to rapidly form connections when they need specific knowledge (Leonardi 2017).

The advent of modern knowledge management tools has also produced second-order effects for organizational networks. For example, the visibility afforded by these tools can make users highly aware the information they post affects how others assess their expertise, which means they may carefully curate their information to manage other's impressions of them (Wasko and Faraj 2006). Users may even "game" these systems in hopes of shaping their access to resources at work and enhancing their reputations (Leonardi and Treem 2012).

Hiring

Recent surveys indicate that around 70% of organizations use some form of "cybervetting," which involves searching online for web pages, social media sites, and other information on applicants (CareerBuilder 2017). Berkelaar (2014) found that during cybervetting, pictures had more impact on managers' opinions of applicants than did verbal information, and negative information had greater impact than positive information. She found that cybervetting had the potential to replace more interactive forms of interviewing, resulting in candidates not advancing based on online information. Despite the fact that cybervetting often yields information illegal to use in hiring decisions (information on gender, race, sexual orientation), organizations continue to utilize it. This affects the pool of individuals available to organizational networks, and potentially reduces diversity in the network.

Surveillance

One cornerstone of management is control and monitoring of employees. ICTs facilitate surveillance through digital records and the potential for 24/7 awareness of what employees are doing, and as a result networks and the activities within them are much more visible to management. For example, ICTs can record time online, keystrokes, websites visited, time on customer calls, and the degree to which employees interact and work together, among other types of information. This may have positive effects for the organization in that it ensures that employees stay on task, work collaboratively, and use the organization's resources for work purposes. It can also benefit employees by documenting their successes and providing records so that if they are harassed or otherwise abused, they have evidence to pursue a case.

Surveillance, however, also has well-known downsides. It can lead to anxieties among employees who are surveilled, greatly reducing spontaneity and satisfaction and alienating employees (Kuhn et al. 2017). In some cases this leads to resistance and organizational dissent, manifested in disregard for rules and procedures and sometimes even sabotage or gaming of surveillance technologies.

Telework

Statistics from 2017 suggest that 50% of all jobs in the US are suitable for full or part-time telework and that 80% of workers surveyed would like to telework part time (Global Workplace Analytics 2017). This same source indicates that 3.7 million workers in the US telecommute more than 50% of the time. In this case telework extends the organization into the home or some other external location (e.g. the worker's car in the case of insurance adjusters estimating hurricane damage). Teleworkers are more satisfied with their jobs than in-place workers, they report less work-life conflict, and lower levels of stress (Fonner and Roloff 2010, Gajendran and Harrison 2007). Telecommuters also had somewhat higher levels of performance. Gajendaran and Harrison (2007) found that these positive results depended on the degree of autonomy workers felt, suggesting that how the telework was set up and supervised had an effect; workers who reported lower levels of autonomy did not enjoy the benefits. Relationships with coworkers were not affected for those who teleworked less than 50% time, but for those who worked remotely more than half-time, relationships suffered.

Algorithmic Connections

The advent of algorithms has made it all the more pertinent to examine the active role that technology plays in the reticulation of network structures of all types. Most visibly, we have become accustomed to algorithms recommending social connections for us as with the "people you may know" function on Facebook. This computer program actively suggests connections by looking at attributes and positioning of the user within their existing social network. Algorithms are everywhere—they suggest the shows we should watch (e.g. Netflix and Hulu), the items we should buy (e.g. Amazon), where we should eat (e.g. Yelp), and even who we should date (e.g. Tinder). As such, truly understanding how we form relationships in the modern age requires us to account for the role of programs like these in the process of reticulation.

Network Organizations

The affordances of network technologies have enabled the emergence of whole new types of organizational network forms. *Distributed organizations* have multiple units with wide geographical separation that are linked by ICTs. In software development, for example, some large organizations support 24-hour product or software development cycles by having three teams (for example, one in the United States, one in Europe, and one in India) work an 8-hour day and then pass it off to the next team, effectively moving the work around the world.

Virtual organizations are composed of multiple different organizations held together by ICTs. Calyx and Corolla, an online florist, was an early example of a virtual organization (Lucas 1995). Its small central office handles online orders, which are then sent to various flower growers, who prepare the orders and then pass them off to a delivery service, which takes them to customers. Payment is handled by a credit card company. Although Calyx and Corolla appears to be a coherent organization, it is really comprised of five or six organizations in different places that are brokered by management and coordinated via ICTs.

Network organizational forms have the advantage of flexibility, compared to traditional hierarchical organizations (Burton et al. 2006). They can be reconfigured much more easily than traditional organizations, and so can adapt to changes in their environments and technological change much more quickly. Trust is essential in these organizations, because every part of the network depends on other parts (Poole 1999). Members of network organizations tend to rely on "swift trust," assuming others will uphold their end of the bargain, and later revise perceptions of trust based on behavior.

Q2: How has the shifting nature of technology affected how we study social networks?

Perhaps the greatest influence that ICTs have had on social network research has been their impact on how we collect network data. The massive adoption of ICTs has given researchers access to mountains of behavioral data that enable analyses never before imagined. By behavioral data we mean any traces of social interaction that are left behind when using ICTs. This data enables researchers to study very large networks over time and incorporate the attributes of actors, and attributes of links.

Before the advent of large scale behavioral network data, the primary technique available to capture social networks was to ask people who they spoke with using sociometric surveys. When administering a sociometric survey, researchers ask members of an organization to recall their social relationships (e.g. "Who do you talk to in your day to day work?") and to elaborate on the nature of each of those relationships (e.g. "Which of these people do you go to for advice?"). Based on this data, the researcher maps the network and calculates the various measures we reviewed previously. However, there are significant challenges in doing sociometric surveys. They are labor intensive in their data collection for both the researcher, who needs to poll every individual in an organization, and for the respondent, who needs to comment on every potential relationship with every other individual inside their organization. They often result in missing data which is a challenge because a response rate of 80% is sometimes needed to accurately calculate important statistics like centrality (Borgatti et al. 2006). There is also a problem because participants often misreport or just do not recall who they interact with (there is a tendency for them to overestimate how often they interact with high status people and underestimate or forget other contacts) (Brashears and Quintane 2015).

Rather than using sociometric surveys, networks scholars can now rely on traces of interactions that occur on digital media to capture network structure and behavior. Why ask people who they interact with when you have records of all their interactions on an email server? One of the earliest large behavioral datasets to impact network science was the "Enron Dataset" a record of about a half-million internal emails from an energy company that was released to the public during the jury proceedings of a major financial scandal in the early 2000's. A number of studies have focused on communication networks using this dataset (e.g. Diesner et al. 2005). Other types of data, such as server records of play in massive multiplayer online games (e.g. World of WarCraft) (Williams et al. 2011) and records of Wikipedia entries (Matei and Britt 2017) have also been used to generate networks.

A number of new tools for computational analysis and data gathering have been applied to network studies of large corpuses of digitally captured data. These include tools for identifying who is connected with whom, such as C-IKNOW (http://sonic.northwestern.edu/software/software-archive/c-iknow/) and web crawlers that identify links between organizations online via hyperlinks (e.g. SocSciBot, http://socscibot.wlv.ac.uk/). Sociometric badges (Lederman et al. 2016) are small wearable devices with sensors that capture interactions among wearers, measuring conversational time, physical proximity, and physical activity levels. Data from these devices can be transformed into network data with high spatial and temporal resolution.

Q3: How has our growing understanding of social networks affected the technological landscape?

The third quadrant in our framework leads the analyst to examine how advances in social network analysis have influenced the nature of modern

ICTs. The clearest influence is the growth of network logics as a defining characteristic of the communication tools. The popularization of social platforms such as LinkedIn, Facebook, and Twitter was one of the most defining aspects of public culture in the 2000s. As these platforms became more popular, technology developers started similarly featured tools intended for use within the organization such as Yammer, Facebook@Work, and Hootsuite. It is no mistake we call these technologies "social network sites," as the tenets of network analysis are central to their underlying infrastructure, feature base, and in public definitions of these tools.

Although the term "social network site" is meaningfully distinct from "social network analysis," the former relies heavily on the application of network concepts. Consider some of the key affordances of these technologies: Users establish and maintain ties with other users (friends, followers, connections, etc.). The amalgamation of these connections produces a network of information that permits unique capabilities for sharing and relationship formation. Algorithms that drive content on these platforms draw on network concepts such as triadic closure to recommend users new content (e.g. I'm likely to have more in common with my friends' friends than with a random stranger, so I'll be more likely to be interested in their posts). Other algorithms, such the recommender engine on LinkedIn, draw on classic ideas of brokerage to help users connect with knowledge and jobs of interest. We could enumerate a much lengthier list, but these examples should suffice to demonstrate how central network logics have become to the types of ICTs we encounter on a daily basis.

Network logics are also central to the technologies we depend upon to provide instantaneous access to relevant information. Modern Internet search tools, in particular, rely on network analysis to provide high quality search results. Google's creators revolutionized how we search for information on the Internet when they introduced PageRank, an algorithm that uses the network structure of webpages to estimate which pages are likely to be the most important on the Web (Brin and Page n.d.). PageRank was designed to crawl a network of websites (nodes) connected by hyperlinks (links) to figure out which pages were the most influential, and thereby most likely to be relevant for search results. Centrality is the operating logic here: pages with more hyperlinks pointing to them tend to be higher quality. Although the intricacies of Google's current search algorithms are proprietary, PageRank remains an important component of this process. Before this technique, internet search was notoriously slow and performed poorly. Popular hubs like Yahoo! and AltaVista relied more on the categorical logics similar to telephone directories. Can you imagine flipping through all of the webpages on "communication" sequentially to figure out which concepts were relevant for your term paper?

The network perspective is increasingly used by organizations to develop technologies to organize their own work, their structures, and the challenges they face. For example, the U.S. military has spent decades developing a doctrine of "netcentric warfare," in which technological networks including networked communications and networks of data are used to provide a shared awareness of the battle space for U.S. forces (Wilson 2007). This shared awareness enables units to coordinate better and quickly respond to changes on the battlefield. Originally driven by the potential of ICTs such as networks of sensors, this movement soon brought a network perspective on military operations into play, which shaped the types of technologies that the military utilized. The nation of Crete designed an interorganizational information infrastructure for its healthcare system based on network concepts to offer connectivity and communality (Constantinides and Barrett 2015).

Q4:   How has our growing understanding of social networks affected how we study the technological landscape?

In the early 2000s, Manuel Castells (2001) published an iconic text arguing that truly understanding how ICTs were impacting our world required us to view them as embedded within complex social networks. As we described earlier, this viewpoint has led to a vibrant array of research examining how technology has influenced society. But this also asks us to consider how the advent of network thinking has influenced the way that scholars study ICTs.

Early research on ICTs tended to examine how the features of specific communication media influenced communication processes. Scholars observed, for example, that textual communication technologies like email and instant messaging reduced participants' access to important social cues such as facial expressions and tone of voice. This reduced access to social cues was shown to produce several influences on interaction such as increased conflict (Garner and Poole 2013), lack of awareness of partners' social context (Cramton 2001), and difficulties conveying complex topics (Daft and Lengel 1986). Others focused on ICTs' capacity to bridge distance affording collaboration opportunities that never previously existed.

It is increasingly apparent that studying the impacts of single communication tools is insufficient to characterize how people communicate in a world where many of us text, post, tweet, snap, and speak all within a matter of minutes. One way to consider the complexities of technology use in the modern era is to think of our technology use in network terms. From a network perspective, technologies like mobile devices and the Internet can each be considered nodes in a multimodal network where individuals are connected via multiple forms of technology (Contractor et al. 2011). This perspective encourages scholars to ask different types of questions about how individuals appropriate multiple technologies to maintain the complexities of their relationships.

Several current areas of study exemplify these different types of questions. For example, one line of research has examined how the appropriation of multiple communication technologies has influenced the way that we engage in social interaction, such as when we use text messaging to have back-channel conversations during meetings (Stephens 2019). Other scholars have examined how individuals appropriate a constellation of communication tools to perform complex relational maintenance tasks (Rainie and Wellman 2012, Stephens 2019). Finally, others have shown that individuals' media consumption is increasingly fragmented across multiple communication platforms, which is a dramatic shift from traditional studies of media use (Kim 2014, Taneja et al. 2012).

Contrary to early critiques that claimed the Internet was causing individuals to become more isolated (e.g. Putnam 2000, Sunstein 2002), research taking a network perspective toward technology use indicates that certain individuals can craftily use the constellation of technologies available to them to maintain wider social networks. One implication of these findings is that scholarship examining interactions on a single technical platform might increasingly provide misleading results. For example, if we were to only examine your face-to-face interactions, we might conclude you have a relatively isolated social network, whereas if we examined those interactions alongside those you have through texts, tweets, posts, and snaps we would likely see something very different. Another implication of the rise of media multiplexity is the advent of a new form of digital divide, whereby individuals who have access to multiple technological platforms and the skills to meaningfully adopt them increasingly realize disproportionate advantages over those without these skills (Hargittai 2010).

Conclusion

The sociotechnical revolution has arrived, and we have ventured in this chapter to demonstrate just how tangled ICTs have become with our understandings of social networks. To close, we offer a few observations about our findings to guide the reader. First, we would like to challenge you to keep the duality of networks and technology in mind. We still frequently hear people make claims like "technology has changed the world!" and, while these claims may be partially true, they only tell part of the story. An appropriate response to this might be, "Yes, but the world has also changed technology! And we can't tell the whole story without considering both." Second, it is not clear that the revolution has ended. In fact, some indicators suggest that the revolution is still particularly nascent in organizations, where ESM is still a relatively new form of technology and job calls for big-data analysts are only on the rise.

This is clearly an area that will produce fruitful research for much time to come. Finally, as the structure of our review indicates, we perceive an imbalance in how scholars have approached the study of networks in technology. Specifically, scholars have spent considerable efforts examining how shifts in technology have impacted social networks. Our other quadrants, however, are home to less scholarship. We think there is much fertile areas for research examining how network logics have influenced the development of technology and in examining technology use from an explicitly network oriented perspective.

Discussion Questions

1. In a small group, brainstorm a list of technological networks that you use. More heads are better than one in this task.
2. Pick a couple of the networks from your list. Identify their positive and negative second-order effects. Do the positives outweigh the negatives, or vice versa?
3. Conduct an online search using the term "internet of things." What does this mean? How will it change your technological networks in the future?
4. Is the internet leading to increased isolation among people you know? Is it polarizing their positions and beliefs? Why or why not?

References

Berkelaar, B. L. 2014. "Cybervetting, Online Information, and Personnel Selection New Transparency Expectations and the Emergence of a Digital Social Contract," *Management Communication Quarterly*, 28, 479–506.

Borgatti, S. P., Carley, K. M. and Krackhardt, D. 2006. "On the Robustness of Centrality Measures under Conditions of Imperfect Data," *Social Networks*, 28, 124–136.

Brandon, D. P. and Hollingshead, A. B. 2004. "Transactive Memory Systems in Organizations: Matching Tasks, Expertise, and People," *Organization Science*, 15, 633–644.

Brashears, M. E. and Quintane, E. 2015. "The Microstructures of Network Recall: How Social Networks are Encoded and Represented in Human Memory," *Social Networks*, 41, 113–126.

Brin, S. and Page, L. (n.d.) "The Anatomy of a Large-Scale Hypertextual Web Search Engine," [online] Retrieved from http://infolab.stanford.edu/~backrub/google.html [Accessed April 8 2018].

Burton, R., DeSanctis, G. and Obel, B. 2006. *Organizational Design: A Step-By-Step Approach* (2nd ed.). Cambridge, UK: Cambridge University Press.

CareerBuilder. (2017). *Number of Employers Using Social Media to Screen Candidates at All-Time High, Finds Latest CareerBuilder Study* [Press release]. Retrieved on 5 November 2018 from http://press.careerbuilder.com/2017-06-15-Number-of-Employers-Using-Social-Media-to-Screen-Candidates-at-All-Time-High-Finds-Latest-CareerBuilder-Study

Castells, M. 2001. *The Internet Galaxy: Reflections on Economy, Society, and Culture*, Oxford, UK: Oxford University Press.

Constantinides, P. and Barrett, M. 2015. "Information Infrastructure Development and Governance as Collective Action," *Information Systems Research*, 26, 40–56.

Contractor, N., Monge, P. and Leonardi, P. 2011. "Multidimensional Networks and the Dynamics of Sociomateriality: Bringing Technology Inside the Network," *International Journal of Communication*, 5, 682–720.

Cramton, K. D. 2001. "The Mutual Knowledge Problem and Its Consequences for Dispersed Collaboration," *Organization Science*, 12, 346–371.

Daft, R. L. and Lengel, R. H. 1986. "Organizational Information Requirements, Media Richness and Structural Design," *Management Science*, 32, 554–571.

DeSanctis, G., Poole, M. S., Zigurs, I., DeSharnais, G., D'Onofrio, M., Gallupe, B., Holmes, M., Jackson, B., Jackson, M., Lewis, H. and Limayem, M. 2008 "The Minnesota GDSS Research Project: Group Support Systems, Group Processes, and Outcomes," *Journal of the Association for Information Systems*, 9, 551–568.

Diesner, J., Frantz, T. L. and Carley, K. M. 2005. "Communication Networks from the Enron Email Corpus 'It's Always About the People. Enron is no Different'," *Computational & Mathematical Organization Theory*, 11, 201–228.

Faraj, S. and Sproull, L. 2000. "Coordinating Expertise in Software Development Teams," *Management Science*, 46, 1554–1568.

Fonner, K. and Roloff, M. E. 2010. "Why Teleworkers are More Satisfied with Their Jobs Than Are Office-Based Workers: When Less Contact is Beneficial," *Journal of Applied Communication Research*, 8, 336–361.

Fulk, J. and Steinfield, C. (eds). 1990. *Organizations and Communication Technology*, Newbury Park, CA: SAGE.

Gajendron, R. S. and Harrison, D. A. 2007. The Good, the Bad, and the Unknown About Telecommuting: Meta-Analysis of Psychological Mediators and Individual Consequences," *Journal of Applied Psychology*, 92, 1524–1541.

Garner, J. and Poole, M. S. 2013. "Perspectives on Workgroup Conflict and Communication. In Oetzel, J. G. and Ting-Toomey, S. (eds.) *The SAGE Handbook of Conflict Communication* (2nd ed.), Thousand Oaks, CA: SAGE. pp. 321–347.

Global Workplace Analytics 2017. "Latest Telecommuting Statistics," [online] Retrieved from http://globalworkplaceanalytics.com/telecommuting-statistics [Accessed 8 April 2018].

Hargittai, E. 2010. "Digital Na(t)ives? Variation in Internet Skills and Uses among Members of the 'Net Generation'," *Sociological Inquiry*, 80, 92–113.

Kiesler, S. and Sproull, L. 1991. *Connections: New Ways of Working in the Networked World*, Cambridge, MA: MIT Press.

Kilduff, M. and Brass, D. J. 2010. "Organizational Social Network Research: Core Ideas and Key Debates," *The Academy of Management Annals*, 4, 317–357.

Kim, S. J. 2014. "A Repertoire Approach to Cross-Platform Media Use Behavior," *New Media & Society*, 18, 353–372.

Krackhardt, D. and Kilduff, M. 1999. "Whether Close or Far: Social Distance Effects on Perceived Balance in Friendship Networks," *Journal of Personality and Social Psychology*, 76, 770–782.

Kuhn, T. R., Ashcraft, K. L. and Cooren, F. 2017. *The Work of Communication: Relational Perspectives on Working and Organizing in Contemporary Capitalism*, New York: Routledge.

Kuwabara, K., Hildebrand, C. A. and Zou, X. 2018. "Lay Theories About Networking: How Laypeople's Beliefs about Networks Affect Their Attitude Toward and Engagement in Instrumental Networking," *Academy of Management Review*, 43, 50–64.

Lederman, O., Calacci, D., MacMullen, A., Fehder, D. C., Murray, F. E. and Pentland, A. 2016. Open Badges: A Low-Cost Toolkit for Measuring Team Communication and Dynamics. *2016 International Conference on Social Computing*, Washington DC, USA.

Lee, S. and Monge, P. 2011. "The Coevolution of Multiplex Communication Networks in Organizational Communities," *Journal of Communication*, 61, 758–779.

Leonardi, P. M. 2012. "Materiality, Sociomateriality, and Socio-Technical Systems: What Do These Terms Mean? How are they Different? Do We Need Them?" in Leonardi P. M., Nardi, B. A. and Kallinikos, J. (eds.), *Materiality and Organizing: Social Interaction in a Technological World*, Oxford, UK: Oxford University Press, pp. 25–48.

Leonardi, P. M. 2017. "The Social Media Revolution: Sharing and Learning in the Age of Leaky Knowledge," *Information and Organization*, 27, 47–59.

Leonardi, P. M. and Treem, J. W. 2012. "Knowledge Management Technology as a Stage for Strategic Self-Presentation: Implications for Knowledge Sharing in Organizations," *Information and Organization*, 22, 37–59.

Lucas, H. J. 1995. *The T-Form Organization*, San Francisco, CA: Jossey-Bass.

Matei, S. A. and Britt, B. C. 2017. *Structural Differentiation in Social Media: Adhocracy, Entropy, and the '1% Effect'*, Chaim, Switzerland: Springer.

Monge, P. R., Fulk, J., Kalman, M. E., Flanagin, A. J., Parnassa, C. and Rumsey, S. 1998. "Production of Collective Action in Alliance-Based Interorganizational Communication and Information Systems," *Organization Science*, 9, 411–433.

Monge, P. and Contractor, N. 2003. *Theories of Communication Networks*, Oxford, UK: Oxford University Press.

Norman, D. 1999. "Affordances, Conventions, and Design," *Interactions*, 6, 38–43.

Pew Research Center, 2018. "Social Media Use in 2018," [online] Retrieved from www.pewinternet.org/2018/03/01/social-media-use-in-2018/. [Accessed 2 April 2018].

Poole, M. S. 1999. "Organizational Challenges for the New Forms," in DeSanctis, G. and Fulk, J. (eds.), *Shaping Organization Form: Communication, Connection, and Community*, Thousand Oaks, CA: SAGE, pp. 453–472.

Putnam, R. D. 2000. *Bowling Alone: The Collapse and Revival of American Community*, New York: Simon & Schuster.

Rainie, L. and Wellman, B. 2012. *Networked: The New Social Operating System*, Cambridge, MA: MIT Press.

Rice, R. E. 1984. (ed.). *The New Media: Communication, Research, and Technology*, Beverly Hills, CA: SAGE.

Shumate, M. and Contractor, N. S. 2014. "The Emergence of Multidimensional Communication Networks," in Putnam L. & Mumby, D. (eds.), *The SAGE*

Handbook of Organizational Communication, Thousand Oaks, CA: SAGE, pp. 449–475.

Stephens, K. 2019. *Negotiating Control: Organizations and Mobile Communication*, New York: Oxford University Press.

Stephens, K., Fulk, J. and Monge, P. 2009. "Constrained Choices in Alliance Formation: Cupids and Organizational Marriages," *Human Relations*, 62, 501–536.

Sunstein, C. R. 2002. *Republic.com*, Princeton, NJ: Princeton University Press.

Taneja, H., Webster, J. G., Malthouse, E. C. and Ksiazek, T. B. 2012. "Media Consumption Across Platforms: Identifying User-Defined Repertoires," *New Media & Society*, 14, 951–968.

Treem, J. W. and Leonardi, P. M. 2013. "Social Media Use in Organizations: Exploring the Affordances of Visibility, Editability, Persistence, and Association," *Annals of the International Communication Association*, 36, 143–189.

Walther, J. B. and Bazarova, N. N. 2008. "Validation and Application of Electronic Propinquity Theory to Computer-Mediated Communication in Groups," *Communication Research*, 35, 622–645.

Williams, D., Contractor, N., Poole, M. S., Srivastava, J. and Cai, D. 2011. "The Virtual Worlds Exploratorium: Using Large-Scale Data and Computational Techniques for Communication Research," *Communication Methods and Measures*, 5, 163–180.

Wilson, C. 2007. *Network Centric Operations: Background and Oversight Issues for Congress*, Washington, DC: Congressional Research Service.

Yuan, Y. C., Fulk, J. and Monge, P. 2007. "Access to Information in Connective and Communal Transactive Memory Systems," *Communication Research*, 34, 131–155.

14 Crisis and Resilience

Matthew W. Seeger and Rahul Mitra

Crises and disasters, large and small, are part of almost all of our lives. While these events may vary widely depending on scope, scale, cause, and context, they share some features. A *crisis* may be defined as a specific, unexpected, non-routine event or a series of events that creates high levels of uncertainty and a significant or perceived threat to high-priority goals (Seeger et al. 2005, Sellnow and Seeger 2013). Threat, uncertainty, and the need for some form of immediate response are generally considered common features of crises. Crises may be intentional (e.g. terrorism, sabotage, sustained unethical management) or unintentional (e.g. natural disasters, economic downturns, product failures). Importantly, both types of crisis are increasingly "a consistent part of our existence" (Ulmer et al. 2011: 13). The interconnected and dynamic structures of world finance and technologies, as well as human migration, climate change, and depleted resources, have increased the frequency of crises.

This confluence of organizational structures and social events makes effectively communicating about crises crucial. Effective crisis communication is not limited to a single event or time frame. Rather, it involves adopting a broader, holistic perspective to the interconnected and ongoing nature of risks, and recognizing that a variety of message forms, channels, and strategies are necessary to reach multiple stakeholders. Crisis communication is an ongoing process of creating shared meaning between groups, communities, individuals, and agencies, within the context of a crisis, for the purpose of preparing for and reducing, limiting, and responding to threats and harm (Sellnow and Seeger 2013). We also note that crises can be very powerful sources of positive and negative organizational, community, and societal change. In fact, many significant changes are driven by crises and associated communication processes that "create high levels of uncertainty and simultaneously present an organization with both opportunities for and threats to its high-priority goals" (Ulmer et al. 2011: 7).

While crisis communication is a diverse and multidisciplinary area of research and practice, communication scholars have primarily approached the topic from the standpoint of public relations, strategic communication, and organizational rhetoric. This is not to say that organizational communication researchers do not study crisis—as evidenced through scholarship on high-reliability organizations (e.g. firefighters, police), disaster response policies and strategies, and worker safety (e.g. Doerfel et al. 2013, Myers and McPhee 2006, Scott and Trethewey 2008, Stephens et al. 2013)—but that it is often addressed in the context of corporate social responsibility, leadership, change management, decision-making, and other themes (for more in-depth treatment of these topics, see Chapters 4, 11, and 12 in this volume, respectively). In recent years, however, organizational communication scholars have begun to appreciate crisis communication on its own terms, even as they have sought to theorize resilience as an inherently communicative concept (e.g. Buzzanell 2010). The recent special issue of the interdisciplinary journal *Corporate Communications* on communicating/organizing for reliability, resilience, and safety is a promising development, wherein the guest editors urge for greater attention to how these crisis themes are interconnected and foundational to organizational communication (Barbour et al. 2018).

In this chapter, we first describe our own experiences as communication researchers exploring crisis and resilience. We then briefly review four primary research traditions in crisis communication scholarship, along with some practical applications. Our goal is to describe crisis as a communicative phenomenon, and focus on the ways organizations, agencies, and communities may learn from a crisis. To do so, we describe two post-crisis concepts—resilience and discourse(s) of renewal.

Personal Narratives to Crisis and Resilience

Matt's Story: The Purple Aces Tragedy

In 1977, I was an undergraduate student studying communication at the University of Evansville in southern Indiana. On December 13, 1977, at 7:22 pm CST, a Douglas DC-3, carrying the University basketball team, the Purple Aces, crashed at the Evansville Regional Airport. The plane lost control in harsh weather and crashed shortly after takeoff. All 22 passengers, including players, coaches, and staff, died in the crash. The National Transportation Safety Board later determined that the crash was caused by the pilot's failure to remove gust locks on the right-wing aileron and the rudder before takeoff, as well as an overloaded baggage compartment. The crisis was devastating for a small college campus of 3,000 students. Faculty, administration, staff, students, alumni, and members of the community were shocked, confused, and profoundly saddened by the loss. The only campus offices open that night were the student newspaper (*The Crescent*) and the student radio station (WUEV). I was working in both those offices that night and experienced the crisis in a very personal way. For a short time, these offices became the communication center for the crisis, providing information to the media, community, friends, and family. The campus community came together in grief, and to provide comfort and support.

Eventually, the community recovered and the story of the 1977 Purple Aces became an important part of the university's history and identity. Those who experienced the tragedy were profoundly changed, as was the university.

Rahul's Story: From Singur to Resilience

When I began my master's study in 2007 in the United States, a furor was raging in my home state of West Bengal in India, from where I hail. India's largest automotive company, Tata Motors, and the state's government had procured 997 acres of agricultural land to build a gargantuan factory, leading to protracted protests by rural sharecroppers who claimed they had been dispossessed. These protests came to a head when 50 protesters met their death in ensuing riots, and Tata Motors suspended construction and eventually moved from the state. I analyzed the organization's response during this crisis, noting how it positioned itself as a noble beneficent and played down the protests as isolated and malicious, as well as how this rhetorical strategy backfired (Mitra 2013). That project led to a research program of studying the social responsibility of organizations, which—I gradually realized—was often used by companies to stave off consumer and activist boycotts, and highlight their good conduct during crisis situations. Moreover, I came to trace how not all crises manifest in flash points, like Singur or the Purple Aces, but in some cases they may be "sleeper" crises, reflecting long-term decline in socioecological systems, as with climate change and rapidly eroding natural resources (Mitra 2018). Throughout these instances, a crucial part of crisis response is forestalling risks and building system resilience, engaging stakeholders as widely as possible. Far from being polar opposites, crises and resilience go hand in hand—so that organizations engaged in crisis response realize they must create spaces for long-term resilience and adaptation not just to prevent censure from stakeholders, but also to live to see another day.

Having thus explained our respective entry-points to crisis research, we now describe four primary frameworks used by scholars and practitioners to study crisis events.

Crisis Frameworks

Crises are ubiquitous and can be intensely emotional, memorable and transformational events. They are profound forces for social change and they can fundamentally shift how we understand and respond to risks and threats. These events create very high levels of uncertainty, disorder, and confusion. They disrupt meaning systems, break established routines, create instability, and call into question agreed-upon understandings of risk (Seeger and Sellnow 2016). Crisis communication, therefore, is an essential area for inquiry from a variety of standpoints, theoretical orientations and methodological perspectives. Crisis communication is a diverse, rich, and complex field that has grown significantly in the last two decades. It is also an essential area of practice necessary to successfully manage any risk or crisis event. In its most essential form, crisis communication is the process of exchanging messages between interdependent senders and receivers within the intense, threatening, consequential, and uncertain conditions created by a crisis.

In addition, investigations of crises have developed from very different disciplinary traditions including psychology, sociology, medicine, emergency management, and political science, as well as communication. These disciplines have emphasized different aspects of crises. The literature is diverse, and includes explorations of warnings and evacuations (e.g. Cole and Fellows 2008, Eisenman et al. 2007, Mileti and Sorenson 1990, Mileti and O'Brien 1992), apologetic and repair-oriented communication (e.g. Benoit 1995, Coombs 2007), role of social media (e.g. Veil et al. 2011), and functional approaches, including best practices (Seeger 2006) and the Crisis and Emergency Risk Communication framework. We describe these approaches in the following sections, in some detail.

Warnings and Evacuations

A warning is a functional message or system of messages for informing an audience or audiences of some probable threat or danger (Sellnow and Seeger 2013). Warnings address risks, such as tornados, water contamination, earthquakes, mud slides, water and food contaminations, and floods. A warning generally follows an alert, issued when there is a general concern, or when something has happened or may happen to potentially jeopardize public security, health, and well-being. A warning follows the alert, when the threat has been confirmed, and includes more specific information about the nature of the threats and sometimes advice about how to respond (National Research Council 2011). For example, a tornado watch is an alert that is issued when the conditions are right for tornados to form. A tornado warning suggests that a threat is imminent and that immediate action is required (NOAA 2018). Alerts and warnings are designed to promote risk reducing or mitigating behaviors by target audiences. The process whereby warnings promote decisions and actions has been described by Mileti and Sorensen (1990) as a process of "Hear-Confirm-Understand-Decide-Respond."

As informational messages, warnings seek to convey to an audience an understanding of specific threats, the likely severity of the potential harm and the probability of its occurring. They function, therefore, to reduce uncertainty about a risk (Sutton et al. 2014). Warnings often include recommendations about actions that those at risk can take to avoid, reduce, or mitigate the threats. These recommendations, such as boil water before drinking, shelter in place, or evacuate, are designed to be matched to the specific threat. Warning messages are also persuasive, seeking to influence behaviors in response to the crisis. That is, both informative and persuasive roles must function together during a crisis. It is also important to contextualize warnings within the larger context of *risk communication*, defined as "an interactive process of exchange of information and opinion among individuals, groups, and institutions (National Research Council 1989: 21).

Warning systems have been part of the public response to threats for decades. Early systems used bells and word of mouth to disseminate alerts and warnings. Sirens have been used widely for weather, industrial, and transportation risks where an immediate audience must be notified of risk. The Emergency Broadcasting System (EBS), and later, the Emergency Alert System, was developed in 1963 as a television and radio-based system. The system was established to provide government officials with an expeditious method of communicating with the American public in the event of war, threat of war, or grave national crisis (U.S. Defense Civil Preparedness Agency 1978). The media also has a critical role in disseminating warnings. Local officials, weather reporters, and community members are often used to disseminate warnings and persuade the public to take recommended actions. Many agencies and communities, including universities, are now turning to instant messaging (IM) and text-based alert systems as part of their warning systems.

Apologetic and Image Repair-Oriented Communication

A dominant approach to post-crisis communication concerns itself with how organizations respond to the accusations of wrongdoing that often accompany crises (Sellnow and Seeger 2013). Following these accusations, organizations need to respond with explanations, accounts, justifications and in some cases apologies. Efforts to explain how organizations respond include Image Repair Theory (Benoit 1995) and Situated Crisis Communication Theory (Coombs 2007). These approaches share a focus on the damaged organizational image or reputation, and suggested efforts to use communication strategically to offset or repair that damage.

Image repair theory consists largely of a typology of communication strategies individuals or organizations can use to project a more favorable image, or to repair an image following a crisis. The potential harm of a damaged organizational image is significant. Customers turn away from, seek to punish, and stop doing business with organizations whose images are tarnished by crises. Politicians and the public may demand new regulations. Stock values may fall dramatically, causing stockholders to demand drastic changes, including changes to leadership and management. Investigations and lawsuits may linger. There is, therefore, a significant benefit to repairing a damaged image. Image repair, however, is not intended to serve those who wish to deceive the public. Rather, as Benoit (2005: 409) states, "Effective image repair suggests that those who are truly at fault should admit it immediately and take appropriate corrective action."

To engage in image repair, Benoit (2005: 407) explains that the party accused of wrongdoing must first address two questions: "(1) what accusation(s) or suspicion(s) threaten the image, and (2) who is or are the most important audiences?" The specific nature of the accusations will help determine the most effective response. Understanding the audience is also important, because the audience will determine whether the response strategy is effective. Image repair theory describes a typology of five general response strategies: denial, evading responsibility, reducing offensiveness, corrective action, and mortification. Benoit also identifies secondary strategies for denial, including evading responsibility and reducing offensiveness of the event.

Situational crisis communication theory (SCCT) also addresses the need to respond to the public's perceptions of organizational wrongdoing, following crises or similar controversy. SCCT offers a specific set of strategies from which organizations can choose, and these strategies are matched to specific circumstances of the crisis. Coombs and Holladay (2002: 183) argued that SCCT "develops a prescriptive system for matching crisis response strategies to the crisis situation" (also see Coombs 2014, 2007). SCCT is based largely on maintaining or reestablishing a favorable organizational reputation and is used extensively in public relations research. Coombs (2014: 109) notes that "SCCT organizes previously delineated crisis response strategies using Attribution theory as a guiding light." Attribution theory describes ways inferences are systematically inferred about actions to make sense of ongoing events (Weiner 1985). SCCT expands the application of attribution to the ways organizational "stakeholders make attributions about the cause of a crisis" (Coombs 2014: 110). The key consideration in SCCT is the degree to which stakeholders view the organization as responsible for the crisis. First, managers must identify the crisis type and accountability level (i.e. how much blame is due the organization) on the basis of the gravity of the situation, the organization's crisis history (if any), and its relationship with the stakeholders. Second, they must select a crisis response strategy that is proportionate to the expected reputational damage.

SCCT describes strategies that are organized into four clusters "that stakeholders perceive as similar to one another" (Coombs 2014: 156). These include denial strategies, diminishment strategies, rebuilding strategies, and bolstering strategies. Coombs suggests that denial strategies seek to diminish connections between the crisis and the organization,

whereas diminishment strategies try to downplay organizational control over the crisis. Third, rebuilding strategies are designed to enhance
organizational reputation, and finally, bolstering strategies supplement
the other three strategies by building a "positive connection between the
organization and the stakeholders" (Coombs 2014: 157). Importantly,
Coombs (2014) argues that these crisis response strategies can be used
in a variety of combinations, within limits. For example, an organization
could accept that there is a crisis and offer a strategic response, by simultaneously applying diminishment and rebuilding. Claeys, Caubherge and
Vyncke's (2010) experimental study largely verified Coombs' model, also
noting that individuals' locus of control moderated how they perceived
the crisis response strategy to impact organizational reputation. Specifically, those with an external locus of control preferred the denial strategy
more than people with an internal locus of control. Moreover, while the
SCCT was conceived with corporate reputation in mind, Sisco, Collins,
and Zoch (2010) showed that SCCT could also be applied in the case of
nonprofit organizations in their case study of the American Red Cross.

Social Media for Crisis Management

Kaplan and Haenlein (2010: 61) define *social media* as "a group of Inter-
net-based applications that build on the ideological and technological
foundations of Web 2.0, and that allow the creation and exchange of user
generated content." Central to this definition is the understanding that
content is not only shared, but also potentially modified continuously
in a collaborative fashion (Web 2.0), and that this communicative process occurs on a publicly accessible platform that goes above and beyond
mainstream institutional structures. Prominent social media technologies
include text-messaging, mobile phones, and online social networking
sites (SNSs). For Baym et al. (2012), seven key concepts distinguish social
media (or *new media*, as they are also termed) from traditional forms;
viz., synchronicity, availability of social cues, mobility, storage capability,
ability to replicate, interactivity, and the extent of reach to audience.

Both crisis communication researchers and practitioners have embraced
developments within social media. The relevance of social media in crisis situations has been vividly demonstrated during the 2010 Colorado
Wildfires, United Airlines flight 3411 involving the forcible removal of
a passenger, and during Hurricane Harvey in 2017. The inherently fast-
paced, viral nature of social media networks can affect the reputation of
a company—sometimes within a matter of minutes. Particularly during
crisis situations, the rapid sharing of user-generated content means that
stakeholders are no longer passive participants waiting to be informed
about particular developments. Rather, they generate and disseminate
their own information, which may sometimes be at odds with organizations' preferred reality (Eriksson 2012). At the same time, such rapid

distribution of information is crucial, especially during the early stages of crises, when fast action is critical, and can thus serve as an important tool in managing crises by disseminating vital information. Its importance is increasingly evident as more of the public, and government agencies embrace the capacity of social media technologies, such as Twitter, YouTube, and Facebook, to disseminate information quickly and widely. Veil, Buehner and Palenchar (2011: 120) argued that "used thoughtfully, social media, can improve risk and crisis communication efforts."

Social media can serve several key functions in crisis communication. First, it can help monitor for emerging risks and provide information about how they are developing, since many crises will be reported first on social media. For instance, Yates and Paquette (2011) examined the design and usage of social media technologies to coordinate the relief effort following the devastating 2010 earthquake in Haiti, while Eriksson's (2012) "descriptive model approach" sought to understand online crisis communication processes, based on interviews with 24 Swedish practitioners. Second, social media can facilitate two-way communication between organizations and stakeholders about risks and crises, thus enriching organizations' interactive capacity. For instance, Yang, Kang, and Johnson (2010) found that crisis narratives in organizational blogs that emphasized dialogic communication were more successful in engaging audiences and resulted in positive post-crisis perceptions.

Third, social media can assist in controlling rumors. Veil, Sellnow and Petrun (2011: 119) noted that interaction using social media "is essential in addressing misinformation and establishing the organization as a credible source." Rumors and misinformation during crises are hard to counter and can be especially destructive, so that the more quickly an organization can respond to rumors, the more effective its control measures. Researchers using the social-mediated crisis communication (SMCC) model to examine how publics respond to crisis communication via social media found that such technologies significantly influenced individuals' attribution of their emotions (Fisher Liu et al. 2011). Moreover, sharing of information occurs along a multi-tiered system across different types of publics (Austin et al. 2012). A fourth way social media contributes to effective crisis communication is by including alternative (and potentially richer) message forms and content. For instance, social media can include interactive maps, videos, and links to other data sources. Interactive maps have been especially helpful in facilitating evacuations. Images can enrich the story and provide vivid illustrations of emerging risks, while videos also engage audiences at different levels and in myriad ways. Finally, social media functions as a very direct form of communication that is not filtered by gatekeepers, as with legacy media. Organizations and agencies thus have the ability to disseminate messages in a very direct and targeted way. According to a study by Schultz et al. (2011), there was a significant difference between the impact of social

versus traditional media in influencing respondents' perceptions of corporate reputation and their secondary crisis communication (e.g. sharing
information, commenting).

Functional Approaches

Crisis communication is also a set of practices and activities with enormous functionality. Functional approaches to crises thus concern the
results or outcomes of communication behaviors and processes. That is
to say, crisis communication is a tool that senders and receivers use to
accomplish crisis-related goals, solve problems, make decisions, influence
others, and coordinate actions for preparing, responding and recovering
(Sellnow and Seeger 2013). Communication may be more, or less, effective in accomplishing these outcomes, depending on its structure, how
it is used, what audiences it targets, and what channels are employed,
among many other factors. Two such approaches are the Crisis and
Emergency Risk Communication framework developed by the Centers
for Disease Control and Prevention (Reynolds, Hunter-Galdo and Sokler
2002, Reynolds and Seeger 2005), and the Best Practices in Crisis Communication framework (Covello 2003, Seeger 2006).

Crisis and Emergency Risk Communication (CERC) is an integrated
approach to communicating risk and crisis in public health contexts. Following the Hong Kong avian influenza outbreak in 1997, the 9/11 terrorist attack, and anthrax letter contamination, the Centers for Disease
Control and Prevention (CDC) developed a comprehensive guide for crisis and risk communication, media and community relations, cultural
factors, public health law, and related issues (Reynolds et al. 2002). The
CERC framework and associated manual includes a number of resources,
frameworks, and models for practicing crisis communication within the
public health context. Among these resources was a five-phase model of
crisis stages, and a comprehensive and integrated approach to risk, crisis,
and emergency response communication (Reynolds and Seeger 2005).
The model includes (1) pre-crisis, (2) initial event, (3) maintenance, (4)
resolution, and (5) evaluation.

The pre-crisis stage is an incubation stage, where the communication
functions are focused around risk messages, warnings, and information about preparation (Reynolds and Seeger 2005). Risk messages are
designed to inform and persuade those at risk about how to prepare for
a crisis. One familiar example is the Ready.gov campaign, which encourages people to prepare for a wide range of disasters. The initial event stage
begins with some form of trigger event, which results in perceived threats
and high levels of uncertainty. Communication functions in this stage to
reduce uncertainty and provide the public with strategies of self-efficacy.
In this way, the public is able to take actions to contain and mitigate the
harm, such as shelter in place or evacuate. The maintenance stage requires

ongoing efforts to reduce uncertainty by providing additional information about how the crisis is developing and its potential impacts. In this stage, it is also possible to educate people about risks. Communication in the fourth stage, resolution, focuses on updating affected audiences regarding resolution and initiating frank discussions about the cause of the crisis. This is the point where questions of blame and responsibility are usually raised along with associated efforts to repair damaged images. The resolution stage is also associated with new understandings of risk and procedures for risk avoidance. This may include the development of increased resilience. The last stage is the evaluation stage. This is a point where communication functions to promote learning through things such as after action reports, debriefs, and lessons learned documents.

Through the CERC framework, the CDC sought to develop crisis communication capacity at various levels of public health operations. As a general conceptual framework for integrating crisis and risk communication, CERC may be summarized as a loosely connected set of guidelines and principles, grounded in key concepts and research that function to addressing the needs of the public health community. Accordingly, it has been applied broadly in a wide variety of cases, where the public's health is threatened by an emergency.

A second functional approach involves articulating a set of standards for effective crisis communication, within the context of a best-practices framework. *Best practices* describe techniques or methods that have consistently been demonstrated as effective, within given contexts or circumstances, in achieving desired outcomes. That is, they are standards and accepted ways of doing business. Best practices are widely used in business and professional contexts including, medicine, law, education, and engineering, among others. This approach can be especially useful in contexts where there are questions and confusion about what might be the most effective approach (Covello 2003, Seeger 2006). A crisis is a very complex, intense and dynamic situation, where guidelines and standards can be especially helpful in informing decisions. These principles may be understood as decision rules or guidelines for informing practice. Two best practice approaches are described as follows.

Seeger (2006) identified ten best practices in crisis and emergency risk communication. These include the following:

1. Develop process approaches to risk and crisis communication, and include participation of the communication function in the policy development process;
2. Engage in pre-event planning for the initial crisis communication response;
3. Develop pre-event relationships and partnerships with the public;
4. Listen to the public's concerns, and understand concerns and needs of different audiences;

5.   Communicate in an honest, candid and open manner;
6.   Collaborate and coordinate with credible sources;
7.   Meet the needs of the media, and remain accessible to media;
8.   Communicate with compassion, concern, and empathy;
9.   Accept the uncertainty and ambiguity of a crisis; and
10.   Communicate messages of self-efficacy.

Covello (2003: 5) offered a similar set of best practices, which he described as a checklist "that should be included in any public health risk and crisis communication plan." These seven best practices are largely consistent with those described by Seeger (2006). They include (1) accepting and involving stakeholders as legitimate partners; (2) listening to people; (3) being truthful, honest, frank, and open; (4) coordinating, collaborating, and partnering with other credible sources; (5) meeting the needs of the media; (6) communicating clearly and with compassion; (7) planning thoroughly and carefully.

These best practices can serve as guidelines for communicating under the uncertainty and confusion that often accompany a crisis. They encapsulate a variety of functional and foundational principles for effective communication. Functional frameworks such as CERC and Best Practices are designed to guide and inform practices. They summarize and synthesize existing evidence in ways that are useful within the dynamic and threatening context of a crisis.

Understanding the Impact of Crises

Crises can fundamentally change how we understand and respond to risks and threats, since they often result in fundamental reordering of systems, processes, norms, and operations to increase resilience and reduce the probabilities of similar events. Usually, there are enough opportunities for these changes to lead to growth and improvement, influenced by a variety of communicative processes. Two approaches to post-crisis change concern the ways in which systems manage and recover from crises; these are resilience and renewal.

Resilience

For Ayyub (2014: 4),

> Resilience notionally means the ability to prepare for and adapt to changing conditions and withstand and recover rapidly from disruptions. Resilience includes the ability to withstand and recover from disturbances of the deliberate attack types, accidents, or naturally occurring threats or incidents.

Organizations and communities that are resilient can absorb distur-
bances, improvise and reorganize during a crisis, so that they retain their
functionality, structure, and essential identity. Resilience is an emergent,
rather than a static, characteristic and is the "outcome of a recursive
process that includes sensing, anticipation, learning, and adaptation"
(Ayyub 2014: 2). Often, this recursive process is enacted following a crisis, as part of larger efforts to learn from these events. Resilience may
thus be understood as the emergent capacity of a system to accommodate
risks, avoid crises, cope with disruption, bounce back, pull through, or
adapt to the disruption of a crisis (see also Boin and McConnell 2007,
Kendra and Wachtendorf 2007).

Two sets of factors related to resilience are crucial: system characteristics (i.e. features of communities, organizations and agencies) and event
characteristics (i.e. scope, scale, frequency, level of disruption, surprise,
and the specific threat). *System characteristics* include such things as
capacity; skill; availability of resources; those resources' robustness; the
speed with which resources can be rapidly deployed; level of training
and preparation, including both width and depth; and the level of system integration. In addition, connections between systems allowing for
coordination and cooperation are factors in resilience. *Event characteristics* include the scope, scale, duration, and nature of the event. Crises
that have broader scope, address larger geographic areas, and that are
more intense, as measure by a variety of factors, create more destruction.
Moreover, crises that are based in novel or exotic risk factors are generally more challenging to manage.

Recent work by communication scholars has highlighted the communicative processes and structures that enact resilience in different contexts and levels, such as local communities, families, organizations, and
nations (see the 2018 Special Forum on "communication and resilience"
in *Journal of Applied Communication Research*). Buzzanell and Houston
(2018: 2) note, "When viewed from a communication lens, resilience
operates as a process embedded or situated in everyday life at ordinary
moments of loss as well as at extraordinary and profound disruptions
caused by war, disaster, death, and mass violence." They draw from and
extend communicative theorizing on resilience, noting how it involves five
key processes: crafting a new normalcy, affirming or anchoring important identities, drawing on salient communication networks, adopting
alternative logics, and foregrounding positive and action-oriented themes
(Buzzanell 2010). This perspective is in line with Norris et al. (2008:
130), who argue that resilience is a function of system adaptability, rather
than stability; it is "a process linking a set of adaptive capacities to a
positive trajectory of functioning and adaptation after a disturbance."
For instance, studying multi-stakeholder initiatives (MSIs) for water
stewardship, Mitra (2018) demonstrated how, it was through the communicative framing and management of stakeholder tensions that such

MSIs were able to adapt to ongoing tensions, and thereby cultivate resilience in the complex social-ecological systems at stake. Similarly, Doerfel et al. (2013) observe that recovery and rebuilding after disaster requires not just maintaining and strengthening interorganizational networks, but also being flexible enough to forge new connections and cultivate communities of practice intimately familiar with ground realities of the crisis.

Discourse(s) of Renewal

A second emerging framework seeking to explain how community and organizational systems respond to crises pertains to the discourse(s) of renewal. The discourse of renewal framework is unique, in that it views crisis from the lens of an optimistic, future oriented vision of moving beyond the crisis rather than determining legal liability or responsibility for the crisis (Ulmer et al. 2007). Renewal seeks to explain how organizations can learn, grow, and improve following a crisis—well beyond merely repairing organizational image and reputation, to fundamentally change the nature and structure of the organization (Ulmer et al. 2007). Anderson (2013: 21) suggests that the discourse of renewal is "a rhetorical response that illuminates the opportunities associated with the crisis and emphasizes the future." Renewal involves narratives of growth, learning, rebirth, resurrection and restoration. They are forward-looking or prospective communication processes projecting an optimistic future after crises have occurred (Seeger et al. 2005, Sellnow and Seeger 2013).

As an approach to post-crisis discourse, discourse of renewal is an alternative to the dominant strategic approaches grounded in image repair and the SCCT, discussed earlier. *Image repair* describes a set of rhetorical strategies designed to reduce, limit, or address the question, "Who is to blame?" On the other hand, renewal addresses the question, "What do we do now?" The renewal narrative develops after a crisis has created severe disruption in a region, community or organization. Often, basic elements of the established system have been swept away and components of order and organization—including people, processes, and structures—are gone, or no longer function as they have in the past. A crisis then can create an immediate need, and both a literal and symbolic space for change. Instead of blame, apology, or liability, the focus is on organizational (re)learning, and co-building a "vision" for the future based on stakeholder consensus, so that the organization can "reemerge, re-envision or reconstitute" itself (Seeger and Griffin-Padgett 2010: 136). Discourses that focus on the future and opportunities to rethink fundamental assumptions can result in stronger, more effective, and more resilient systems.

Research adopting this framework has largely used the case study approach to trace how renewal plays out discursively. For instance, Ulmer and Sellnow (2002) noted three categories of renewal that were rhetorically effective in the aftermath of 9/11: signaling commitment to affected parties and stakeholders, commitment to self-correction, and commitment to core organizational values. More recently, Carlson (2018) analyzed the public relations efforts of energy giant Enbridge, after its 2010 oil spill in the Kalamazoo river, and used the discourse of renewal framework to theorize "vigilant resilience" for organizations and communities. Her study highlighted theoretical connections between resilience and renewal, foregrounding how stakeholder dialogue—at the heart of both concepts—can create unexpected discursive openings to critique and reimagine the status quo.

To conclude, renewal narratives address questions about the meaning of the crisis for the future and opportunities to learn, grow and improve. They may fundamentally reorder the community or organization down to its core purpose and values (Seeger et al. 2005: 92). These narratives are based on "connecting with core values, establishing the importance of the past in the present, and spurring efforts and energy toward process and the future" (Reierson et al. 2009: 116), articulated by credible leaders and spokespersons. They feature calls to learn, rebuild, recover, and come back better and stronger.

Directions for Future Research

Crises and disasters are ubiquitous, and communication is an essential part of understanding how these events develop, how they affect individuals, organizations, and society, how they are managed, and how they are understood. Investigators have created a very robust and interdisciplinary body of research in crises, which has informed practice in a variety of areas. Important questions remain, nevertheless, about the development of new methods and technologies of crisis communication, about intercultural factors, about new areas of emerging risk, and about crisis narratives.

First, future scholars should disrupt traditional boundaries of internal versus external communication. Organizational communication and public relations scholars should engage in depth with crises, resilience, and renewal. With the exception of more recent resilience and discourse of renewal frameworks, most crisis communication literature adopts a transmission-oriented view of communication, and an organization-centric perspective of the system. Thus, there remains a need for studies that involve both more constitutive, meaning-oriented approaches, and adopt a broader stakeholder-oriented view of crises and resilience. For instance, organizational communication researchers might examine how renewal is enacted through organizational learning, how complex stakeholder networks spanning multiple boundaries shape organizational and system-level resilience, and how crisis strategies and stakeholder responses are influenced by underlying themes of power and resistance.

More critical, feminist, and postcolonial approaches to crisis communication are also crucial, to deconstruct power relations and structures, which are rarely interrogated in mainstream crisis communication scholarship (for an exception, see Mitra 2013).

Also important for further study is the impact of social media, which have fundamentally changed the dynamics of crisis communication. Even as social media have positioned those experiencing crises as credible sources of real-time information, while allowing communities to organize and coordinate in more immediate ways in response (Yates and Paquette 2011), there are few longitudinal and embedded studies, utilizing ethnographic methods (for instance), or tracing how crises may be experienced simultaneously by different stakeholders. For the most part, crisis research in this area has focused on individual interpretations of crisis messages, issued by fictional organizations in artificial, experimental settings, to posit causal relations between message type and individual reception (e.g. Fisher Liu et al. 2011, Yang et al. 2010). Questions thus persist about how people adapt social media to crises in real time; how rumors develop, intensify and may be defused; how social media can empower public responses to crises; and how social media function as a system for monitoring and situational awareness.

Intercultural factors also play an important role in crisis communication and should be probed further. Increasingly, crises are international and multicultural events that require a more global approach to communication. Pandemics, for example, are infectious disease outbreaks that spread rapidly across regions, countries, continents, and cultures. In these cases, no single response agency or government is solely responsible for the managing the event. Rather, intergovernmental agencies, such as the World Health Organization must manage coordinated responses. In addition, cultural values, norms, traditions, and practices can be important factors in how a community receives and processes information and responds to a crisis. Significantly more effort thus needs to be directed toward understanding how culture influences crisis communication.

Finally, new areas of emerging and interactive risks challenge what we know about managing crises. New infectious disease threats, emerging technology-based crises, environmental disasters, and the interaction of these threats create especially high levels of uncertainty that merit concerted and collaborative action. The burning crises of today's interconnected global era are associated with the functioning of complex, dynamic systems and interactive complexity (Sellnow et al. 2002). These crises are especially fluid, hard to predict, difficult to manage, and can result in widespread harm over extended periods of time, as they cascade—creating additional levels of impact. For instance, consider the cascading effects of natural disasters (e.g. Hurricane Harvey) creating disease outbreaks, water contamination, energy shortages, and related secondary shocks. It is thus crucial to examine the communication demands for these interactive, cascading events that defy traditional parameters and boundaries.

Conclusion

The Purple Aces disaster at the University of Evansville in 1977 helped illustrate that crises cannot be understood, avoided, or managed without communication. It was also a vivid example of how a community experiences and responds to a crisis. Meanwhile, the Singur protests in India demonstrate how, when organizations do not engage in meaningful collaboration and engagement with stakeholders, both it and the community lose on potential opportunities, and system resilience suffers. More generally, crisis events, such as health pandemics, earthquakes, floods, hurricanes, toxic spills and water contaminations, fires, protests, radiological events, product recalls, mass shootings and terrorist events, can be important forces of change. Communication is essential to the management of these events and helps determine the shape and direction of that change.

Discussion Questions

1. Consider a recent crisis event and discuss how the situation might be managed by community, government or organizational representatives using each of the following frameworks: (1) warnings and evacuations, (2) image repair, (3) SCCT, and (4) best practices.
2. How can organizations and agencies use social media more effectively to manage crises? What key factors related to social media become pertinent? How can crisis managers use social media in such circumstances to engage stakeholders productively?
3. What communication processes might help an organization or community learn from a crisis? How would these differ, or be the same, if you used a resilience or a discourse of renewal framework?
4. How do image repair approaches to post-crisis situations contrast with renewal and resilience perspectives?
5. How would the practice of crisis communication vary according to the cultural context? Think about the audience and the risk factor, in particular.

References

Anderson, L. 2013. "Recalling Toyota's Crisis: Utilizing the Discourse of Renewal," *Journal of Professional Communication*, 2, 21–42.
Austin, L., Fisher Liu, B. and Jin, Y. 2012. "How Audiences Seek Out Crisis Information: Exploring the Social-Mediated Crisis Communication Model," *Journal of Applied Communication Research*, 40, 188–207.

Ayyub, B. M. 2014. "Systems Resilience for Multihazard Environments: Definition, Metrics, and Valuation for Decision Making," *Risk Analysis*, 34, 340–355.

Barbour, J. B., Buzzanell, P. M., Kinsella, W. J. and Stephens, K. K. 2018. "Communicating/Organizing for Reliability, Resilience, and Safety: Special Issue Introduction," *Corporate Communications: An International Journal*, 23, 154–161.

Baym, N., Campbell, S. W., Horst, H., Kalyanaraman, S., Oliver, M. B., Rothenbuhler, E., Weber, R. and Miller, K. 2012. "Communication Theory and Research in the Age of New Media: A Conversation from the CM Café," *Communication Monographs*, 79, 256–267.

Benoit, W. L. 1995. *Accounts, Excuses, and Apologies: A Theory of Image Restoration Strategies*, Albany, NY: State University of New York Press.

Boin, A. and McConnell, A. 2007. "Preparing for Critical Infrastructure Breakdowns: The Limits of Crisis Management and the Need for Resilience," *Journal of Contingencies and Crisis Management*, 15, 50–59.

Buzzanell, P. M. 2010. "Resilience: Talking, Resisting, and Imagining New Normalcies into Being," *Journal of Communication*, 60, 1–14.

Buzzanell, P. M. and Houston, B. J. 2018. "Communication and Resilience: Multilevel Applications and Insights," *Journal of Applied Communication Research*, 46, 1–4.

Carlson, E. 2018. "Vigilant Resilience: The Possibilities for Renewal through Preparedness," *Corporate Communications: An International Journal*, 23, 212–225.

Claeys, A-S., Caubherge, V. and Vyncke, P. 2010. "Restoring Reputations in Times of Crisis: An Experimental Study of the Situational Crisis Communication Theory and the Moderating Effects of Locus of Control," *Public Relations Review*, 36, 256–262.

Cole, T. W. and Fellows, K. L. 2008. "Risk Communication Failure: A Case Study of New Orleans and Hurricane Katrina," *Southern Communication Journal*, 73, 211–228.

Coombs, W. T. 2014. *Ongoing Crisis Communication: Planning, Managing, and Responding*, Thousand Oaks, CA: SAGE.

Coombs, W. T. 2007. "Protecting Organization Reputations During a Crisis: The Development and Application of Situational Crisis Communication Theory," *Corporate Reputation Review*, 10, 163–176.

Coombs, W. T. and Holladay, S. J. 2002. "Helping Crisis Managers Protect Reputational Assets: Initial Tests of the Situational Crisis Communication Theory," *Management Communication Quarterly*, 16, 165–186.

Covello, V. T. 2003. "Best Practices in Public Health Risk and Crisis Communication," *Journal of Health Communication*, 8, 5–8.

Doerfel, M., Chewning, L. and Lai, C.-H. 2013. "The Evolution of Networks and the Resilience of Interorganizational Relationships after Disaster," *Communication Monographs*, 80, 553–559.

Eriksson, M. 2012. "On-Line Strategic Crisis Communication: In Search of a Descriptive Model Approach," *International Journal of Strategic Communication*, 6, 309–327.

Eisenman, D. P., Cordasco, K. M., Asch, S., Golden, J. F. and Glik, D. 2007. "Disaster Planning and Risk Communication with Vulnerable Communities: Lessons from Hurricane Katrina," *American Journal of Public Health*, 97, S109–S115.

Fisher Liu, B., Austin, L. and Jun, Y. 2011. "How Publics Respond to Crisis Communication Strategies: The Interplay of Information Form and Source," *Public Relations Review*, 37, 345–353.

Kaplan, A. M. and Haenlein, M. 2010. "Users of the World, Unite! The Challenges and Opportunities of Social Media," *Business Horizons*, 53, 59–68.

Kendra, J. M. and Wachtendorf, T. 2007. "Community Innovation and Disasters," in Rodriguez, H., Quarantelli, E. and Dynes, R. (eds.), *Handbook of Disaster Research*, New York: Springer, pp. 316–334.

Mileti, D. S. and O'Brien, P. W. 1992. "Warnings during Disaster: Normalizing Communicated Risk," *Social Problems*, 39, 40–57.

Mileti, D. S. and Sorensen, J. H. 1990. *Communication of Emergency Public Warnings: A Social Science Perspective and State-of-the-Art Assessment* (No. ORNL-6609), Oak Ridge National Lab., TN.

Mitra, R. 2013. "The Neo-Capitalist Firm in Emerging India: Organization-State-Media Linkages," *International Journal of Business Communication*, 50, 3–33.

Mitra, R. 2018. "Communicative Management of Tensions by Multi-Stakeholder Initiatives (MSIs) for Water Resilience," *Corporate Communications: An International Journal*, 23, 257–273.

Myers, K. K. and McPhee, R. D. 2006. "Influences on Member Assimilation in Workgroups in High-Reliability Organizations: A Multilevel Analysis," *Human Communication Research*, 32, 440–468.

National Oceanic and Atmospheric Administration (NOAA) (2018). *Tornado Social Media*. Retrieved Nov 5, 2018 from www.weather.gov/wrn/spring2018-tornado-sm

National Research Council (Ed.). 1989. *Improving Risk Communication*, National Academies Press, Washington, DC.

National Research Council. 2011. *Public Response to Alters and Warnings*, National Academies Press, Washington, DC.

Norris, F. H., Stevens, S. P., Pfefferbaum, B., Wyche, K. F. and Pfefferbaum, R. L. 2008. "Community Resilience as a Metaphor, Theory, Set of Capacities, and Strategy for Disaster Readiness," *American Journal of Community Psychology*, 41, 127–150.

Reierson, J. L., Sellnow, T. L. and Ulmer, R. R. 2009. "Complexities of Crisis Renewal Over Time: Learning from the Tainted Odwalla Apple Juice Case," *Communication Studies*, 60, 114–129.

Reynolds, B. and Seeger, M. W. 2005. "Crisis and Emergency Risk Communication as an Integrative Model," *Journal of Health Communication*, 10, 43–55.

Reynolds, B., Hunter-Galdo, J. and Sokler, L. 2002. "Crisis and Emergency Risk Communication," Atlanta, GA: Centers for Disease Control and Prevention.

Schultz, F., Utz, S. and Goritz, A. 2011. "Is the Medium the Message? Perceptions of and Reactions to Crisis Communication via Twitter, Blogs and Traditional Media," *Public Relations Review*, 37, 20–27.

Scott, C. W. and Trethewey, A. 2008. "Organizational Discourse and the Appraisal of Occupational Hazards: Interpretive Repertoires, Heedful Interrelating, and Identity at Work," *Journal of Applied Communication Research*, 36, 298–317.

Seeger, M. W. 2006. "Best Practices in Crisis Communication: An Expert Panel Process," *Journal of Applied Communication Research*, 34, 232–244.

Seeger, M. W. and Sellnow, T. L. 2016. *Narratives of Crisis: Telling Stories of Ruin and Renewal*. Palo Alto, CA: Stanford University Press.

Seeger, M. W., Ulmer, R. R., Novak, J. M. and Sellnow, T. 2005. "Post-Crisis Discourse and Organizational Change, Failure and Renewal," *Journal of Organizational Change Management*, 18, 78–95.

Seeger, M. W. and Griffin Padgett, D. R. 2010. "From Image Restoration to Renewal: Approaches to Understanding Post Crisis Communication," *The Review of Communication*, 10, 127–141.

Sellnow, T. L. and Seeger, M. W. 2013. *Theorizing Crisis Communication* (Vol. 4). Malden, MA: John Wiley & Sons.

Sellnow, T. L., Seeger, M. W. and Ulmer, R. R. 2002. "Chaos Theory, Informational Needs, and Natural Disasters," *Journal of Applied Communication Research*, 30, 269–292.

Sisco, H. F., Collins, E. L. and Zoch, L. M. 2010. "Through the Looking Glass: A Decade of Red Cross Crisis Response and Situational Crisis Communication Theory," *Public Relations Review*, 36, 21–27.

Stephens, K. K., Barrett, A. K. and Mahometa, M. J. 2013. "Organizational Communication in Emergencies: Using Multiple Channels and Sources to Combat Noise and Capture Attention," *Human Communication Research*, 39, 230–251.

Sutton, J., Spiro, E. S., Johnson, B., Fitzhugh, S., Gibson, B. and Butts, C. T. 2014. "Warning Tweets: Serial Transmission of Messages during the Warning Phase of a Disaster Event," *Information, Communication & Society*, 17, 765–787.

Ulmer, R. R., Seeger, M. W. and Sellnow, T. L. 2007. "Post-Crisis Communication and Renewal: Expanding the Parameters of Post-Crisis Discourse," *Public Relations Review*, 33, 130–134.

Ulmer, R. R. and Sellnow, T. L. 2002. "Crisis Management and the Discourse of Renewal: Understanding the Potential for Positive Outcomes of Crisis," *Public Relations Review*, 28, 361–365.

Ulmer, R. R., Sellnow, T. L. and Seeger, M. W. 2011. *Effective Crisis Communications: Moving from Crisis to Opportunity*, Thousand Oaks, CA: SAGE.

U.S. Defense Civil Preparedness Agency. (1978). *Emergency Broadcast System: The Life-Saving Public Service Program*, Washington, DC: Department of Defense.

Veil, S. R., Buehner, T. and Palenchar, M. J. 2011. "A Work-in-Process Literature Review: Incorporating Social Media in Risk and Crisis Communication," *Journal of Contingencies and Crisis Management*, 19, 110–122.

Veil, S. R., Sellnow, T. L. and Petrun, E. L. 2011. "Hoaxes and Paradoxical Challenges of Restoring Legitimacy: Domino's Responses to Its YouTube Crisis," *Management Communication Quarterly*, 26, 322–345.

Weiner, B. 1985. "An Attributional Theory of Achievement Motivation and Emotion," *Psychological Review*, 92, 548–573.

Yang, S-U., Kang, M. and Johnson, P. 2010. "Effects of Narratives, Openness to Dialogic Communication, and Credibility on Engagement in Crisis Communication through Organizational Blogs," *Communication Research*, 37, 473–497.

Yates, D. and Paquette, S. 2011. "Emergency Knowledge Management and Social Media Technologies: A Case Study of the 2010 Haitian Earthquake," *International Journal of Information Management*, 31, 6–13.

15 Moving Forward: Future Directions in Organizational Communication

Rahul Mitra and Jamie McDonald

In high school, or perhaps college, you may have learned about German physicist Werner Heisenberg (1901–1976) and his famous Uncertainty Principle. Notwithstanding his questionable association with the Third Reich's nuclear arms race during World War II, he was awarded the Nobel Prize in Physics in 1932, and his Uncertainly Principle is widely regarded as one of the cornerstones of Quantum Mechanics. Simple yet elegant in its succinctness, the Uncertainty Principle (sometimes called the Indeterminacy Principle) states that it is impossible (not just practically, but also theoretically) to simultaneously obtain the precise location and velocity of a particle. Rather, as the uncertainty in one variable diminishes, uncertainty in the other increases to compensate, so that Heisenberg concluded that causal determinism—which required exact knowledge of both position and momentum—was implausible (Beyler, n.d.). Although this could be read as a limiting condition for scientific inquiry, reiterating how some things are simply not knowable, it might be interpreted as evidence for another fundamental truth—that all things are interrelated and complex, shaped by each other in unforeseen ways and processes, and constantly shifting and evolving over time.

What do quantum mechanics have to do with organizational communication?

Although we certainly do not aver that the social sciences and humanities should unreflexively adopt the standards, procedures and dictums of the physical sciences, we believe that this underlying truth of constant and indeterminate movement in the physical world is mirrored by social relationships, structures, and interactions. Put simply, organizations—and organizational communication by association—have always been and will continue to be in flux (see especially Chapters 1, 2, and 3 in this volume). Organizations will accomplish great feats and result in complex social formations, while also provoking unforeseen events and forces, many of which might be destructive, setting off chain reactions that go well beyond "opposite and equal," even as the teachings of quantum physics disrupt traditional Newtonian science. Moreover, despite the immense urge to uncover causal mechanisms and proclaim these to hold beyond a doubt (e.g. Why and when is leadership effective? Why do some groups flounder while others soar? What instruments will change the culture of an organization to the precise degree desired?), Heisenberg reminds us that not everything—perhaps, *nothing*—is entirely measurable, discernable, or absolute. As particles shift constantly, changing their speed and directions, so too do organizations—although they may not be quite as miniscule or vibrate quite as erratically—and boundaries, attributions, and structures are rarely defined, distinct, or even desirable. As it turns out, there's a little bit of physics in organizational communication after all!

Our volume recognizes this flux and indeterminacy through the theme of "movement," which is centered by each of the contributed chapters. As we noted in Chapter 1, each of the contributors has been urged to engage in intergenerational and interconceptual conversations pertaining to the chapters they have cowritten. The result has been a stimulating discussion, wherein the coauthors describe various shifts and movements, both in their personal lives and the life span of the topic studied. Our goal was never to provide *the* definitive guide to organizational communication scholarship—indeed, such a guide would not remain definitive for very long, even if it was possible to include every single perspective, concept, and story from the field—but to provide fragments and vignettes to inspire and empower you, the reader, to figure out where *you* fit. How do these stories align with yours? How do these topics and their epochal shifts—admittedly not exhaustive—speak to your own personal and professional life? How would you draw from the theories, lessons, and discussion questions posed here to understand the ongoing social and organizational changes unfolding around you? Thus, our goal has always been, by depicting the movement in organizational communication theory and practice, to *move you*—so that you may find your own set of catalyzing agents in this book, and decide on your personalized course of action and reflection.

In the remaining sections of this concluding chapter, we consider some future directions for organizational communication research, as evidenced through the tumultuous social, ecological, cultural, and institutional movements around us. First, we use a movement-inspired lens to theorize both communication and organization (and their concomitant meanings of communicati*ng*, communication*s*, organizi*ng*, and organizatio*ns*). Second, we identify clusters of technological, social-ecological, and cultural-generational changes to ponder about future shifts in organizational communication theory, method, and practice.

Further Unpacking Communication and Organization

One of our pet peeves as communication scholars is when laypersons, or even academics from other disciplines, misname our field as communication*s*—not communica*tion*. That seemingly innocuous extra letter often equates us with the study of information technologies, tele-communications, and media channels, and although some of this lies within the domain of communication, our field is broad enough to include several other combinations and permutations of communicative action (e.g. face-to-face interaction). Communication*s* are things, whereas communica*tion* is a process, a subject of study to shed light on the organization of social life. Yet, perhaps, in our disciplinary fervor, we are too hasty to dismiss communication*s* from our lexicon. Indeed, we argue in this section, that a movement-inspired lens to organizational communication centers an ongoing interplay of action, subject or social phenomenon, and object(s) in the world—or, in other words, shifts between communica*ting* and organi*zing* (action), communica*tion* and organiza*tion* (subject), and communication*s* and organization*s* (object), as depicted by Figure 15.1.

Let us begin with the communication side of things. If we are to pay attention to how social phenomena—such as communica*tion*—are constantly in flux, it stands to reason that the material artifacts and objects—that is, communication*s*—by which these phenomena are manifested matter a great deal. This is amply clear in chapters throughout this book, from the review of organizational networks and technology (Chapter 13), to crisis communication (Chapter 14), to research on group decision-making (Chapter 10). To understand the broader meaning of this social phenomenon or subject (i.e. what is communica*tion?*), we need to understand the constitution of and underlying processes of communication*s*, or the everyday objects, tools, and technologies that shape this subject (and are shaped by it in turn). Thus, rather than merely resist how communica*tion* is often likened to communication*s* in lay speech, we should strive to broaden

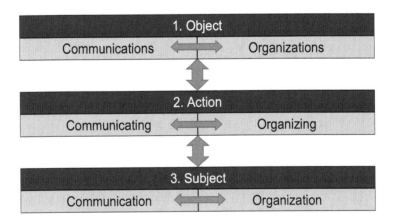

Figure 15.1 A Movement-Inspired Lens to Organizational Communication

societal understanding of communications beyond a relatively narrow set of tools, to other roles and forms, both deceptively simple and extravagantly complex (e.g. Barrett and Stephens 2017, Leonardi and Vaast 2017).

The connective tissue between communication and communications is the verb form communicat*ing*, which denotes practice and action. Robert Craig (1999, 2006), for instance, termed communication a practical discipline over all others because the subject of our study is not something ethereal "out there" but rooted in everyday life, occurring in *every moment* of it. We cannot *not* communicate, because communicat*ing* is inevitably bound with human action (Watzlawick et al. 1967, also see Chapter 2 of this volume). It is by communicat*ing* with different stakeholders, or even with oneself, that we give voice *and* action to ideas, perspectives, and strategies—that is, we *move* solutions from ideas to implementation. Paradoxically, even as we culturally privilege action over talk (at least in the United States), it is through talking—and other forms of communicat*ing*, lest we overly privilege the auditory sense—that action comes about. Thus, communicat*ing is* action, rather than just portentous of action (Austin 1975, Taylor and Van Every 2000). It is the ever-shifting, constantly moving element that gives shape to the broader subject at hand (i.e. communicat*ion*) through the implementation of various sensory tools and objects (i.e. communication*s*) that may also change the arc of communicat*ing*, as its movement is countered and addressed via fluid conversations and interactions. Our movement-inspired lens thus unpacks the process of communication into a tripartite schema of object/action/subject, or communication*s*/communicat*ing*/communicat*ion*, and encourages us to trace the interplay across these elements rather than focusing solely on any one of these.

The organization side in Figure 15.1 elaborates on the context of communication that most concerns us here. The movement-inspired object/action/subject schema is useful here as well, to unpack organizational communication more fully. In Chapter 1, we noted that,

> Rather than take organizations as taken-for-granted and already formed entities, much organizational communication scholarship is concerned with the ways in which organizing and organizations are accomplished through communication. This area of research thus underscores how organizations are dynamic entities that are constantly (re)produced through organizing processes, which are fundamentally communicative (Brummans et al. 2014, Weick 1979). In this sense, organizations can be conceptualized as discursive constructions that cannot exist without communication (Fairhurst and Putnam 2004).

The recognition of constant flux is apparent in this excerpt, such that "organizations are dynamic entities." Moreover, there is a link between the two columns of Figure 15.1, or between communication*s*/ communicat*ing*/communica*tion* and organization*s*/organiz*ing*/organiza*tion*, so that organization*s* are "constantly (re)produced through organiz*ing* processes, which are fundamentally communicative" (italics added). Thus, again, at the center we have the action of organiz*ing*, which involves the alignment of practices on the ground—practices that involve the use and creation of specific objects or entities (i.e. organization*s*)—in order to give meaning to (and perhaps contest extant interpretations of) the broader subject, organiza*tion*, or what it means to organize. Organization*s*, like Amazon, GM, and the United States federal government, may be discursive constructions, owing to the primordial links between organiz*ing* and communicat*ing*, but they are also grounded in material structures and conditions, such as bodies, genders, physical materials, and technologies, and are thus also tangible objects (Ashcraft et al. 2009, Fairhurst and Putnam 2004).

As a field, organizational communication has long been concerned with the study of communicative processes within such organization*s*—a mode of inquiry widely described as employing the "container metaphor," since the object is seen to enclose the action (Putnam et al. 1996). Following the interpretive, critical, and discursive turns, disciplinary focus has arguably shifted more toward organiz*ing*, or the actions themselves, so that communication-as-constitutive (CCO) approaches invert the lens from object-containing-action to action-constituting-object. Along the way, some frameworks, such as (but not limited to) the Montréal School, have also sought to problematize the subject, interrogating organiza*tion* as a social phenomenon—although, perhaps due to its (widespread) use of ethnolinguistic methods, far more attention has been paid to the action of organiz*ing* (Boivin et al. 2017, Brummans et al. 2014)

How does this translate in terms of the movement-inspired lens of Figure 15.1? As an example, the container metaphor perspective studies the impact of organization*s* on communicat*ing* and specific communication*s*—with perhaps some research tackling the reverse effect as well, or how communicat*ing* and communication*s* affected organization*s* on the ground. Thus, container-themed studies tend to examine the upward and downward flows between boxes 1 and 2, or between object(s) and action; largely missing, however, are interrogations of the subjects of communica*tion* and organiza*tion*, or the flows connecting box 3 to the others. For that matter, the nature of organiz*ing* and communicat*ing* actions were rarely interrogated either, with preset categories generally used. Discursive approaches, in contrast, focus on the upward flows from box 2 (action) toward box 1 (object), or how organiz*ing* and communicat*ing* shape specific communication*s* and organization*s*, or flows within box 2 between the actions, with some Montréal School projects also examining the downward flows of box 2 (action) on organiza*tion*, within box 3 (subject). A movement-inspired lens recognizes, however, that upward and downward flows occur across the three categories of object, action, and subject. Moreover, there are bound to be multiple meanings, types, and contestations within each category or box, such that organizations, organizing, and organization are rarely the same in different contexts. Time is another key factor, shaping not just direct and indirect effects, but also mediating and moderating impacts between and betwixt these categories. Objects, actions, and subjects are thus interconnected and fluid, despite the material conditions underlying specific contexts, so that studying how things, processes, and themes *are* is inevitably bound to shift and impact how they *might be* or *should be*.

A movement-inspired lens also blurs normative, descriptive, and predictive research by noting the deeper implications—both local and systemic—of research, and by disrupting traditional boundaries between what is and what might be. At the very least, this means greater reflexivity and self-awareness on the part of organizational communication researchers, who must realize that the impacts of their endeavors simply do not "stop" when data collection does, or after the publication of a manuscript. At the most ambitious level, recognizing the movement of object/action/subject would urge designing studies that marry functionalist and normative paradigms of thinking, and multiple methods that can effectively study (or at least account for) upward and downward flows across these categories. Meta-questions to be posed might include the following: How do actions (communicating, organizing) shape both objects (communications, organizations) and the underlying subject (communication, organization), or how do societal shifts in subject affect actions and objects, or, how do different objects create competing yet compelling actions and subjects for society?

These meta-questions become especially important, as we consider in the next section some widespread social-ecological-cultural shifts—such as Big Data, the Gig Economy, and populist political movements—that potentially transform organizing practices, the contested realities of organizations, and what counts as organization.

Moving Forward

Our goal in outlining these clusters of societal movements is not so much to demonstrate the current and ongoing relevance of organizational communication research, as it is to encourage you to think deeply about how you fit in, and where and how you might use our movement-inspired lens to render organizations, organizing, and organization more ethical, erudite, and efficient. How do these themes and shifts *move you*? *How might you move the institutional make-up around you*, using organizational communication research, to address these ongoing shifts?

Technological Changes

This is the cluster of themes that probably springs first in most people's minds, when asked to reflect on future directions for the field. Technological changes are profound not merely because they change—and are constantly changing—our everyday lives, how we use different objects and artifacts, and the very creation of such artifacts, but also because they transform the very tools that we use for research to trace these unfolding patterns.

The rapidity of these technological changes reorganizing our everyday lives makes it seem as if obsolescence is always just around the corner, if you're not looking far and wide. It was not too long ago when research on virtual organizations was considered cutting-edge (DeSanctis and Monge 1998), and now we realize that practically every organization has both a virtual and brick-and-mortar presence, so that even that moniker—"virtual organizations"—seems increasingly arcane. Telework is not something that happens to only workers in the information technology sector, but to each and every one us answering emails on our smartphone while waiting in line to board a flight or hailing a cab across town (Fonner and Roloff 2012). Our bodies are increasingly connected to our technologies and our workplaces through Fitbit and other devices that keep tabs on our healthy behaviors, with deep implications for how our employers treats us, the insurance packages and other benefits we enjoy, and the knowing look your boss gives you when she asks you why your Fitbit score is so low (Dailey and Zhu 2016). Big Data is not just something that technology wonks discuss at high-level symposiums anymore, it's with you whenever you "like" a friend's status on Facebook, or order a cute T-shirt on Target.com, or leave a review of your favorite restaurant on Yelp (Bharati et al. 2017). Whether you realize it, or not, there are new algorithms, apps, computer chips, and technology workers laboring to accurately predict your subjective and objective modes of decision-making in all spheres of life (Kemper and Kolkman 2018).

At the same time, these technological forces enable new forms of research, such as Big Data analysis on social and policy trends that might have been unknowable less than ten years ago, similar to how advances in social network analysis software during the early 2000s enabled the tracking and predictive capacity of sophisticated research on technology, institutional interconnections, social and professional relationships, and a host of other organizational issues (Bharati et al. 2017, Bisel et al. 2014, Pilny and Atouba 2018). For instance, data tracked on wearable technology (e.g. body cameras and chips, Fitbit) might contribute to research projects combining behavioral and biomedical information to better understand individual responses to changing work and life circumstances. Computational approaches might be used to ascertain organizational variables, measures, and processes ranging from group interaction to decision-making (Pilny and Poole 2017)

The impact of such technologies is probably most profound at the level of objects (box 1 of Figure 15.1), shaping the complex communications we use, and the organizations that employ both us and them. Technologies are objects, after all, and the constant flux in technological development has severe implications for different objects and artifacts connected to each other by virtue of human use and habit. Welcome to the Internet-of-Things, where your Alexa or Siri adjusts the thermostat, changes the refrigerator setting, lowers your window blinds and the lights when the sun gets too hot, and, oh, controls your music and telecommunication needs (Tham 2018). Thus, at the object level, how might such far-reaching technological changes shape the structures and processes of organizations? Given the ongoing flows across objects, actions and subjects, how might these technological changes also affect everyday practices of communicat*ing* and organiz*ing* (i.e. box 2), especially as these new technologies are deeply woven with(in) our bodies and embodied practices? How might they affect underlying meanings, norms, and values related to organiz*ation* and communic*ation* (box 3)—what might it mean, for instance, to communicate when new technologies seemingly predict your behaviors and intentions without your verbalization (or making them public in some other way)? What is the role of such organiz*ation* and organizations in our social collective, and might it/they become more powerful, sentient, and responsive than what the collective is prepared for, or even desires?

Social-Ecological Changes

A second cluster of themes pertains to the profound societal shifts underway, which we see as closely related to—if not directly precipitated by—widespread environmental changes. In noting these interconnections between the social and ecological, our goal is to highlight how broad social movements do not occur in an institutional or environmental vacuum. Rather, ongoing political and cultural shake-ups are inevitably tied to grievances related to the competition over scarce resources, inequality, and ownership of key ecologies (Berkes et al. 2003).

The most prominent examples pertain to climate change, and how societies, governments, and multinational companies have strived to adapt accordingly—noting instances of both successful resilience and capacity-building, as well as failed attempts to adequately recognize ongoing social-ecological risks, or deliberate attempts to prevent meaningful action to protect vested economic interests (Chapter 4 in this volume). Ecological disasters—occurring more frequently owing to "global weirding," as volatile environmental shifts have been termed—also highlight the efforts and capacity (in some cases, inadequacy) of communities, governments, and key institutions to engage in effective crisis relief and communication (Chapter 14). Communities displaced by governments or multinational companies increasingly draw on both local and global networks (and technologies) to expose institutional malpractices and battle conventional power hierarchies (Chapter 3). Energy politics continue to have far-reaching consequences, ranging from the 1973 oil crisis to more recent shifts toward natural gas and clean energy technologies—even as the dominance of energy sector companies provokes changes in social, political, and institutional cultures (Barrett and Dailey 2017, Mitra 2016). Institutional and international conflict (and alliances) are at stake, evidenced by acrimony around global efforts to mitigate climate change. Long-simmering tensions in volatile regions (e.g. Syria, Sudan) can be exacerbated by environmental forces, such as prolonged drought—which, in turn, intensify wicked problems like the refugee crises unfolding across Europe, Asia and Africa (Gemenne et al. 2014). Social and political anxieties over scarce natural and economic resources feed existing streams of xenophobia and populism, creating a potent cocktail of authoritarian and illiberal forces even in democracies long considered to be stable.

Social-ecological changes may be traced and unpacked at every category of the object/action/subject schema of Figure 15.1. A useful example is the broader movement toward "mobility" among both traditional automakers and high-growth, high-tech institutions in the U.S., which seeks to redefine decades-long reliance on individually owned (and gas-guzzling) automobiles by adopting alternative themes of collective ownership and affordability, clean energy technologies, embeddedness with local neighborhoods and environments, and monitoring/surveillance technologies for higher predictive capacity (Cohen et al. 2014, Remane et al. 2016). Mobility has both impacted legacy automaker companies (e.g. GM, Ford) and spawned a complex ecosystem of startups around auto parts, clean-tech, artificial intelligence, urban planning, and other ventures—shaping not just existing organizational structures, artifacts, and technologies (i.e. objects), but also on-the-ground practices and processes of enacting what it means to be mobile (i.e. actions) (Willing et al. 2017). As these organizations and institutional leaders increasingly collaborate with grassroots communities and impacted stakeholders, a negotiation ensues as to the role and nature of organiz*ation* and communic*ation* in shaping mobility—and the urban environment—for a new generation of users (and workers). At the same time, mobility advocates have largely ignored broader questions of how this might shape global supply chains, rural contexts, as well as local spaces in the Global South, which remain ripe for study by organizational communication scholars. Researchers might also consider the complex flows across object/action/subject for any of the "wicked" (Rittel and Webber 1973) social-ecological problems reviewed earlier, not just mobility, as well as how these issues are interlinked (e.g. climate change provoking social conflict provoking a institutional outcries), even when such linkages are not readily visible to policymakers or grassroots communities.

Cultural-Generational Changes

Finally, we consider some key shifts in cultures and generations, which shape organizational communication. Several of these changes intersect with both technological and social-ecological themes—as per our movement-inspired lens—although they do not stem directly from them; rather, they emphasize the relentless march of time on/in open societies, inevitably shifting broader values, practices, and discourses.

In the U.S., a shift in workplace values and behavior is apparent with the millennial generation beginning to dominate workplace composition, so that there is a need to study in-depth intergenerational communication and work practices. On the one hand, millennial workers reshape prevalent work norms and expectations, job engagement, and organizational commitment (O'Connor and Ralie 2015, Walden et al. 2017). On the other hand, older workers are exploring new avenues and "bridge employment" pathways toward retirement, rather than simply exiting their jobs and careers (Anderson and Guo 2018). Meanwhile, in China, scholars are tracing the impact of the "Post-80s" generation, who came of age after economic reforms were instituted, and are thus strongly oriented toward the global economy, even as the country remains strongly autocratic (Long et al. 2018). Post-Fordist organizational forms and the gig economy (often termed the *sharing economy* or *platform economy*) are evidence of global cultural-generational change, redefining both the scope and values of liberal capitalism (Mumby 2016). Working in the gig economy reframes extant norms and rules of employability (Carr et al. 2017), even as it enshrines precariousness and uncertainty for employees, employers, and customers (Kuhn 2018)—as evidenced by ongoing debates on the status of Uber drivers as independent contractors versus bona fide employees (due full benefits), and Airbnb's responsibility for some of its hosts' bigotry toward historically marginalized groups.

Broadly speaking, these cultural-generational shifts have strong implications for how workers progressively identify with and at their organizations (Chapter 5 in this volume), how leaders and groups interact and make key decisions (Chapters 10 and 11), how specific workplace and work-life policies are designed, implemented and enacted over time (Chapters 6 and 12), and ongoing considerations of diversity, equity and inclusion in multicultural and global workplaces (Chapter 8). Along with these shifts have come the need for institutions to grapple far more with the hitherto unspoken reality of feelings and emotions at work and in life (Chapter 9), recognizing both the tensions and overlaps between personal and professional space(s), so that being heartfelt and reflexive is increasingly valued compared to mere efficiency and competence.

With respect to the object/action/subject schema of Figure 15.1, cultural-generational changes are likely to provoke the most impact in the realm of subjects (box 3) and actions (box 2) undertaken by organizational members and stakeholders. Many of the examples outlined earlier are closely related to deeply held identities, beliefs, norms, and values of individuals, and are thus likely to impact ongoing practices, habits, and behaviors on the ground—that is, their actions, both in terms of everyday communica*ting* and organi*zing*, which are closely interlinked. Moreover, changing values and identities tend to shape how new generations of stakeholders interpret the broader purpose, role, and scope of communica*tion* and organiza*tion* subjects in their own right—suggesting new forms of organiza*tion* (e.g. the gig economy), which in turn require rethinking the role of communica*tion*. Crucial to further unpack are the flows across actions and subjects, and how they in turn affect tangible objects—communication*s*, organization*s*, and other material conditions and entities relevant to the changing life-world.

Themes of power disparities, experiences of difference and diversity, and identification are likely to figure deeply in ongoing negotiations of workplace culture, norms, and socialization. Notably, it is not just bona fide employees who must undertake these complex negotiations, but a potentially broader set of impacted stakeholders in these new generation economies—such as contract workers, temp workers, supply chain workers, and distributing agency workers. Finally, as generations of community members and organizational stakeholders evolve, so too do generations of researchers, who might find it increasingly urgent to blend empirical and normative voices in their scholarship, and focus on evocative strains to reach broader audiences and research participants. This shift is already underway—witness, for instance, our emphasis on reflection and movement in this volume, along with the contributing coauthors' deep conversations on the value and import of organizational communication research. We look forward, humbly and with bated breath, to further such shifts in tone, topic, and method.

Conclusion

This chapter had a twofold goal. The first goal was to, as most concluding chapters of edited volumes do, draw connections—however tenuous—among the various chapters contributed by our illustrious authors, so as to present a coherent whole for you, our reader. The second goal was to explicate on the underlying theme of "movement" that we see everywhere in the field of organizational communication, hoping that we may move *you* to embark on your own scholarly journey. For us, talking about movement in the field is not so much about describing the various paradigms of research—such as from scientific management to human relations to systems theory, or even from functionalist to interpretive to the linguistic turn. Several other volumes and articles have already done an admirable job of outlining these particular shifts. Instead, *our* challenge was to demonstrate the ongoing movement within key areas of the field—crucial topics that hold much practical relevance in contemporary organizations and organizing—by juxtaposing the personal with the professional, and the conceptual with the generational.

For us, organizational communication theory is profoundly practical and personal; we see ourselves, our research participants, colleagues, students, and surrounding organizations moved inevitably toward greater realization and self-awareness as a result of theory. We wanted to capture precisely this sentiment through our volume. In closing, this chapter elaborated on what a movement-inspired lens might mean for a truly personal and practical philosophy of organizational communication. We also considered some yet-unfolding technological, social-ecological, and cultural-generational changes that we suspect will produce even further movement and volatility in the field (and the world at large). We are profoundly hopeful that organizational communication scholars and practitioners may weather these ongoing changes with a semblance of calm and continuity. Like Heisenberg, we are resigned to the inevitability of never knowing absolutely every minute aspect of organizational practice in the fast-approaching future, but remain attuned to the ongoing intersections and dependencies of the social (and natural) world. Along the way—informed by our past experiences, successes and failures—we are determined to stake out what we may, from current issues to those not-entirely-unknowable future directions.

Discussion Questions

1. Think of two to three specific concepts, theories, or issues related to organizational communication that you thought you knew fairly well enough about prior to reading our book. How has your understanding changed or otherwise affected, as a result of engaging with the chapters you have read? How has this book inspired or motivated you to think differently about these concepts, theories, or issues?
2. Do you think organizations and/or the social world are constantly in movement? Why, or why not? Do you think constant movement for organizations (and organizational communication) is good or bad for different stakeholders, and society in general? Discuss.
3. Identify one or two key topics addressed by organizational communication scholarship. Now, using the movement-inspired lens discussed in this chapter, think about what the different objects, actions, and subjects at stake might be for these organizational topics identified by you? How might they impact each other? What should researchers be looking out for?

4. Think of some societal changes or issues that you see impacting you personally, or your loved ones, or the region you live in. Would you categorize these changes as technological, social-ecological, cultural-generational, or a combination of these? Why? How might these changes identified by you affect different organizations (e.g. corporations, nonprofit organizations, government agencies), and organizational communication?

5. What were some of the best or most useful aspects of this book? What spoke to you personally, or moved you to reflect deeply on your circumstances, or inspired you to pursue a specific research project? How and why did the chapters make you think about the everyday applicability of organizational communication theory to organizational practice?

6. Conversely, what were some blind spots or drawbacks to the structure, tone and/or content of this book? What was perhaps ambiguous or confusing to you? (Mind you, we do not always think that what is ambiguous at first is a drawback; on the contrary, we have both found that graduate school is full of ambiguities that require in-depth engagement and reflection to enable greater understanding!) What are some specific changes that you would like to see, or modifications you might suggest for how we have designed this book?

References

Anderson, L. B. and Guo, S. J. 2018. "The Changing Face of Retirement: Exploring Retirees' Communicative Construction of Tensions through Bridge Employment," *Communication Studies*, 69, 196–212.

Ashcraft, K. L., Kuhn, T. and Cooren, F. 2009. "Constitutional Amendments: 'Materializing' Organizational Communication," in Brief, A. and Walsh, J. (eds.), *The Academy of Management Annals*, New York: Routledge, pp. 1–64.

Austin, J. L. 1975. *How to Do Things with Words*, Cambridge, MA: Harvard University Press.

Barrett, A. K. and Dailey, S. 2018. "A New Normal? Competing National Cultural Discourses and Workers' Constructions of Identity and Meaningful Work in Norway," *Communication Monographs*, 85, 284–307.

Barrett, A. K. and Stephens, K. K. 2017. "The Pivotal Role of Change Appropriation in the Implementation of Health Care Technology," *Management Communication Quarterly*, 31, 163–193.

Berkes, F., Colding, J. and Folke, C. (eds.) 2003. *Navigating Social-Ecological Systems: Building Resilience for Complexity and Change*, New York: Cambridge University Press.

Beyler, R. n. d. "Werner Heisenberg: German physicist and philosopher," *Encyclopedia Brittanica*, Retrieved fro: www.britannica.com/biography/Werner-Heisenberg#ref524688

Bharati, P., Beaulieu, T., Davidson, E. and Syed, R. 2017. "At the Interface of Social Media Analytics, Big Data and Social Movements: Research Challenges," *Academy of Management Proceedings, 1*.

Bisel, R. S., Barge, J. K., Dougherty, D. S., Lucas, K. and Tracy, S. J. 2014. "A Round-Table Discussion of 'Big Data' in Qualitative Organizational Communication Research," *Management Communication Quarterly*, 28, 625–649.

Boivin, G., Brummans, B. H. and Barker, J. R. 2017. "The Institutionalization of CCO Scholarship: Trends from 2000 to 2015," *Management Communication Quarterly*, 31, 331–355.

Brummans, B. H. J. M., Cooren, F., Robichaud, D. and Taylor, J. R. 2014. "Approaches to the Communicative Constitution of Organizations," in Putnam, L. L. and Mumby, D. K. (eds.), *The SAGE Handbook of Organizational Communication: Advances in Theory, Research, and Methods*, Thousand Oaks, CA: SAGE, pp. 173–194.

Carr, C. T., Hall, R. D., Mason, A. J. and Varney, E. J. 2017. "Cueing Employability in the Gig Economy: Effects of Task-Relevant and Task-Irrelevant Information on Fiverr," *Management Communication Quarterly*, 31, 409–428.

Cohen, B. and Kietzmann, J. 2014. "Ride On! Mobility Business Models for The Sharing Economy," *Organization & Environment*, 27, 279–296.

Craig, R. T. 1999. "Communication Theory as a Field," *Communication Theory*, 9, 119–161.

Craig, R.T. 2006. "Communication as practice," in Shepherd, G.J., St. John, J. and Striphas, T. (eds.), *Communication as…: Perspectives on Theory*, Thousand Oaks, CA: SAGE, pp. 38–48.

Dailey, S. L. and Zhu, Y. 2017. "Communicating Health at Work: Organizational Wellness Programs as Identity Bridges," *Health Communication*, 32, 261–268.

DeSanctis, G. and Monge, P. (1998). "Communication Processes for Virtual Organizations," *Journal of Computer-Mediated Communication*, 3. doi:10.1111/j.1083–6101.1998.tb00083.x

Fairhurst, G. T. and Putnam, L. L. 2004. "Organizations as Discursive Constructions," *Communication Theory*, 14, 5–26.

Fonner, K. L. and Roloff, M. E. 2012. "Testing the Connectivity Paradox: Linking Teleworkers' Communication Media Use to Social Presence, Stress from Interruptions, and Organizational Identification," *Communication Monographs*, 79, 205–231.

Gemenne, F., Barnett, J., Adger, W. N. and Dabelko, G. D. 2014. "Climate and Security: Evidence, Emerging Risks, and A New Agenda," *Climate Change*, 123, 1–9.

Kemper, J. and Kolkman, D. 2018. "Transparent to Whom? No Algorithmic Accountability Without A Critical Audience," *Information, Communication & Society*, Advance online publication.

Kuhn, T. 2018. "Working and Organizing as Social Problems: Reconceptualizing Organizational Communication's Domain," in Salem, P.J. and Timmerman, E. (eds.), *Transformative Practice and Research in Organizational Communications*, Hershey, PA: IGI Global, pp. 30–42.

Leonardi, P. M. and Vaast, E. 2017. "Social Media and Their Affordances for Organizing: A Review and Agenda for Research," *Academy of Management Annals*, 11, 150–188.

Long, Z., Buzzanell, P. M. and Kuang, K. 2018. "Chinese Post80s Generational Resilience: Chengyu (成语) as Communicative Resources for Adaptation and Change," *International Journal of Business Communication*. Advance online publication.

Mitra, R. 2016. "Re-constituting 'America': The Clean Energy Economy Ventriloquized," *Environmental Communication*, 10, 269–288.

Mumby, D. K. 2016. "Organizing Beyond Organization: Branding, Discourse, and Communicative Capitalism," *Organization*, 23, 884–907.

O'Connor, A. and Raile, A.N.W. 2015. "Millennials' Get a 'Real Job': Exploring Generational Shifts in the Colloquialism's Characteristics and Meanings," *Management Communication Quarterly*, 29, 276–290.

Pilny, A. and Atouba, Y. 2018. "Modeling Valued Organizational Communication Networks Using Exponential Random Graph Models," *Management Communication Quarterly*, 32, 250–264.

Pilny, A. and Poole, M. S. (eds.). 2017. *Group Processes: Data-Driven Computational Approaches*, Cham, Switzerland: Springer.

Putnam, L. L., Phillips, N. and Chapman, P. 1996. "Metaphors of Communication and Organization," in Clegg, S., Hardy, C. and Nord, W. (eds.), *Handbook of Organization Studies*, Thousand Oaks, CA: SAGE, pp. 375–408.

Remane, G., Hildebrandt, B., Hanelt, A. and Kolbe, L.M. 2016. "Discovering New Digital Business Model Types: A Study of Technology Startups from The Mobility Sector," *PACIS 2016 Proceedings*, 289.

Rittel, H. W. J. and Webber, M. M. 1973. "Dilemmas in a General Theory of Planning," *Policy Sciences*, 4, 155–169.

Taylor, J. R. and Van Every, E. J. 2000. *The Emergent Organization: Communication as Its Site and Surface*, Mahwah, NJ: Lawrence Erlbaum.

Tham, J. C. K. 2018. "Interactivity in an Age of Immersive Media: Seven Dimensions for Wearable Technology, Internet of Things, and Technical Communication," *Technical Communication*, 65, 46–65.

Walden, J., Jung, E. H. and Westerman, C. Y. K. 2017. "Employee Communication, Job Engagement, and Organizational Commitment: A Study of Members of the Millennial Generation," *Journal of Public Relations Research*, 29, 73–89.

Watzlawick, P., Bavelas, J. B. and Jackson, D. D. 1967. *Pragmatics of Human Communication: A Study of Interactional Patterns, Pathologies and Paradoxes*, New York: Norton & Company.

Weick, K. E. 1979. *The Social Psychology of Organizing*, Reading, MA: Addison-Wesley.

Willing, C., Brandt, T. and Neumann, D. 2017. "Intermodal Mobility," *Business & Information Systems Engineering*, 59, 173–179.

Index

Made in the USA
Columbia, SC
13 May 2025